Lecture Notes in Computer Science 11497

Commenced Publication in 1973
Founding and Former Series Editors:
Gerhard Goos, Juris Hartmanis, and Jan van Leeuwen

Michael Kirkedal Thomsen ·
Mathias Soeken (Eds.)

Reversible Computation

11th International Conference, RC 2019
Lausanne, Switzerland, June 24–25, 2019
Proceedings

 Springer

Editors
Michael Kirkedal Thomsen (iD)
University of Copenhagen
Copenhagen, Denmark

Mathias Soeken (iD)
École Polytechnique Fédérale de Lausanne
Lausanne, Switzerland

ISSN 0302-9743   ISSN 1611-3349 (electronic)
Lecture Notes in Computer Science
ISBN 978-3-030-21499-9   ISBN 978-3-030-21500-2 (eBook)
https://doi.org/10.1007/978-3-030-21500-2

LNCS Sublibrary: SL2 – Programming and Software Engineering

This Springer imprint is published by the registered company Springer Nature Switzerland AG
The registered company address is: Gewerbestrasse 11, 6330 Cham, Switzerland

Preface

This volume contains the proceedings of RC 2019, the 11th International Conference on Reversible Computation, held in Lausanne, Switzerland, during June 24–25, 2019. RC 2019 was the 11th event in a series of annual meetings designed to gather researchers from different scientific disciplines for the discussion and dissemination of recent developments in all aspects of reversible computation. Previous RC events took place in York, UK (2009), Bremen, Germany (2010), Ghent, Belgium (2011), Copenhagen, Denmark (2012), Victoria, Canada (2013), Kyoto, Japan (2014), Grenoble, France (2015), Bologna, Italy (2016), Kolkata, India (2017), and Leicester, UK (2018). Reversible computation concerns models of computation where programs or processes are logically reversible (as, for example, in undoing of program execution for reversible debugging), or physically reversible (as, for example, in quantum circuits and robotics). The main areas of research presented at the conference were reversible formal models for computation and physical systems, reversible programming languages, and reversible circuits.

The conference received 22 submissions, and we would like to thank everyone who submitted. Each submission was reviewed by at least three reviewers, who provided detailed evaluations as well as constructive comments and recommendations. After careful reviewing and extensive discussions, the Program Committee (PC) accepted 13 full papers, and two short papers for presentation at the conference. We would like to thank the PC members and all the additional reviewers for their truly professional work and strong commitment to the success of RC 2019. We are also grateful to the authors for taking into account the comments and suggestions provided by the referees during the preparation of the final versions of their papers.

This year the conference program included two invited talks: Glynn Winskel spoke on concurrent strategies and his work relating to quantum computation and Renato Renner discussed his research on quantum information theory. The papers that accompany the invited talks are included in these proceedings. Furthermore, the program included a tutorial by Ali Javadi-Abhari's groups at IBM research on Qiskit and IBMQ. Finally, the program also included a poster session, which was the first time for an RC conference.

We would like to thank everyone who contributed to the organization of RC 2019, especially Giulia Meuli, Bruno Schmitt, Fereshte Mozafari, Carole Burget, Chantal Demont, and Giovanni De Micheli. We thank the EPFL, École Polytechnique Fédérale de Lausanne for their support. Finally, we acknowledge EasyChair for facilitating PC discussions and the production of the proceedings.

June 2019

Michael Kirkedal Thomsen
Mathias Soeken

Organization

Program Chairs

Michael Kirkedal Thomsen   University of Copenhagen, Denmark
Mathias Soeken   EPFL, Switzerland

Steering Committee

Rolf Drechsler   University of Bremen, Germany
Robert Glück   University of Copenhagen, Denmark
Ivan Lanese   University of Bologna/Inria, Italy/France
Irek Ulidowski   University of Leicester, UK
Robert Wille   Johannes Kepler University Linz, Austria

Program Committee

Earl Campbell   University of Sheffield, UK
Anupam Chattopadhyay   Nanyang Technological University, Singapore
Gerhard Dueck   University of New Brunswick, Canada
Carla Ferreira   Universidade Nova de Lisboa, Portugal
Robert Glück   University of Copenhagen, Denmark
Jarkko Kari   University of Turku, Finland
Nader Khammassi   Delft University of Technology, The Netherlands
Ivan Lanese   University of Bologna/Inria, Italy/France
Krzysztof Podlaski   University of Lodz, Poland
Ulrik Pagh Schultz   University of Southern Denmark, Denmark
Iain Phillips   Imperial College London, UK
Robert Rand   University of Pennsylvania, USA
Mariusz Rawski   Warsaw University of Technology, Poland
Irek Ulidowski   University of Leicester, UK
Benoît Valiron   Université Paris-Saclay, France
Germán Vidal   Universitat Politecnica de Valencia, Spain
Robert Wille   Johannes Kepler University of Linz, Austria
Shigeru Yamashita   Ritsumeikan University, Japan
Tetsuo Yokoyama   Nanzan University, Japan

Additional Reviewers

Torben Ægidius Mogensen   Giulia Meuli
James Hoey   Maja Hanne Kirkeby
Eva Graversen   Claudio Mezzina
Kesha Hietala   Robin Kaarsgaard

Contents

Invited Talk

Concurrent Quantum Strategies

Pierre Clairambault[1], Marc de Visme[1], and Glynn Winskel[2(✉)]

[1] Univ Lyon, ENS de Lyon, CNRS, UCB Lyon 1, LIP, Lyon, France
[2] Computer Laboratory, University of Cambridge, Cambridge, UK
gw104@cam.ac.uk

Abstract. A game-semantics foundation for quantum computation is presented. It draws on two lines of work: for its temporal dynamics, on concurrent games and strategies, based on event structures; for its quantum interactions, on the mathematical foundations of positive operators and completely positive maps. The two lines are married in the definition of quantum concurrent strategy, obtained via an operator generalisation of the conditions on a probabilistic concurrent strategy. The result is a compact-closed (bi)category of quantum games, whose finite configurations carry finite dimensional Hilbert spaces, and quantum strategies, whose finite configurations carry operators.

1 Introduction

We describe how concurrent strategies, based on event structures, can be extended with quantum effects. The motivation is threefold:

(1) Concurrent strategies have been advanced as a possible foundation for a generalised domain theory, in which concurrent games and strategies take over the roles of domains and continuous functions [1,2]. A major reason has been to broaden the applicability of denotational semantics. It became important to see how concurrent strategies could be adapted to quantitative semantics, to probabilistic and quantum settings. Although a previous extension of concurrent strategies [3] did generalise quantum game theory as then developed [4], it did not provide a framework rich enough to represent quantum computation; it was insufficient to express the mix of classical and quantum behaviour of quantum lambda-calculi [5]. The extension to truly quantum strategies, has proved elusive. The pioneering attempt [6] placed severe restrictions on entanglement and the recent dynamic account of the execution of a quantum programming language via the geometry of interaction [7] is not compositional.

(2) As quantum information and computation become more sophisticated there is a need to reconcile quantum theory with causality [8], and put any attempt through the strictures of computer science, with its emphasis on compositionality, adequacy and full abstraction. Concurrent quantum strategies expose the causal nature of a quantum process as an event structure, and provide a means to compose quantum processes, in the manner of strategies.

© Springer Nature Switzerland AG 2019
M. K. Thomsen and M. Soeken (Eds.): RC 2019, LNCS 11497, pp. 3–19, 2019.
https://doi.org/10.1007/978-3-030-21500-2_1

(3) We aim to broaden the semantic basis for quantum programming. The breakthroughs in the denotational semantics of quantum programming of the last decade or so, *e.g.* [5,9], have been based on insightful generalisations of those categories used in quantum information, specifically by extending completely positive maps with extra structure to more fully address mixes of classical and quantum effects. But we are now seeing their limitations. Because the generalisations do not capture the dynamics of quantum programs directly it is hard to see whether the models are fully abstract or how they might be refined to fully abstract models. Concurrent quantum strategies form a marriage of concurrent strategies with completely positive maps. They extend to nonlinear features, through symmetry in games, and support the fine-tuning needed to obtain full-abstraction results, along the lines of [10,11].

An adequate denotational semantics to the full quantum lambda calculus [12] in terms of concurrent quantum strategies is given in [13]. This paper is intended to complement that work by focussing on the fundamental, *linear* concurrent quantum strategies and how they generalise concurrent probabilistic strategies.

2 Event Structures

An *event structure* comprises $(E, \leq, \mathrm{Con})$, consisting of a set E of *events* which are partially ordered by $\leq$, the *causal dependency relation*, and a nonempty *consistency* relation Con consisting of finite subsets of E. The relation $e' \leq e$ expresses that event e causally depends on the previous occurrence of event e'. That a finite subset of events is consistent conveys that its events can occur together. The relations satisfy several axioms:

$$[e] =_{\mathrm{def}} \{e' \mid e' \leq e\} \text{ is finite for all } e \in E,$$
$$\{e\} \in \mathrm{Con} \text{ for all } e \in E,$$
$$Y \subseteq X \in \mathrm{Con} \text{ implies } Y \in \mathrm{Con}, \text{ and}$$
$$X \in \mathrm{Con} \ \& \ e \leq e' \in X \text{ implies } X \cup \{e\} \in \mathrm{Con}.$$

There is an accompanying notion of state, or history, those events that may occur up to some stage in the behaviour of the process described. A *configuration* is a, possibly infinite, set of events $x \subseteq E$ which is: *consistent*, $X \subseteq x$ and X is finite implies $X \in \mathrm{Con}$; and *down-closed*, $e' \leq e \in x$ implies $e' \in x$.

Two events e, e' are considered to be causally independent, and called *concurrent* if the set $\{e, e'\}$ is in Con and neither event is causally dependent on the other; then we write $e \ co \ e'$. In games the relation of *immediate* dependency $e \rightarrowtail e'$, meaning e and e' are distinct with $e \leq e'$ and no event in between, plays a very important role. We write $[X]$ for the down-closure of a subset of events X. Write $\mathcal{C}^{\infty}(E)$ for the configurations of E and $\mathcal{C}(E)$ for its finite configurations. (Sometimes we shall need to distinguish the precise event structure to which a relation is associated and write, for instance, $\leq_E$, $\rightarrowtail_E$ or co_E.)

A *map* of event structures $f : E \rightharpoonup E'$ is a partial function f from E to E' such that the image of a configuration x is a configuration fx and any event of fx arises as the image of a unique event of x. When f is total, then written $f : E \to E'$, it induces a bijection $x \cong fx$. Maps compose as functions.

A map $f : E \rightharpoonup E'$ reflects causal dependency locally, in the sense that if e, e' are events in a configuration x of E for which $f(e') \leq f(e)$ in E', then $e' \leq e$ also in E; the event structure E inherits causal dependencies from the event structure E' via the map f. Consequently, a map $f : E \rightharpoonup E'$ preserves concurrency. In general a map of event structures need not preserve causal dependency; a total map which does is called *rigid*.

Let $(E, \leq, \mathrm{Con})$ be an event structure. Let $V \subseteq E$ be a subset of 'visible' events. Define the *projection* of E on V, to be $E{\downarrow}V =_{\mathrm{def}} (V, \leq_V, \mathrm{Con}_V)$, where $v \leq_V v'$ iff $v \leq v'$ & $v, v' \in V$ and $X \in \mathrm{Con}_V$ iff $X \in \mathrm{Con}$ & $X \subseteq V$. Projection hides all events outside V. It is associated with a *partial-total factorization system*. Consider a partial map of event structures $f : E \rightharpoonup E'$. Let

$$V =_{\mathrm{def}} \{e \in E \mid f(e) \text{ is defined}\}.$$

Then f clearly factors into the composition

$$E \xrightarrow{f_0} E{\downarrow}V \xrightarrow{f_1} E'$$

of f_0, a partial map of event structures taking $e \in E$ to itself if $e \in V$ and undefined otherwise, and f_1, a total map of event structures acting like f on V. Note that any $x \in \mathcal{C}^\infty(E{\downarrow}V)$ is the image under f_0 of a *minimum* configuration, *viz.* $[x]_E \in \mathcal{C}^\infty(E)$. We call f_1 the *defined part* of the partial map f.

It is sometimes useful to build an event structure out of computation paths. A computation path is described by a partial order $(p, \leq_p)$ for which the set $\{e' \in p \mid e' \leq_p e\}$ is finite for all $e \in p$. We can identify such a path with an event structure in which the consistency relation consists of all finite subsets of events. Between two paths $p = (p, \leq_p)$ and $q = (q, \leq_q)$, we write $p \hookrightarrow q$ when $p \subseteq q$ and the inclusion is a rigid map of event structures.

Proposition 1. *A rigid family $\mathcal{R}$ comprises a non-empty subset of finite partial orders which is down-closed w.r.t. rigid inclusion, i.e. $p \hookrightarrow q \in \mathcal{R}$ implies $p \in \mathcal{R}$. A rigid family determines an event structure $\mathrm{Pr}(\mathcal{R})$ whose order of finite configurations is isomorphic to $(\mathcal{R}, \hookrightarrow)$. The event structure $\mathrm{Pr}(\mathcal{R})$ has events those elements of $\mathcal{R}$ with a top event; its causal dependency is given by rigid inclusion; and its consistency by compatibility w.r.t. rigid inclusion. The order isomorphism $\mathcal{R} \cong \mathcal{C}(\mathrm{Pr}(\mathcal{R}))$ takes $q \in \mathcal{R}$ to $\{p \in \mathrm{Pr}(\mathcal{R}) \mid p \hookrightarrow q\}$.*

The *pullback* of total maps of event structures is essential in composing strategies. We can define it via a rigid family of *secured bijections*. Let $\sigma : S \to B$ and $\tau : T \to B$ be total maps of event structures. There is a composite bijection

$$\theta : x \cong \sigma x = \tau y \cong y,$$

between $x \in \mathcal{C}(S)$ and $y \in \mathcal{C}(T)$ such that $\sigma x = \tau y$; because σ and τ are total they induce bijections between configurations and their image. The bijection is *secured* when the transitive relation generated on θ by $(s,t) \le (s',t')$ if $s \le_S s'$ or $t \le_T t'$ is a partial order.

Theorem 1. *Let $\sigma : S \to B$ and $\tau : T \to B$ be total maps of event structures. The family $\mathcal{R}$ of secured bijections between $x \in \mathcal{C}(S)$ and $y \in \mathcal{C}(T)$ such that $\sigma x = \tau y$ is a rigid family. The functions $\pi_1 : \mathrm{Pr}(\mathcal{R}) \to S$ and $\pi_2 : \mathrm{Pr}(\mathcal{R}) \to T$, taking a secured bijection with top to, respectively, the left and right components of its top, are maps of event structures. $\mathrm{Pr}(\mathcal{R})$ with π_1 and π_2 is the pullback of σ and τ in the category of event structures.*

Notation 2 From Proposition 1, finite configurations of the pullback of $\sigma : S \to B$ and $\tau : T \to B$ are order-isomorphic to the rigid family of secured bijections. Define $x \wedge y$ to be the configuration of the pullback which corresponds via this isomorphism to a secured bijection between $x \in \mathcal{C}(S)$ and $y \in \mathcal{C}(T)$, necessarily with $\sigma x = \tau y$; any finite configuration of the pullback takes the form $x \wedge y$ for unique x and y.

3   Games and Strategies

Both a game and a strategy will be represented by an *event structure with polarity*, which comprises (A, pol_A) where A is an event structure and a polarity function $pol_A : A \to \{+, -, 0\}$ ascribing a polarity $+$ (Player), $-$ (Opponent) or 0 (neutral) to its events. The events correspond to (occurrences of) moves. It will be technically useful to allow events of neutral polarity; they arise, for example, in a play between a strategy and a counterstrategy. Maps are those of event structures which preserve polarity. A *game* is represented by an event structure with polarities restricted to $+$ or $-$, with no neutral events.

Definition 1. In an event structure with polarity, with configurations x and y, write $x \subseteq^- y$ to mean inclusion in which all the intervening events are Opponent moves. Write $x \subseteq^+ y$ for inclusion in which the intervening events are neutral or Player moves. The *Scott order*, between $x, y \in \mathcal{C}^\infty(A)$, where A is a game, is defined by: $y \sqsubseteq_A x \iff y \supseteq^- x \cap y \subseteq^+ x$. (The order $\supseteq^-$ is converse to $\subseteq^-$.)

There are two fundamentally important operations on two-party games. One is that of forming the *dual game*. On a game A this amounts to reversing the polarities of events to produce the dual $A^\perp$. The other operation, a *simple parallel composition* $A\|B$, is achieved on games A and B by simply juxtaposing them, ensuring a finite subset of events is consistent if its overlaps with the two games are individually consistent; any configuration x of $A\|B$ decomposes into $x_A\|x_B$ where x_A and x_B are configurations of A and B respectively.

A *strategy in a game A* is a total map $\sigma : S \to A$ of event structures with polarity such that

(i) if $\sigma x \subseteq^- y$, where $x \in \mathcal{C}(S)$ and $y \in \mathcal{C}(A)$, there is a unique $x' \in \mathcal{C}(S)$ with $x \subseteq x'$ and $\sigma x' = y$;

(ii) if $s \rightarrow s'$ in S & $pol(s) = +$ or $pol(s') = -$, then $\sigma(s) \rightarrow \sigma(s')$ in A.

The first condition is one of receptivity, ensuring that the strategy is open to all moves of Opponent permitted by the game. The second condition ensures that the only additional immediate causal dependencies a strategy can enforce are those in which a Player move awaits a move of Opponent.

A strategy *from* a game A *to* a game B is a strategy in the game $A^{\perp}\|B$. A map $f : \sigma \Rightarrow \sigma'$ of strategies $\sigma : S \rightarrow A$ and $\sigma' : S' \rightarrow A$ is a map $f : S \rightarrow S'$ s.t. $\sigma = \sigma' f$; this determines isomorphism of strategies.

The conditions defining a strategy are precisely those needed to ensure that the copycat strategy behaves as identity w.r.t. composition.

3.1 Copycat

Let A be a game. The copycat strategy $\alpha_A : \mathbb{C}_A \rightarrow A^{\perp}\|A$ is an instance of a strategy from A to A. The event structure $\mathbb{C}_A$ is based on the idea that Player moves in one component of the game $A^{\perp}\|A$ always copy previous corresponding moves of Opponent in the other component. For $c \in A^{\perp}\|A$ we use $\bar{c}$ to mean the corresponding copy of c, of opposite polarity, in the alternative component. The event structure $\mathbb{C}_A$ comprises $A^{\perp}\|A$ with extra causal dependencies $\bar{c} \leq c$ for all events c with $pol_{A^{\perp}\|A}(c) = +$; together with the additional causal dependency they generate a partial order; take a finite subset to be consistent in $\mathbb{C}_A$ iff its down-closure w.r.t. the relation $\leq$ is consistent in $A^{\perp}\|A$.

Lemma 1. *Let A be a game. Let $x \in \mathcal{C}(A^{\perp})$ and $y \in \mathcal{C}(A)$,*

$$x\|y \in \mathcal{C}(\mathbb{C}_A) \quad \textit{iff} \quad y \sqsubseteq_A x.$$

3.2 Composition

Two strategies $\sigma : S \rightarrow A^{\perp}\|B$ and $\tau : T \rightarrow B^{\perp}\|C$ compose via pullback and hiding summarised below.

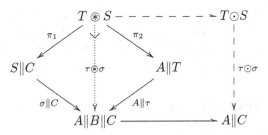

Ignoring polarities, by forming the pullback of $\sigma\|C$ and $A\|\tau$ we obtain the synchronisation of complementary moves of S and T over the common game B; subject to the causal constraints of S and T, the effect is to instantiate the Opponent moves of T in $B^{\perp}$ by the corresponding Player moves of S in B, and *vice versa*. Reinstating polarities we obtain the *interaction* of σ and τ

$$\tau \circledast \sigma : T \circledast S \rightarrow A^{\perp}\|B^0\|C,$$

where we assign neutral polarities to all moves in or over B. Moves over the common game B remain unhidden. The map $A\|B\|C \rightharpoonup A\|C$ is undefined on B and otherwise mimics the identity. Pre-composing this map with $\tau \circledast \sigma$ we obtain a partial map $T \circledast S \rightharpoonup A^\perp \|C$; it is undefined on precisely the neutral events of $T \circledast S$. The defined parts of its partial-total factorization yields

$$\tau \odot \sigma : T \odot S \to A^\perp \| C$$

on reinstating polarities; this is the *composition* of σ and τ.

Notation 3. For $x \in \mathcal{C}(S)$ and $y \in \mathcal{C}(T)$, let $\sigma x = x_A \| x_B$ and $\tau y = y_B \| y_C$ where $x_A \in \mathcal{C}(A)$, $x_B, y_B \in \mathcal{C}(B)$, $y_C \in \mathcal{C}(C)$. Define $y \circledast x = (x\|y_C) \wedge (x_A\|y)$. This is a partial operation. Any finite configuration of $T \circledast S$ has the form $y \circledast x =_{\text{def}} (x\|y_C) \wedge (x_A\|y)$ for unique $x \in \mathcal{C}(S)$ and $y \in \mathcal{C}(T)$.

3.3   A Bicategory of Strategies

We obtain a bicategory for which the objects are games, the arrows $\sigma : A \nrightarrow B$ are strategies $\sigma : S \to A^\perp\|B$; with 2-cells $f : \sigma \Rightarrow \sigma'$ maps of strategies. The vertical composition of 2-cells is the usual composition of maps. Horizontal composition is given by the composition of strategies $\odot$ (which extends to a functor on 2-cells via the universality of pullback and partial-total factorisation).

As $A^\perp\|B \cong (B^\perp)^\perp\|A^\perp$, a strategy $\sigma : A \nrightarrow B$ corresponds to a strategy $\sigma^\perp : B^\perp \nrightarrow A^\perp$. The bicategory of strategies is compact-closed; the *unit* $\emptyset \nrightarrow A^\perp\|A$ and *counit* $A\|A^\perp \nrightarrow \emptyset$ being the obvious modifications of the copycat strategy.

We can restrict the 2-cells to be rigid maps and still obtain a bicategory. This is important later, when the 2-cells for probabilistic and quantum strategies will be rigid.

A strategy $\sigma : S \to A$ is *deterministic* if S is deterministic, *viz.*

$$\forall X \subseteq_{\text{fin}} S. \ [X]^- \in \text{Con}_S \implies X \in \text{Con}_S,$$

where $[X]^- =_{\text{def}} \{s' \in S \mid \exists s \in X. \ pol_S(s') = - \ \& \ s' \leq s\}$. In other words, a strategy is deterministic if consistent behaviour of Opponent is answered by consistent behaviour of Player. Copycat $\mathfrak{cc}_A$ is deterministic iff the game A is *race-free*, *i.e.* if $x \subseteq^- y$ and $x \subseteq^+ z$ in $\mathcal{C}(A)$ then $y \cup z \in \mathcal{C}(A)$.

4   Quantum Foundations

The category **FdHilb** of finite dimensional Hilbert spaces has as objects finite dimensional vector spaces, over the complex numbers $\mathbb{C}$, with an inner product $\langle \phi | \psi \rangle$, which is conjugate-linear in the first argument and linear in the second. Its arrows are linear maps between the underlying vector spaces. Any map $f : H \to K$ has an adjoint $f^\dagger : K \to H$ specified by $\langle f^\dagger(\phi) | \psi \rangle_H = \langle \phi | f(\psi) \rangle_K$.

The category **FdHilb** is symmetric monoidal w.r.t. the well-known operation of tensor product of Hilbert spaces, where the tensor unit I is the one-dimensional vector space, comprising the complex numbers $\mathbb{C}$ with inner product $\langle c|d \rangle = c^* \cdot d$ where c^* is the complex conjugate of c.

As observed in [9], the category **FdHilb** is compact-closed w.r.t. the operation of dual space. A finite dimensional Hilbert space H with inner product $\langle \phi | \psi \rangle_H$ has a *dual space* H^* given concretely as the vector space of linear maps from H to I; as any linear map from H to I can be represented by $\phi^* = \langle \phi | = \langle \phi |_- \rangle_H$, for some $\phi \in H$, its inner product is specified by taking $\langle \phi^* | \psi^* \rangle_{H^*} =_{\text{def}} \langle \psi | \phi \rangle_H$. The *unit* of the compact-closure $\eta_H : I \to H^* \otimes H$ takes $1 \in I$ to the identity matrix $\sum_i \langle i | \otimes | i \rangle$ w.r.t. an orthonormal basis $|1\rangle, \cdots, |n\rangle$, of size the dimension $\dim(H)$. The *counit*, $\epsilon_H : H \otimes H^* \to I$ is given by the inner product and takes $\phi \otimes \psi$ to $\langle \psi | \phi \rangle$.

As is well-known, via this compact-closed structure, **FdHilb** admits a *partial trace* to form a traced monoidal category [14]. Given a map $f : H \otimes L \to K \otimes L$ in **FdHilb** its partial trace is a map $\text{Tr}_L(f) : H \to K$. When H and K are the unit space, $\text{tr}(f) = \text{Tr}_L(I \otimes f) : I \to I$, so is a scalar factor, which coincides with the usual trace of the matrix of the operator f.

We reserve the term *operator* for a linear map with the same domain and codomain. An operator preserving the inner product is called *unitary*; unitaries are associated with the undisturbed evolution of a quantum system. An operator $f : H \to H$ in **FdHilb** is *positive* if $\langle \phi | f(\phi) \rangle$ is a non-negative real for all $\phi \in H$. Write $\textbf{Op}(H)$, and $\textbf{Pos}(H)$, for the set of operators, respectively positive operators, on a finite dimensional Hilbert space H. Given operators f and g on a finite dimensional Hilbert space H we can define the *Löwner order* on $\textbf{Op}(H)$ by taking $f \leq_L g$ iff $g - f$ is positive. Those $\rho \in \textbf{Pos}(H)$ for which $\text{tr}(\rho) \leq 1$ are called subdensity operators. They play the role of "mixed" quantum states to be thought of as subprobabilistic combinations of pure quantum states.[1]

In order to represent operations on quantum systems, such as those taking quantum states to quantum states, one derives a category **CPM** based on a rich class of completely positive maps. The objects of **CPM** are again finite dimensional Hilbert spaces but now a *completely positive map* $f : H \to K$ in **CPM** is a linear map $f : H^* \otimes H \to K^* \otimes K$ in **FdHilb** such that its correspondent $\bar{f} : H^* \otimes K \to H^* \otimes K$ in **FdHilb**, got via compact-closure, is a positive operator. We write $\text{CJ} : f \mapsto \bar{f}$ for the 1-1 correspondence between completely positive maps $f \in \textbf{CPM}(H, K)$ and positive operators $\bar{f} \in \textbf{Pos}(H^* \otimes K)$; it is the well-known *Choi-Jamiolkowski isomorphism*.

We represent the Hilbert space $H^* \otimes H$ as that of matrices of the isomorphic space of operators $\textbf{Op}(H)$; w.r.t. an orthonormal basis of H, an operator on H can be described as a vector $\sum_{i,j} c_{ij} |i\rangle \langle j|$ or as a matrix with entries c_{ij}. It is helpful conceptually and technically to regard a map $f : H \to K$ in **CPM** as taking operators on H to operators on K, so as a map $f : \textbf{Op}(H) \to \textbf{Op}(K)$ in **FdHilb**. A linear map $f : \textbf{Op}(H) \to \textbf{Op}(K)$ is *positive* if it takes positive operators to positive operators. Those $f : \textbf{Op}(H) \to \textbf{Op}(K)$ arising from completely positive maps are those for which $f \otimes \text{id}_L$ is positive for any $\text{id}_L : \textbf{Op}(L) \to \textbf{Op}(L)$.

---

[1] The use of subdensity rather than density operators, where $\text{tr}(\rho) = 1$, is natural in quantum systems which may stick with a non-trivial probability.

If a completely positive map f further satisfies $\text{tr}(f(A)) \leq \text{tr}(A)$ it is called a *superoperator*. Superoperators represent the physically realisable operations on quantum states. In strategies, due to the presence of Opponent moves, we shall have call for completely positive maps which are not superoperators, for maps of **CPM** which act on positive operators which are not identifiable with the usual states of quantum mechanics.

We can describe a map in **CPM**, regarded as a map between operators, as function from matrices of the argument to matrices of the result. A qubit is represented by a vector so a column matrix in $\mathbb{C}^2$, w.r.t. the standard basis, and an operator on qubits by a 2-by-2 matrix. The measurement of a value 0 or 1 of a qubit in $\mathbb{C}^2$ is described, respectively, by the two superoperators $\text{meas}_0, \text{meas}_1 \in \mathbf{CPM}(\mathbb{C}^2, \text{I})$ where

$$\text{meas}_0 : \begin{pmatrix} a & b \\ c & d \end{pmatrix} \mapsto a \quad \text{and} \quad \text{meas}_1 : \begin{pmatrix} a & b \\ c & d \end{pmatrix} \mapsto d.$$

The two superoperators representing the creation of qubit initially set to 0 or 1, respectively, are given by $\text{new}_0, \text{new}_1 \in \mathbf{CPM}(\text{I}, \mathbb{C}^2)$ where

$$\text{new}_0 : a \mapsto \begin{pmatrix} a & 0 \\ 0 & 0 \end{pmatrix} \quad \text{and} \quad \text{new}_1 : d \mapsto \begin{pmatrix} 0 & 0 \\ 0 & d \end{pmatrix}.$$

For U a unitary on H, the superoperator $\hat{U} \in \mathbf{CPM}(H, H)$ takes an operator $M \in \mathbf{Op}(H)$ to $U^\dagger M U$, which restricts to the usual application of a unitary operation to a quantum state.

Two maps in **CPM** play an early role. They derive from the unit and counit associated with the compact closure of **FdHilb**. Let H be a finite dimensional Hilbert. The unit η_H^{Hilb} of **FdHilb** viewed as completely positive map gives $1_H \in \mathbf{CPM}(\text{I}, H)$ which on argument 1 returns the identity operator id_H; it is not a superoperator. The counit $\epsilon_{H^*}^{Hilb}$, makes a completely positive map $\text{tr}_H \in \mathbf{CPM}(H, \text{I})$ which on an operator on H returns its trace.

The category **CPM** inherits its symmetric monoidal structure from **FdHilb**. Its compact-closed structure, $\eta_H^{cpm} \in \mathbf{CPM}(\text{I}, H^* \otimes H)$ and $\epsilon_H^{cpm} \in \mathbf{CPM}(H \otimes H^*, \text{I})$, is also induced by the compact-closed structure of **FdHilb** once we identify an object H in **CPM** with its space of operators $\mathbf{Op}(H)$:

$$\eta_H^{cpm} = \eta_{\mathbf{Op}(H)}^{Hilb} : \text{I} \to \mathbf{Op}(H)^* \otimes \mathbf{Op}(H);$$
$$\epsilon_H^{cpm} = \epsilon_{\mathbf{Op}(H)}^{Hilb} : \mathbf{Op}(H) \otimes \mathbf{Op}(H)^* \to \text{I}.$$

More explicitly, w.r.t. an orthonormal basis $|1\rangle, \cdots |n\rangle$ of H, we have an orthornormal basis $E_{ij} =_{\text{def}} |i\rangle\langle j|$ of $\mathbf{Op}(H)$. The unit η_H^{cpm} takes 1 to the identity $\sum_{i,j} E_{ij}^* \otimes E_{ij}$. The counit ϵ_H^{cpm} takes $v \otimes f$ to $f(v)$; explicitly, on the basis, it takes $E_{ij} \otimes E_{kl}^*$ to $\delta_{ik}\delta_{jl}$, described using the Kronecker delta.

CPM provides a conveniently rich category, supporting all quantum operations, and the diagrammatic reasoning which derives from compact-closure. In fact, **CPM** inherits a *dagger (a.k.a. strong) compact-closed* structure from

FdHilb [9,15]. The mathematics that follows could be explained more axiomatically w.r.t. dagger compact-closed categories enriched over cancellative commutative monoids; the enrichment is needed to support subtraction in the "monotone" condition on quantum strategies.

In what follows, often Hilbert spaces will come presented as explicit tensor products $A = \bigotimes_{a \in x} H(a)$ or $B = \bigotimes_{b \in y} H(b)$; in such cases we adopt the convention that $A \otimes B = \bigotimes_{c \in x \cup y} H(c)$ when $x \cap y = \emptyset$; the associated structural maps, symmetry and the left and right unit maps, will become identities.

5 From Probabilistic to Quantum Strategies

Taking guidance from probabilistic strategies we are led to a definition of quantum strategy in a quantum game. Probabilistic strategies are recovered as a special case, when the quantum game is classical.

5.1 Probabilistic Strategies

A *probabilistic strategy* in a game A is a strategy $\sigma : S \to A$ together with a probability valuation which endows S with probability, while taking account of the fact that in the strategy Player can't be aware of the probabilities assigned by Opponent. We should restrict to race-free games, precisely those for which copycat is deterministic, so that we have probabilistic identity strategies; it follows that S is race-free. Precisely, a *probability valuation* is a function $v : \mathcal{C}(S) \to [0, \infty)$ which is

(normalised) $v(\emptyset) = 1$;
(oblivious) if $x \subseteq^- y$ then $v(x) = v(y)$, for $x, y \in \mathcal{C}(S)$; and
(monotone) if $y \subseteq^+ x_1, \cdots, x_n$ then $d_v[y; x_1, \cdots, x_n] \geq 0$,

where the *drop function*,

$$d_v[y; x_1, \cdots, x_n] =_{\text{def}} v(y) - \sum_{\emptyset \neq I \subseteq \{1, \cdots, n\}} (-1)^{|I|+1} v(x_I),$$

$y, x_1, \cdots, x_n \in \mathcal{C}(S)$ and we take $x_I = \bigcup_{i \in I} x_i$ and $v(x_I) = v(\bigcup_{i \in I} x_i)$ when the union x_I is a configuration and 0 otherwise. Together the three conditions ensure that the range of a probability valuation stays within the interval $[0, 1]$.

When there are no Opponent moves in S, a probability valuation v makes S into a probabilistic event structure [16]. Then v extends to a continuous valuation w on the Scott-open[2] sets of $\mathcal{C}^\infty(S)$, one in which $w(\{y \in \mathcal{C}^\infty(S) \mid x \subseteq y\}) = v(x)$; this yields a 1-1 correspondence between valuations on configurations and

---

[2] A *Scott-open* subset of configurations is upwards-closed w.r.t. inclusion and such that if it contains the union of a directed subset S of configurations then it contains an element of S. A *continuous valuation* is a function w from the Scott-open subsets of $\mathcal{C}^\infty(E)$ to $[0, 1]$ which is *((normalised)* $w(\mathcal{C}^\infty(E)) = 1$; *(strict)* $w(\emptyset) = 0$; *(monotone)* $U \subseteq V \implies w(U) \leq w(V)$; *(modular)* $w(U \cup V) + w(U \cap V) = w(U) + w(V)$; and *(continuous)* $w(\bigcup_{i \in I} U_i) = \sup_{i \in I} w(U_i)$, for *directed* unions.

continuous valuations on open sets [16]. Hence, by [17], the valuation v determines a probability distribution on the Borel sets. In this case $v(x)$ reads as Prob(x), the probability that the result includes the events of the finite configuration x. When S has Opponent moves, the reading of v involves conditional probabilities. When $x \subseteq^+ y$ in $\mathcal{C}(S)$, provided $v(x) \neq 0$, the conditional probability of Player making moves y given x, is expressed by Prob$(y \mid x) = v(y)/v(x)$. Player is *oblivious* to Opponent in the sense that if two events, $\oplus, \ominus$, of opposite polarities can occur at a configuration x, then not only are they causally independent there (because S is race-free), they are also probabilistically independent: Prob$(\oplus|x) = $ Prob$(\oplus|x, \ominus)$. The *monotone* condition expresses that we assign non-negative probabilities to generalised intervals $[y; x_1, \cdots, x_n]$, consisting of those configurations which include the finite configuration y but do not include any of the finite configurations $x_1, \cdots, x_n$.

The composition of strategies extends to probabilistic strategies, $\sigma : S \to A^\perp \| B$ with valuation v_σ and $\tau : T \to B^\perp \| C$ with v_τ. A configuration of their interaction, of the form $y \circledast x \in \mathcal{C}(T \circledast S)$ for $x \in \mathcal{C}(S)$ and $y \in \mathcal{C}(T)$, is assigned valuation $v_{\tau \circledast \sigma}(y \circledast x) = v_\tau(y) \cdot v_\sigma(x)$. Their composition $\tau \odot \sigma$ has probability valuation $v_{\tau \odot \sigma}(z) = v_{\tau \circledast \sigma}([z]_{T \circledast S})$ for z a finite configuration of $T \odot S$. The proof that we so obtain probability valuations relies heavily on properties of drop functions.

We obtain a bicategory of probabilistic strategies on race-free games. Because copycat is deterministic it can be assigned the constantly 1 valuation and remains an identity w.r.t. composition. The 2-cells are rigid maps of strategies which relate probability valuations across 2-cells via a *push-forward* result:

Lemma 2. *Let $f : \sigma \Rightarrow \sigma'$ be a rigid 2-cell between strategies $\sigma : S \to A$ and $\sigma' : S' \to A$. Let v be a probability valuation for σ. Taking, for $y \in \mathcal{C}(S')$, $(fv)(y) =_{\mathrm{def}} \sum_{x:fx=y} v(x)$ defines a probability valuation fv for σ', the push-forward of v.*

A 2-cell between probabilistic strategies σ, v to σ', v' is a rigid 2-cell $f : \sigma \Rightarrow \sigma'$ of strategies for which $(fv)(x') \leq v'(x')$, for all configurations $x' \in \mathcal{C}(S')$. Vertical and horizontal composition are inherited from strategies.

5.2   Quantum Strategies

The probabilistic case provides loose guidelines in extending to quantum strategies. As usual probabilities are replaced by operators but there is now the question of their type, which we take as given by the game.[3]

A *quantum game* (A, H) comprises A, a race-free event structure with polarity, together with H assigning a finite dimensional Hilbert space $H(a)$ to each event $a \in A$. It is convenient to extend the assignment to any finite $y \subseteq A$ and

---

[3] We eschew the other obvious possibility in which the game also determines the operators because we want strategies to be quantum, not just probabilistic, in line with the quantum lambda-calculus [5] and earlier definition [6].

write $H(y) =_{\text{def}} \bigotimes_{a \in y} H(a)$; in particular $H(\emptyset) = \text{I}$, the one-dimensional Hilbert space.

At this point we are guided to a quantum extension of strategies in which finite configurations of a strategy are positive operators of type given by the game. (In order to extend the probabilistic case and model the non-local nature of quantum theory we do not assign operators just to events.) Once here, it is hard to escape the quantum generalisations of the first two conditions on quantum strategies. There is though the issue of how to generalise the remaining monotone condition and the drop function on which it is based. For reasons explained shortly we adopt a strong condition in which positivity is expressed by the Löwner order between operators.

A *quantum strategy* in a quantum game (A, H) is a strategy $\sigma : S \to A$ together with a *quantum valuation* for σ, an assignment $Q(x)$ of a positive operator on $H(\sigma x)$ to each $x \in \mathcal{C}(S)$, which is

  (normalised) $Q(\emptyset) = 1$, the identity on I;
  (oblivious) if $x \subseteq^- y$ then $Q(x) \otimes \text{id}_{H(\sigma y \backslash \sigma x)} = Q(y)$; and
  (monotone) if $y \subseteq^+ x_1, \cdots, x_n$ then $d_Q[y; x_1, \cdots, x_n] \geq_L 0$,

where $d_Q[y; x_1, \cdots, x_n] =_{\text{def}} Q(y) - \sum_{\emptyset \neq I \subseteq \{1, \cdots, n\}} (-1)^{|I|+1} \text{Tr}_{H(\sigma x_I \backslash \sigma y)} Q(x_I)$.

Analogously to the probabilistic case, we take $x_I = \bigcup_{i \in I} x_i$ and $Q(x_I) = Q(\bigcup_{i \in I} x_i)$ when the union is a configuration and to be 0, the zero operator, otherwise. The role of the partial trace in the "monotone" condition is to hide the effects of operators outside the space $H(\sigma y)$, and reduce an operator on larger spaces $H(\sigma x_I)$ to one on $H(\sigma y)$.

Note a special case, when the quantum game is *classical*, in the sense that each $H(a)$ is the one-dimensional Hilbert space. Then, by the "monotone" condition, every non-zero operator $Q(x)$ is necessarily multiplication by a positive scalar, less than or equal to 1. Identifying operators on one-dimensional Hilbert space with scalars, we recover probabilistic strategies.

Another special case is that in which all the moves in the game A are those of Player. Then, by "monotone", each $Q(x)$ is a subdensity operator; so in this case states of an event structure, *viz.* configurations, are assigned *quantum states*. In moving from probabilistic to quantum strategies what were formerly probabilistic states have become quantum states. Without Opponent events we have uncovered a notion of quantum event structure (in some ways stricter, in others more general, than those defined previously [16].)

When the games contain Opponent events the operators $Q(x)$ need not have trace less than or equal to one; consider, for instance, the identity operator assigned to the singleton configuration of a strategy over a quantum game comprising a single Opponent event with a space of dimension 2. The operators $Q(x)$ will however be *1-bounded*—the output's norm never exceeds that of the input, see Proposition 3.

There is the issue of the choice of "monotone" condition. Why not weaken it to one in which the drop is reduced to a real number using the full trace operation? Because the weaker form is not preserved by composition of strategies.

Quantum Strategies and Superoperators. We characterise those positive operators $Q(x)$ on $H(\sigma x)$ which are assigned to $x \in \mathcal{C}(S)$ in a quantum strategy $\sigma : S \to A$ w.r.t. a quantum game (A, H). This involves splitting a configuration x into its Opponent and Player events, x^- and x^+ respectively.

Lemma 3. *Let $\sigma : S \to A$ with Q be a quantum strategy in a quantum game (A, H). For any $x \in \mathcal{C}(S)$, $Q(x)$ is a positive operator for which*

$$\mathrm{Tr}_{H(\sigma x^+)}(Q(x)) \leq_L \mathrm{id}_{H(\sigma x^-)} \text{ in the Löwner order.}$$

Given a positive operator Q on $N \otimes P$, for which $\mathrm{Tr}_P(Q) \leq_L \mathrm{id}_N$, it is easy to arrange a quantum strategy in which Q is assigned to a finite configuration.

Example 1. Let A be the quantum game $\ominus \rightarrowtail \oplus$ with $\ominus$ assigned Hilbert space N and $\oplus$ the space P. Imagine a quantum strategy $\sigma : S \to A$ where S has the same shape as A, *viz.* $\ominus \rightarrowtail \oplus$. It will necessarily assign id_N to the configuration $\{\ominus\}$ and the operators Q that can be assigned to $\{\ominus, \oplus\}$ are precisely those positive operators Q on $N \otimes P$, for which $\mathrm{Tr}_P(Q) \leq_L \mathrm{id}_N$.

Lemma 3 informs us how to rescale a quantum valuation to obtain subdensity operators whose trace is a probability valuation:

Proposition 2. *Let Q be a quantum valuation for a strategy $\sigma : S \to A$. Defining $\rho(x) = Q(x)/\dim(H(\sigma x^-))$ we obtain subdensity operators for all $x \in \mathcal{C}(S)$. Their trace $v(x) = \mathrm{tr}(\rho(x)) = \mathrm{tr}(Q(x)/\dim(H(\sigma x^-)))$, for $x \in \mathcal{C}(S)$, yields a probability valuation v for σ.*

Via the Choi-Jamiolkowski isomorphism, the positive operators $Q(x)$ assigned to a strategy correspond to superoperators. In more detail, a positive operator $Q(x) \in \mathbf{Pos}(H(\sigma x))$ is an operator

$$Q(x) \in \mathbf{Pos}((H(\sigma x^-)^*)^* \otimes H(\sigma x^+))$$

which corresponds under Choi-Jamiolkowski to a completely positive map

$$^-Q^+(x) : \mathbf{CPM}(H(\sigma x^-)^*, H(\sigma x^+)).$$

In quantum strategies, the operators $Q(x)$ are precisely those which correspond to superoperators $^-Q^+(x)$ —a corollary of the following refinement of the Choi-Jamiolkowski isomorphism (read $H(\sigma x^-)$ for N and $H(\sigma x^+)$ for P):

Lemma 4. *Let N and P be finite dimensional Hilbert spaces. Positive operators $Q \in \mathbf{Pos}(N \otimes P)$, for which $\mathrm{Tr}_P(Q) \leq_L \mathrm{id}_N$ in the Löwner order, correspond via the Choi-Jamiolkowski isomorphism to trace non-increasing completely positive maps $\mathrm{CJ}^{-1}(Q) \in \mathbf{CPM}(N^*, P)$, i.e. superoperators.*

The view espoused by Leifer and Spekkens of this refinement of the CJ-isomorphism is that it establishes a correspondence between *conditional* quantum states of P, conditional on N, and superoperators from N to P, understood as the quantum analogue of stochastic maps [18]. Their view is underscored here in strategies where the explicit contingency on the environment through Opponent moves leads to matching intuitions.

It follows as a corollary of Lemma 4 that any positive operator $Q(x)$, where $x \in \mathcal{C}(S)$, is necessarily 1-bounded:

Proposition 3. *A positive operator Q on $N \otimes P$ for which $\mathrm{Tr}_P(Q) \leq_L \mathrm{id}_N$ in the Löwner order is 1-bounded.*

Let $\sigma : S \to A$ be a strategy in a race-free game A, expanded to a quantum game (A, H). In summary, in moving from a probabilistic valuation v to a quantum valuation Q, w.r.t. $x \in \mathcal{C}(S)$, we replace: the valuation $v(x) \in [0, \infty)$, at $x \in \mathcal{C}(S)$, by a bounded positive operator $Q(x)$; that the value $v(x)$ is in $[0, 1]$, by $Q(x)$ being a 1-bounded positive operator; the order $\leq$ on the reals by the Löwner order $\leq_L$ on operators; that $v(x) = \mathrm{Prob}(x)$, when $x = x^+$, by $Q(x)$ being a sub-density operator, *i.e.* a quantum state; the conditional probability $v(x)$ by a conditional state $Q(x)$; multiplication in the reals by composition in **CPM**. Indeed, in the next section, composition in **CPM** will play a central role in the composition of quantum valuations, replacing the role of multiplication in composing probabilistic valuations.

6   Quantum Strategies Between Games

We extend the operations on games, simple parallel composition and dual, to quantum games (A, H_A) and (B, H_B). Any finite subset z of $A \| B$ splits as $z = x \| y$ for unique finite subsets x of A and y of B; we take $H_{A \| B}(z) = H_A(x) \otimes H_B(y)$. A quantum game (A, H_A) has *dual* $(A^\perp, H_{A^\perp})$ where $H_{A^\perp}(z)$ is the dual Hilbert space $H_A(z)^*$, for any finite subset z of $A^\perp$.

6.1   Quantum Valuations as Completely Positive Maps

Before we compose quantum strategies we reformulate quantum valuations as maps in **CPM**. Let $\sigma : S \to A^\perp \| B$ be a quantum strategy with valuation Q_S. For $x \in \mathcal{C}(S)$ its image in the game $A^\perp \| B$ decomposes into $x_A \| x_B = \sigma x$, where $x_A \in \mathcal{C}(A)$ and $x_B \in \mathcal{C}(B)$. Thus $Q_S(x)$ is a positive operator on $H_{A^\perp \| B}(\sigma x) = H_A(x_A)^* \otimes H_B(x_B)$. As such, it corresponds via the Choi-Jamiolkowski isomorphism to a completely positive map

$$Q_S(x) \in \mathbf{CPM}(H_A(x_A), H_B(x_B)).$$

(The map need not be a superoperator, but note, in general, it acts between conditional quantum states not merely mixed states.)

Via the compact-closure of **FdHilb**, we can reformulate the conditions required of a quantum strategy now with the corresponding assignments Q of completely positive maps. In the reformulation, when $x \subseteq^- y$, we shall require the *expansion* of a map $Q \in \mathbf{CPM}(H_A(x_A), H_B(x_B))$ to

$$\Uparrow^y (Q) = Q \otimes (1_{H_B(y_B \setminus x_B)} \circ \mathrm{tr}_{H_A(y_A \setminus x_A)})$$

in $\mathbf{CPM}(H_A(y_A), H_B(y_B))$. Similarly, in rephrasing the "monotone" condition, when $y \subseteq^+ x$, we need the *reduction* of a map $Q \in \mathbf{CPM}(H_A(x_A), H_B(x_B))$ to

$$\Downarrow_y (Q) = (\mathrm{id}_{H_B(y_B)} \otimes \mathrm{tr}_{H_B(x_B \setminus y_B)}) \circ Q \circ (\mathrm{id}_{H_A(y_A)} \otimes 1_{H_A(x_A \setminus y_A)})$$

in $\mathbf{CPM}(H_A(y_A), H_B(y_B))$. The expansion and reduction operations on completely positive maps correspond via the CJ-isomorphism to the earlier operations (tensoring with an identity and partial trace) we saw earlier on positive operators. The conditions on a quantum valuation become

(*normalised*) $Q(\emptyset) = 1 \in \mathbf{CPM}(\mathrm{I}, \mathrm{I})$;
(*oblivious*) if $x \subseteq^- y$ then $\Uparrow^y (Q(x)) = Q(y)$; and
(*monotone*) if $y \subseteq^+ x_1, \cdots, x_n$ then $d_Q[y; x_1, \ldots, x_n]$ is in
$\mathbf{CPM}(H(x_A), H(x_B))$, where

$$d_Q[y; x_1, \ldots, x_n] = Q(y) - \sum_{\emptyset \neq I \subseteq \{1, \ldots, n\}} (-1)^{|I|+1} \Downarrow_y (Q(x_I)),$$

again with the understanding that $Q(x_I) = Q(\bigcup_{i \in I} x_i)$ when the union is a configuration and the zero map otherwise.

6.2   Quantum Copycat

Let (A, H_A) be a race-free quantum game. We can extend a copycat strategy $\propto_A : \mathbb{C}_A \to A^\perp \| A$ with a quantum valuation. Recall a finite configuration of $\mathbb{C}_A$ comprises $x \| y$ where $x, y \in \mathcal{C}(A)$ are in the Scott order $y \sqsubseteq x$, so $y \supseteq^- x \cap y \subseteq^+ x$. We thus have the inclusion $(x \cap y) \| (x \cap y) \subseteq x \| y$ in $\mathcal{C}(\mathbb{C}_A)$. Define the quantum valuation of copycat as

$$Q_{\propto_A}(x \| y) = \Uparrow^{x \| y} (\mathrm{id}_{H_A(x \cap y)}) \in \mathbf{CPM}(H_A(x), H_A(y)),$$

the expansion of the identity on $H_A(x \cap y)$ in $\mathbf{CPM}$. Its being a quantum valuation depends on A being race-free to validate the "monotone" condition.

6.3   Composition of Quantum Strategies

Consider quantum strategies $\sigma : S \to A^\perp \| B$, Q_σ and $\tau : T \to B^\perp \| C$, Q_τ. We assign a quantum valuation, $Q_{\tau \circledast \sigma}$ to their interaction. Recall, the interaction

$$\tau \circledast \sigma : T \circledast S \to A^\perp \| B^0 \| C,$$

in which the events of B are reset to have neutral polarity, and are now additionally assigned the one-dimensional Hilbert space. Recall a configuration of $T \circledast S$ has the form $y \circledast x$, for unique $x \in \mathcal{C}(S)$ and $y \in \mathcal{C}(T)$. We have

$$Q_\sigma(x) \in \mathbf{CPM}(H_A(x_A), H_B(x_B)),$$

where $x_A \| x_B = \sigma x$, with $x_A \in \mathcal{C}(A)$ and $x_B \in \mathcal{C}(B)$. Similarly,

$$Q_\tau(y) \in \mathbf{CPM}(H_B(y_B), H_C(y_C)),$$

for a decomposition $y_B \| y_C = \tau y$. Define

$$Q_{\tau \circledast \sigma}(y \circledast x) =_{\mathrm{def}} Q_\tau(y) \circ Q_\sigma(x) \in \mathbf{CPM}(H_A(x_A), H_C(y_C)).$$

The composition is well-defined because for $y \circledast x$ to be defined configurations x and y must share a common image, $x_B = y_B$, in the game B.

The composition $\tau \odot \sigma : T \odot S \to A^\perp \| C$ has quantum valuation $Q_{\tau \odot \sigma}(z) = Q_{\tau \odot \sigma}([z]_{T \circledast S})$ for z a finite configuration of $T \odot S$.

In particular, the interaction $\tau \circledast \sigma : T \circledast S \to B^0$, of a strategy $\sigma : S \to B$ against a counterstrategy $\tau : T \to B^\perp$, has $Q_{\tau \circledast \sigma}$ assign a non-negative real to each finite configuration of $T \circledast S$ to form a probability valuation, making $T \circledast S$ into a probabilistic event structure. We can push forward the probability valuation of $T \circledast S$ to a probability valuation of B (via the continuous valuation induced on the Scott open sets of $\mathcal{C}^\infty(T \circledast S)$) and consequently to a probability distribution over $\mathcal{C}^\infty(B)$, the possible resulting end positions of the play.

The proof that composition yields a quantum strategy mimics that in the probabilistic case, but generalising from the reals to quantum operations.

Theorem 4. *The composition of two quantum strategies is a quantum strategy and, up to isomorphism, has quantum copycat is its identity.*

6.4 A Bicategory of Quantum Strategies

In analogy with the probabilistic case, 2-cells between quantum strategies are rigid maps of strategies which relate quantum valuations across 2-cells via a *push-forward* result:

Lemma 5. *Let $f : \sigma \Rightarrow \sigma'$ be a rigid 2-cell between strategies $\sigma : S \to A$ and $\sigma' : S' \to A$. Let Q be a quantum valuation for σ. Taking, for $y \in \mathcal{C}(S')$,*

$$(fQ)(y) =_{\mathrm{def}} \sum_{x : fx = y} Q(x)$$

defines a quantum valuation fQ for σ', the quantum push-forward.

A bicategory of quantum strategies on race-free quantum games ensues. Its maps are quantum strategies. A 2-cell between quantum strategies from σ, Q to σ', Q' is a rigid 2-cell $f : \sigma \Rightarrow \sigma'$ of strategies for which $Q'(x') - (fQ)(x')$ is completely positive for all configurations $x' \in \mathcal{C}(S')$. The bicategory of quantum strategies inherits compact-closure from that of plain strategies and $\mathbf{CPM}$.

There are notable special cases.

Proposition 4. *The sub-bicategory of quantum strategies on games (A, H_A), in which H_A is constantly the one-dimensional Hilbert space, is isomorphic to the bicategory of probabilistic strategies.*

Consider the sub-(bi)categories in which the games consist purely of Player moves. When there is no additional quantum structure, the strategies in this case yield a sub-bicategory equivalent to *stable spans*, a model which underlies treatments of nondeterministic dataflow [19]; restricting to deterministic strategies on countable games, the sub-bicategory is equivalent to Berry's dI-domains and stable functions. Broadened to quantum games and quantum strategies, all the quantum assignments $Q(x)$ will be a superoperators and we obtain a framework for quantum dataflow and, in particular, for the semantics of quantum flowcharts [20]. Of more interest though, are interpretations of higher-order languages such as quantum λ-calculi where interactions are more complicated and in which polarities play a more intricate role [13].

Acknowledgments. We are grateful to the ERC for Advanced Grant ECSYM. Discussions with Frank Roumen and Benoît Valiron have been very helpful.

References

1. Winskel, G.: Events, causality and symmetry. Comput. J. **54**, 42–57 (2011)
2. Winskel, G.: Distributed games and strategies. Festschrift for pierre-louis curien on the occasion of his 60th birthday (2014, as yet unpublished)
3. Winskel, G.: Distributed probabilistic and quantum strategies. Electr. Notes Theor. Comput. Sci. **298**, 403–425 (2013)
4. Grabbe, J.: An introduction to quantum game theory. arXiv preprint quant-ph/0506219 (2005)
5. Pagani, M., Selinger, P., Valiron, B.: Applying quantitative semantics to higher-order quantum computing. In: POPL 2014 (2014)
6. Delbecque, Y., Panagaden, P.: Game semantics for quantum stores. MFPS XXIV, Electr. Notes Theor. Comput. Sci. **218**, 153–170 (2008)
7. Dal Lago, U., Faggian, C., Valiron, B., Yoshimizu, A.: The geometry of parallelism, classical, probabilistic, and quantum effects. In: POPL 2017 (2017)
8. Brukner, C.: Quantum causality. Nat. Phys. **10**, 259 (2014)
9. Abramsky, S., Coecke, B.: A categorical semantics of quantum protocols. In: LICS 2004 (2004)
10. Castellan, S., Clairambault, P., Winskel, G.: The parallel intensionally fully abstract games model of PCF. In: LICS 2015 (2015)
11. Castellan, S., Clairambault, P., Paquet, H., Winskel, G.: The concurrent game semantics of probabilistic PCF. In: LICS 2018 (2018)
12. Selinger, P., Valiron, B.: On a fully abstract model for a quantum linear functional language. Electr. Notes Theor. Comput. Sci. **210**, 123–137 (2008)
13. Clairambault, P., de Visme, M., Winskel, G.: Game semantics for quantum programming. In: POPL 2019 (2019)
14. Joyal, A., Street, R., Verity, D.: Traced monoidal categories. In: Mathematical Proceedings of the Cambridge Philosophical Society (1996)
15. Selinger, P.: Dagger compact closed categories and completely positive maps: (extended abstract). Electr. Notes Theor. Comput. Sci. **170**, 139–163 (2007)
16. Winskel, G.: Probabilistic and quantum event structures. In: van Breugel, F., Kashefi, E., Palamidessi, C., Rutten, J. (eds.) Horizons of the Mind. A Tribute to Prakash Panangaden. LNCS, vol. 8464, pp. 476–497. Springer, Cham (2014). https://doi.org/10.1007/978-3-319-06880-0_25

17. Alvarez-Manilla, M., Edalat, A., Saheb-Djahromi, N.: An extension result for continuous valuations. J. LMS **61**, 629–640 (2000)
18. Leifer, M.S., Spekkens, R.W.: Towards a formulation of quantum theory as a causally neutral theory of Bayesian inference. Phys. Rev. **88**, 052130 (2013)
19. Saunders-Evans, L., Winskel, G.: Event structure spans for nondeterministic dataflow. Electr. Notes Theor. Comput. Sci. **175**(3), 109–129 (2007)
20. Selinger, P.: Towards a quantum programming language. Math. Struct. Comput. Sci. **14**, 527–586 (2004)

Theory and Foundation

A Birkhoff Connection Between Quantum Circuits and Linear Classical Reversible Circuits

Alexis De Vos[1(✉)] and Stijn De Baerdemacker[2]

[1] Vakgroep Elektronica en Informatiesystemen, Universiteit Gent,
9000 Ghent, Belgium
alexis.devos@ugent.be
[2] Department of Chemistry, University of New Brunswick,
Fredericton E3B 5A3, Canada

Abstract. Birkhoff's theorem tells how any doubly stochastic matrix can be decomposed as a weighted sum of permutation matrices. Similar theorems on unitary matrices reveal a connection between quantum circuits and linear classical reversible circuits. It triggers the question whether a quantum computer can be regarded as a superposition of classical reversible computers.

1 Introduction

Let D be an arbitrary $n \times n$ doubly stochastic matrix. This means that all entries D_{jk} are real and satisfy $0 \leq D_{jk} \leq 1$ and that all line sums (i.e. the n row sums and the n column sums) are equal to 1. Let $P(n)$ be the group of $n \times n$ permutation matrices. Birkhoff [1] has demonstrated

Theorem 1. *Any $n \times n$ doubly stochastic matrix D can be written*

$$D = \sum_j c_j P_j$$

with all $P_j \in P(n)$ and the weights c_j real, satisfying both $0 \leq c_j \leq 1$ and $\sum_j c_j = 1$.

Because unitary matrices describe quantum circuits [2] and permutation matrices describe classical reversible circuits [3], the question arises whether a similar theorem holds for matrices from the unitary group $U(n)$. In a sloppy way, one might reformulate the question as:

Is a quantum computer a quantum superposition of a finite number of classical (reversible) computers?

It is a surprise that (to our knowledge) this problem has not been discussed in the literature.

© Springer Nature Switzerland AG 2019
M. K. Thomsen and M. Soeken (Eds.): RC 2019, LNCS 11497, pp. 23–33, 2019.
https://doi.org/10.1007/978-3-030-21500-2_2

It is clear that a simple positive answer to the above question is not possible. Indeed, any sum $\sum_j c_j P_j$ is a matrix with identical line sums (equal to $\sum_j c_j$), whereas an arbitrary unitary matrix usually does not have identical line sums. Moreover, if all c_j are real, then the matrix $\sum_j c_j P_j$ has exclusively real entries, again a property not shown by an arbitrary unitary matrix. Nevertheless, below we will present some Birkhoff-like theorems concerning $n \times n$ unitary matrices in general and $2^w \times 2^w$ unitary matrices in peculiar.

2   The ZXZ Decomposition of a Unitary Matrix

Each quantum circuit acting on w qubits is represented by a $2^w \times 2^w$ unitary matrix. Such matrix thus is a member of the unitary group $U(n)$ with $n = 2^w$. In light of quantum circuit decomposition, the (sub)group structure of $U(n)$ is particularly important. We note the following two useful subgroups [4,5]:

- XU(n), i.e. the group of U(n) matrices with all line sums equal to 1 and
- ZU(n), i.e. the group of diagonal U(n) matrices with upper-left entry equal to 1.

Whereas U(n) is a group of dimension n^2, XU(n) is a group of dimension $(n-1)^2$ and ZU(n) is a group of dimension $n - 1$.

Idel and Wolf [6] proved the following theorem:

Theorem 2. *Every $n \times n$ unitary matrix U can be decomposed as*

$$U = a\, Z_1 X Z_2, \tag{1}$$

where both Z_1 and Z_2 are ZU(n) matrices, where X is an XU(n) matrix, and a is a unit-modulus scalar.

Proof of the theorem is based on simplectic topology and, unfortunately, is not constructive. There exists an iterative method [7] for, given a matrix U, finding a set (a, Z_1, X, Z_2) with arbitrary numerical precision. If n equals 2^w, then the matrix decomposition expresses the decomposition of a quantum circuit acting on w qubits [8]. The 3-qubit case ($n = 8$) looks like

3   The Birkhoff Decomposition of the XU Matrix

De Baerdemacker et al. [9] proved the following theorem:

Theorem 3. *Every XU(n) matrix X can be decomposed as*

$$X = \sum_{j=1}^{n!} c_j P_j,$$

where P_j are the $n \times n$ permutation matrices and c_j are complex numbers, such that both $\sum c_j = 1$ and $\sum |c_j|^2 = 1$.

De Baerdemacker et al. provide an algorithm to find any possible set of appropriate weights c_j. This set is far from unique (except if $n = 2$).

De Vos and De Baerdemacker [10,11] demonstrated, in case n equals a power of 2 (say, $n = 2^w$), the following theorem:

Theorem 4. *Every XU(2^w) matrix X can be decomposed as*

$$X = \sum_{j=1}^{N(w)} c_j E_j,$$

where j runs over all $2^w \times 2^w$ epicirculant permutation matrices E_j, where c_j are complex numbers, such that both $\sum c_j = 1$ and $\sum |c_j|^2 = 1$, and $N(w)$ equals $2^w(2^w - 1)(2^w - 2)(2^w - 2^2)...(2^w - 2^{w-1})$.

In next section will be explained what is meant with 'epicirculant matrix'. Theorem 4 is stronger than Theorem 3, because $N(w)$ scales much better than $(2^w)!$ for large w, as can be seen in the table:

w	2^w	$(2^w)!$	$N(w)$
1	2	2	2
2	4	24	24
3	8	40,320	1,344
4	16	20,922,789,888,000	322,560

One possible set of weights c_j is given by

$$c_j = \delta_{1,j} + \frac{2^w - 1}{N(w)} \left[\text{Trace}\left(E_j^{-1} X\right) - \text{Trace}\left(E_j\right) \right],$$

where the Kronecker delta assumes that the epicirculant matrix E_1 is the $2^w \times 2^w$ unit matrix.

4   Epicirculant Matrices

Before giving the definition of a $2^w \times 2^w$ epicirculant matrix, it is useful to introduce some convenient conventions:

Remark 1. *In the present paper, rows and columns of any $2^w \times 2^w$ matrix are numbered from 0 to $2^w - 1$ (instead of the conventional numbering from 1 to 2^w) and each such number is represented by the $w \times 1$ matrix consisting of the w bits of the binary notation of the row-or-column number.*

E.g. the upper-left entry of the 8×8 matrix A is entry $A_{0,0} = A_{(0,0,0)^T,(0,0,0)^T}$, whereas its lower-right entry is denoted $A_{7,7} = A_{(1,1,1)^T,(1,1,1)^T}$. Further, we choose to order bits from least significant to most significant bit. E.g., for $w = 3$, the vector $(1,1,0)^T$ denotes the number 3.

Definition 1. *A $2^w \times 2^w$ epicirculant matrix M is a $2^w \times 2^w$ matrix, such that each entry $M_{j,k}$ equals the entry $M_{0,c}$ with $c = k - xj$, where the multiplication xj is a matrix multiplication performed modulo 2, and where x is some invertible $w \times w$ matrix with entries from $\{0,1\}$, called the pitch matrix. The subtraction $k - xj$ is a vector addition performed modulo 2.*

E.g. the following matrix is an 8×8 epicirculant matrix with pitch matrix $x = \begin{pmatrix} 1 & 0 & 0 \\ 0 & 0 & 1 \\ 0 & 1 & 1 \end{pmatrix}$:

$$
\begin{pmatrix}
m_0 & m_1 & m_2 & m_3 & m_4 & m_5 & m_6 & m_7 \\
m_1 & m_0 & m_3 & m_2 & m_5 & m_4 & m_7 & m_6 \\
m_4 & m_5 & m_6 & m_7 & m_0 & m_1 & m_2 & m_3 \\
m_5 & m_4 & m_7 & m_6 & m_1 & m_0 & m_3 & m_2 \\
m_6 & m_7 & m_4 & m_5 & m_2 & m_3 & m_0 & m_1 \\
m_7 & m_6 & m_5 & m_4 & m_3 & m_2 & m_1 & m_0 \\
m_2 & m_3 & m_0 & m_1 & m_6 & m_7 & m_4 & m_5 \\
m_3 & m_2 & m_1 & m_0 & m_7 & m_6 & m_5 & m_4
\end{pmatrix}.
\tag{2}
$$

Thanks to the fact that matrix x is invertible, not only each of the eight rows but also each of the eight columns contains exactly one m_0, one m_1, ..., and one m_7. If all entries of its upper row (i.e. row 0) are equal to 0, except one entry equal to 1 (in column s), then an epicirculant matrix is an epicirculant permutation matrix. The vector representing position s is called the shift vector. There exist as many different epicirculant permutation matrices as there exist possible shift vectors (i.e. 2^w) times the number of possible pitch matrices (i.e. $(2^w - 1)(2^w - 2)(2^w - 2^2)...(2^w - 2^{w-1})$). Because

- the shift vectors form a group isomorphic to the direct product $(\mathbf{C_2})^w$ of w cyclic groups, each of order 2, and therefore of order 2^w and
- the pitch matrices form a group isomorphic to the general linear group $GL(w,2)$ of order $(2^w - 1)(2^w - 2)(2^w - 2^2)...(2^w - 2^{w-1})$,

the epicirculant permutation matrices form a group [12] isomorphic to the general affine group $GA(w,2)$ of order $N(w)$, isomorphic to the semidirect product $(\mathbf{C_2})^w : GL(w,2)$. E.g. the following matrix is an 8×8 epicirculant permutation matrix with shift vector $s = \begin{pmatrix} 0 \\ 1 \\ 0 \end{pmatrix}$ and pitch matrix $x = \begin{pmatrix} 1 & 0 & 0 \\ 0 & 0 & 1 \\ 0 & 1 & 1 \end{pmatrix}$:

$$\begin{pmatrix} 0\,0\,1\,0\,0\,0\,0\,0 \\ 0\,0\,0\,1\,0\,0\,0\,0 \\ 0\,0\,0\,0\,0\,0\,1\,0 \\ 0\,0\,0\,0\,0\,0\,0\,1 \\ 0\,0\,0\,0\,1\,0\,0\,0 \\ 0\,0\,0\,0\,0\,1\,0\,0 \\ 1\,0\,0\,0\,0\,0\,0\,0 \\ 0\,1\,0\,0\,0\,0\,0\,0 \end{pmatrix}. \tag{3}$$

It is obtained from matrix (2) by choosing $m_2 = 1$ and $m_k = 0$ for $k \neq 2$. We note that, if s is the $w \times 1$ zero matrix and x is the $w \times w$ unit matrix, then the corresponding epicirculant permutation matrix is the $2^w \times 2^w$ unit matrix E_1.

We have [11]:

Lemma 1. *Each epicirculant permutation matrix E can be written as the product of a zero-shift epicirculant permutation matrix L and a unit-pitch epicirculant permutation matrix N:*

$$E = LN.$$

E.g. matrix (3) has the decomposition

$$\begin{pmatrix} 1\,0\,0\,0\,0\,0\,0\,0 \\ 0\,1\,0\,0\,0\,0\,0\,0 \\ 0\,0\,0\,0\,1\,0\,0\,0 \\ 0\,0\,0\,0\,0\,1\,0\,0 \\ 0\,0\,0\,0\,0\,0\,1\,0 \\ 0\,0\,0\,0\,0\,0\,0\,1 \\ 0\,0\,1\,0\,0\,0\,0\,0 \\ 0\,0\,0\,1\,0\,0\,0\,0 \end{pmatrix} \begin{pmatrix} 0\,0\,1\,0\,0\,0\,0\,0 \\ 0\,0\,0\,1\,0\,0\,0\,0 \\ 1\,0\,0\,0\,0\,0\,0\,0 \\ 0\,1\,0\,0\,0\,0\,0\,0 \\ 0\,0\,0\,0\,0\,0\,1\,0 \\ 0\,0\,0\,0\,0\,0\,0\,1 \\ 0\,0\,0\,0\,1\,0\,0\,0 \\ 0\,0\,0\,0\,0\,1\,0\,0 \end{pmatrix}. \tag{4}$$

The left matrix has shift equal to $\begin{pmatrix} 0 \\ 0 \\ 0 \end{pmatrix}$ and pitch equal to $\begin{pmatrix} 1\,0\,0 \\ 0\,0\,1 \\ 0\,1\,1 \end{pmatrix}$, whereas the right matrix has shift vector $\begin{pmatrix} 0 \\ 1 \\ 0 \end{pmatrix}$ and pitch matrix $\begin{pmatrix} 1\,0\,0 \\ 0\,1\,0 \\ 0\,0\,1 \end{pmatrix}$.

From classical reversible computation [3, 13–15], we know the following two lemmas:

Lemma 2. *An arbitrary zero-shift epicirculant permutation matrix L represents a linear circuit, i.e. a circuit consisting exclusively of singly controlled NOT gates (a.k.a. FEYNMAN gates).*

and

Lemma 3. *An arbitrary unit-pitch epicirculant permutation matrix N represents a circuit consisting merely of a stack of w single-qubit gates, each either an IDENTITY gate or a NOT gate. We call such stack a NOT stack.*

E.g. the product (4) represents the circuit cascade

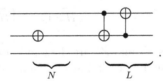

In general, N consists of 0 to w NOTs and L consists of $\mathcal{O}(w^2)$ or $\mathcal{O}(\frac{w^2}{\log(w)})$ controlled NOTs, depending on the synthesis method applied [13,14].

5   The Birkhoff Decomposition of the Two ZU Matrices

Because a member Z of the group $\mathrm{ZU}(n)$ is diagonal, it cannot be decomposed as a weighted sum $\sum c_j P_j$ of permutation matrices P_j, such that the weight sum $\sum c_j$ equals 1. Indeed, if $\sum c_j = 1$, then all line sums of the matrix $\sum c_j P_j$ are equal to 1. Except for the $n \times n$ unit matrix, no diagonal matrix has this property. For this reason, we decompose the matrices Z_1 and Z_2 of (1) according to

$$Z_1 = GX_1G^{-1} \quad \text{and} \quad Z_2 = GX_2G^{-1}, \tag{5}$$

where G is a constant $n \times n$ (dephased) Hadamard matrix [16]. As the unitary matrices Z_1 and Z_2 have unit upper-left entry, automatically, X_1 and X_2 (equal to $G^{-1}Z_1G$ and $G^{-1}Z_2G$, respectively) have all line sums equal to 1.

If $n = 2^w$, we choose the following Hadamard matrix:

$$G = H \otimes H \otimes \dots \otimes H, \tag{6}$$

i.e. the Kronecker product of w small (i.e. 2×2) Hadamard matrices

$$H = \frac{1}{\sqrt{2}} \begin{pmatrix} 1 & 1 \\ 1 & -1 \end{pmatrix}. \tag{7}$$

The matrix G has following entries:

$$G_{a,b} = \frac{1}{\sqrt{2^w}} (-1)^{f(a,b)},$$

where $f(x, y)$ is the sum of the bitwise product of the binary numbers x and y and hence the matrix product of the row vector x^T and the column vector y:

$$f(x, y) = \sum_j x_j y_j \bmod 2 = x^T y.$$

With this choice of G, the two matrix decompositions (5) represent the following circuit decomposition:

As the unitary matrices Z_1 and Z_2 are diagonal, automatically, X_1 and X_2 are epicirculant with unit pitch matrix. Indeed, if a $2^w \times 2^w$ matrix D is diagonal and G is given by (6, 7), then an arbitrary entry of the product $G^{-1}DG$ is given by

$$
\begin{aligned}
(G^{-1}DG)_{j,k} &= \sum_r \sum_s (G^{-1})_{j,r} D_{r,s} G_{s,k} \\
&= \sum_r \frac{1}{\sqrt{2^w}} (-1)^{-r^T j} D_{r,r} \frac{1}{\sqrt{2^w}} (-1)^{r^T k} \\
&= \frac{1}{2^w} \sum_r (-1)^{r^T (k-j)} D_{r,r}.
\end{aligned}
$$

We note that $(G^{-1}DG)_{0,k-j} = \frac{1}{2^w} \sum_r (-1)^{r^T (k-j)} D_{r,r}$ equals $(G^{-1}DG)_{j,k}$, which means that $G^{-1}DG$ is epicirculant according to Definition 1 with x equal to the $w \times w$ unit matrix.

Any $2^w \times 2^w$ epicirculant matrix M satisfies

$$
M = \sum_{m=0}^{2^w-1} M_{0,m} F_m,
$$

with F_m the epicirculant permutation matrix with shift vector equal to m and same pitch matrix as M. Hence, X_1 and X_2 satisfy the (short) Birkhoff sums:

$$
X_1 = \sum_{j=1}^{2^w} a_j E_j \quad \text{and} \quad X_2 = \sum_{j=1}^{2^w} b_j E_j,
$$

where the E_j are the epicirculant permutation matrices with unit pitch matrix. Because X_1 and X_2 are unitary, we immediately have $\sum |a_j|^2 = \sum |(X_1)_{0,j}|^2 = 1$ and $\sum |b_j|^2 = \sum |(X_2)_{0,j}|^2 = 1$. Moreover, because both X_1 and X_2 have row sums equal to 1, we have $\sum a_j = \sum (X_1)_{0,j} = 1$ and $\sum b_j = \sum (X_2)_{0,j} = 1$.

The unit-pitch epicirculant permutation matrices form a group isomorphic to the direct product $(\mathbf{C}_2)^w$ of order 2^w. According to Lemma 3, such permutation matrix E_j represents a NOT stack.

6   The Birkhoff Decomposition of the Scalar Factor

The unit-modulus scalar a in (1) is to be interpreted as a $2^w \times 2^w$ unitary matrix A, i.e. a times the $2^w \times 2^w$ unit matrix. It thus is also a times the $2^w \times 2^w$ identity permutation matrix. Therefore it is a weighted 'sum' of permutation matrices:

$$
A = \sum_j d_j P_j = a P_1.
$$

We have $\sum |d_j|^2 = |a|^2 = 1$; however, the sum $\sum_j d_j = a$ usually is <u>not</u> equal to 1.

The matrix A equals the Kronecker product

$$I \otimes I \otimes I \otimes ... \otimes I \otimes \begin{pmatrix} a & 0 \\ 0 & a \end{pmatrix} \otimes I \otimes I \otimes I \otimes ... \otimes I,$$

with $w-1$ appearances of the factor $I = \begin{pmatrix} 1 & 0 \\ 0 & 1 \end{pmatrix}$ and, within the product, arbitrary position of the factor $\begin{pmatrix} a & 0 \\ 0 & a \end{pmatrix}$. The scalar a thus represents a w-qubit quantum circuit with merely one single-qubit gate acting on an arbitrary wire.

7   The Birkhoff Decomposition of the U Matrix

From the above discussion, we see that any w-qubit quantum circuit can be constructed as the following cascade:

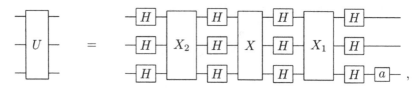

containing

- $4w + 1$ single-qubit gates represented by U(2) matrices:
  - $4w$ HADAMARD gates and
  - one PHASE-SHIFT gate
  and
- three w-qubit circuits represented by $\mathrm{XU}(2^w)$ matrices:
  - one decomposable as a weighted sum of classical reversible circuits consisting of 2-bit gates (controlled NOT gates) and single-bit gates (NOT gates) and
  - two decomposable as a weighted sum of classical reversible circuits consisting exclusively of single-bit gates (NOT gates).

We have

$$U = a\,Z_1 X Z_2$$
$$= a\,G X_1 G^{-1} X G X_2 G^{-1}$$
$$= a\,G\,(\sum_{j_1=1}^{2^w} a_{j_1} E_{j_1})\,G^{-1}\,(\sum_{j=1}^{N(w)} c_j E_j)\,G\,(\sum_{j_2=1}^{2^w} b_{j_2} E_{j_2})\,G^{-1}$$
$$= a \sum_{j_1=1}^{2^w} \sum_{j=1}^{N(w)} \sum_{j_2=1}^{2^w} a_{j_1} c_j b_{j_2}\,G E_{j_1} G^{-1} E_j G E_{j_2} G^{-1}. \tag{8}$$

We note that the identities

$$-\boxed{H}-\boxed{H}- \quad = \quad \text{———}$$

and

imply that each of the two compositions $GE_{j_1}G^{-1}$ and $GE_{j_2}G^{-1}$ can be replaced by a stack of w gates, each either an IDENTITY gate, representing the unit matrix $\begin{pmatrix} 1 & 0 \\ 0 & 1 \end{pmatrix}$, or a Z gate, representing the matrix

$$Z = \begin{pmatrix} 1 & 0 \\ 0 & -1 \end{pmatrix}.$$

Thus:

Lemma 4. *A* NOT *stack sandwiched between two* HADAMARD *stacks is a* Z *stack.*

The Z stacks form a group isomorphic to $(\mathbf{C}_2)^w$ and are represented by diagonal $2^w \times 2^w$ matrices with an upper-left entry equal to 1 and all other diagonal entries equal to ± 1. Thus the matrix $GE_{j_1}G^{-1}E_jGE_{j_2}G^{-1}$ within Eq. (8) represents an epicirculant permutation matrix sandwiched between two Z stacks and hence is a signed epicirculant permutation matrix. We summarise the present section by a new theorem:

Theorem 5. *Every* $U(2^w)$ *matrix* U *can be decomposed as*

$$U = a \sum_{j=1}^{M(w)} c_j S_j,$$

where a is a complex (unit-modulus) scalar, where j runs over $2^w \times 2^w$ signed epicirculant permutation matrices S_j, where c_j are complex numbers, such that both $\sum c_j = 1$ and $\sum |c_j|^2 = 1$, and $M(w)$ equals $4^w \times 2^w(2^w - 1)(2^w - 2)(2^w - 2^2)...(2^w - 2^{w-1})$.

8   Conclusion

We conclude that an arbitrary quantum computer can be regarded as a weighted sum of almost-classical reversible computers. Each of these reversible computers consists of two surprisingly simple classical parts:

- one linear circuit (composed of exclusively controlled NOTs) and
- one NOT stack

and three small quantum parts:

- one complex scalar and
- two Z stacks.

Whereas a matrix product represents a circuit cascade, a matrix sum does not represent a simple circuit structure. Recently, there have been some attempts [17,18] to apply a weighted matrix sum for quantum circuit synthesis. However, this so-called 'reuse method' is only efficient (in terms of gate count and ancilla count) in very specific cases. Further research may reveal the full impact of the unitary Birkhoff theorems on quantum computation. Future work may lead to applications in simulation of quantum systems by means of classical computers.

Acknowledgement. Support by the European Cost Action IC 1405 'Reversible computation' is greatly acknowledged.

References

1. Birkhoff, G.: Tres observaciones sobre el algebra lineal. Universidad Nacional de Tucumán: Revista Matemáticas y Física Teórica **5**, 147–151 (1946)
2. Nielsen, M., Chuang, I.: Quantum Computation and Quantum Information. Cambridge University Press, Cambridge (2000). ISBN 9780521635035
3. De Vos, A.: Reversible Computing. Wiley, Weinheim (2010). ISBN 9783642295164
4. De Vos, A., De Baerdemacker, S.: The NEGATOR as a basic building block for quantum circuits. Open Syst. Inf. Dyn. **20**, 1350004 (2013)
5. De Vos, A., De Baerdemacker, S.: On two subgroups of $U(n)$, useful for quantum computing. J. Phy. Conf. Ser. **597**, 012030 (2015). Proceedings of the 30th International Colloquium on Group-Theoretical Methods in Physics, Gent, July (2014)
6. Idel, M., Wolf, M.: Sinkhorn normal form for unitary matrices. Linear Algebra Appl. **471**, 76–84 (2015)
7. De Vos, A., De Baerdemacker, S.: Scaling a unitary matrix. Open Syst. Inf. Dyn. **21**, 1450013 (2014)
8. De Vos, A., De Baerdemacker, S., Van Rentergem, Y.: Synthesis of Quantum Circuits Versus Synthesis of Classical Reversible Circuits. Morgan & Claypool, La Porte (2018). ISBN 9781681733814
9. De Baerdemacker, S., De Vos, A., Chen, L., Yu, L.: The Birkhoff theorem for unitary matrices of arbitrary dimension. Linear Algebra Appl. **514**, 151–164 (2017)
10. De Vos, A., De Baerdemacker, S.: The Birkhoff theorem for unitary matrices of prime dimension. Linear Algebra Appl. **493**, 455–468 (2016)
11. De Vos, A., De Baerdemacker, S.: The Birkhoff theorem for unitary matrices of prime-power dimension. arXiv:1812.08833 [math-ph] (accepted for publication in Linear Algebra Appl.)
12. Wikipedia: Affine group (2018). https://wikipedia.org/wiki/Affine_group
13. Beth, T., Rötteler, M.: Quantum algorithms: applicable algebra and quantum physics. In: Alber, G., et al. (eds.) Quantum Information, vol. 173, pp. 96–150. Springer, Berlin (2001). https://doi.org/10.1007/3-540-44678-8_4. ISBN 3540416668
14. Patel, K., Markov, I., Hayes, J.: Optimal synthesis of linear reversible circuits. Quant. Inf. Comput. **8**, 282–294 (2008)
15. De Vos, A., De Baerdemacker, S.: Decomposition of a linear reversible computer: digital versus analog. Int. J. Unconventional Comput. **6**, 239–263 (2010)
16. Tadej, W., Życzkowski, K.: A concise guide to complex Hadamard matrices. Open Syst. Inf. Dyn. **13**, 133–177 (2006)

17. Klappenecker, A., Rötteler, M.: Quantum software reusability. Int. J. Found. Comput. Sci. **14**, 777–796 (2003)
18. Allouche, C., Baboulin, M., de Brugière, T.G., Valiron, B.: Reuse method for quantum circuit synthesis. In: International Conference on Applied Mathematics, Modeling and Computational Science, Waterloo, August (2017)

Inversion, Iteration, and the Art of Dual Wielding

Robin Kaarsgaard[✉][iD]

DIKU, Department of Computer Science, University of Copenhagen, Copenhagen, Denmark
robin@di.ku.dk

Abstract. The humble † ("dagger") is used to denote two different operations in category theory: Taking the *adjoint* of a morphism (in dagger categories) and finding the *least fixed point* of a functional (in categories enriched in domains). While these two operations are usually considered separately from one another, the emergence of reversible notions of computation shows the need to consider how the two ought to interact.

In the present paper, we wield both of these daggers at once and consider dagger categories enriched in domains. We develop a notion of a monotone dagger structure as a dagger structure that is well behaved with respect to the enrichment, and show that such a structure leads to pleasant inversion properties of the fixed points that arise as a result. Notably, such a structure guarantees the existence of *fixed point adjoints*, which we show are intimately related to the *conjugates* arising from a canonical involutive monoidal structure in the enrichment. Finally, we relate the results to applications in the design and semantics of reversible programming languages.

Keywords: Reversible computing · Dagger categories · Iteration categories · Domain theory · Enriched categories

1 Introduction

Dagger categories are categories in which each morphism $X \xrightarrow{f} Y$ can be assigned an *adjoint* $Y \xrightarrow{f^\dagger} X$ subject to certain equations. In recent years, dagger categories have been used to capture aspects of *inversion* in both reversible [27,28,30] and quantum [2,12,35] computing. Likewise, domain theory and categories enriched in domains (see, *e.g.*, [3,4,6,14,15,38]) have been successful since their inception in modelling both recursive functions and data types in programming via *fixed points*.

The author would like to thank Martti Karvonen, Mathys Rennela, Robert Glück, and the anonymous reviewers for their useful comments, corrections, and suggestions; and to acknowledge the support given by *COST Action IC1405 Reversible computation: Extending horizons of computing.*

M. K. Thomsen and M. Soeken (Eds.): RC 2019, LNCS 11497, pp. 34–50, 2019.
https://doi.org/10.1007/978-3-030-21500-2_3

A motivating example of the interaction between adjoints and fixed points is found in the reversible functional programming language Rfun [40], as the interaction between program inversion and recursion. In this language, inverses of recursive functions can be constructed in a particularly straightforward way, namely as recursive functions with function body the inverse of the function body of the original function. Previously, the author and others showed that this phenomenon appears in *join inverse categories*, a particular class of domain-enriched dagger categories suitable for modelling classical reversible computing, as *fixed point adjoints* [30] to the functionals (*i.e.*, second-order continuous functions) used to model recursive functions.

Several questions remain about these fixed point adjoints, however. Notably: Are these fixed point adjoints canonical? Why do they arise in classical reversible computing, and do they arise elsewhere as well? To answer these questions requires us to develop the art of wielding the two daggers offered by dagger categories and domain-enriched categories at once. We argue that well-behaved interaction between the dagger and domain-enrichments occurs when the dagger is locally monotone, *i.e.*, when $f \sqsubseteq g$ implies $f^\dagger \sqsubseteq g^\dagger$. We show that the functionals on $\mathscr{C}$ form an involutive monoidal category, which also proves surprisingly fruitful in unifying seemingly disparate concepts from the literature under the banner of *conjugation of functionals*. Notably, we show that the conjugate functionals arising from this involutive structure coincide with fixed point adjoints [30], and that they occur naturally both in proving the ambidexterity of dagger adjunctions [22] and in natural transformations that preserve the dagger (including dagger traces [36]).

While these results could be applied to model a reversible functional programming language with general recursion and parametrized functions (such as an extended version of Theseus [28]), they are general enough to account for even certain probabilistic and nondeterministic models of computation, such as the category **Rel** of sets and relations, and the category **DStoch**$_{\leq 1}$ of finite sets and subnormalized doubly stochastic maps.

Overview: A brief introduction to the relevant background material on dagger categories, (**DCPO-**)enriched categories, iteration categories, and involutive monoidal categories is given in Sect. 2. In Sect. 3 the concept of a *monotone dagger structure* on a **DCPO**-category is introduced, and it is demonstrated that such a structure leads to the existence of fixed point adjoints for (ordinary and externally parametrized) fixed points, given by their conjugates. We also explore natural transformations in this setting, and develop a notion of *self-conjugate natural transformations*, of which †-trace operators are examples. Finally, we discuss potential applications and avenues for future research in Sect. 4, and end with a few concluding remarks in Sect. 5.

2   Background

Though familiarity with basic category theory, including monoidal categories, is assumed, we recall here some basic concepts relating to dagger categories,

(**DCPO**)-enriched categories, iteration categories, and involutive monoidal categories [7,25]. The material is only covered here briefly, but can be found in much more detail in the numerous texts on dagger category theory (see, *e.g.*, [2,20,31,35]), enriched category theory (for which [33] is the standard text), and domain theory and iteration categories (see, *e.g.*, [3,15]).

2.1   Dagger Categories

A dagger category (or †-category) is a category equipped with a suitable method for flipping the direction of morphisms, by assigning to each morphism an *adjoint* in a manner consistent with composition. They are formally defined as follows.

Definition 1. *A dagger category is a category $\mathscr{C}$ equipped with an functor $(-)^\dagger :$ $\mathscr{C}^{\mathrm{op}} \to \mathscr{C}$ satisfying that $\mathrm{id}_X^\dagger = \mathrm{id}_X$ and $f^{\dagger\dagger} = f$ for all identities $X \xrightarrow{\mathrm{id}_X} X$ and morphisms $X \xrightarrow{f} Y$.*

Dagger categories, dagger functors (*i.e.*, functors F satisfying $F(f^\dagger) = F(f)^\dagger$), and natural transformations form a 2-category, **DagCat**.

A given category may have several different daggers which need not agree. An example of this is the groupoid of finite-dimensional Hilbert spaces and linear isomorphisms, which has (at least!) two daggers: One maps linear isomorphisms to their linear inverse, the other maps linear isomorphisms to their hermitian conjugate. The two only agree on the unitaries, *i.e.*, the linear isomorphisms which additionally preserve the inner product. For this reason, one would in principle need to specify *which* dagger one is talking about on a given category, though this is often left implicit (as will also be done here).

Let us recall the definition of the some interesting properties of morphisms in a dagger category: By theft of terminology from linear algebra, say that a morphism $X \xrightarrow{f} X$ in a dagger category is *hermitian* or *self-adjoint* if $f = f^\dagger$, and *unitary* if it is an isomorphism and $f^{-1} = f^\dagger$. Whereas objects are usually considered equivalent if they are isomorphic, the "way of the dagger" [22,31] dictates that all structure in sight must cooperate with the dagger; as such, objects ought to be considered equivalent in dagger categories only if they are isomorphic via a unitary map.

We end with a few examples of dagger categories. As discussed above, **FHilb** is an example (*the* motivating one, even [35]) of dagger categories, with the dagger given by hermitian conjugation. The category **PInj** of sets and partial injective functions is a dagger category (indeed, it is an *inverse category* [11,32]) with $f^\dagger$ given by the partial inverse of f. Similarly, the category **Rel** of sets and relations has a dagger given by $R^\dagger = R^\circ$, *i.e.*, the relational converse of R. Noting that a dagger subcategory is given by the existence of a faithful dagger functor, it can be shown that **PInj** is a dagger subcategory of **Rel** with the given dagger structures.

2.2   DCPO-categories and Other Enriched Categories

Enriched categories (see, *e.g.*, [33]) capture the idea that homsets on certain categories can (indeed, ought to) be understood as something other than sets – or in other words, as objects of another category than **Set**. A category $\mathscr{C}$ is *enriched* in a monoidal category $\mathscr{V}$ if all homsets $\mathscr{C}(X, Y)$ of $\mathscr{C}$ are objects of $\mathscr{V}$, and for all objects X, Y, Z of $\mathscr{C}$, $\mathscr{V}$ has families of morphisms $\mathscr{C}(Y, Z) \otimes \mathscr{C}(X, Y) \to \mathscr{C}(X, Z)$ and $I \to \mathscr{C}(X, X)$ corresponding to composition and identities in $\mathscr{C}$, subject to commutativity of diagrams corresponding to the usual requirements of associativity of composition, and of left and right identity. As is common, we will often use the shorthand "$\mathscr{C}$ is a $\mathscr{V}$-category" to mean that $\mathscr{C}$ is enriched in the category $\mathscr{V}$.

We focus here on categories enriched in the category of *domains* (see, *e.g.*, [3]), *i.e.*, the category **DCPO** of pointed directed complete partial orders and continuous maps. A partially ordered $(X, \sqsubseteq)$ is said to be directed complete if every directed set (*i.e.*, a *non-empty* $A \subseteq X$ satisfying that any pair of elements of A has a supremum in A) has a supremum in X. A function f between directed complete partial orders is monotone if $x \sqsubseteq y$ implies $f(x) \sqsubseteq f(y)$ for all x, y, and continuous if $f(\sup A) = \sup_{a \in A} \{f(a)\}$ for each directed set A (note that continuity implies monotony). A directed complete partial order is *pointed* if it has a least element $\bot$ (or, in other words, if also the empty set has a supremum), and a function f between such is called *strict* if $f(\bot) = \bot$ (*i.e.*, if also the supremum of the empty set is preserved[1]). Pointed directed complete partial orders and continuous maps form a category, **DCPO**.

As such, a category enriched in **DCPO** is a category $\mathscr{C}$ in which homsets $\mathscr{C}(X, Y)$ are directed complete partial orders, and composition is continuous. Additionally, we will require that composition is strict (meaning that $\bot \circ f = \bot$ and $g \circ \bot = \bot$ for all suitable morphisms f and g), so that the category is actually enriched in the category **DCPO!** of directed complete partial orders and strict continuous functions, though we will not otherwise require functions to be strict.

Enrichment in **DCPO** provides a method for constructing morphisms in the enriched category as least fixed points of continuous functions between homsets: This is commonly used to model recursion. Given a continuous function $\mathscr{C}(X, Y) \xrightarrow{\varphi} \mathscr{C}(X, Y)$, by Kleene's fixed point theorem there exists a least fixed point $X \xrightarrow{\text{fix}\,\varphi} Y$ given by $\sup_{n \in \omega} \{\varphi^n(\bot)\}$, where φ^n is the n-fold composition of φ with itself.

2.3   Parametrized Fixed Points and Iteration Categories

Related to the fixed point operator is the *parametrized fixed point operator*, an operator pfix assigning morphisms of the form $X \times Y \xrightarrow{\psi} X$ to a morphism

---

[1] This is *not* the case in general, as continuous functions are only required to preserve least upper bounds of directed sets, which, by definition, does not include the empty set.

$Y \xrightarrow{\text{pfix}\,\psi} X$ satisfying equations such as the *parametrized fixed point identity*

$$\text{pfix}\,\psi = \psi \circ \langle \text{pfix}\,\psi, \text{id}_Y \rangle$$

and others (see, *e.g.*, [14,24]). Parametrized fixed points are used to solve domain equations of the form $x = \psi(x,p)$ for some given parameter $p \in Y$. Indeed, if for a continuous function $X \times Y \xrightarrow{\psi} X$ we define $\psi^0(x,p) = x$ and $\psi^{n+1}(x,p) = \psi(\psi^n(x,p),p)$, we can construct its parametrized fixed point in **DCPO** in a way reminiscent of the usual fixed point by

$$(\text{pfix}\,\psi)(p) = \sup_{n \in \omega}\{\psi^n(\bot_X, p)\} \ .$$

In fact, a parametrized fixed point operator may be derived from an ordinary fixed point operator by $(\text{pfix}\,\psi)(p) = \text{fix}\,\psi(-,p)$. Similarly, we may derive an ordinary fixed point operator from a parametrized one by considering a morphism $X \xrightarrow{\varphi} X$ to be parametrized by the terminal object 1, so that the fixed point of $X \xrightarrow{\varphi} X$ is given by the parametrized fixed point of $X \times 1 \xrightarrow{\pi_1} X \xrightarrow{\varphi} X$.

The parametrized fixed point operation is sometimes also called a *dagger operation* [14], and denoted by $f^\dagger$ rather than pfix f. Though this is indeed the other dagger that we are wielding, we will use the phrase "parametrized fixed point" and notation "pfix" to avoid unnecessary confusion.

An *iteration category* [15] is a cartesian category with a parametrized fixed point operator that behaves in a canonical way. The definition of an iteration category came out of the observation that the parametrized fixed point operator in a host of concrete categories (notably **DCPO**) satisfy the same identities. This lead to an elegant semantic characterization of iteration categories, due to [15].

Definition 2. *An* iteration category *is a cartesian category with a parametrized fixed point operator satisfying all identities (of the parametrized fixed point operator) that hold in* **DCPO**.

Note that the original definition defined iteration categories in relation to the category $\mathbf{CPO}_m$ of ω-complete partial orders and monotone functions, rather than to **DCPO**. However, the motivating theorem [15, Theorem 1] shows that the parametrized fixed point operator in $\mathbf{CPO}_m$ satisfies the same identities as the one found in **CPO** (*i.e.*, with continuous rather than monotone functions). Since the parametrized fixed point operator of **DCPO** is constructed *precisely* as it is in **CPO** (noting that ω-chains are directed sets), this definition is equivalent to the original.

2.4 Involutive Monoidal Categories

An involutive category [25] is a category in which every object X can be assigned a *conjugate* object $\overline{X}$ in a functorial way such that $\overline{\overline{X}} \cong X$. A novel idea by Egger [13] is to consider dagger categories as categories enriched in an *involutive monoidal category*. We will return to this idea in Sect. 3.1, and recall the relevant definitions in the meantime (due to [25], compare also with *bar categories* [7]).

Definition 3. *A category $\mathcal{V}$ is involutive if it is equipped with a functor $\mathcal{V} \xrightarrow{\overline{(-)}} \mathcal{V}$ (the involution) and a natural isomorphism* id $\xRightarrow{\iota} \overline{\overline{(-)}}$ *satisfying* $\iota_{\overline{X}} = \overline{\iota_X}$.

Borrowing terminology from linear algebra, we call $\overline{X}$ (respectively $\overline{f}$) the *conjugate* of an object X (respectively a morphism f), and say that an object X is *self-conjugate* if $X \cong \overline{X}$. Note that since conjugation is covariant, any category $\mathscr{C}$ can be made involutive by assigning $\overline{X} = X$, $\overline{f} = f$, and letting id $\xRightarrow{\iota} \overline{\overline{(-)}}$ be the identity in each component; as such, an involution is a structure rather than a property. Non-trivial examples of involutive categories include the category of complex vector spaces **Vect**$_\mathbb{C}$, with the involution given by the usual conjugation of complex vector spaces; and the category **Poset** of partially ordered sets and monotone functions, with the involution given by order reversal.

When a category is both involutive and (symmetric) monoidal, we say that it is an *involutive (symmetric) monoidal category* when these two structures play well together, as in the following definition [25].

Definition 4. *An* involutive (symmetric) monoidal category *is a (symmetric) monoidal category $\mathcal{V}$ which is also involutive, such that the involution is a monoidal functor, and* id $\Rightarrow \overline{\overline{(-)}}$ *is a monoidal natural isomorphism.*

This specifically gives us a natural family of isomorphisms $\overline{X \otimes Y} \cong \overline{X} \otimes \overline{Y}$, and when the monoidal product is symmetric, this extends to a natural isomorphism $\overline{X \otimes Y} \cong \overline{Y} \otimes \overline{X}$. This fact will turn out to be useful later on when we consider dagger categories as enriched in certain involutive symmetric monoidal categories.

3   Domain Enriched Dagger Categories

Given a dagger category that also happens to be enriched in domains, we ask how these two structures ought to interact with one another. Since domain theory dictates that the well-behaved functions are precisely the continuous ones, a natural first answer would be to that the dagger should be locally continuous; however, it turns out that we can make do with less.

Definition 5. *Say that a dagger structure on* **DCPO***-category is* monotone *if the dagger is locally monotone, i.e., if $f \sqsubseteq g$ implies $f^\dagger \sqsubseteq g^\dagger$ for all f and g.*

In the following, we will use the terms "**DCPO**-category with a monotone dagger structure" and "**DCPO**-†-category" interchangably. That this is sufficient to get what we want – in particular to obtain local continuity of the dagger – is shown in the following lemma.

Lemma 1. *In any* **DCPO***-†-category, the dagger is an order isomorphism on morphisms; in particular it is continuous and strict.*

Proof. For $\mathscr{C}$ a dagger category, $\mathscr{C} \cong \mathscr{C}^{\mathrm{op}}$ so $\mathscr{C}(X,Y) \cong \mathscr{C}^{\mathrm{op}}(X,Y) = \mathscr{C}(Y,X)$ for all objects X, Y; that this isomorphism of hom-objects is an order isomorphism follows directly by local monotony. $\qquad\square$

Let us consider a few examples of **DCPO**-†-categories.

Example 1. The category **Rel** of sets and relations is a dagger category, with the dagger given by $R^{\dagger} = R^{\circ}$, the relational converse of R (*i.e.*, defined by $(y,x) \in R^{\circ}$ iff $(x,y) \in R$) for each such relation. It is also enriched in **DCPO** by the usual subset ordering: Since a relation $\mathcal{X} \to \mathcal{Y}$ is nothing more than a subset of $\mathcal{X} \times \mathcal{Y}$, equipped with the subset order $-\subseteq-$ we have that $\sup(\Delta) = \bigcup_{R \in \Delta} R$ for any directed set $\Delta \subseteq \mathbf{Rel}(\mathcal{X}, \mathcal{Y})$. It is also pointed, with the least element of each homset given by the empty relation.

To see that this is a monotone dagger structure, let $\mathcal{X} \xrightarrow{R,S} \mathcal{Y}$ be relations and suppose that $R \subseteq S$. Let $(y,x) \in R^{\circ}$. Since $(y,x) \in R^{\circ}$ we have $(x,y) \in R$ by definition of the relational converse, and by the assumption that $R \subseteq S$ we also have $(x,y) \in S$. But then $(y,x) \in S^{\circ}$ by definition of the relational converse, so $R^{\dagger} = R^{\circ} \subseteq S^{\circ} = S^{\dagger}$ follows by extensionality.

Example 2. We noted earlier that the category **PInj** of sets and partial injective functions is a dagger subcategory of **Rel**, with $f^{\dagger}$ given by the partial inverse (a special case of the relational converse) of a partial injection f. Further, it is also a **DCPO**-subcategory of **Rel**; in **PInj**, this becomes the relation that for $X \xrightarrow{f,g} Y$, $f \sqsubseteq g$ iff for all $x \in X$, if f is defined at x and $f(x) = y$, then g is also defined at x and $g(x) = y$. Like **Rel**, it is pointed with the nowhere defined partial function as the least element of each homset. That $\sup(\Delta)$ for some directed $\Delta \subseteq \mathbf{PInj}(X, Y)$ is a partial injection follows straightforwardly, and that this dagger structure is monotone follows by an argument analogous to the one for **Rel**.

Example 3. More generally, any *join inverse category* (see [16]), of which **PInj** is one, is a **DCPO**-†-category. Inverse categories are canonically dagger categories enriched in partial orders. That this extends to **DCPO**-enrichment in the presence of joins is shown in [30]; that the canonical dagger is monotonous with respect to the partial order is an elementary result (see, *e.g.*, [30, Lemma 2]).

Example 4. The category **DStoch**$_{\leq 1}$ of finite sets and *subnormalized doubly stochastic maps* is an example of a probabilistic **DCPO**-†-category. A subnormalized doubly stochastic map $X \xrightarrow{f} Y$, where $|X| = |Y| = n$, is given by an $n \times n$ matrix $A = [a_{ij}]$ with non-negative real entries such that $\sum_{i=1}^{n} a_{ij} \leq 1$ and $\sum_{j=1}^{n} a_{ij} \leq 1$. Composition is given by the usual multiplication of matrices.

This is a dagger category with the dagger given by matrix transposition. It is also enriched in **DCPO** by ordering subnormalized doubly stochastic maps entry-wise (*i.e.*, $A \leq B$ if $a_{ij} \leq b_{ij}$ for all i, j), with the everywhere-zero matrix as the least element in each homset, and with suprema of directed sets given by computing suprema entry-wise. That this dagger structure is monotone follows by the fact that if $A \leq B$, so $a_{ij} \leq b_{ij}$ for all i, j, then also $a_{ji} \leq b_{ji}$ for all j, i, which is precisely to say that $A^{\dagger} = A^{T} \leq B^{T} = B^{\dagger}$.

As such, in terms of computational content, these are examples of deterministic, nondeterministic, and probabilistic **DCPO**-†-categories. We will also discuss the related category **CP*(FHilb)**, used to model quantum phenomena, in Sect. 4.

3.1   The Category of Continuous Functionals

We illustrate here the idea of dagger categories as categories enriched in an involutive monoidal category by an example that will be used throughout the remainder of this article: Enrichment in a suitable subcategory of **DCPO**. It is worth stressing, however, that the construction is *not* limited to dagger categories enriched in **DCPO**; any dagger category will do. As we will see later, however, this canonical involution turns out to be very useful when **DCPO**-†-categories are considered.

Let $\mathscr{C}$ be a **DCPO**-†-category. We define an induced (full monoidal) subcategory of **DCPO**, call it **DcpoOp$(\mathscr{C})$**, which enriches $\mathscr{C}$ (by its definition) as follows:

Definition 6. *For a* **DCPO**-†-*category* $\mathscr{C}$, *define* **DcpoOp$(\mathscr{C})$** *to have as objects all objects* Θ, Λ *of* **DCPO** *of the form* $\mathscr{C}(X,Y)$, $\mathscr{C}^{\mathrm{op}}(X,Y)$ *(for all objects* X, Y *of* $\mathscr{C}$), 1, *and* $\Theta \times \Lambda$ *(with* 1 *initial object of* **DCPO**, *and* $- \times -$ *the cartesian product), and as morphisms all continuous functions between these.*

In other words, **DcpoOp$(\mathscr{C})$** is the (full) cartesian subcategory of **DCPO** generated by objects used in the enrichment of $\mathscr{C}$, with all continuous maps between these. That the dagger on $\mathscr{C}$ induces an involution on **DcpoOp$(\mathscr{C})$** is shown in the following theorem.

Theorem 1. **DcpoOp$(\mathscr{C})$** *is an involutive symmetric monoidal category.*

Proof. On objects, define an involution $\overline{(-)}$ with respect to the cartesian (specifically symmetric monoidal) product of **DCPO** as follows, for all objects Θ, Λ, Σ of **DcpoOp$(\mathscr{C})$**: $\overline{\mathscr{C}(X,Y)} = \mathscr{C}^{\mathrm{op}}(X,Y)$, $\overline{\mathscr{C}^{\mathrm{op}}(X,Y)} = \mathscr{C}(X,Y)$, $\overline{1} = 1$, and $\overline{\Theta \times \Lambda} = \overline{\Theta} \times \overline{\Lambda}$. To see that this is well-defined, recall that $\mathscr{C} \cong \mathscr{C}^{\mathrm{op}}$ for any dagger category $\mathscr{C}$, so in particular there is an isomorphism witnessing $\mathscr{C}(X,Y) \cong \mathscr{C}^{\mathrm{op}}(X,Y)$ given by the mapping $f \mapsto f^{\dagger}$. But then $\mathscr{C}^{\mathrm{op}}(X,Y) = \{f^{\dagger} \mid f \in \mathscr{C}(X,Y)\}$, so if $\mathscr{C}(X,Y) = \mathscr{C}(X',Y')$ then $\overline{\mathscr{C}(X,Y)} = \mathscr{C}^{\mathrm{op}}(X,Y) = \{f^{\dagger} \mid f \in \mathscr{C}(X,Y)\} = \{f^{\dagger} \mid f \in \mathscr{C}(X',Y')\} = \mathscr{C}^{\mathrm{op}}(X',Y') = \overline{\mathscr{C}(X',Y')}$. That $\overline{\mathscr{C}^{\mathrm{op}}(X,Y)} = \mathscr{C}(X,Y)$ is well-defined follows by analogous argument.

On morphisms, we define a family ξ of isomorphisms by $\xi_I = \mathrm{id}_I$, $\xi_{\mathscr{C}(X,Y)} = (-)^{\dagger}$, $\xi_{\mathscr{C}^{\mathrm{op}}(X,Y)} = (-)^{\dagger}$, and $\xi_{\Theta \times \Lambda} = \xi_{\Theta} \times \xi_{\Lambda}$, and then define

$$\overline{\Theta \xrightarrow{\varphi} \Lambda} = \overline{\Theta} \xrightarrow{\xi_{\Theta}^{-1}} \Theta \xrightarrow{\varphi} \Lambda \xrightarrow{\xi_{\Lambda}} \overline{\Lambda}.$$

This is functorial as $\overline{\mathrm{id}_{\Theta}} = \xi_{\Theta} \circ \mathrm{id}_{\Theta} \circ \xi_{\Theta}^{-1} = \xi_{\Theta} \circ \xi_{\Theta}^{-1} = \mathrm{id}_{\overline{\Theta}}$, and for $\Theta \xrightarrow{\varphi} \Lambda \xrightarrow{\psi} \Sigma$,

$$\overline{\psi \circ \varphi} = \xi_{\Sigma} \circ \psi \circ \varphi \circ \xi_{\Theta}^{-1} = \xi_{\Sigma} \circ \psi \circ \xi_{\Lambda}^{-1} \circ \xi_{\Lambda} \circ \varphi \circ \xi_{\Theta}^{-1} = \overline{\psi} \circ \overline{\varphi}.$$

Finally, since the involution is straightforwardly a monoidal functor, and since the natural transformation id $\Rightarrow \overline{\overline{(-)}}$ can be chosen to be the identity since all objects of $\mathbf{DcpoOp}(\mathscr{C})$ satisfy $\overline{\overline{\Theta}} = \Theta$ by definition, this is an involutive symmetric monoidal category. $\square$

The resulting category $\mathbf{DcpoOp}(\mathscr{C})$ can very naturally be thought of as the induced *category of (continuous) functionals* (or second-order functions) of $\mathscr{C}$.

Notice that this is a special case of a more general construction on dagger categories: For a dagger category $\mathscr{C}$ enriched in some category $\mathscr{V}$ (which could simply be **Set** in the unenriched case), one can construct the category $\mathscr{V}\mathbf{Op}(\mathscr{C})$, given on objects by the image of the hom-functor $\mathscr{C}(-, -)$ closed under monoidal products, and on morphisms by all morphisms of $\mathscr{V}$ between objects of this form. Defining the involution as above, $\mathscr{V}\mathbf{Op}(\mathscr{C})$ can be shown to be involutive monoidal.

Example 5. One may question how natural (in a non-technical sense) the choice of involution on $\mathbf{DcpoOp}(\mathscr{C})$ is. One instance where it turns out to be useful is in the context of dagger adjunctions (see [22] for details), that is, adjunctions between dagger categories where both functors are dagger functors.

Dagger adjunctions have no specified left and right adjoint, as all such adjunctions can be shown to be ambidextrous in the following way: Given $F \dashv G$ between endofunctors on $\mathscr{C}$, there is a natural isomorphism $\mathscr{C}(FX, Y) \xrightarrow{\alpha_{X,Y}} \mathscr{C}(X, GY)$. Since $\mathscr{C}$ is a dagger category, we can define a natural isomorphism $\mathscr{C}(X, FY) \xrightarrow{\beta_{X,Y}} \mathscr{C}(GX, Y)$ by $f \mapsto \alpha_{Y,X}(f^\dagger)^\dagger$, *i.e.*, by the composition

$$\mathscr{C}(X, FY) \xrightarrow{\xi} \mathscr{C}(FY, X) \xrightarrow{\alpha_{Y,X}} \mathscr{C}(Y, GX) \xrightarrow{\xi} \mathscr{C}(GX, Y)$$

which then witnesses $G \dashv F$ (as it is a composition of natural isomorphisms). But then $\beta_{X,Y}$ is defined precisely to be $\overline{\alpha_{Y,X}}$ when F and G are endofunctors.

3.2   Daggers and Fixed Points

In this section we consider the morphisms of $\mathbf{DcpoOp}(\mathscr{C})$ in some detail, for a **DCPO**-†-category $\mathscr{C}$. Since least fixed points of morphisms are such a prominent and useful feature of **DCPO**-enriched categories, we ask how these behave with respect to the dagger. To answer this question, we transplant the notion of a *fixed point adjoint* from [30] to **DCPO**-†-categories, where an answer to this question in relation to the more specific *join inverse categories* was given:

Definition 7. *A functional* $\mathscr{C}(Y, X) \xrightarrow{\varphi_{\ddagger}} \mathscr{C}(Y, X)$ *is* fixed point adjoint to *a functional* $\mathscr{C}(X, Y) \xrightarrow{\varphi} \mathscr{C}(X, Y)$ *iff* $(\mathrm{fix}\,\varphi)^\dagger = \mathrm{fix}\,\varphi_{\ddagger}$.

Note that this is symmetric: If $\varphi_{\ddagger}$ is fixed point adjoint to φ then $\mathrm{fix}\,(\varphi_{\ddagger})^\dagger = (\mathrm{fix}\,\varphi)^{\dagger\dagger} = \mathrm{fix}\,\varphi$, so φ is also fixed point adjoint to $\varphi_{\ddagger}$. As shown in the following theorem, it turns out that the conjugate $\overline{\varphi}$ of a functional φ is precisely fixed point adjoint to it. This is a generalization of a theorem from [30], where a more ad-hoc formulation was shown for join inverse categories, which constitute a non-trivial subclass of **DCPO**-†-categories.

Theorem 2. *Every functional is fixed point adjoint to its conjugate.*

Proof. The proof applies the exact same construction as in [30], since being a **DCPO**-†-category suffices, and the constructed fixed point adjoint turns out to be the exact same. Let $\mathscr{C}(X,Y) \xrightarrow{\varphi} \mathscr{C}(X,Y)$ be a functional. Since $\overline{\varphi} = \xi_{\mathscr{C}(X,Y)} \circ \varphi \circ \xi^{-1}_{\mathscr{C}(X,Y)}$,

$$\overline{\varphi}^n = \left(\xi_{\mathscr{C}(X,Y)} \circ \varphi \circ \xi^{-1}_{\mathscr{C}(X,Y)} \right)^n = \xi_{\mathscr{C}(X,Y)} \circ \varphi^n \circ \xi^{-1}_{\mathscr{C}(X,Y)}$$

and so

$$\mathrm{fix}\,\overline{\varphi} = \sup\{\overline{\varphi}^n(\bot_{Y,X})\}_{n\in\omega} = \sup\{\varphi^n(\bot^{\dagger}_{Y,X})^{\dagger}\} = \sup\{\varphi^n(\bot_{X,Y})^{\dagger}\}$$
$$= \sup\{\varphi^n(\bot_{X,Y})\}^{\dagger} = (\mathrm{fix}\,\varphi)^{\dagger}$$

as desired. □

This theorem is somewhat surprising, as the conjugate came out of the involutive monoidal structure on $\mathbf{DcpoOp}(\mathscr{C})$, which is not specifically related to the presence of fixed points. As previously noted, had $\mathscr{C}$ been enriched in another category $\mathscr{V}$, we would still be able to construct a category $\mathscr{V}\mathbf{Op}(\mathscr{C})$ of $\mathscr{V}$-functionals with the *exact same* involutive structure.

As regards recursion, this theorem underlines the slogan that *reversibility is a local phenomenon*: To construct the inverse to a recursively defined morphism $\mathrm{fix}\,\varphi$, it suffices to invert the local morphism φ at each step (which is essentially what is done by the conjugate $\overline{\varphi}$) in order to construct the global inverse $(\mathrm{fix}\,\varphi)^{\dagger}$.

Parametrized functionals and their external fixed points are also interesting to consider in this setting, as some examples of **DCPO**-†-categories (*e.g.*, **PInj**) fail to have an internal hom. For example, in a dagger category with objects $L(X)$ corresponding to "lists of X" (usually constructed as the fixed point of a suitable functor), one could very reasonably construe the usual map-function not as a higher-order function, but as a family of morphisms $LX \xrightarrow{\mathrm{map}\langle f\rangle} LY$ indexed by $X \xrightarrow{f} Y$ – or, in other words, as a functional $\mathscr{C}(X,Y) \xrightarrow{\mathrm{map}} \mathscr{C}(LX,LY)$. Indeed, this is how certain higher-order behaviours are mimicked in the reversible functional programming language Theseus (see also Sect. 4).

To achieve such parametrized fixed points of functionals, we naturally need a parametrized fixed point operator on $\mathbf{DcpoOp}(\mathscr{C})$ satisfying the appropriate equations – or, in other words, we need $\mathbf{DcpoOp}(\mathscr{C})$ to be an *iteration category*. That $\mathbf{DcpoOp}(\mathscr{C})$ is such an iteration category follows immediately by its definition (*i.e.*, since $\mathbf{DcpoOp}(\mathscr{C})$ is a full subcategory of **DCPO**, we can define a parametrized fixed point operator in $\mathbf{DcpoOp}(\mathscr{C})$ to be precisely the one in **DCPO**), noting that parametrized fixed points preserve continuity.

Lemma 2. $\mathbf{DcpoOp}(\mathscr{C})$ *is an iteration category.*

For functionals of the form $\mathscr{C}(X,Y) \times \mathscr{C}(P,Q) \xrightarrow{\psi} \mathscr{C}(X,Y)$, we can make a similar definition of a *parametrized fixed point adjoint*:

Definition 8. *A functional* $\mathscr{C}(X,Y) \times \mathscr{C}(P,Q) \xrightarrow{\psi_{\ddagger}} \mathscr{C}(X,Y)$ *is* parametrized fixed point adjoint *to a functional* $\mathscr{C}(X,Y) \times \mathscr{C}(P,Q) \xrightarrow{\psi} \mathscr{C}(X,Y)$ *iff* $(\mathrm{pfix}\,\psi)(p)^{\dagger} = (\mathrm{pfix}\,\psi_{\ddagger})(p^{\dagger})$.

We can now show a similar theorem for parametrized fixed points of functionals and their conjugates:

Theorem 3. *Every functional is parametrized fixed point adjoint to its conjugate.*

Proof. Let $\mathscr{C}(X,Y) \times \mathscr{C}(P,Q) \xrightarrow{\psi} \mathscr{C}(X,Y)$ be a functional. We start by showing that $\bar{\psi}^n(f,p) = \psi^n(f^{\dagger},p^{\dagger})^{\dagger}$ for all $Y \xrightarrow{f} X$, $Q \xrightarrow{p} P$, and $n \in \mathbb{N}$, by induction on n. For $n = 0$ we have

$$\bar{\psi}^0(f,p) = f = f^{\dagger\dagger} = (f^{\dagger})^{\dagger} = \psi^0(f^{\dagger},p^{\dagger})^{\dagger}.$$

Assuming now the induction hypothesis for some n, we have

$$\bar{\psi}^{n+1}(f,p) = \bar{\psi}(\bar{\psi}^n(f,p),p) = \bar{\psi}(\psi^n(f^{\dagger},p^{\dagger})^{\dagger},p) = \psi(\psi^n(f^{\dagger},p^{\dagger})^{\dagger\dagger},p^{\dagger})^{\dagger}$$
$$= \psi(\psi^n(f^{\dagger},p^{\dagger}),p^{\dagger})^{\dagger} = \psi^{n+1}(f^{\dagger},p^{\dagger})^{\dagger}$$

Using this fact, we now get

$$(\mathrm{pfix}\,\bar{\psi})(p^{\dagger}) = \sup_{n\in\omega}\{\bar{\psi}^n(\bot_{Y,X},p^{\dagger})\} = \sup_{n\in\omega}\{\psi^n(\bot^{\dagger}_{Y,X},p^{\dagger\dagger})^{\dagger}\}$$
$$= \sup_{n\in\omega}\{\psi^n(\bot_{X,Y},p)\}^{\dagger} = (\mathrm{pfix}\,\psi)(p)^{\dagger}$$

which was what we wanted. □

Again, this theorem highlights the local nature of reversibility, here in the presence of additional parameters. We observe further the following highly useful property of parametrized fixed points in $\mathbf{DcpoOp}(\mathscr{C})$:

Lemma 3. *Parametrized fixed points in* $\mathbf{DcpoOp}(\mathscr{C})$ *preserve conjugation.*

Proof. Let $\mathscr{C}(X,Y) \times \mathscr{C}(P,Q) \xrightarrow{\psi} \mathscr{C}(X,Y)$ be continuous, and $P \xrightarrow{p} Q$. Then $\overline{\mathrm{pfix}\,\psi(p)} = (\xi \circ \overline{(\mathrm{pfix}\,\psi)} \circ \xi^{-1})(p) = (\mathrm{pfix}\,\psi)(p^{\dagger})^{\dagger} = (\mathrm{pfix}\,\bar{\psi})(p)^{\dagger\dagger} = (\mathrm{pfix}\,\bar{\psi})(p)$, so $\overline{\mathrm{pfix}\,\psi} = \mathrm{pfix}\,\bar{\psi}$. □

Note that a lemma of this form only makes sense for parametrized fixed points, as the usual fixed point of a functional $\mathscr{C}(X,Y) \xrightarrow{\varphi} \mathscr{C}(X,Y)$ results in a morphism $X \xrightarrow{\mathrm{fix}\,\varphi} Y$ in $\mathscr{C}$, not a functional in $\mathbf{DcpoOp}(\mathscr{C})$.

3.3   Naturality and Self-conjugacy

We now consider the behaviour of functionals and their parametrized fixed points when they are natural. For example, given a natural family of functionals $\mathscr{C}(FX, FY) \xrightarrow{\alpha_{X,Y}} \mathscr{C}(GX, GY)$ natural in X and Y (for dagger endofunctors F and G on $\mathscr{C}$), what does it mean for such a family to be well-behaved with respect to the dagger on $\mathscr{C}$? We would certainly want that such a family preserves the dagger, in the sense that $\alpha_{X,Y}(f)^\dagger = \alpha_{Y,X}(f^\dagger)$ in each component X, Y. It turns out that this, too, can be expressed in terms of conjugation of functionals.

Lemma 4. *Let* $\mathscr{C}(FX, FY) \xrightarrow{\alpha_{X,Y}} \mathscr{C}(GX, GY)$ *be a family of functionals natural in* X *and* Y. *Then* $\alpha_{X,Y}(f)^\dagger = \alpha_{Y,X}(f^\dagger)$ *for all* $X \xrightarrow{f} Y$ *iff* $\alpha_{X,Y} = \overline{\alpha_{Y,X}}$.

Proof. Suppose $\alpha_{X,Y}(f)^\dagger = \alpha_{Y,X}(f^\dagger)$. Then $\alpha_{X,Y}(f) = \alpha_{X,Y}(f)^{\dagger\dagger} = \alpha_{Y,X}(f^\dagger)^\dagger = \overline{\alpha_{Y,X}}(f)$, so $\alpha_{X,Y} = \overline{\alpha_{Y,X}}$. Conversely, assuming $\alpha_{X,Y} = \overline{\alpha_{Y,X}}$ we then have for all $X \xrightarrow{f} Y$ that $\alpha_{X,Y}(f) = \alpha_{Y,X}(f^\dagger)^\dagger$, so $\alpha_{X,Y}(f)^\dagger = \alpha_{Y,X}(f^\dagger)^{\dagger\dagger} = \alpha_{Y,X}(f^\dagger)$. □

If a natural transformation α satisfies $\alpha_{X,Y} = \overline{\alpha_{Y,X}}$ in all components X, Y, we say that it is *self-conjugate*. An important example of a self-conjugate natural transformation is the *dagger trace operator*, as detailed in the following example.

Example 6. A trace operator [29] on a braided monoidal category $\mathscr{D}$ is family of functionals

$$\mathscr{D}(X \otimes U, Y \otimes U) \xrightarrow{\mathrm{Tr}^U_{X,Y}} \mathscr{D}(X, Y)$$

subject to certain equations (naturality in X and Y, dinaturality in U, etc.). Traces have been used to model features from partial traces in tensorial vector spaces [19] to tail recursion in programming languages [1,8,18], and occur naturally in tortile monoidal categories [29] and unique decomposition categories [17,23].

A *dagger trace operator* on a dagger category (see, *e.g.*, [36]) is precisely a trace operator on a dagger monoidal category (*i.e.*, a monoidal category where the monoidal functor is a dagger functor) that satisfies $\mathrm{Tr}^U_{X,Y}(f)^\dagger = \mathrm{Tr}^U_{Y,X}(f^\dagger)$ in all components X, Y. Such traces have been used to model reversible tail recursion in reversible programming languages [27,28,30], and also occur in the *dagger compact closed categories* (see, *e.g.*, [37]) used to model quantum theory. In light of Lemma 4, dagger traces are important examples of self-conjugate natural transformations on dagger categories.

Given the connections between (di)naturality and parametric polymorphism [5,39], one would wish that parametrized fixed points preserve naturality. Luckily, this does turn out to be the case:

Theorem 4. *If* $\mathscr{C}(FX, FY) \times \mathscr{C}(GX, GY) \xrightarrow{\alpha_{X,Y}} \mathscr{C}(FX, FY)$ *is natural in* X *and* Y, *so is its parametrized fixed point.*

This theorem can be read as stating that, just like reversibility, a recursive polymorphic map can be obtained from one that is only locally polymorphic. Combining this result with Lemma 4 regarding self-conjugacy, we obtain the following corollary.

Corollary 1. *If* $\mathscr{C}(FX, FY) \times \mathscr{C}(GX, GY) \xrightarrow{\alpha_{X,Y}} \mathscr{C}(FX, FY)$ *is a self-conjugate natural transformation, so is* $\mathrm{pfix}\,\alpha_{X,Y}$.

Proof. If $\alpha_{X,Y} = \overline{\alpha_{Y,X}}$ for all X, Y then also $\mathrm{pfix}\,\alpha_{X,Y} = \mathrm{pfix}\,\overline{\alpha_{Y,X}}$, which is further natural in X and Y by Theorem 4. But then $\overline{\mathrm{pfix}\,\alpha_{X,Y}} = \mathrm{pfix}\,\overline{\alpha_{X,Y}} = \mathrm{pfix}\,\alpha_{Y,X}$, as parametrized fixed points preserve conjugation.   □

4   Applications and Future Work

Reversible Programming Languages. Theseus [28] is a typed reversible functional programming language similar in syntax and spirit to Haskell. It has support for recursive data types, as well as reversible tail recursion using so-called *typed iteration labels* as syntactic sugar for a dagger trace operator. Theseus is based on the Π-family of reversible combinator calculi [27], which bases itself on dagger traced symmetric monoidal categories augmented with a certain class of algebraically ω-compact functors.

Theseus also supports *parametrized functions*, that is, families of reversible functions indexed by reversible functions of a given type, with the proviso that parameters must be passed to parametrized maps statically. For example, (if one extended Theseus with polymorphism) the reversible map function would have the signature $map :: (a \leftrightarrow b) \rightarrow ([a] \leftrightarrow [b])$, and so map is not in itself a reversible function, though $map\,\langle f \rangle$ is (for some suitable function f passed statically). This gives many of the benefits of higher-order programming, but without the headaches of higher-order reversible programming.

The presented results show very directly that we can extend Theseus with a fixed point operator for general recursion while maintaining desirable inversion properties, rather than making do with the simpler tail recursion. Additionally, the focus on the continuous functionals of $\mathscr{C}$ given by the category $\mathbf{DcpoOp}(\mathscr{C})$ also highlights the feature of parametrized functions in Theseus, and our results go further to show that even parametrized functions that use general recursion not only have desirable inversion properties, but also preserve naturality, the latter of which is useful for extending Theseus with parametric polymorphism.

Quantum Programming Languages. An interesting possibility as regards quantum programming languages is the category $\mathbf{CP^*}(\mathbf{FHilb})$ (see [12] for details on the $\mathbf{CP^*}$-construction), which is dagger compact closed and equivalent to the category of finite-dimensional C^*-algebras and completely positive maps [12]. Since finite-dimensional C^*-algebras are specifically von Neumann algebras, it follows (see [9,34]) that this category is enriched in the category of *bounded* directed complete partial orders; and since it inherits the dagger from $\mathbf{FHilb}$ (and is locally ordered by the pointwise extension of the Löwner order restricted to positive operators), the dagger structure is monotone, too. As such, the presented results ought to apply in this case as well – modulo concerns of boundedness – though this warrants more careful study.

Dagger Traces in **DCPO**-†-*Categories.* Given a suitable monoidal tensor (*e.g.*, one with the zero object as tensor unit) and a partial additive structure on morphisms, giving the category the structure of a *unique decomposition category* [17,23], a trace operator can be canonically constructed. In previous work [30], the author (among others) demonstrated that a certain class of **DCPO**-†-categories, namely join inverse categories, had a dagger trace under suitably mild assumptions. It is conjectured that this theorem may be generalized to other **DCPO**-†-categories that are not necessarily inverse categories, again provided that certain assumptions are satisfied.

Involutive Iteration Categories. As it turned out that the category **DcpoOp**($\mathscr{C}$) of continuous functionals on $\mathscr{C}$ was both involutive and an iteration category, an immediate question to ask is how the involution functor ought to interact with parametrized fixed points in the general case. A remarkable fact of iteration categories is that they are defined to be cartesian categories that satisfy all equations of parametrized fixed points that hold in the category **CPO**$_m$ of ω-complete partial orders and *monotone* functions, yet also have a complete (though infinite) equational axiomatization [15].

We have provided an example of an interaction between parametrized fixed points and the involution functor here, namely that **DcpoOp**($\mathscr{C}$) satisfies $\overline{\text{pfix}\,\psi} = \text{pfix}\,\overline{\psi}$. It could be interesting to search for examples of involutive iteration categories in the wild (as candidates for a semantic definition), and to see if Ésik's axiomatization could be extended to accomodate for the involution functor in the semantic category.

5   Conclusion and Related Work

We have developed a notion of **DCPO**-categories with a monotone dagger structure (of which **PInj**, **Rel**, and **DStoch**$_{\leq 1}$ are examples, and **CP***(**FHilb**) is closely related), and shown that these categories can be taken to be enriched in an induced involutive monoidal category of continuous functionals. With this, we were able to account for (ordinary and parametrized) fixed point adjoints as arising from conjugation of the functional in the induced involutive monoidal category, to show that parametrized fixed points preserve conjugation and naturality, and that natural transformations that preserve the dagger are precisely those that are self-conjugate. We also described a number of potential applications in connection with reversible and quantum computing.

A great deal of work has been carried out in recent years on the domain theory of quantum computing, with noteworthy results in categories of von Neumann algebras (see, *e.g.*, [9,10,26,34]). Though the interaction between dagger structure and the domain structure on homsets was not the object of study, Heunen considers the similarities and differences of **FHilb** and **PInj**, also in relation to domain structure on homsets, in [21], though he also notes that **FHilb** fails to enrich in domains as composition is not even monotone (this is not to say that domain theory and quantum computing do not mix; only that **FHilb** is the wrong category to consider for this purpose). Finally, dagger traced symmetric monoidal categories, with the dagger trace serving as an operator for reversible tail recursion, have been studied in connection with reversible combinator calculi [27] and functional programming [28].

References

1. Abramsky, S.: Retracing some paths in process algebra. In: Montanari, U., Sassone, V. (eds.) CONCUR 1996. LNCS, vol. 1119, pp. 1–17. Springer, Heidelberg (1996). https://doi.org/10.1007/3-540-61604-7_44
2. Abramsky, S., Coecke, B.: A categorical semantics of quantum protocol. In: 2004 Proceedings on Logic in Computer Science, pp. 415–425. IEEE (2004)
3. Abramsky, S., Jung, A.: Domain theory. In: Handbook of Logic in Computer Science, No. 3, pp. 1–168. Clarendon Press (1994)
4. Adámek, J.: Recursive data types in algebraically ω-complete categories. Inf. Comput. **118**, 181–190 (1995)
5. Bainbridge, E.S., Freyd, P.J., Scedrov, A., Scott, P.J.: Functorial polymorphism. Theor. Comput. Sci. **70**(1), 35–64 (1990)
6. Barr, M.: Algebraically compact functors. J. Pure Appl. Algebra **82**(3), 211–231 (1992)
7. Beggs, E.J., Majid, S.: Bar categories and star operations. Algebras Represent. Theory **12**(2), 103–152 (2009)
8. Benton, N., Hyland, M.: Traced premonoidal categories. Theor. Inform. Appl. **37**(4), 273–299 (2003)
9. Cho, K.: Semantics for a quantum programming language by operator algebras. Master's thesis, University of Tokyo (2014)
10. Cho, K., Jacobs, B., Westerbaan, B., Westerbaan, A.: An introduction to effectus theory. arXiv:1512.05813 [cs.LO] (2015)
11. Cockett, J.R.B., Lack, S.: Restriction categories I: categories of partial maps. Theor. Comput. Sci. **270**(1–2), 223–259 (2002)
12. Coecke, B., Heunen, C., Kissinger, A.: Categories of quantum and classical channels. Quant. Inf. Process. **15**(12), 5179–5209 (2016)
13. Egger, J.: Involutive monoidal categories and enriched dagger categories. Seminar talk, University of Oxford (2008)
14. Ésik, Z.: Fixed point theory. In: Droste, M., Kuich, W., Vogler, H. (eds.) Handbook of Weighted Automata, pp. 29–65. Springer, Berlin (2009). https://doi.org/10.1007/978-3-642-01492-5_2
15. Ésik, Z.: Equational properties of fixed point operations in cartesian categories: an overview. In: Italiano, G.F., Pighizzini, G., Sannella, D.T. (eds.) MFCS 2015. LNCS, vol. 9234, pp. 18–37. Springer, Heidelberg (2015). https://doi.org/10.1007/978-3-662-48057-1_2
16. Guo, X.: Products, joins, meets, and ranges in restriction categories. Ph.D. thesis, University of Calgary (2012)
17. Haghverdi, E.: Unique decomposition categories, geometry of interaction and combinatory logic. Math. Struct. Comput. Sci. **10**(2), 205–230 (2000)

18. Hasegawa, M.: Recursion from cyclic sharing: traced monoidal categories and models of cyclic lambda calculi. In: de Groote, P., Roger Hindley, J. (eds.) TLCA 1997. LNCS, vol. 1210, pp. 196–213. Springer, Heidelberg (1997). https://doi.org/10.1007/3-540-62688-3_37

19. Hasegawa, M., Hofmann, M., Plotkin, G.: Finite dimensional vector spaces are complete for traced symmetric monoidal categories. In: Avron, A., Dershowitz, N., Rabinovich, A. (eds.) Pillars of Computer Science. LNCS, vol. 4800, pp. 367–385. Springer, Heidelberg (2008). https://doi.org/10.1007/978-3-540-78127-1_20

20. Heunen, C.: Categorical quantum models and logics. Ph.D. thesis, Radboud University Nijmegen (2009)

21. Heunen, C.: On the Functor ℓ^2. In: Coecke, B., Ong, L., Panangaden, P. (eds.) Computation, Logic, Games, and Quantum Foundations. The Many Facets of Samson Abramsky. LNCS, vol. 7860, pp. 107–121. Springer, Heidelberg (2013). https://doi.org/10.1007/978-3-642-38164-5_8

22. Heunen, C., Karvonen, M.: Monads on dagger categories. Theory Appl. Categories **31**(35), 1016–1043 (2016)

23. Hoshino, N.: A representation theorem for unique decomposition categories. Electron. Notes Theor. Comput. Sci. **286**, 213–227 (2012)

24. Hyland, M.: Abstract and concrete models for recursion. In: Proceedings of the NATO Advanced Study Institute on Formal Logical Methods for System Security and Correctness, pp. 175–198. IOS Press (2008)

25. Jacobs, B.: Involutive categories and monoids, with a GNS-correspondence. Found. Phys. **42**(7), 874–895 (2012)

26. Jacobs, B.: New directions in categorical logic, for classical, probabilistic and quantum logic. Logical Methods Comput. Sci. **11**(3), 1–76 (2015)

27. James, R.P., Sabry, A.: Information effects. In: Proceedings, POPL 2012, pp. 73–84. ACM (2012)

28. James, R.P., Sabry, A.: Theseus: a high level language for reversible computing (2014). Work-in-progress report presented at RC 2014

29. Joyal, A., Street, R., Verity, D.: Traced monoidal categories. Math. Proc. Cambridge Philos. Soc. **119**(3), 447–468 (1996)

30. Kaarsgaard, R., Axelsen, H.B., Glück, R.: Join inverse categories and reversible recursion. J. Logical Algebraic Methods Program. **87**, 33–50 (2017)

31. Karvonen, M.: The way of the dagger. Ph.D. thesis, School of Informatics, University of Edinburgh (2019)

32. Kastl, J.: Inverse categories. In: Algebraische Modelle, Kategorien und Gruppoide, Studien zur Algebra und ihre Anwendungen, vol. 7, pp. 51–60. Akademie-Verlag (1979)

33. Kelly, G.M.: Basic Concepts of Enriched Category Theory. London Mathematical Society Lecture Note Series, vol. 64. Cambridge University Press, Cambridge (1982)

34. Rennela, M.: Towards a quantum domain theory: order-enrichment and fixpoints in W*-algebras. Electron. Notes Theor. Comput. Sci. **308**, 289–307 (2014)

35. Selinger, P.: Dagger compact closed categories and completely positive maps. Electron. Notes Theor. Comput. Sci. **170**, 139–163 (2007)

36. Selinger, P.: A survey of graphical languages for monoidal categories. In: Coecke, B. (ed.) New Structures for Physics, pp. 289–355. Springer, Berlin (2011). https://doi.org/10.1007/978-3-642-12821-9_4

37. Selinger, P.: Finite dimensional Hilbert spaces are complete for dagger compact closed categories. Logical Methods Comput. Sci. **8**, 1–12 (2012)

38. Smyth, M.B., Plotkin, G.D.: The category-theoretic solution of recursive domain equations. SIAM J. Comput. **11**(4), 761–783 (1982)

39. Wadler, P.: Theorems for free! In: Proceedings of the Fourth International Conference on Functional Programming Languages and Computer Architecture, FPCA 1989, pp. 347–359. ACM (1989)
40. Yokoyama, T., Axelsen, H.B., Glück, R.: Towards a reversible functional language. In: De Vos, A., Wille, R. (eds.) RC 2011. LNCS, vol. 7165, pp. 14–29. Springer, Heidelberg (2012). https://doi.org/10.1007/978-3-642-29517-1_2

Reversibility *vs* Local Creation/Destruction

Pablo Arrighi[1,2], Nicolas Durbec[1(✉)], and Aurélien Emmanuel[3]

[1] Aix-Marseille Univ., Université de Toulon, CNRS, LIS, Marseille, France
nicolas.durbec@lis-lab.fr
[2] IXXI, Lyon, France
[3] École Normale Supérieure, CNRS, Paris, France

Abstract. Consider a network that evolves reversibly, according to nearest neighbours interactions. *Can its dynamics create/destroy nodes?* On the one hand, since the nodes are the principal carriers of information, it seems that they cannot be destroyed without jeopardising bijectivity. On the other hand, there are plenty of global functions from graphs to graphs that are non-vertex-preserving and bijective. The question has been answered negatively—in three different ways. Yet, in this paper we do obtain reversible local node creation/destruction—in three relaxed settings, whose equivalence we prove for robustness. We motivate our work both by theoretical computer science considerations (reversible computing, cellular automata extensions) and theoretical physics concerns (basic formalisms towards discrete quantum gravity).

1 Introduction

Cellular Automata (CA) consist in a $\mathbb{Z}^n$ grid of identical cells, each of which may take a state in Σ. Thus the configurations are in $\Sigma^{\mathbb{Z}^n}$. The next state of a cell is given by applying a fixed local rule f to the cell and its neighbours, synchronously and homogeneously across space. CA thus have a number of physics-like symmetries: shift-invariance (the dynamics acts everywhere and everywhen the same) and causality (information has a bounded speed of propagation). They constitute one of the most established models of computation that accounts for Euclidean space: they are widely used to model spatially-dependent computational problems (self-replicating machines, synchronization. . .), and multi-agents phenomena (traffic jams, demographics. . .). But their origin lies in Physics, where they are constantly used to model waves or particles (e.g. as numerical schemes for Partial Differential Equations).

Since both quantum and classical mechanics are reversible, it was natural to endow CA with this other, physics-like symmetry. The study of Reversible CA (RCA) was further motivated by the promise of lower energy consumption in reversible computation. RCA have turned out to have an elegant mathematical theory, which relies on a topological characterization in order to prove for instance that the inverse of a CA is a CA [20]—which clearly is non-trivial due

© Springer Nature Switzerland AG 2019
M. K. Thomsen and M. Soeken (Eds.): RC 2019, LNCS 11497, pp. 51–66, 2019.
https://doi.org/10.1007/978-3-030-21500-2_4

to [21].Another fundamental property of RCA is that they can be expressed as a finite-depth circuits of local reversible permutations or 'blocks' [13,22,23].

Causal Graph Dynamics (CGD) [1,3,6,26,27] are a twofold extension of CA. First, the underlying grid is extended to arbitrary bounded-degree graphs. Informally, this means that each vertex of a graph G may take a state among a set Σ, so that configurations are in $\Sigma^{V(G)}$, whereas edges dictate the locality of the evolution: the next state of a vertex v depends only upon the subgraph G_u^r induced by the vertices lying at graph distance at most r of u. Second, the graph itself is allowed to evolve over time. Informally, this means that configurations are in the union of $\Sigma^{V(G)}$ for every possible bounded-degree graph G, i.e. $\bigcup_G \Sigma^{V(G)}$. This leads to a model where the local rule f is applied synchronously and homogeneously on every possible sub-disk of the input graph, thereby producing small patches of the output graphs, whose union constitutes the output graph. Figure 1 illustrates the concept. CGD were motivated by the countless situations featuring nearest-neighbours interactions with time-varying neighbourhood (e.g. agents exchange contacts, move around...). Many existing models (of complex systems, computer processes, biochemical agents, economic agents, social networks...) fall into this category, thereby generalizing CA for their specific sake (e.g. self-reproduction as in [32], discrete general relativity à la Regge calculus [30], etc.). CGD are a theoretical framework, for these models. Some graph rewriting models, such as Amalgamated Graph Transformations [10] and Parallel Graph Transformations [14,31], also work out rigorous ways of applying a local rewriting rule synchronously throughout a graph, albeit with a different, category-theory-based perspective, of which the latest and closest instance is [26]. In [7,8] one of the authors studied CGD in the reversible regime, i.e. Reversible CGD. Specific examples of Reversible CGD had been described in [19,24].

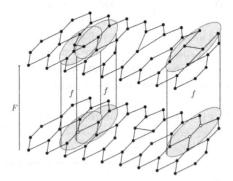

Fig. 1. Informal illustration of Causal Graph Dynamics.

From a theoretical Computer Science perspective, the point was to generalize RCA theory to arbitrary, bounded-degree, time-varying graphs. Indeed the two main results in [7,8] were the generalizations of the two above-mentioned fundamental properties of RCA. However, the results were limited to (almost–) vertex – preserving CGD. We show that this limitation can be lifted.

From a mathematical perspective, questions related to the bijectivity of CA over certain classes of graphs (more specifically, whether pre-injectivity implies surjectivity for Cayley graphs generated by certain groups [9,15,17]) have received quite some attention. The present paper on the other hand provides a context in which to study "bijectivity of CA over time-varying graphs". We answer the question: *Is it the case that bijectivity necessarily rigidifies space (i.e. forces the conservation of each vertex)?* Our analysis pinpoints the assumptions that lead to this rigidification—and how to circumvent them.

From a theoretical physics perspective, the question whether the reversibility of small scale physics (quantum mechanics, newtonian mechanics), can be reconciled with the time-varying topology of large scale physics (relativity), is a major challenge. This paper provides a rigorous discrete, toy model where reversibility and time-varying topology coexist and interact—in a way which does allow for space expansion. In fact these results open the way for Quantum Causal Graph Dynamics [5] allowing for vertex creation/destruction—which could provide a rigorous basic formalism to use in Quantum Gravity [18,25].

2 The Conflict Between Reversibility and Node Creation/Destruction

The Question. Consider a network that evolves reversibly, according to nearest neighbours interactions. *Can its dynamics create/destroy nodes?*

Issue 1. Because the network evolves according to nearest neighbours interactions only, the same local causes must produce the same local effects. In other words if the neighbourhood of a node u looks the same as that of a node v, then the same must happen at u and v. Therefore the names of the nodes must be irrelevant to the dynamics. Surely the most natural way to formalize this invariance under isomorphisms is as follows. Let F be the function from graphs to graphs that captures the time evolution; we require that for any renaming R, $F \circ R = R \circ F$. But it turns out that this commutation condition forbids node creation, even in the absence any reversibility condition—as proven in [1]. Intuitively, say that a node $u \in V(G)$ creates a node $u' \in V(G')$ through F, and consider an R that just interchanges the u' name for some fresh name v'. Then $F(RG) = F(G)$, which has no v', differs from $RF(G)$, which has a v'.

Issue 2. The above issue can be fixed by making it explicit that new names are constructed from the locally available ones (e.g. u' from u in the above example), so that renaming the new names (e.g. u' into v' through some R') necessarily implies having renamed the available ones (e.g. u into v through R). Then invariance under isomorphisms is formalized by requiring that for any renaming R, there exists R', such that $F \circ R = R' \circ F$. But it turns out that this conjugation condition, taken together with reversibility, still forbids node creation, as proven in [3]. To get a taste of the difficulty, say that a node u creates two nodes $u.l$ and $u.r$. Then F^{-1} should merge these back into a single node u. However, we expect F^{-1} to have the same conjugation property that for any renaming S, there exists S', such that $F^{-1} \circ S = S' \circ F^{-1}$. Consider an S that leaves $u.l$ unchanged, but renames $u.r$ into some fresh v'. What will be the name of the merger between $u.l$ and v' through F^{-1}, now? What should S' do upon u in order to obtain that name? Generally speaking, node creation between G and $F(G)$ augments the naming space and endangers the bijectivity that should hold between $\{RG\}$ the set of renamings of G and $\{RF(G)\}$ the set of renamings of $F(G)$.

Issue 3. Both the above no-go theorems rely on naming issues. In order to bypass them, one may drop names altogether, and work with graphs modulo isomorphisms. Doing this, however, is quite inconvenient. Basic statements such as "the neighbourhood of u determines what will happen at u"—needed to formalize the fact the network evolves according to nearest-neighbours interactions—are no longer possible if we cannot speak of u.

Still, having chosen networks that are not mere graphs (edges are between the ports of the nodes) we can designate a node relative to another by giving a path from one to the other (the successive ports that lead to it). It then suffices to have one privileged pointed vertex acting as 'the origin', to be able to designate any vertex relative to it. Then, the invariance under isomorphisms is almost trivial, as nodes have no name. The one thing that remains to enforce is invariance under shifting the origin. Namely, if X_u stands for X with its origin shifted along path u, then there must exist some successor function $R_X : V(X) \longrightarrow V(F(X))$ such that $F(X_u) = F(X)_{R_X(u)}$. But it turns out that this seemingly mild condition, when taken together with reversibility, again forbids node creation but for a finite number of graphs—as was proven in [8].

Intuitively, node creation between X and $F(X)$ augments the number of ways in which the graph can be pointed at, i.e. the number or possible origins. This again endangers the bijectivity that should hold between the sets of shifts $\{X_u\}_{u \in V(X)}$ and $\{F(X)_{u'}\}_{u' \in V(F(X))}$.

Three Solutions and a Plan. In [19], Hasslacher and Meyer describe a great example of a nearest-neighbours driven dynamics, which exhibits a rather surprising thermodynamical behaviour in the long-run. The HM example consists of particles moving around a circle, with collisions causing the circle to shrink or grow, according to the way in which particles meet. The HM example is clearly non-vertex-preserving, but it is also reversible, in some sense which was left informal, and really is not obvious.

We will see that most direct approach to formalizing the HM example and its properties, is to work with pointed graphs modulo just when they are useful, e.g. for stating causality, and to drop the pointer everywhen else, e.g. for stating reversibility. This relaxed setting reconciles reversibility and local creation/destruction—it can be thought of as a direct response to Issue 3. Section 4 presents this solution.

A second approach is to simulate the HM example with a strictly reversible, vertex-preserving dynamics, where each 'visible' node of the network is equipped with its own reservoir of 'invisible' nodes—in which it can tap in order to create an visible node. The obtained relaxed setting thus circumvents the above three issues. Section 5 presents this solution.

A third approach is to work with standard, named graphs. Remarkably it turns out that naming our nodes within the algebra of variables over everywhere-infinite binary trees directly resolves Issue 2. Section 6 presents this solution.

The question of reversibility versus local creation/destruction, is thus, to some extent, formalism-dependent. Fortunately, we were able to prove that the three proposed relaxed settings are equivalent, as synthesized in Sect. 7. Thus we have reached a robust formalism allowing for both the features. Section 3 recalls the definitions and results that constitute our point of departure. Section 8 summarizes the contributions and perspectives. *This paper is an extended abstract designed to work on its own, but the full-blown details and proofs are made available in the appendices of the corresponding arXiv preprint* [4].

3   In a Nutshell: Reversible Causal Graph Dynamics

The following provides an intuitive introduction to Reversible CGD. A thorough formalization was given in [6].

Networks. Whether for CA over graphs [28], multi-agent modeling [12] or agent-based distributed algorithms [11], it is common to work with graphs whose nodes have numbered neighbours. Thus our 'graphs' or networks are the usual, connected, undirected, possibly infinite, bounded-degree graphs, but with a few additional twists:

- The set π of available ports to each vertex is finite.
- The vertices are connected through their ports: an edge is an unordered pair $\{u : a, v : b\}$, where u, v are vertices and $a, b \in \pi$ are ports. Each port is used at most once per node: if both $\{u : a, v : b\}$ and $\{u : a, w : c\}$ are edges, then $v = w$ and $b = c$. As a consequence the degree of the graph is bounded by $|\pi|$.
- The vertices and edges can be given labels taken in finite sets Σ and Δ respectively, so that they may carry an internal state.
- These labeling functions are partial, so that we may express our partial knowledge about part of a graph.

The set of all graphs (see Fig. 2(a)) is denoted $\mathcal{G}_{\Sigma,\Delta,\pi}$.

Compactness. In order to both drop the irrelevant names of nodes and obtain a compact metric space of graphs, we need 'pointed graphs modulo' instead:

- The graphs have a privileged pointed vertex playing the role of an origin.
- The pointed graphs are considered modulo isomorphism, so that only the relative position of the vertices can matter.

The set of all pointed graphs modulo (see Fig. 2(c)) is denoted $\mathcal{X}_{\Sigma,\Delta,\pi}$.

If, instead, we drop the pointers but still take equivalence classes modulo isomorphism, we obtain just graphs modulo, aka 'anonymous graphs'. The set of all anonymous graphs (see Fig. 2(d)) is denoted $\widetilde{\mathcal{X}}_{\Sigma,\Delta,\pi}$.

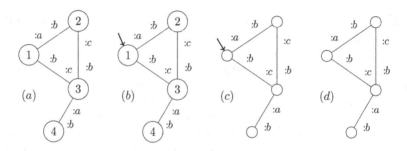

Fig. 2. *The different types of graphs.* (a) A graph G. (b) A pointed graph $(G, 1)$. (c) A pointed graph modulo X. (d) An anonymous graph $\tilde{X}$.

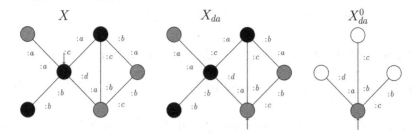

Fig. 3. *Operations over pointed graphs modulo.* The pointer of X is shifted along edge da, yielding X_{da}, and then the disk of radius 0 around the pointer, yielding X_{da}^0.

Paths and Vertices. Over pointed graphs modulo isomorphism, vertices no longer have a unique identifier, which may seem impractical when it comes to designating a vertex. Fortunately, any vertex of the graph can be designated by a sequence of ports in $(\pi^2)^*$ that lead from the origin to this vertex. For instance, say two vertices are designated by paths u and v, respectively. Suppose there is an edge $e = \{u : a, v : b\}$. Then, v can be designated by the path $u.ab$, where "." stands for the word concatenation. The origin is designated by ε.

Operations Over Graphs. Given a pointed graph modulo X, X^r denotes the sub-disk of radius r around the pointer. The pointer of X can be moved along a path u, leading to $Y = X_u$. We use the notation X_u^r for $(X_u)^r$ i.e., first the pointer is moved along u, then the sub-disk of radius r is taken (Fig. 3).

Causal Graph Dynamics. We will now recall their topological definition. It is important to provide a correspondence between the vertices of the input pointed graph modulo X, and those of its image $F(X)$, which is the role of R_X:

Definition 1 (Dynamics). *A dynamics $(F, R_\bullet)$ is given by*

- *a function $F \colon \mathcal{X}_{\Sigma, \Delta, \pi} \to \mathcal{X}_{\Sigma, \Delta, \pi}$;*
- *a map $R_\bullet$, with $R_\bullet \colon X \mapsto R_X$ and $R_X \colon V(X) \to V(F(X))$.*

Next, continuity is the topological way of expressing causality:

Definition 2 (Continuity). *A dynamics* $(F, R_\bullet)$ *is said to be* continuous *if and only if for any* X *and* m, *there exists* n, *such that*

- $F(X)^m = F(X^n)^m$ • *dom* $R_X^m \subseteq V(X^n)$ *and* $R_X^m = R_{X^n}^m$

where R_X^m *denotes the partial map obtained as the restriction of* R_X *to the co-domain* $F(X)^m$, *using the natural inclusion of* $F(X)^m$ *into* $F(X)$.

Notice that the second condition states the continuity of $R_\bullet$ itself. A key point is that by compactness, continuity entails uniform continuity, meaning that n does not depend upon X—so that the above really expresses that information has a bounded speed of propagation of information.

We now express that the same causes lead to the same effects:

Definition 3 (Shift-invariance). *A dynamics* $(F, R_\bullet)$ *is said to be* shift-invariant *if for every* X, $u \in V(X)$, *and* $v \in V(X_u)$,

- $F(X_u) = F(X)_{R_X(u)}$ • $R_X(u.v) = R_X(u).R_{X_u}(v)$

Finally we demand that graphs do not expand in an unbounded manner:

Definition 4 (Boundedness). *A dynamics* $(F, R_\bullet)$ *is said to be* bounded *if there exists a bound* b *such that for any* X *and any* $w' \in V(F(X))$, *there exists* $u' \in Im(R_X)$ *and* $v' \in V(F(X)_{u'}^b)$ *such that* $w' = u'.v'$.

Putting these conditions together yields the topological definition of CGD:

Definition 5 (Causal Graph Dynamics). *A CGD is a shift-invariant, continuous, bounded dynamics.*

Reversibility. Invertibility is imposed in the most general and natural fashion.

Definition 6 (Invertible dynamics). *A dynamics* $(F, R_\bullet)$ *is said to be* invertible *if* F *is a bijection.*

Unfortunately, this condition turns out to be very limiting. It is the following limitation that the present paper seeks to circumvent:

Theorem 1 (Invertible implies almost-vertex-preserving [8]**).** *Let* $(F, R_\bullet)$ *be an invertible CGD. Then there exists a bound* p, *such that for any graph* X, *if* $|V(X)| > p$ *then* R_X *is bijective.*

On the face of it reversibility is stronger a condition than invertibility:

Definition 7 (Reversible Causal Graph Dynamics). *A CGD* $(F, R_\bullet)$ *is* reversible *if there exists* $S_\bullet$ *such that* $(F^{-1}, S_\bullet)$ *is a CGD.*

Fortunately, invertibility gets you reversibility:

Theorem 2 (Invertible implies reversible [8]**).** *If* $(F, R_\bullet)$ *is an invertible CGD, then* $(F, R_\bullet)$ *is reversible.*

As a simple example we provide an original, general scheme for propagating particles on an arbitrary network in a reversible manner:

Example 1 (General reversible advection). Consider $\pi = \{a, b, \ldots\}$ a finite set of ports, and let $\Sigma = \mathcal{P}(\pi)$ be the set of internal states, where: $\varnothing$ means 'no particle is on that node'; $\{a\}$ means 'one particle is set to propagate along port a'; $\{a, b\}$ means 'one particle is set to propagate along port a and another along port b'.... Let s be a bijection over the set of ports, standing for the successor direction. Figure 4(a) specifies how individual particles propagate. Basically, when reaching its destination, the particle set to propagate along the successor of the port it came from. Missing edges behave like self-loops. Applying this to all particles synchronously specifies the graph dynamic.

4   The Anonymous Solution

Having a pointer is essential in order to express causality, but cumbersome when it comes to reversibility. Here is the direct way to get the best of both worlds.

Definition 8 (Anonymous Causal Graph Dynamics). *Consider $\widetilde{F}$ a function over $\widetilde{\mathcal{X}}_{\Sigma,\Delta,\pi}$. We say that $\widetilde{F}$ is an ACGD if and only if there exists $(F, R_\bullet)$ a CGD such that F over $\mathcal{X}_{\Sigma,\Delta,\pi}$ naturally induces $\widetilde{F}$ over $\widetilde{\mathcal{X}}_{\Sigma,\Delta,\pi}$.*

Invertibility, then, just means that $\widetilde{F}$ is bijective. Fortunately, this time the condition is not so limiting, and we are able to implement non-vertex-preserving dynamics, as can be seen from this slight generalization of the HM example:

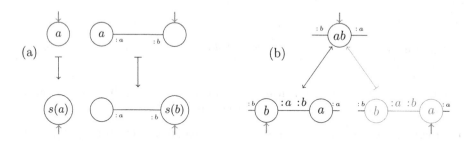

Fig. 4. *(a) General reversible advection. (b) The Hasslacher-Meyer example's collision step.* The anonymous dynamics is in plain black, the underlying regular dynamics is in grey.

Example 2 (Anonymous HM). Consider the state space of Example 1 and alternate: 1. a step of advection as in Fig. 4(a), 2. a step of collision, where the collision is the specific graph replacement provided in Fig. 4(b). The composition of these two specifies the ACGD.

So, ACGD feature local vertex creation/destruction. Yet they are clearly less constructive than CGD, as $R_\bullet$ is no longer explicit. In spite of this lack of constructiveness, we still have

Theorem 3 (Anonymous invertible implies reversible). *If an ACGD in invertible, then the inverse function is an ACGD.*

Proof outline. By Theorem 6 the invertible ACGD $\widetilde{F}$ can be directly simulated by an invertible IMCGD, see next. By Theorem 4 the inverse IMCGD is also an IMCGD. Dropping the invisible matter of this inverse provides the CGD that underlines $\widetilde{F}^{-1}$. □

5   The Invisible Matter Solution

Reversible CGD are vertex-preserving. Still, we could think of using them to simulate a non-vertex-preserving dynamics by distinguishing 'visible' and 'invisible matter', and making sure that every visible node is equipped with its own reservoir of 'invisible' nodes—in which it can tap. For this scheme to iterate, and for the created nodes to be able to create nodes themselves, it is convenient to shape the reservoirs as everywhere infinite binary trees.

Definition 9 (Invisible Matter Graphs).
Consider $\mathcal{X} = \mathcal{X}_{\Sigma,\Delta,\pi}$, $\mathcal{T} = \mathcal{X}_{\{m\},\emptyset,\{m,l,r\}}$ and $\mathcal{X}' = \mathcal{X}_{\Sigma\cup\{m\},\Delta,\pi\cup\{m,l,r\}}$, assuming that $\{m\}\cap\Sigma = \emptyset$ and $\{m,l,r\}\cap\pi = \emptyset$. Let $T \in \mathcal{T}$ be the infinite binary tree whose origin ε has a copy of T at vertex lm, and another at vertex rm. Every $X \in \mathcal{X}$ can be identified to an element of $\mathcal{X}'$ obtained by attaching an instance of T at each vertex through path mm. The hereby obtained graphs will be denoted by $\mathcal{Y}$ and referred to as invisible matter graphs.

We will now consider those CGD over $\mathcal{X}'$ that leave $\mathcal{Y}$ stable. In fact we want them trivial as soon as we dive deep enough into the invisible matter:

Definition 10 (Invisible-matter quiescence). *A dynamic $(F, R_\bullet)$ over $\mathcal{Y}$ is said* invisible matter quiescent *if there exists a bound b such that, for all $X \in \mathcal{Y}$, and for all s,t in $\{lm, rm\}^*$, we have $|s| \geq b \implies R_{X_{mms}}(t) = t$.*

Notice that this condition is similar to boundedness, as it prevents nodes from splitting infinitely.

Definition 11 (Invisible Matter Causal Graph Dynamics). *A CGD over $\mathcal{Y}$ is said to be an IMCGD if and only if it is vertex-preserving and invisible matter quiescent.*

Fortunately, we are indeed able to encode non-vertex-preserving dynamics in the visible sector of an invertible IMCGD:

Example 3 (Invisible Matter HM). Consider $\mathcal{X}$ as in Example 1 and extend it to $\mathcal{Y}$. Alternate: 1. a step of advection as in Examples 1 and 4(a), 2. a step of collision, where the collision is the specific graph replacement provided in Fig. 5. The composition of these two specifies the invertible IMCGD.

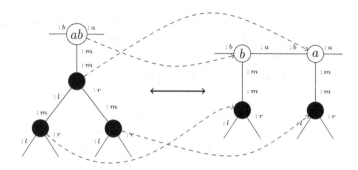

Fig. 5. *HM example's collision step with pointers and invisible matter.* Black vertices are 'invisible'. The dotted lines show where to place the pointer in the image according to its position in the antecedent.

Notice how the graph replacement of Fig. 4(b)—with the grey color taken into account—would fail to be invertible, due to the collapsing of two pointer positions into one.

Fortunately also, invertibility still implies reversibility:

Theorem 4 (Invertible implies reversible). *If $(F, R_\bullet)$ is an invertible IMCGD, then $(F^{-1}, R^{-1}_{F^{-1}(\bullet)})$ is an IMCGD.*

Proof outline. Intuitively this property is inherited from that of CGD over $\mathcal{X}'$. Theorem 2, however, relies on the compactness of $\mathcal{X}'$, and as matter of fact $\mathcal{Y}$ is not compact. Still it admits a compact closure $\overline{\mathcal{Y}}$, over which IMCGD have a natural, continuous extension.   □

6   The Name Algebra Solution

So far we worked with (pointed) graphs modulo. But named graphs are often more convenient e.g. for implementation, and sometimes mandatory e.g. for studying the quantum case [5]. In this context, being able to locally create a node implies being able to locally make up a new name for it—just from the locally available ones. For instance if a dynamics F splits a node u into two, a natural choice is to call these $u.l$ and $u.r$. Now, apply a renaming R that maps $u.l$ into v and $u.r$ into w, and apply F^{-1}. This time the nodes v and w get merged into one; in order not to remain invertible a natural choice is to call the resultant node $(v \vee w)$. Yet, if R is chosen trivial, then the resultant node is $(u.l \vee u.r)$, when $F^{-1} \circ F = Id$ demands that this to be u instead. This suggests considering a name algebra where $u = (u.l \vee u.r)$.

Definition 12 (Name Algebra). *Let $\mathcal{N}$ be a countable set (eg $\mathcal{N} = \mathbb{N}$). Consider the terms produced by the grammar $V ::= \mathcal{N} \mid V.\{l, r\}^* \mid V \vee V$ together with the equivalence induced by the term rewrite systems*

- $(u \vee v).l \longrightarrow u$ $(u \vee v).r \longrightarrow v$ (S) *and*   - $(u.l \vee u.r) \longrightarrow u$ (M)

i.e. u and v are equivalent if and only if their normal forms $u\!\downarrow_{S\cup M}$ and $v\!\downarrow_{S\cup M}$ are equal.

Well-foundedness outline. The term rewriting system (TRS) was checked terminating and locally confluent using CiME [16], hence its confluence and the unicity of normal forms via Church-Rosser. □

This is the algebra of symbolic everywhere infinite binary trees. Indeed, each element x of $\mathcal{N}$ can be thought of as a variable representing an infinite binary tree. The $.l$ (resp. $.r$) projection operation recovers the left (resp. right) subtree. The 'join' operation $\vee$ puts a node on top of its left and right trees to form another—it is therefore neither commutative nor associative. This infinitely splittable/mergeable tree structure is reminiscent of Sect. 5, later we shall prove that named graphs arise by abstracting away the invisible matter.

No graph can have two distinct nodes called the same. Nor should it be allowed to have a node called x and two others called $x.r$ and $x.l$, because the latter may merge and collide with the former.

Definition 13 (Intersectant). *Two terms v, v' in $\mathcal{V}$ and are said to be* intersectant *if and only if there exists t, t' in $\{l, r\}^*$ such that $v.t = v'.t'$. We write $v \cap v'$ as a shorthand notation for $\{v.t \mid t \in \{l, r\}^*\} \cap \{v'.t \mid t \in \{l, r\}^*\}$. We also write $v \cap V$ for $v \cap \bigcap_{v' \in V} v'$.*

Definition 14 (Well-named graphs). *We say that a graph G is* well-named *if and only if for all v, v' in $V(G) \subseteq \mathcal{V}$, $v \cap v' \neq \emptyset$ implies $v = v'$. We denote by $\mathcal{W}$ the subset of well-named graphs.*

We now have all the ingredients to define Named Causal Graph Dynamics. As before, we want our dynamic to be *continuous* and *bounded*:

Definition 15 (Continuity). *A function $\overline{F}$ over $\mathcal{W}$ is said to be* continuous *if and only if for any G and any $n \geq 0$, there exists $m \geq 0$, such that for all $v, v' \in V$, $v \cap v' = \emptyset$ implies $\overline{F}(G)_{v'}^n = \overline{F}(G_v^m)_{v'}^n$.*

Definition 16 (Boundedness). *A function $\overline{F}$ over $\mathcal{W}$ is said to be* bounded *if and only if there exists a bound b such that for all G, for all $v \in V(G)$, for all $v' \in V(\overline{F}G))$ such that there exist $t, t' \in \{l, r\}^*$ with $v.t = v'.t'$, then $|t| \leq b$ and $|t'| \leq b$.*

Next, we prevent our dynamics from relying on the names of the nodes:

Definition 17 (Renaming). *Consider R an injective function from $\mathcal{N}$ to V such that for any $x, y \in \mathcal{N}$, $R(x)$ and $R(y)$ are not intersectant. The natural extension of R to the whole of V, according to*

$$R(u.l) = R(u).l \qquad R(u.r) = R(u).r \qquad R(u \vee v) = R(u) \vee R(v)$$

is referred to as a renaming.

Definition 18 (Shift-invariance). *A function $\overline{F}$ over $\mathcal{W}$ is said to be* shift-invariant *if and only if for any $G \in \mathcal{W}$ and any renaming R, $F(RG) = RF(G)$.*

Our dynamics may split and merge names, but not drop them:

Definition 19 (Name-preservation). *Consider $\overline{F}$ a function over $\mathcal{W}$. The function $\overline{F}$ is said to be* name-preserving *if and only if for all u in V and G in $\mathcal{W}$ we have that $u \cap V(G) = u \cap V(\overline{F}(G))$.*

Definition 20 (Named Causal Graph Dynamics). *A function $\overline{F}$ over $\mathcal{W}$ is said to be a* Named Causal Graph Dynamics (NCGD) *if and only if is shift-invariant, continuous, and name-preserving.*

Fortunately, invertible NCGD do allow for local creation/destruction of vertices:

Fig. 6. The HM example's collision step for Named CGD.

Example 4 (Named HM example). Consider $\mathcal{W}$ with ports and labels as in Example 1. Alternate: 1. a step of advection as in Examples 1 and 4(a), 2. a step of collision, where the collision is the specific graph replacement provided in Fig. 6. That the latter is an involution follows from the three equalities holding in V.

Fortunately also, invertibility still implies reversibility.

Theorem 5 (Named invertible implies reversible). *If an NCGD in invertible, then the inverse function is an NCGD.*

Proof outline. By Theorem 8 the invertible NCGD $\overline{F}$ can be directly simulated by an invertible IMCGD $(F, R_\bullet)$, whose pointer mimics the behaviour of atomic names. Its inverse $(F^{-1}, R^{-1}_{F^{-1}(\bullet)})$ thus captures the full behaviour of $\overline{F}^{-1}$ over graphs including vertex names. By Theorem 4 $(F^{-1}, R^{-1}_{F^{-1}(\bullet)})$ is continuous, and thus so is $\overline{F}^{-1}$. □

7 Robustness

Previous works gave three negative results about the ability to locally create/destroy nodes in a reversible setting. But we just described three relaxed settings in which this is possible. The question is thus formalism-dependent. How sensitive is it to changes in formalism, exactly? We show that the three solutions directly simulate each other. They are but three presentations, in different levels of details, of a single robust solution.

In what follows α is the natural, surjective map from $\mathcal{Y}$ to $\widetilde{\mathcal{X}}$, which (informally): 1. Drops the pointer and 2. Cuts out the invisible matter. Whatever an ACGD does to a $\alpha(Y)$, an IMCGD can do to Y—moreover the notions of invertibility match:

Theorem 6 (IMCGD simulate ACGD). *Consider $\widetilde{F}$ an ACGD. Then there exists $(F, R_\bullet)$ an IMCGD such that for all but a finite number of graphs Y in $\mathcal{Y}$, $\widetilde{F}(\alpha(Y)) = \alpha(F(Y))$. Moreover if $\widetilde{F}$ is invertible, then this $(F, R_\bullet)$ is invertible.*

Proof outline. Any ACGD $\widetilde{F}$ has an underlying CGD $(F, R_\bullet)$. We show it can be extended to invisible matter, an then mended to make $R_\bullet$ bijective, thereby obtaining an IMCGD. The precise way this is mended relies on the fact vertex creation/destruction cannot happen without the presence of a local asymmetry—except in a finite number of cases. Next, bijectivity upon anonymous graphs induces bijectivity upon pointed graphs modulo.   □

Similarly, whatever an IMCGD does to a Y, a ACGD can do to $\alpha(Y)$:

Theorem 7 (ACGD simulate IMCGD). *Consider $(F, R_\bullet)$ an IMCGD. Then there exists an ACGD such that $\widetilde{F} \circ \alpha = \alpha \circ F$. Moreover if $(F, R_\bullet)$ is invertible, then this $\widetilde{F}$ is invertible.*

Proof outline. The ACGD is obtained by dropping the pointer and the invisible matter. The preservation of the invertibility is due to the shift invariance.   □

In what follows, if G is a graph in $\mathcal{W}$, then G' is the graph obtained from G by attaching invisible–matter trees to each vertex, and naming the attached vertices in $V(G).\{l, r\}^*$ according to Fig. 7.

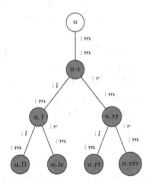

Fig. 7. Conventions for naming the invisible–matter.

Theorem 8 (IMCGD simulate NCGD). *Consider $\overline{F}$ an NCGD. There exists $\overline{R}_\bullet$ such that for all G, $\overline{R}_G$ is a bijection from $V(G).\{l, r\}^*$ to $V(F(G)).\{l, r\}^*$. This induces an IMCGD $(F, R_\bullet)$ via*

- $F((\widetilde{G', u.t})) = (\widetilde{\overline{F}(G)', \overline{R}_G(u.t)})$.
- $R_{(\widetilde{G', u.t})}(p)$ *is the path between $\overline{R}_G(u.t)$ and $\overline{R}_G(v.s)$ in $\overline{F}(G)'$, where $v.s$ is obtained by following path p from $u.t$ in G'.*

Moreover if $\overline{F}$ is invertible, then this $(F, R_\bullet)$ is invertible.

Proof outline. The names $V(\overline{F}(G))$ can be understood as keeping track of the splits and mergers that have happened through the application of $\overline{F}$ to G, as in Fig. 6. $\overline{R}_\bullet$ uses this to build a bijection from $V(G')$ to $V(\overline{F}(G)')$, following conventions as in Fig. 5.   □

Theorem 9 (NCGD simulate IMCGD). *Consider* $(F, R_\bullet)$ *an IMCGD. Then there exists $\overline{F}$ an NCGD such that for all graphs $Y = \widetilde{(G, u)}$ in $\mathcal{Y}$, $F(Y) = (\overline{F}(G), u)$. Moreover F is invertible if and only if $\overline{F}$ is invertible.*

Proof outline. Each vertex of Y can be named so that the resulting graph G is well-named. Then $R_\bullet$ is used to construct the behaviour of $\overline{F}$ over names of vertices. As $(F, R_\bullet)$ does not merge nor split vertices, F preserves the name of each vertex.   □

Thus, NCGD are more detailed than IMCGD, which are more detailed than ACGD. But, if one is thought of as retaining just the interesting part of the other, it does just what the other would do to this interesting part—and no more.

8   Conclusion

Summary of contributions. We have raised the question whether parallel reversible computation allows for the local creation/destruction of nodes. Different negative answers had been given in [1,3,8] which inspired us with three relaxed settings: Causal Graph Dynamics over fully-anonymized graphs (ACGD); over pointer graphs modulo with invisible matter reservoirs (IMCGD); and finally CGD over graphs whose vertex names are in the algebra of 'everywhere infinite binary trees' (NCGD). For each of these formalism, we proved non-vertex-preservingness by implementing the Hasslacher-Meyer example [19]—see Examples 2, 3 and 4. We also proved that we still had the classic Cellular Automata (CA) result that invertibility (i.e. mere bijectivity of the dynamics) implies reversibility (i.e. the inverse is itself a CGD)—via compactness—see Theorems 3, 4 and 5. The answer to the question of reversibility versus local creation/destruction is thus formalism-dependent to some extent. We proceeded to examine the extent in which this is the case, and were able to show that (Reversible) ACGD, IMCGD and NCGD directly simulate each other—see Theorems 6, 7, 8 and 9. They are but three presentations, in different levels of details, of a single robust setting in which reversibility and local creation/destruction are reconciled.

Perspectives. Just like Reversible CA were precursors to Quantum CA [2,29], Reversible CGD have paved the way for Quantum CGD [5]. Toy models where time-varying topologies are reconciled with quantum theory, are of central interest to the foundations of theoretical physics [18,25]—as it struggles to have general relativity and quantum mechanics coexist and interact. The 'models of computation approach' brings the clarity and rigor of theoretical CS to the table, whereas the 'natural and quantum computing approach' provides promising new abstractions based upon 'information' rather than 'matter'. Quantum CGD [5], however, lacked the ability to locally create/destroy nodes—which is necessary in order to model physically relevant scenarios. Our next step will be to apply the lessons hereby learned, to fix this.

References

1. Arrighi, P., Dowek, G.: Causal graph dynamics. In: Czumaj, A., Mehlhorn, K., Pitts, A., Wattenhofer, R. (eds.) ICALP 2012. LNCS, vol. 7392, pp. 54–66. Springer, Heidelberg (2012). https://doi.org/10.1007/978-3-642-31585-5_9

2. Arrighi, P., Nesme, V., Werner, R.: Unitarity plus causality implies localizability. J. Comput. Syst. Sci. **77**, 372–378 (2010). QIP 2010 (long talk)

3. Arrighi, P., Dowek, G.: Causal graph dynamics (long version). Inf. Comput. **223**, 78–93 (2013)

4. Arrighi, P., Durbec, N., Emmanuel, A.: Reversibility vs local creation/destruction. CoRR, abs/1805.10330 (2018). http://arxiv.org/abs/1805.10330

5. Arrighi, P., Martiel, S.: Quantum causal graph dynamics. Phys. Rev. D **96**, 024026 (2017). https://doi.org/10.1103/PhysRevD.96.024026

6. Arrighi, P., Martiel, S., Nesme, V.: Cellular automata over generalized cayley graphs. Math. Struct. Comput. Sci. **28**(3), 340–383 (2018). https://doi.org/10.1017/S0960129517000044

7. Arrighi, P., Martiel, S., Perdrix, S.: Block representation of reversible causal graph dynamics. In: Kosowski, A., Walukiewicz, I. (eds.) FCT 2015. LNCS, vol. 9210, pp. 351–363. Springer, Cham (2015). https://doi.org/10.1007/978-3-319-22177-9_27

8. Arrighi, P., Martiel, S., Perdrix, S.: Reversible causal graph dynamics. In: Devitt, S., Lanese, I. (eds.) RC 2016. LNCS, vol. 9720, pp. 73–88. Springer, Cham (2016). https://doi.org/10.1007/978-3-319-40578-0_5

9. Bartholdi, L.: Gardens of Eden and amenability on cellular automata. J. Eur. Math. Soc. **12**(1), 241–248 (2010)

10. Boehm, P., Fonio, H.R., Habel, A.: Amalgamation of graph transformations: a synchronization mechanism. J. Comput. Syst. Sci. **34**(2–3), 377–408 (1987)

11. Chalopin, J., Das, S., Widmayer, P.: Deterministic symmetric rendezvous in arbitrary graphs: overcoming anonymity, failures and uncertainty. In: Alpern, S., Fokkink, R., Gąsieniec, L., Lindelauf, R., Subrahmanian, V. (eds.) Search Theory, pp. 175–195. Springer, Berlin (2013). https://doi.org/10.1007/978-1-4614-6825-7_12

12. Danos, V., Laneve, C.: Formal molecular biology. Theor. Comput. Sci. **325**(1), 69–110 (2004). https://doi.org/10.1016/j.tcs.2004.03.065. http://www.sciencedirect.com/science/article/pii/S0304397504002336. Computational Systems Biology

13. Durand-Lose, J.O.: Representing reversible cellular automata with reversible block cellular automata. Discrete Math. Theor. Comput. Sci. **145**, 154 (2001)

14. Ehrig, H., Lowe, M.: Parallel and distributed derivations in the single-pushout approach. Theor. Comput. Sci. **109**(1–2), 123–143 (1993)

15. Ceccherini-Silberstein, T., Fiorenzi, F., Scarabotti, F.: The garden of Eden theorem for cellular automata and for symbolic dynamical systems. In: Random Walks and Geometry. Proceedings of a Workshop at the Erwin Schrödinger Institute, Vienna, 18 June–13 July 2001. Collaboration with Klaus Schmidt and Wolfgang Woess. Collected papers, pp. 73–108. de Gruyter, Berlin (2004)

16. Ganzinger, H. (ed.): RTA 1996. LNCS, vol. 1103. Springer, Heidelberg (1996). https://doi.org/10.1007/3-540-61464-8
17. Gromov, M.: Endomorphisms of symbolic algebraic varieties. J. Eur. Math. Soc. 1(2), 109–197 (1999). https://doi.org/10.1007/pl00011162
18. Hamma, A., et al.: A quantum Bose-Hubbard model with evolving graph as toy model for emergent spacetime. Arxiv preprint arXiv:0911.5075 (2009)
19. Hasslacher, B., Meyer, D.A.: Modelling dynamical geometry with lattice gas automata. Expanded Version of a Talk Presented at the Seventh International Conference on the Discrete Simulation of Fluids Held at the University of Oxford, June 1998
20. Hedlund, G.A.: Endomorphisms and automorphisms of the shift dynamical system. Math. Syst. Theory 3, 320–375 (1969)
21. Kari, J.: Reversibility of 2D cellular automata is undecidable. In: Cellular Automata: Theory and Experiment, vol. 45, pp. 379–385. MIT Press (1991)
22. Kari, J.: Representation of reversible cellular automata with block permutations. Theory Comput. Syst. 29(1), 47–61 (1996)
23. Kari, J.: On the circuit depth of structurally reversible cellular automata. Fundam. Inf. 38(1–2), 93–107 (1999)
24. Klales, A., Cianci, D., Needell, Z., Meyer, D.A., Love, P.J.: Lattice gas simulations of dynamical geometry in two dimensions. Phys. Rev. E 82(4), 046705 (2010). https://doi.org/10.1103/PhysRevE.82.046705
25. Konopka, T., Markopoulou, F., Smolin, L.: Quantum graphity. Arxiv preprint hep-th/0611197 (2006)
26. Maignan, L., Spicher, A.: Global graph transformations. In: Proceedings of the 6th International Workshop on Graph Computation Models, L'Aquila, Italy, 20 July 2015, pp. 34–49 (2015)
27. Martiel, S., Martin, B.: Intrinsic universality of causal graph dynamics. In: Neary, T., Cook, M. (eds.) Electronic Proceedings in Theoretical Computer Science, Proceedings, Machines, Computations and Universality 2013, Zürich, Switzerland, 9 September 2013–11 September 2013, vol. 128, pp. 137–149. Open Publishing Association (2013). https://doi.org/10.4204/EPTCS.128.19
28. Papazian, C., Rémila, E.: Hyperbolic recognition by graph automata. In: Widmayer, P., Eidenbenz, S., Triguero, F., Morales, R., Conejo, R., Hennessy, M. (eds.) ICALP 2002. LNCS, vol. 2380, pp. 330–342. Springer, Heidelberg (2002). https://doi.org/10.1007/3-540-45465-9_29
29. Schumacher, B., Werner, R.: Reversible quantum cellular automata. arXiv preprint quant-ph/0405174 (2004)
30. Sorkin, R.: Time-evolution problem in Regge calculus. Phys. Rev. D. 12(2), 385–396 (1975)
31. Taentzer, G.: Parallel high-level replacement systems. Theor. Comput. Sci. 186(1–2), 43–81 (1997)
32. Tomita, K., Kurokawa, H., Murata, S.: Graph automata: natural expression of self-reproduction. Phys. D: Nonlinear Phenom. 171(4), 197–210 (2002). https://doi.org/10.1016/S0167-2789(02)00601-2. http://www.sciencedirect.com/science/article/pii/S0167278902006012

Characterizing Compatible View Updates in Syntactic Bidirectionalization

Naoki Nishida[1] and Germán Vidal[2]($\boxtimes$)

[1] Graduate School of Informatics, Nagoya University,
Furo-cho, Chikusa-ku, 464-8603 Nagoya, Japan
nishida@i.nagoya-u.ac.jp
[2] MiST, DSIC, Universitat Politècnica de València,
Camino de Vera, s/n, 46022 Valencia, Spain
gvidal@dsic.upv.es

Abstract. Given a function that takes a *source* data and returns a *view*, bidirectionalization aims at producing automatically a new function that takes a modified view and returns the corresponding, modified source. In this paper, we consider simple first-order functional programs specified by (conditional) term rewrite systems. Then, we present a bidirectionalization technique based on the injectivization and inversion transformations from [24]. We also prove a number of relevant properties which ensure that changes in both the source and the view are correctly propagated and that no undesirable side-effects are introduced. Furthermore, we introduce the use of narrowing—an extension of rewriting that replaces matching with unification—to precisely characterize *compatible* (also called *in-place*) view updates so that the resulting bidirectional transformations are well defined. Finally, we discuss some directions for dealing with view updates that are not compatible.

Keywords: Bidirectional transformations ·
Functional programming languages · Term rewriting · Narrowing

1 Introduction

The framework of bidirectional transformations (bx) considers two representations of some data and the functions that convert one representation into the other and vice versa (see, e.g., [18] for an overview). Typically, we have a function called "get" that takes a *source* and returns a *view*. In turn, the function "put" takes a possibly updated view and returns the corresponding source. In

This work has been partially supported by the EU (FEDER) and the *Spanish Ministerio de Ciencia, Innovación y Universidades*/AEI under grant TIN2016-76843-C4-1-R, by the *Generalitat Valenciana* under grants PROMETEO-II/2015/013 (SmartLogic) and Prometeo/2019/098 (DeepTrust), by the COST Action IC1405 on Reversible Computation - extending horizons of computing, and by JSPS KAKENHI Grant Number JP17H01722.

© Springer Nature Switzerland AG 2019
M. K. Thomsen and M. Soeken (Eds.): RC 2019, LNCS 11497, pp. 67–83, 2019.
https://doi.org/10.1007/978-3-030-21500-2_5

this context, *bidirectionalization* [22] aims at automatically producing one of the functions, typically producing a function put from the corresponding function get (but the opposite approach is also possible, see, e.g., [10]). For this purpose, a so called *complement* function is often introduced so that the get function becomes injective (see, e.g., [12]).

Somewhat independently, reversible computation considers execution principles that can proceed both forward (i.e., normal computation) and backward. Moreover, *reversibilization* aims at transforming an irreversible computation principle into a reversible one. In particular, Landauer's seminal work [20] states how any computation principle can be made reversible by adding the history of the computation to each state. Although it may seem impractical at first, there are several useful reversibilization techniques that are roughly based on this idea (e.g., [8, 22, 24, 27]).

In this work, we consider a simple first-order functional programming language for our developments.[1] Consider, e.g., the following simple function:[2]

$$\mathsf{fn}\; [\,] = [\,]$$
$$\mathsf{fn}\; ((\mathsf{Name}\; n\; l){:}xs) = n{:}ys \;\; \mathsf{where}\; ys = \mathsf{fn}\; xs$$
$$\mathsf{fn}\; ((\mathsf{City}\; c){:}xs) = ys \;\; \mathsf{where}\; ys = \mathsf{fn}\; xs$$

The function fn takes a list of names of the form (Name *first_name last_name*) and cities of the form (City *name*), and returns a list of *first_names*. E.g.,

$$\mathsf{fn}\; [\mathsf{Name\; John\; Smith, City\; London, Name\; Ada\; Lovelace}]$$

evaluates to [John, Ada].

Trivially, function fn is not injective and, thus, its inverse is not a function. The framework of [24] introduces a Landauer embedding to make term rewriting reversible, which is then mapped to an *injectivization* transformation on (conditional) term rewrite systems. For the above function fn, it would return the following injective version:

$$\mathsf{fn}^i\; [\,] = \langle [\,], \beta_1 \rangle$$
$$\mathsf{fn}^i\; ((\mathsf{Name}\; n\; l){:}xs) = \langle n{:}ys, \beta_2\; l\; ws \rangle \;\; \mathsf{where}\; \langle ys, ws \rangle = \mathsf{fn}^i\; xs$$
$$\mathsf{fn}^i\; ((\mathsf{City}\; c){:}xs) = \langle ys, \beta_3\; c\; ws \rangle \;\; \mathsf{where}\; \langle ys, ws \rangle = \mathsf{fn}^i\; xs$$

In contrast to the original function, the inversion of function fn^i can easily be obtained by switching the left- and right-hand sides of every equation (see Definition 2). Here, the call fn^i [Name John Smith, City London, Name Ada Lovelace] now returns $\langle [\mathsf{John, Ada}], \beta_2\; \mathsf{Smith}\; (\beta_3\; \mathsf{London}\; (\beta_2\; \mathsf{Lovelace}\; (\beta_1))) \rangle$.

The net effect is essentially equivalent to the introduction of a complement in the syntactic bidirectionalization approach of Matsuda et al. [22]. There, a complement function is first derived, which is then merged with the original function using tupling. While [24] considers a slightly more general class of programs (as

---

[1] In this section, we denote programs using a Haskell-like notation, but they will be specified using conditional term rewrite systems in the remainder of the paper.

[2] As it is common practice, we use ":" and [] as list constructors.

we do), [22] defines several optimizations to avoid introducing unnecessary symbols in the computed complements (which might improve the number of updates their "put" function can deal with).

In this paper, we present a syntactic bidirectionalization technique based on the injectivization and inversion transformations of [24]. We prove that the so called GetPut law (using the terminology from the literature on *lenses* [11]) always holds for our bidirectional transformations, while the PutGet and PutPut laws hold for *compatible* view updates only. Then, we introduce the use of narrowing to formally characterize the class of view updates that are compatible. Finally, we consider other possible situations—namely, view updates that are not compatible—and discuss some possible approaches to deal with them.

More details and missing proofs can be found in [26].

2 Term Rewriting

In this paper, we will use (conditional) term rewrite systems to specify first-order functional programs. Therefore, in this section, we recall some basic concepts of term rewriting. We refer the reader to, e.g., [2, 30] for further details.

Terms and Substitutions. A *signature* $\mathcal{F}$ is a set of ranked function symbols (i.e., function symbols with an associated arity). Given a set of variables $\mathcal{V}$ with $\mathcal{F} \cap \mathcal{V} = \varnothing$, we denote the domain of *terms* by $\mathcal{T}(\mathcal{F}, \mathcal{V})$. We use $f, g, \ldots$ to denote function symbols and $x, y, \ldots$ to denote variables. Positions are used to address the nodes of a term viewed as a tree. A *position* p in a term t, in symbols $p \in \mathcal{P}os(t)$, is represented by a finite sequence of natural numbers, where the empty sequence ϵ denotes the root position. We let $t|_p$ denote the *subterm* of t at position p and $t[s]_p$ the result of *replacing the subterm* $t|_p$ by the term s. $\mathcal{V}ar(t)$ denotes the set of variables appearing in t. A term t is *ground* if $\mathcal{V}ar(t) = \varnothing$.

A *substitution* $\sigma : \mathcal{V} \mapsto \mathcal{T}(\mathcal{F}, \mathcal{V})$ is a mapping from variables to terms such that $\mathcal{D}om(\sigma) = \{x \in \mathcal{V} \mid x \neq \sigma(x)\}$ is its domain. A substitution σ is *ground* if $\sigma(x)$ is ground for all $x \in \mathcal{D}om(\sigma)$. Substitutions are extended to morphisms from $\mathcal{T}(\mathcal{F}, \mathcal{V})$ to $\mathcal{T}(\mathcal{F}, \mathcal{V})$ in the natural way. We denote the application of a substitution σ to a term t by $t\sigma$ (postfix notation). The identity substitution is denoted by id. We let "$\circ$" denote the composition of substitutions, i.e., $\sigma \circ \theta(x) = (x\theta)\sigma = x\theta\sigma$. The *restriction* $\theta \restriction_V$ of a substitution θ to a set of variables V is defined as follows: $x\theta \restriction_V = x\theta$ if $x \in V$ and $x\theta \restriction_V = x$ otherwise.

A substitution σ is *more general* than a substitution θ, denoted by $\sigma \leqslant \theta$, if there is a substitution δ such that $\delta \circ \sigma = \theta$. A *unifier* of two terms s and t is a substitution σ with $t\sigma = s\sigma$; furthermore, σ is the *most general unifier* of t and s, denoted by $\mathsf{mgu}(t, s)$ if, for every other unifier θ of t and s, we have $\sigma \leqslant \theta$.

Term Rewrite Systems. A set of rewrite rules $l \to r$ such that l is a nonvariable term and r is a term whose variables appear in l is called a *term rewrite system* (TRS for short); terms l and r are called the left-hand side and the right-hand side of the rule, respectively. We restrict ourselves to finite signatures and TRSs.

Given a TRS $\mathcal{R}$ over a signature $\mathcal{F}$, the *defined* symbols $\mathcal{D}_\mathcal{R}$ are the root symbols of the left-hand sides of the rules and the *constructors* are $\mathcal{C}_\mathcal{R} = \mathcal{F} \setminus \mathcal{D}_\mathcal{R}$. *Constructor terms* of $\mathcal{R}$ are terms over $\mathcal{C}_\mathcal{R}$ and $\mathcal{V}$, denoted by $\mathcal{T}(\mathcal{C}_\mathcal{R}, \mathcal{V})$. We sometimes omit $\mathcal{R}$ from $\mathcal{D}_\mathcal{R}$ and $\mathcal{C}_\mathcal{R}$ if it is clear from the context. A substitution σ is a *constructor substitution* (of $\mathcal{R}$) if $x\sigma \in \mathcal{T}(\mathcal{C}_\mathcal{R}, \mathcal{V})$ for all variables x.

In the following, we denote by $\overline{o_n}$ a sequence of elements $o_1, \ldots, o_n$ for some n. We write $\overline{o}$ when the number of elements is not relevant.

Given a TRS $\mathcal{R}$, we say that a term t is *basic* [17] if it has the form $f(\overline{t_n})$ with $f \in \mathcal{D}_\mathcal{R}$ a defined function symbol and $\overline{t_n} \in \mathcal{T}(\mathcal{C}_\mathcal{R}, \mathcal{V})$ constructor terms.

For a TRS $\mathcal{R}$, we define the associated rewrite relation $\to_\mathcal{R}$ as the smallest binary relation on terms satisfying the following: given terms $s, t \in \mathcal{T}(\mathcal{F}, \mathcal{V})$, we have $s \to_\mathcal{R} t$ iff there exist a position p in s, a rewrite rule $l \to r \in \mathcal{R}$, and a substitution σ such that $s|_p = l\sigma$ and $t = s[r\sigma]_p$; the rewrite step is sometimes denoted by $s \to_{p,l\to r} t$ to make explicit the position and rule used in this step. The instantiated left-hand side $l\sigma$ is called a *redex*. A term s is called *irreducible* or in *normal form* with respect to a TRS $\mathcal{R}$ if there is no term t with $s \to_\mathcal{R} t$. A *derivation* is a (possibly empty) sequence of rewrite steps. Given a binary relation $\to$, we denote by $\to^*$ its reflexive and transitive closure, i.e., $s \to_\mathcal{R}^* t$ means that s can be reduced to t in $\mathcal{R}$ in zero or more steps.

Programs. In this work, *programs* are denoted by so called *conditional* term rewrite systems (CTRSs) where rules have now the form $l \to r \Leftarrow C$ with C a *condition* (i.e., a sequence of equations). In particular, we consider *oriented* 3-CTRSs where $Var(r) \subseteq Var(l) \cup Var(C)$ and the equations are *oriented*, i.e., C has the form $s_1 \twoheadrightarrow t_1, \ldots, s_n \twoheadrightarrow t_n$ with $\twoheadrightarrow$ interpreted as *reachability* $\to_\mathcal{R}^*$. Also, we focus on a subclass of oriented 3-CTRSs called pcDCTRS [5,23] ("pc" stands for *pure constructor*) where, for each conditional rule $l \to r \Leftarrow s_1 \twoheadrightarrow t_1, \ldots, s_n \twoheadrightarrow t_n$, the following conditions hold:

- l and $\overline{s_n}$ are basic terms and r and $\overline{t_n}$ are constructor terms, and
- $Var(s_i) \subseteq Var(l, \overline{t_{i-1}})$ for all $i = 1, \ldots, n$ (i.e., it is a *deterministic* CTRS; see below).

Finally, we also require the left-hand sides of the rules in a pcDCTRS to be non-overlapping, i.e., there is no pair of (different) rules $l_1 \to r_1 \Leftarrow C_1$ and $l_2 \to r_2 \Leftarrow C_2$ such that $l_1\sigma = l_2\sigma$ for some substitution σ. This is still quite a general class of CTRSs and it is particularly appropriate to represent typical (first-order) functional programs (e.g., so called *treeless* functional programs [32] or *extended top-down tree transducers* [28] can be seen as subclasses of pcDCTRSs). Intuitively speaking, a rule like $l \to r \Leftarrow s_1 \twoheadrightarrow t_1, \ldots, s_n \twoheadrightarrow t_n$ resembles a typical functional definition of the form

$$l_1 = r_1 \text{ where } t_1 = s_1, \ldots, t_n = s_n$$

Example 1. Function fn in Sect. 1 can be specified using a pcDCTRS as follows:

$$\mathsf{fn}([\,]) \to [\,]$$
$$\mathsf{fn}(\mathsf{name}(n, l){:}xs) \to n{:}ys \Leftarrow \mathsf{fn}(xs) \twoheadrightarrow ys$$
$$\mathsf{fn}(\mathsf{city}(c){:}xs) \to ys \Leftarrow \mathsf{fn}(xs) \twoheadrightarrow ys$$

where the constructor symbols name and city are now denoted using small letters (in contrast to the Haskell-like notation used in Sect. 1).

Given a pcDCTRS $\mathcal{R}$, the associated (constructor-based) rewrite relation $\to_{\mathcal{R}}$ is defined as the smallest binary relation satisfying the following: given ground terms $s, t \in \mathcal{T}(\mathcal{F})$, we have $s \to_{\mathcal{R}} t$ iff there exist a position p in s with $s|_p$ a basic subterm, a rewrite rule $l \to r \Leftarrow \overline{s_n \twoheadrightarrow t_n} \in \mathcal{R}$, and a ground constructor substitution σ such that $s|_p = l\sigma$, $s_i\sigma \to_{\mathcal{R}}^* t_i\sigma$ for all $i = 1, \ldots, n$, and $t = s[r\sigma]_p$. Since the left-hand sides of a pcDCTRS are basic terms and there are no overlappings, every computation can be made deterministic by fixing a strategy (e.g., by always selecting the leftmost innermost redex).

Moreover, the fact that pcDCTRSs are *deterministic* CTRSs [13] (which does not necessarily imply that computations are deterministic) allows us to compute the bindings for the variables in the condition in a deterministic way. E.g., given a ground term s and a rule $l \to r \Leftarrow \overline{s_n \twoheadrightarrow t_n}$ with $s|_p = l\theta$, we have that $s_1\theta$ is ground. Therefore, one can reduce $s_1\theta$ to some term s_1' such that s_1' is an instance of $t_1\theta$ with some ground substitution θ_1. Now, we have that $s_2\theta\theta_1$ is ground and we can reduce $s_2\theta\theta_1$ to some term s_2' such that s_2' is an instance of $t_2\theta\theta_1$ with some ground substitution θ_2, and so forth. If all equations in the condition hold using $\theta_1, \ldots, \theta_n$, we have that $s \to s[r\sigma]_p$ with $\sigma = \theta\theta_1 \ldots \theta_n$.

Remark 1. In the remainder of this paper, we assume for simplicity that all defined symbols of the original pcDCTRS are *unary*. Note that any n-ary defined symbol can be trivially transformed into a unary function by putting all arguments into a fresh tuple symbol. Hence, in the following, program rules will have the following form: $f_0(s) \to r \Leftarrow f_1(s_1) \twoheadrightarrow t_1, \ldots, f_n(s_n) \twoheadrightarrow t_n$.

3 Injectivization and Inversion

In this section, we mostly recall the injectivization and inversion transformations for pcDCTRSs introduced in [24] (with some slight modifications).

Definition 1 (injectivization). *Let $\mathcal{R}$ be a pcDCTRS. We produce a new CTRS $\mathbf{I}(\mathcal{R})$ by replacing each rule*

$$f_0(s) \to r \Leftarrow f_1(s_1) \twoheadrightarrow t_1, \ldots, f_n(s_n) \twoheadrightarrow t_n$$

of $\mathcal{R}$ by a new rule of the form

$$f_0^i(s) \to \langle r, \beta(\overline{y}, \overline{w_n}) \rangle \Leftarrow f_1^i(s_1) \twoheadrightarrow \langle t_1, w_1 \rangle, \ldots, f_n^i(s_n) \twoheadrightarrow \langle t_n, w_n \rangle$$

in $\mathbf{I}(\mathcal{R})$, where

- $f_0^i, \ldots, f_n^i \in \mathcal{D}_{\mathbf{I}(\mathcal{R})}$ *are fresh (not necessarily different) defined function symbols with $f_j^i = f_k^i$ iff $f_j = f_k$, for all j, k,*
- $\beta \in \mathcal{C}_{\mathbf{I}(\mathcal{R})}$ *is a fresh constructor symbol,*
- $\{\overline{y}\} = (\mathcal{V}ar(s) \backslash \mathcal{V}ar(r, \overline{s_n}, \overline{t_n})) \cup \bigcup_{i=1}^n \mathcal{V}ar(t_i) \backslash \mathcal{V}ar(r, s_{i+1}, \ldots, s_n)$,

– and $\overline{w_n}$ *are fresh variables.*

We assume that the variables of $\overline{y}$ *are in lexicographic order. Clearly, we have* $\mathcal{D}_{\mathbf{I}(\mathcal{R})} = \{f^i \mid f \in \mathcal{D}_{\mathcal{R}}\}$ *and* $\mathcal{C}_{\mathbf{I}(\mathcal{R})} = \mathcal{C}_{\mathcal{R}} \cup \{\langle\rangle\} \cup \{\beta \mid l \to \langle\_, \beta(\ldots)\rangle \Leftarrow C \in \mathbf{I}(\mathcal{R})\}$.

Intuitively speaking, the β symbols are needed to know the applied rule, so that the backward steps are computationally deterministic. The variables in $\{\overline{y}\}$ are the variables that are *erased* in the rule (i.e., they are in the left-hand side but not in the corresponding right-hand side or the condition) as well as the variables that are needed for the inverse rule to be deterministic (a more detailed explanation and some examples can be found in [24]).

Now, given a term $f(s)$ that reduces to a normal form v in a pcDCTRS $\mathcal{R}$, we have that $f^i(s)$ reduces to a normal form $\langle v, \pi \rangle$ in $\mathbf{I}(\mathcal{R})$, where π is called the *complement* of the reduction. Although our development originates from the introduction of a *Landauer embedding* [20] to make reductions reversible, complements are similar to the ones obtained by defining a *view complement function* as in [22] (and originally introduced in [3]). Indeed, [22] applies a separated stage of *tupling* [7] to combine the original function and its complement, while this is naturally embedded into the definition above.

Example 2. Let $\mathcal{R}$ be a pcDCTRS defining the function fn of Example 1. Then, we have that $\mathbf{I}(\mathcal{R})$ is defined by the following rules:

$$\mathsf{fn}^i([\,]) \to \langle [\,], \beta_1 \rangle$$
$$\mathsf{fn}^i(\mathsf{name}(n, l){:}xs) \to \langle n{:}ys, \beta_2(l, ws) \rangle \Leftarrow \mathsf{fn}^i(xs) \twoheadrightarrow \langle ys, ws \rangle$$
$$\mathsf{fn}^i(\mathsf{city}(c){:}xs) \to \langle ys, \beta_3(c, ws) \rangle \Leftarrow \mathsf{fn}^i(xs) \twoheadrightarrow \langle ys, ws \rangle$$

E.g., the normal form of $\mathsf{fn}^i([\mathsf{name}(\mathsf{john}, \mathsf{smith}), \mathsf{city}(\mathsf{london}), \mathsf{name}(\mathsf{ada}, \mathsf{lovelace})])$ is $\langle [\mathsf{john}, \mathsf{ada}], \beta_2(\mathsf{smith}, \beta_3(\mathsf{london}, \beta_2(\mathsf{lovelace}, \beta_1))) \rangle$, as expected.

The inversion of an injectivized system now amounts to switching the left- and right-hand sides of the rule and of every equation in the condition, as follows:

Definition 2 (inversion). *Let* $\mathcal{R}$ *be a pcDCTRS and* $\mathcal{R}_f = \mathbf{I}(\mathcal{R})$ *be its injectivization. The inverse system* $\mathcal{R}_b = \mathbf{I}^{-1}(\mathcal{R}_f)$ *is obtained from* $\mathcal{R}_f$ *by replacing each rule*

$$f_0^i(s) \to \langle r, \beta(\overline{y}, \overline{w_n}) \rangle \Leftarrow f_1^i(s_1) \twoheadrightarrow \langle t_1, w_1 \rangle, \ldots, f_n^i(s_n) \twoheadrightarrow \langle t_n, w_n \rangle$$

of $\mathcal{R}_f$ *by a new rule of the form*

$$f_0^{-1}(r, \beta(\overline{y}, \overline{w_n})) \to s \Leftarrow f_n^{-1}(t_n, w_n) \twoheadrightarrow s_n, \ldots, f_1^{-1}(t_1, w_1) \twoheadrightarrow s_1$$

in $\mathcal{R}_b$, *where* $f_0^{-1}, \ldots, f_n^{-1} \in \mathcal{D}_{\mathcal{R}_b}$ *are fresh (not necessarily different) defined function symbols with* $f_j^{-1} = f_k^{-1}$ *iff* $f_j^i = f_k^i$, *for all* j, k. *Here, we have* $\mathcal{D}_{\mathcal{R}_b} = \{f^{-1} \mid f \in \mathcal{R}\}$ *and* $\mathcal{C}_{\mathcal{R}_b} = \mathcal{C}_{\mathcal{R}_f}$.

The correctness of both injectivization and inversion, as well as the fact that $\mathbf{I}(\mathcal{R})$ and $\mathbf{I}^{-1}(\mathbf{I}(\mathcal{R}))$ are also pcDCTRSs, can be found in [24].

Example 3. Inversion of our running example (function fn^i in Example 2) is as follows:

$$\text{fn}^{-1}([\,],\beta_1) \rightarrow [\,]$$
$$\text{fn}^{-1}(n{:}ys, \beta_2(l, ws)) \rightarrow \text{name}(n, l){:}xs \Leftarrow \text{fn}^{-1}(ys, ws) \twoheadrightarrow xs$$
$$\text{fn}^{-1}(ys, \beta_3(c, ws)) \rightarrow \text{city}(c){:}xs \Leftarrow \text{fn}^{-1}(ys, ws) \twoheadrightarrow xs$$

Remark 2. In the following, we let $\text{bx}(\mathcal{R}) = \mathcal{R} \cup \mathbf{I}(\mathcal{R}) \cup \mathbf{I}^{-1}(\mathbf{I}(\mathcal{R}))$. Moreover, given a function $f \in \mathcal{D}_{\mathcal{R}}$, we let $f^i \in \mathcal{D}_{\mathbf{I}(\mathcal{R})}$ denote its injectivization and $f^{-1} \in \mathcal{D}_{\mathbf{I}^{-1}(\mathbf{I}(\mathcal{R}))}$ the inversion of f^i.

4 A Framework for Syntactic Bidirectionalization

In this section, we present a framework for bidirectionalization where narrowing is used to characterize compatible view updates.

4.1 Bidirectionalization

Our bidirectionalization is based on the injectivization and inversion transformations from Sect. 3. Let $\mathcal{R}$ be a pcDCTRS and let $f \in \mathcal{D}_{\mathcal{R}}$ be a function such that

$$f(s) \rightarrow^*_{\text{bx}(\mathcal{R})} v$$

for some constructor terms $s, v \in \mathcal{T}(\mathcal{C}_{\mathcal{R}})$. By construction, there exists a function f^i in $\text{bx}(\mathcal{R})$ such that

$$f^i(s) \rightarrow^*_{\text{bx}(\mathcal{R})} \langle v, \pi \rangle$$

where π (a constructor term) is called the *complement* of the derivation. Conversely, there is also a function f^{-1} in $\text{bx}(\mathcal{R})$ such that

$$f^{-1}(v, \pi) \rightarrow^*_{\text{bx}(\mathcal{R})} s$$

Following the terminology in the bx literature, if f is a "get" function that takes a source and returns a view, we can automatically derive a corresponding "put" function following the so called *constant complement approach* [3] (as in [24]):

Definition 3 (put generation). *Let $\mathcal{R}$ be a pcDCTRS. Given a function $f \in \mathcal{D}_{\mathcal{R}}$, the corresponding "put" function, in symbols, put_f, is defined as follows:*

$$\text{put}_f(v, s) \rightarrow s' \Leftarrow f^i(s) \twoheadrightarrow \langle v', \pi \rangle, f^{-1}(v, \pi) \twoheadrightarrow s'$$

where s, s', v and d' are variables that range over the constructor terms of the original pcDCTRS $\mathcal{R}$, i.e., $\mathcal{T}(\mathcal{C}_{\mathcal{R}})$, while π is a variable that ranges over $\mathcal{T}(\mathcal{C}_{\mathbf{I}(\mathcal{R})})$ to also account for the β symbols introduced in the injectivization stage.

For instance, the corresponding put function for function fn in Example 1 will be defined as follows:

$$\text{put}_{\text{fn}}(v, s) \rightarrow s' \Leftarrow \text{fn}^i(s) \twoheadrightarrow \langle v', \pi \rangle, \text{fn}^{-1}(v, \pi) \twoheadrightarrow s'$$

where functions fn^i and fn^{-1} are defined in Examples 2 and 3, respectively.

Remark 3. In the following, we assume that $bx(\mathcal{R})$ also includes put_f for all $f \in \mathcal{D}_{\mathcal{R}}$, as defined above.

In the following, we prove the usual properties for the bidirectional transformations obtained by our bidirectionalization technique. Basically, we prove that each function f and the corresponding put_f form a so called (very) *well-behaved* lens [11]. Let us start with the following essential property:

Theorem 1 (GetPut). *Let $\mathcal{R}$ be a pcDCTRS. Then, for all defined function $f \in \mathcal{D}_{\mathcal{R}}$ in $\mathcal{R}$ and for all ground constructor term $s \in \mathcal{T}(\mathcal{C}_{\mathcal{R}})$, if the normal form of $f(s)$ is a constructor term, then we have $put_f(f(s), s) \to^*_{bx(\mathcal{R})} s$.*

Example 4. Consider function fn from our running example and the term $s = [name(john, smith), city(london), name(ada, lovelace)]$. Here, the normal form of $fn(s)$ is $[john, ada]$. Then, $put_{fn}([john, ada], s)$ reduces to s since

$$fn^i([name(john, smith), city(london), name(ada, lovelace)])$$
$$\to^* \langle [john, ada], \beta_2(smith, \beta_3(london, \beta_2(lovelace, \beta_1)))\rangle$$

and

$$fn^{-1}([john, ada], \beta_2(smith, \beta_3(london, \beta_2(lovelace, \beta_1)))) \to^* s$$

Other properties, though, do not always hold, since the generated put functions are not always defined. For instance, roughly speaking, the PutGet law states that $f(put_f(v, s)) \to^*_{bx(\mathcal{R})} v$. This law does not hold in general:

Example 5. Consider again function fn from our running example, together with the derivation $fn^i([name(john, smith)]) \to^* \langle [john], \beta_2(smith, \beta_1)\rangle$. Here, the term $fn^{-1}([], \beta_2(smith, \beta_1))$ cannot be reduced to a constructor term. Hence, the Put-Get law does not hold, i.e., $f(put_{fn}([], [name(john, smith)]))$ is not reduced to $[]$.

In the above example, the problem comes from the fact that the view $[]$ and the source $[name(john, smith)]$ are not *compatible*.[3] In this case, a view with exactly one name is required. Thus, in the following, we will consider *partial* versions of some laws [11] as in, e.g., [3, 22].

The notion of compatibility is formalized as follows:

Definition 4 (compatible view). *Let $\mathcal{R}$ be a pcDCTRS. We say that a term v (a view) is compatible with a term s (a source) w.r.t. a function $f \in \mathcal{D}_{\mathcal{R}}$ if $put_f(v, s)$ can be reduced to a constructor term in $bx(\mathcal{R})$.*

For instance, given $s = [name(john, smith), city(london), name(ada, lovelace)]$, the view $v = [rose, ada]$ is compatible with s, while $[ada]$ is not; here, only lists with two elements are compatible with s.

Now, we can prove the PutGet law for compatible view updates:

---

[3] Sometimes, we also say that a view is compatible with a given complement since the complement is fully determined by the source.

Theorem 2 (PutGet). *Let $\mathcal{R}$ be a pcDCTRS, $f \in \mathcal{D}_{\mathcal{R}}$ a defined function and $s \in \mathcal{T}(\mathcal{C}_{\mathcal{R}})$ a ground constructor term. Then, $f(\mathsf{put}_f(v, s)) \to^*_{\mathsf{bx}(\mathcal{R})} v$ for all constructor term v that is compatible with s w.r.t. f.*

Example 6. Consider again function fn and the terms

$$s = [\mathsf{name}(\mathsf{john}, \mathsf{smith}), \mathsf{city}(\mathsf{london}), \mathsf{name}(\mathsf{ada}, \mathsf{lovelace})]$$

and $v = [\mathsf{john}, \mathsf{ada}]$ from Example 4. Given an updated (compatible) view $v' = [\mathsf{rose}, \mathsf{ada}]$, we have $\mathsf{fn}(\mathsf{put}_{\mathsf{fn}}(v', s)) \to^* v'$ since $\mathsf{put}_{\mathsf{fn}}(v', s) \to^* s'$ with $s' = [\mathsf{name}(\mathsf{rose}, \mathsf{smith}), \mathsf{city}(\mathsf{london}), \mathsf{name}(\mathsf{ada}, \mathsf{lovelace})]$ and $\mathsf{fn}(s') \to^* v'$, as expected.

The following result also holds for compatible views. In the following, we say that two terms are *joinable* if they can be reduced to the same constructor term.

Theorem 3 (PutPut). *Let $\mathcal{R}$ be a pcDCTRS, $f \in \mathcal{D}_{\mathcal{R}}$ a defined function and $s \in \mathcal{T}(\mathcal{C}_{\mathcal{R}})$ a ground constructor term. Then, $\mathsf{put}_f(v_1, \mathsf{put}_f(v_2, s))$ and $\mathsf{put}_f(v_1, s)$ are joinable for all constructor terms v_1, v_2 that are compatible with s w.r.t. f.*

Example 7. Consider again function fn and the terms

$$s = [\mathsf{name}(\mathsf{john}, \mathsf{smith}), \mathsf{city}(\mathsf{london}), \mathsf{name}(\mathsf{ada}, \mathsf{lovelace})]$$

$v_1 = [\mathsf{rose}, \mathsf{ada}]$ and $v_2 = [\mathsf{john}, \mathsf{paul}]$. Here, we have $\mathsf{put}_{\mathsf{fn}}(v_1, s) \to^* s_1$, with $s_1 = [\mathsf{name}(\mathsf{rose}, \mathsf{smith}), \mathsf{city}(\mathsf{london}), \mathsf{name}(\mathsf{ada}, \mathsf{lovelace})]$. On the other hand, we have $\mathsf{put}_{\mathsf{fn}}(v_2, s) \to^* s_2$, with $s_2 = [\mathsf{name}(\mathsf{john}, \mathsf{smith}), \mathsf{city}(\mathsf{london}), \mathsf{name}(\mathsf{paul}, \mathsf{lovelace})]$ and $\mathsf{put}_{\mathsf{fn}}(v_1, s_2) \to^* s_1$.

The above result ensures that our put functions do not have undesirable side-effects on the source. In other words, the complement associated to the updated source obtained by a put function will still be the same, no matter the (compatible) view used. A bidirectional transformation fulfilling the above laws is called—in the lenses approach [11]—a *partial very well-behaved lens*. Note that it is "partial" since it is only very well behaved for compatible view updates.

Moreover, when both PutPut and GetPut laws hold, we have

$$\mathsf{put}_f(f(s), \mathsf{put}_f(v, s)) \to^* s$$

i.e., the effects of a view update can always be undone (see, e.g., [12]). Intuitively speaking, the reason for this behaviour in our context is that the computed complement is the same for s and for $\mathsf{put}_f(v, s)$ when v is a compatible view update, as mentioned before.

4.2 Using Narrowing to Characterize Compatible Updates

Let us first briefly introduce the *narrowing* principle [19,29]. It mainly extends term rewriting by replacing pattern matching with unification, so that terms containing logic (i.e., *free*) variables can be (non-deterministically) reduced.

(unification)
$$\frac{n > 1 \ \wedge \ s_1 \in \mathcal{T}(\mathcal{C}, \mathcal{V}) \ \wedge \ \sigma = \mathsf{mgu}(s_1, t_1)}{(s_1 \twoheadrightarrow t_1, \dots, s_n \twoheadrightarrow t_n) \rightsquigarrow_\sigma (s_2 \twoheadrightarrow t_2, \dots, s_n \twoheadrightarrow t_n)\sigma}$$

(narrowing)
$$\frac{p = inn(s_1) \ \wedge \ (l \to r \Leftarrow C) \ll \mathcal{R} \ \wedge \ \sigma = \mathsf{mgu}(s_1|_p, l)}{(s_1 \twoheadrightarrow t_1, \dots, s_n \twoheadrightarrow t_n) \rightsquigarrow_\sigma (C, s_1[r]_p \twoheadrightarrow t_1, \dots, s_n \twoheadrightarrow t_n)\sigma}$$

Fig. 1. Constructor-based conditional narrowing

Example 8. Consider the term $\mathsf{fn}^{-1}(x, \beta_1)$ and the rule "$\mathsf{fn}^{-1}([\,], \beta_1) \to [\,]$". While the term cannot be reduced using rewriting, narrowing performs the following step: $\mathsf{fn}^{-1}(x, \beta_1) \rightsquigarrow_{\{x \mapsto [\,]\}} [\,]$, where $\{x \mapsto [\,]\}$ is a unifier between the term and the left-hand side of the rule.

Now, we present narrowing for pcDCTRSs. For this class of programs, one can naturally extend Bockmayr's *conditional rewriting without evaluation of the premise* [6] to narrowing as follows. In the following, a *goal* is a sequence of equations of the form $s_1 \twoheadrightarrow t_1, \dots, s_n \twoheadrightarrow t_n$, where each s_i is either basic or a constructor term and $t_1, \dots, t_n$ are constructor terms.

Definition 5 (constructor-based conditional narrowing).
Let $\mathcal{R}$ be a pcDCTRS. Constructor-based conditional narrowing is defined as the smallest relation satisfying the transition rules of Fig. 1, where $(l \to r \Leftarrow C) \ll \mathcal{R}$ denotes that $l \to r \Leftarrow C$ is a copy of a rule in $\mathcal{R}$ renamed with fresh variables, and $inn(s)$ selects the position of a basic subterm (i.e., a term of the form $\mathsf{f}(\overline{t_n})$ with f a defined function symbol and $\overline{t_n}$ constructor terms).

Intuitively speaking, given a goal $s_1 \twoheadrightarrow t_1, \dots, s_n \twoheadrightarrow t_n$, we proceed either by unifying the leftmost equation when s_1 is a constructor term and $\mathsf{mgu}(s_1, t_1)$ exists (rule *unification*) or we apply a narrowing step (rule *narrowing*). In the latter case, we select a basic subterm $s_1|_p$ of s_1 that unifies with the left-hand side of a (renamed) rule, say $l \to r \Leftarrow C$, using mgu σ, and return a new goal $(C, s_1[r]_p \twoheadrightarrow t_1, \dots, s_n \twoheadrightarrow t_n)\sigma$.

Let us note that narrowing is often non-deterministic due to the free variables in goals, since the selected subterm might unify with the left-hand sides of several rules (so rule *narrowing* gives rise to some branching). Moreover, narrowing derivations might be infinite even when the rules of a pcDCTRS are terminating (see, e.g., [25]). Indeed, our constructor-based conditional narrowing over pcDCTRSs is essentially equivalent to SLD resolution over equivalent logic programs [21].

In order to narrow a given term s, we start with a goal of the form $s \twoheadrightarrow x$, where x is a fresh variable. A *successful* narrowing derivation for s has the form $(s \twoheadrightarrow x) \rightsquigarrow_\sigma^* (t \twoheadrightarrow x)$ with t a constructor term; here, we say that $\sigma\!\restriction_{\mathcal{V}\mathsf{ar}(s)}$ is the *computed answer substitution* of the successful derivation.

Definition 6 (success set, nwing$_\mathcal{R}$). *Let $\mathcal{R}$ be a pcDCTRS. We denote by* nwing$_\mathcal{R}(s)$ *the success set of a term s in $\mathcal{R}$, where $\sigma \in$ nwing$_\mathcal{R}(s)$ if there is a successful narrowing derivation for the goal $s \twoheadrightarrow x$ in $\mathcal{R}$ with computed answer substitution σ, where x is a fresh variable.*

The following auxiliary result is useful to define the notion of *view skeleton*.

Lemma 1. *Let $\mathcal{R}$ be a pcDCTRS and $\mathsf{f} \in \mathcal{D}$ be a function with $\mathsf{f}^i(s) \rightarrow^*_{\mathsf{bx}(\mathcal{R})}$ $\langle v, \pi \rangle$ for some constructor terms s, v, and π. Then,* nwing$_{\mathsf{bx}(\mathcal{R})}(\mathsf{f}^{-1}(x, \pi))$ *is a singleton up to variable renaming, where x is a fresh variable.*

We observe that the above result does not hold when some β symbols are removed using an optimization like that in [22] which is based on an injectivity analysis. In our approach, the β symbols are essential to drive the narrowing steps and ensure that the derivation is finite and computationally deterministic, no matter if the original function is injective or not.

Definition 7 (view skeleton). *Let $\mathcal{R}$ be a pcDCTRS, $\mathsf{f} \in \mathcal{D}$ be a defined function and s be a constructor term. The view skeleton associated to f and s in* $\mathsf{bx}(\mathcal{R})$ *is defined as follows:*

$$\mathsf{skel}_{\mathsf{bx}(\mathcal{R})}(\mathsf{f}, s) = x\sigma \ \text{where} \ \mathsf{f}^i(s) \rightarrow^* \langle v, \pi \rangle \ \text{and} \ \mathsf{nwing}_{\mathsf{bx}(\mathcal{R})}(\mathsf{f}^{-1}(x, \pi)) = \{\sigma\}$$

with x a fresh variable and v, π constructor terms.

Now, we can precisely characterize the view updates that are compatible with a given source:

Lemma 2. *Let $\mathcal{R}$ be a pcDCTRS, $\mathsf{f} \in \mathcal{D}$ be a defined function, and s be a constructor term. Let* $\mathsf{skel}_{\mathsf{bx}(\mathcal{R})}(\mathsf{f}, s) = v''$. *Then, a constructor term v' is compatible with s w.r.t. f iff there exists a substitution θ such that $v' = v''\theta$.*

Informally speaking, a view skeleton represents the constructors that depend on the *history* of the considered computation, which is represented by a given complement. Variables in a skeleton represent information that is independent of the reduction steps and, thus, the same complement can be used by function f^{-1} in the definition of put_f. In some sense, our notion of skeleton is related to the use of polymorphic functions in the *semantic* approach to bidirectionalization [31], though our approach is in principle rather different.

Example 9. Consider again our running example and function fn as well as its associated functions fn^i and fn^{-1}. Given the source (constructor) term

$$s = [\mathsf{name}(\mathsf{john}, \mathsf{smith}), \mathsf{city}(\mathsf{london}), \mathsf{name}(\mathsf{ada}, \mathsf{lovelace})]$$

we have the following reduction:

$$\mathsf{fn}^i(s) \rightarrow^* \langle [\mathsf{john}, \mathsf{ada}], \pi \rangle \ \text{with} \ \pi = \beta_2(\mathsf{smith}, \beta_3(\mathsf{london}, \beta_2(\mathsf{lovelace}, \beta_1)))$$

Here, the view skeleton associated to s w.r.t. fn is $[n_1, n_2]$ since we have the following narrowing derivation:

$$f^{-1}(x, \pi) \rightarrow y$$
$$\rightsquigarrow^*_{\{x \mapsto [n_1, n_2]\}} [\mathsf{name}(n_1, \mathsf{smith}), \mathsf{city}(\mathsf{london}), \mathsf{name}(n_2, \mathsf{lovelace})] \rightarrow y$$

Therefore, we have that a view update like [richard, ada] will be compatible with s (since it is an instance of $[n_1, n_2]$), while a view update like [john] will not.

4.3   Dealing with Non-compatible View Updates

So far we have only considered compatible (often called "in-place") view updates. A challenging topic for future work involves dealing with view updates which are not compatible. This problem has been considered in the context of the lenses approach to bidirectional transformations (see, e.g., [4]), but we are not aware of any technique that deals with this issue in the context of bidirectionalization.

The problem with non-compatible view updates is that, in general, there are many non-deterministic possibilities to propagate the changes back to the source. Consider again our running example with function fn. Given the source $s = [\mathsf{name}(\mathsf{john}, \mathsf{smith}), \mathsf{city}(\mathsf{london})]$, we get the view [john] with complement $\beta_2(\mathsf{smith}, \beta_3(\mathsf{london}, \beta_1))$. Now, given an arbitrary modified view, say [john, rose], a put function might return any of the following modified sources:

$$s_1 = [\mathsf{name}(\mathsf{john}, \mathsf{smith}), \mathsf{name}(\mathsf{rose}, \bot), \mathsf{city}(\mathsf{london})]$$
$$s_2 = [\mathsf{name}(\mathsf{john}, \mathsf{smith}), \mathsf{city}(\mathsf{london}), \mathsf{name}(\mathsf{rose}, \bot)]$$
$$s_3 = [\mathsf{name}(\mathsf{john}, \mathsf{smith}), \mathsf{name}(\mathsf{rose}, \bot)]$$
$$s_4 = [\mathsf{name}(\mathsf{john}, \mathsf{smith}), \mathsf{city}(\mathsf{london}), \mathsf{city}(\bot), \mathsf{name}(\mathsf{rose}, \bot)]$$
$$\cdots$$

where $\bot$ denotes an undefined value. In all cases, $\mathsf{fn}(s_i)$ reduces to [john, rose], $i = 1, \ldots, 4$, so all these alternatives might—in principle—be considered correct.

Furthermore, *aligning* the views so that the changes can be identified is also a difficult problem. Consider, e.g., that we change [john] to [rose]. Here, one can assume that this is an in-place change and, thus, produce the source [name(rose, smith), city(london)], but it could also be the result of a deletion and an insertion, so that the right source would be [name(rose, $\bot$), city(london)] instead. The larger the views, the more complex the alignment is. Some heuristics have been developed (see, e.g., [4]), but the approach has also some drawbacks (see the discussion in [9]).

Another approach by Diskin, Xiong, and Czarnecki [9] proposes to decompose the view update propagation into two separate operations: computing *deltas* (the differences between two data structures), and propagating deltas. In this context, the authors consider two operations, dget and dput, which are similar to the usual get and put operations from the standard approach but deal with deltas instead.

In our setting, we could specify a delta by means of a function (or a sequence of functions). For instance, the change from [john] to [john, rose] could be specified by using a function that appends a new element at the end of a list, which is defined as follows:

$$\mathsf{app_v}([\,],s) \rightarrow [s]$$
$$\mathsf{app_v}(x:xs,s) \rightarrow x:\mathsf{app_v}(xs,s)$$

so that the change from [john] to [john, rose] is given by the following application: $\mathsf{app_v}([\mathsf{john}],\mathsf{rose})$. Then, one can apply dput to produce an equivalent function, $\mathsf{app_s}$, on the source:

$$\mathsf{app_s}([\,],s) \rightarrow [\mathsf{name}(s,\bot)]$$
$$\mathsf{app_s}(x:xs,s) \rightarrow x:\mathsf{app_s}(xs,s)$$

In general, though, this is not the only possibility; namely, any function that appends the given name after all existing names in the source would be correct, no matter the position and number of cities. E.g., if the source is

$$s = [\mathsf{name}(\mathsf{john},\mathsf{smith}),\mathsf{city}(\mathsf{london})]$$

we have that $\mathsf{app_s}(s,\mathsf{rose})$ returns

$$[\mathsf{name}(\mathsf{john},\mathsf{smith}),\mathsf{name}(\mathsf{rose},\bot),\mathsf{city}(\mathsf{london})]$$

but it could also return

$$[\mathsf{name}(\mathsf{john},\mathsf{smith}),\mathsf{city}(\mathsf{london}),\mathsf{name}(\mathsf{rose},\bot)].$$

Analogously to the case of put, there is some degree of non-determinism that must be fixed using either some user intervention or some heuristic.

We consider the delta-based framework a promising approach for future work.

5   Related Work

First, as mentioned before, the injectivization and inversion transformations for pcDCTRSs are taken from [24]. This paper, though, is concerned with reversible rewriting rather than bidirectional programming. The definition of a put function is sketched with an example (following the constant complement approach as in [12]) to show the potential of these transformations, but no law is formalized, compatibility of view updates is not considered, etc. Other, related approaches to program inversion in functional programming can be found in [14,15]. See also [33] for more details on reversible programming languages.

The closest related work is the *syntactic* approach to the bidirectionalization of functional programs in [22]. While the basic technique shares some similarities with our development (both are based on the constant complement approach), our framework deals with more general programs (e.g., a function producing an inorder traversal of a binary tree can be represented with a pcDCTRS [32] while it cannot be represented with a *treeless* function as required in [22]); moreover, our notion of compatible view updates based on narrowing seems more useful than the *checker* of [22], since we produce a view *skeleton* which represents in a compact way all possible view updates by means of variables that denote updatable subterms.

Indeed, the use of narrowing to identify the parts of the view that are independent of the computed complement (and, thus, of the applied rules) is somehow similar to the requirement of polymorphic functions in the *semantic* approach to bidirectionalization of [31]. In particular, if a function is not polymorphic, our narrowing based approach will easily determine that no compatible view updates are possible. Consider, e.g., the following simple function to check if all the elements of a binary list are zero:

$$f([\,]) \rightarrow \text{true}$$
$$f(0{:}xs) \rightarrow \text{true} \Leftarrow f(xs) \twoheadrightarrow \text{true}$$
$$f(1{:}xs) \rightarrow \text{false}$$

Clearly, the type is $f :: [Bin] \rightarrow Bool$, where Bin is a type with constructors 0 and 1 and $Bool$ is the usual Boolean type. Since the function is not polymorphic, one cannot apply the approach in [31]. Let us now consider our approach. First, injectivization and inversion return the following functions:

$$f^i([\,]) \rightarrow \langle \text{true}, \beta_1 \rangle$$
$$f(0{:}xs) \rightarrow \langle \text{true}, \beta_2(w) \rangle \Leftarrow f^i(xs) \twoheadrightarrow \langle \text{true}, w \rangle$$
$$f^i(1{:}xs) \rightarrow \langle \text{false}, \beta_3(xs) \rangle$$

$$f^{-1}(\text{true}, \beta_1) \rightarrow [\,]$$
$$f^{-1}(\text{true}, \beta_2(w)) \rightarrow 0{:}xs \Leftarrow f^{-1}(\text{true}, w) \twoheadrightarrow xs$$
$$f^{-1}(\text{false}, \beta_3(xs)) \rightarrow 1{:}xs$$

Given an arbitrary source, e.g., $s = [0, 1, 0]$, we have $f^i(s) \rightarrow^* \langle \text{false}, \beta_2(\beta_3([0])) \rangle$ and, then, $\text{skel}_{\text{bx}(\mathcal{R})}(f, s)$ returns just false (since $\text{nwing}_{\text{bx}(\mathcal{R})}(f^{-1}(x, \beta_2(\beta_3([0]))))$ produces the computed answer $\{x \mapsto \text{false}\}$). Therefore, no view different from false would be compatible.

There are other, related works that use narrowing in the context of bidirectional transformations [10, 16]. However, these works consider narrowing (or the *universal resolving algorithm* [1], which is essentially similar) as a mechanism for inverse computation. In their approach, no injectivization is performed and, thus, inverse computation might be non-deterministic. This is rather different to our approach, where inversion is only applied to injective functions and, moreover, narrowing is only applied to terms of the form $f^{-1}(x, \pi)$, with π a ground constructor term, so that narrowing derivations are always finite and computationally deterministic.

6 Discussion

To summarize, we have presented a (syntactic) bidirectionalization technique based on some injectivization and inversion transformations, where programs are specified by means of pcDCTRSs, a general class of conditional term rewrite systems. We have proved a number of laws for our generated put functions, namely that we produce (partial) very well-behaved lenses in the terminology of [11]. Moreover, we have precisely characterized those view updates that are compatible with a given source (also called "in-place" updates) using narrowing [19,29], an extension of rewriting to deal with logic variables. In some way, our approach combines ideas from three previous approaches: reversible rewriting [24], syntactic bidirectionalization [22], and semantic bidirectionalization [31], while it provides new insights by showing that narrowing can easily be used to identify the parts of a view that are updatable without modifying the complement.

As future work, we plan to develop a technique to deal with non-compatible view updates, along the lines presented in Sect. 4.3.

Acknowledgements. We thank the anonymous reviewers for their useful comments and suggestions to improve this paper.

References

1. Abramov, S.M., Glück, R.: The universal resolving algorithm and its correctness: inverse computation in a functional language. Sci. Comput. Program. **43**(2–3), 193–229 (2002)
2. Baader, F., Nipkow, T.: Term Rewriting and All That. Cambridge University Press, Cambridge (1998)
3. Bancilhon, F., Spyratos, N.: Update semantics of relational views. ACM Trans. Database Syst. **6**(4), 557–575 (1981)
4. Barbosa, D.M., Cretin, J., Foster, N., Greenberg, M., Pierce, B.C.: Matching lenses: alignment and view update. In: Hudak, P., Weirich, S. (eds.) Proceedings of the 15th ACM SIGPLAN International Conference on Functional Programming (ICFP 2010), pp. 193–204. ACM (2010)
5. Bergstra, J.A., Klop, J.W.: Conditional rewrite rules: confluence and termination. J. Comput. Syst. Sci. **32**, 323–362 (1986)
6. Bockmayr, A., Werner, A.: LSE narrowing for decreasing conditional term rewrite systems. In: Dershowitz, N., Lindenstrauss, N. (eds.) CTRS 1994. LNCS, vol. 968, pp. 51–70. Springer, Heidelberg (1995). https://doi.org/10.1007/3-540-60381-6_4
7. Chin, W.N.: Towards an automated tupling strategy. In: Proceedings of Partial Evaluation and Semantics-Based Program Manipulation, Copenhagen, Denmark, June 1993, pp. 119–132. ACM, New York (1993)
8. Danos, V., Krivine, J.: Reversible communicating systems. In: Gardner, P., Yoshida, N. (eds.) CONCUR 2004. LNCS, vol. 3170, pp. 292–307. Springer, Heidelberg (2004). https://doi.org/10.1007/978-3-540-28644-8_19
9. Diskin, Z., Xiong, Y., Czarnecki, K.: From state- to delta-based bidirectional model transformations: the asymmetric case. J. Object Technol. **10**(6), 1–25 (2011)
10. Fischer, S., Hu, Z., Pacheco, H.: The essence of bidirectional programming. Sci. China Inf. Sci. **58**(5), 1–21 (2015)
11. Foster, J.N., Greenwald, M.B., Moore, J.T., Pierce, B.C., Schmitt, A.: Combinators for bidirectional tree transformations: a linguistic approach to the view-update problem. ACM Trans. Program. Lang. Syst. **29**(3), 17 (2007)

12. Foster, N., Matsuda, K., Voigtländer, J.: Three complementary approaches to bidirectional programming. In: Gibbons, J. (ed.) Generic and Indexed Programming. LNCS, vol. 7470, pp. 1–46. Springer, Heidelberg (2012). https://doi.org/10.1007/978-3-642-32202-0_1

13. Ganzinger, H.: Order-sorted completion: the many-sorted way. Theor. Comput. Sci. **89**(1), 3–32 (1991)

14. Glück, R., Kawabe, M.: A method for automatic program inversion based on LR(0) parsing. Fundam. Inform. **66**(4), 367–395 (2005)

15. Glück, R., Kawabe, M.: A program inverter for a functional language with equality and constructors. In: Ohori, A. (ed.) APLAS 2003. LNCS, vol. 2895, pp. 246–264. Springer, Heidelberg (2003). https://doi.org/10.1007/978-3-540-40018-9_17

16. Hidaka, S., Hu, Z., Inaba, K., Kato, H., Matsuda, K., Nakano, K.: Bidirectionalizing graph transformations. In: Hudak, P., Weirich, S. (eds.) Proceedings of the 15th ACM SIGPLAN International Conference on Functional programming (ICFP 2010), pp. 205–216. ACM (2010)

17. Hirokawa, N., Moser, G.: Automated complexity analysis based on the dependency pair method. In: Armando, A., Baumgartner, P., Dowek, G. (eds.) IJCAR 2008. LNCS (LNAI), vol. 5195, pp. 364–379. Springer, Heidelberg (2008). https://doi.org/10.1007/978-3-540-71070-7_32

18. Hu, Z., Schürr, A., Stevens, P., Terwilliger, J.F.: Bidirectional transformation "bx" (Dagstuhl Seminar 11031). In: Dagstuhl Reports, vol. 1, no. 1, pp. 42–67 (2011). http://drops.dagstuhl.de/volltexte/2011/3144/

19. Hullot, J.-M.: Canonical forms and unification. In: Bibel, W., Kowalski, R. (eds.) CADE 1980. LNCS, vol. 87, pp. 318–334. Springer, Heidelberg (1980). https://doi.org/10.1007/3-540-10009-1_25

20. Landauer, R.: Irreversibility and heat generation in the computing process. IBM J. Res. Dev. **5**, 183–191 (1961)

21. Lloyd, J.W.: Foundations of Logic Programming, 2nd edn. Springer, Berlin (1987). https://doi.org/10.1007/978-3-642-83189-8

22. Matsuda, K., Hu, Z., Nakano, K., Hamana, M., Takeichi, M.: Bidirectionalization transformation based on automatic derivation of view complement functions. In: Hinze, R., Ramsey, N. (eds.) Proceedings of the 12th ACM SIGPLAN International Conference on Functional Programming, ICFP 2007, pp. 47–58. ACM (2007)

23. Nagashima, M., Sakai, M., Sakabe, T.: Determinization of conditional term rewriting systems. Theor. Comput. Sci. **464**, 72–89 (2012)

24. Nishida, N., Palacios, A., Vidal, G.: Reversible computation in term rewriting. J. Log. Algebr. Methods Program. **94**, 128–149 (2018)

25. Nishida, N., Vidal, G.: Termination of narrowing via termination of rewriting. Appl. Algebra Eng. Commun. Comput. **21**(3), 177–225 (2010)

26. Nishida, N., Vidal, G.: Characterizing compatible view updates in syntactic bidirectionalization. Technical report, DSIC, UPV (2019). http://personales.upv.es/gvidal/german/rc19/tr.pdf

27. Phillips, I.C., Ulidowski, I.: Reversing algebraic process calculi. J. Log. Algebr. Program. **73**(1–2), 70–96 (2007)

28. Rounds, W.C.: Mappings and grammars on trees. Math. Syst. Theory **4**(3), 257–287 (1970)

29. Slagle, J.R.: Automated theorem-proving for theories with simplifiers, commutativity and associativity. J. ACM **21**(4), 622–642 (1974)

30. Terese: Term Rewriting Systems, Cambridge Tracts in Theoretical Computer Science, vol. 55. Cambridge University Press, Cambridge (2003)

31. Voigtländer, J.: Bidirectionalization for free! (pearl). In: Shao, Z., Pierce, B.C. (eds.) Proceedings of the 36th ACM SIGPLAN-SIGACT Symposium on Principles of Programming Languages (POPL 2009), pp. 165–176. ACM (2009)
32. Wadler, P.: Deforestation: transforming programs to eliminate trees. Theor. Comput. Sci. **73**, 231–248 (1990)
33. Yokoyama, T., Axelsen, H., Glück, R.: Principles of a reversible programming language. In: Ramírez, A., Bilardi, G., Gschwind, M. (eds.) Proceedings of the 5th Conference on Computing Frontiers, pp. 43–54. ACM (2008)

Programming Languages

Sized Types for Low-Level Quantum Metaprogramming

Matthew Amy$^{(\boxtimes)}$ (iD)

University of Waterloo, Waterloo, Canada
meamy@uwaterloo.ca

Abstract. One of the most fundamental aspects of quantum circuit design is the concept of *families* of circuits parametrized by an instance size. As in classical programming, metaprogramming allows the programmer to write entire families of circuits simultaneously, an ability which is of particular importance in the context of quantum computing as algorithms frequently use arithmetic over non-standard word lengths. In this work, we introduce metaQASM, a typed extension of the openQASM language supporting the metaprogramming of circuit families. Our language and type system, built around a lightweight implementation of *sized types*, supports subtyping over register sizes and is moreover type-safe. In particular, we prove that our system is strongly normalizing, and as such any well-typed metaQASM program can be statically unrolled into a finite circuit.

Keywords: Quantum programming · Circuit description languages · Metaprogramming

1 Introduction

Quantum computers have the potential to solve a number of important problems, including integer factorization [29], quantum simulation [23], approximating the Jones polynomial [1] and unstructured searching [12] asymptotically faster than the best known classical algorithms. These algorithms are typically described abstractly and make heavy use of classical arithmetic such as modular exponentiation. To make such algorithms concrete, efficient, reversible implementations of large swaths of a classical arithmetic and computation is needed – moreover, due to the limited space constraints and special-purpose nature of quantum circuits, these operations are typically needed in a multitude of bit sizes.

In part due to the increasing viability of quantum computing and the scaling of NISQ [28] devices, there has been a recent explosion in quantum programming tools. Such tools range from software development kits (e.g., Qiskit [5], ProjectQ [32], Strawberry Fields [19], Pyquil [30]) to Embedded domain-specific languages (e.g., Quipper [11], Qwire [27], $Q|SI\rangle$ [22]) and standalone languages and compilers (e.g., QCL [26], QML [2], ScaffCC [16], Q# [33]). Going beyond strict programming tools, software for the synthesis, optimization, and simulation of

© Springer Nature Switzerland AG 2019
M. K. Thomsen and M. Soeken (Eds.): RC 2019, LNCS 11497, pp. 87–107, 2019.
https://doi.org/10.1007/978-3-030-21500-2_6

quantum circuits and programs (e.g., Revkit [31], TOpt [15], Feynman [3], PyZX [20], Quantum++ [9], QX [17]) are becoming more and more abundant.

The proliferation of both hardware and software tools for quantum computing has in turn spurred a need for standardization and portability [14,24]. One such standard which has recently grown in popularity is the Quantum Assembly Language and its many various dialects (e.g., openQASM [6], QASM-HL [16], cQASM [18]). As a lightweight, modular language for specifying simple quantum circuits, programs with a well-defined syntax, QASM support – in particular, for the openQASM dialect – has been built-in to an increasingly large number of software tools, particularly standalone programs like circuit optimizers, as a way to support interoperability.

One feature that is noticeably lacking in these dialects is the ability to define *families* of quantum circuits parametrized over different register sizes, and by extension to *generate* concrete instances. This creates a barrier for the use of QASM in writing portable libraries of quantum circuit families, particularly for classical operations such as arithmetic. As a result, software designers typically end up re-implementing code – typically implemented in the host language for EDSLs, and hence not easily re-usable – for generating instances of simple operations such as adders and multipliers. Alternatively, programmers resort to using other compilers such as Quipper, Q# or ReVerC [4] to generate individual instances, which complicates the compilation or simulation process. While recent progress towards the development of portable libraries of circuit families with high-level non-embedded languages, standardization remains an on-going process, and moreover a low-level approach is preferable in many situations, including as compilation targets and middle-ends.

In this paper we make progress towards the design of a low-level language for quantum programming that supports the metaprogramming of sized circuit families. In particular, we develop a typed extension of the untyped open quantum assembly language (openQASM) with metaprogramming over lightweight *sized types* à la dependent ML [34]. Our language, metaQASM, is further shown to be type-safe and strongly-normalizing, while the non-meta fragment is both more expressive than openQASM and admits a simpler syntax, owing to the type system. For the purposes of this paper, we focus on the type system design and metatheory of such a language, leaving implementation to future work.

1.1   Quantum Metaprogramming

Most QRAM-based quantum programming languages are metaprogramming languages – called *circuit description languages* – in that they typically operate by building quantum circuits to be sent in a single batch to a quantum processor. Such quantum circuits can typically be composed, reversed, and depend on the result of classical computations.

In this paper, we are interested in a particular type of quantum circuit metaprogramming, wherein circuit families are parametrized over *shapes* [11,27], such as the number of input qubits. Existing languages offer varying support for such metaprogramming, either implicitly (e.g., uniform or *transversal* families of circuits in openQASM, iteration and qubit arrays in Q#), or more explicitly (e.g., the generic QData type-class in Quipper, which can be instantiated via explicit type applications). Our approach differs from previous attempts by explicitly parametrizing registers and circuit families with *size* parameters. We adopt a typed approach for a number of reasons:

– it allows the light-weight verification of libraries of circuit generators,
– it provides a means of self-documentation, and
– it allows explicit generation of sized-specialized instances.

The ability to generate instances of circuit families in various sizes *without executing them* is particularly important for the purposes of resource estimation, and for benchmarking tools that operate on fixed-size but arbitrary input circuits, such as circuit optimizers [14].

As an illustration, given an in-place family of adders written in the style of (imperative) Quipper with the type

```
inplace_add :: [Qubit] -> [Qubit] -> Circ (),
```

one may wish to generate a static, optimized instance of inplace_add operating on 2-qubit registers, using an external circuit optimizer. Doing so requires the specialization to (and serialization of) a function

```
inplace_add2 :: (Qubit, Qubit) -> (Qubit, Qubit) -> Circ ().
```

One possible method of generating such a function is to write the body of inplace_add2 using a call to the generic inplace_add applied to the 4 input qubits. However, this quickly gets unwieldy, both in the boilerplate code defining a particular instance, and in the large number of parameters.

A more common solution is to use *dummy parameters*, whereby the generic function is "applied" to lists of qubits, which are then taken by the serialization method as meaning arbitrary inputs. For instance, the following Quipper[1] code [10] prints out a PDF representation of inplace_add2 using dummy parameters qubit :: Qubit

```
print_generic PDF inplace_add [qubit, qubit] [qubit, qubit].
```

The use of dummy parameters is partly a question of style, though it can cause problems when combining optimizations with *initialized* dummy parameters. In either case, the use explicitly sized circuit families carries further benefits to both readability and correctness [27].

---

[1] The function inplace_add2 could instead be directly generated by writing the adder as inplace_add :: QData qa => qa -> qa -> Circ (), then specializing qa to the finite type (Qubit, Qubit) using *type applications*. However, the non-generic serialization functions in Quipper appear to work only for small finite tuple types.

1.2   Organization

The remainder of this paper is organized as follows. Section 2 gives a brief overview of quantum computing. Section 3 reviews the openQASM language and defines a formal semantics for it. Sections 4 and 5 extend openQASM with types and metaprogramming capabilities, and finally Sect. 6 concludes the paper.

2   Quantum Computing

We give a brief overview of the basics of quantum computing. For a more in-depth introduction of quantum computation we direct the reader to [25], while an overview of quantum programming can be found in [8].

In the circuit model, the state of an n-qubit quantum system is described as a unit vector in a dimension 2^n complex vector space. The 2^n elementary basis vectors form the *computational* basis, and are denoted by $|\mathbf{x}\rangle$ for bit strings $\mathbf{x} \in \{0,1\}^n$ – these are called the *classical* states. A general quantum state may then be written as a *superposition* of classical states

$$|\psi\rangle = \sum_{\mathbf{x} \in \mathbb{F}_2^n} \alpha_{\mathbf{x}} |\mathbf{x}\rangle,$$

for complex $\alpha_{\mathbf{x}}$ and having unit norm. The states of two n and m qubit quantum systems $|\psi\rangle$ and $|\psi\rangle$ may be combined into an $n + m$ qubit state by taking their tensor product $|\psi\rangle \otimes |\psi\rangle$. If to the contrary the state of two qubits cannot be written as a tensor product the two qubits are said to be *entangled*.

Quantum circuits, in analogy to classical circuits, carry qubits from left to right along *wires* through *gates* which transform the state. In the unitary circuit model gates are required to implement unitary operators on the state space – that is, quantum gates are modelled by complex-valued matrices U satisfying $UU^\dagger = U^\dagger U = I$, where $U^\dagger$ is the complex conjugate of U. As a result, unitary quantum computations must be *reversible*, and in particular the quantum circuits performing classical computations are precisely the set of reversible circuits.

The standard universal quantum gate set, known as Clifford$+T$, consists of the two-qubit controlled-NOT gate (CNOT), and the single-qubit Hadamard (H) and T gates. As quantum circuits implement linear operators, we may define the above three gates by their effect on classical states:

$$\text{CNOT}|x\rangle|y\rangle = |x\rangle|x \oplus y\rangle, \qquad T|x\rangle = e^{\frac{2\pi i}{8}x}|x\rangle,$$

$$H|x\rangle = \frac{1}{\sqrt{2}} \sum_{x' \in \{0,1\}} (-1)^{x \cdot x'} |x'\rangle.$$

Figure 1 gives a pictorial representation of a quantum circuit over CNOT, H, and T gates. CNOT gates are written as a solid dot on their first argument and an exclusive-OR symbol ($\oplus$) on their second argument.

More general quantum operations include qubit initialization and measurement, which effectively convert between classical and quantum data. As neither operation is unitary and hence not (directly) reversible, we regard them as functions of the classical computer rather than gates in a quantum circuit.

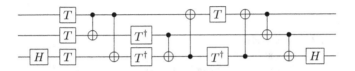

Fig. 1. An example of a quantum circuit implementing the Toffoli gate.

3 openQASM

The open quantum assembly language (openQASM [6]) is a low-level, untyped imperative quantum programming language, developed as a dialect of the informal QASM language. One of the key additions of the openQASM language is that of *modularity*, in the form of a simple module and import system. As this work is largely concerned with the question of *making this modularity more powerful* – specifically, to support the modular definition of entire circuit families – we first give a brief overview of the openQASM language.

The official specification of openQASM can be found in [6]. Programs in openQASM are structured as sequences of declarations and commands. Programmers can declare statically-sized classical or quantum registers, define unitary circuits (called *gates* in openQASM), apply gates or circuits, measure or initialize qubits and condition commands on the value of classical bits. Gate arguments are restricted to individual qubits, where the application of gates to one or more register *of the same size* is syntactic sugar for the application of a single gate in parallel across the registers. The listing below gives an example of an openQASM program performing quantum teleportation:

```
OPENQASM 2.0;
qreg q[3];
creg c0[1];
creg c1[1];

h q[1];
cx q[1],q[2];
cx q[0],q[1];
h q[0];
measure q[0] -> c0[0];
measure q[1] -> c1[0];
if(c0==1) z q[2];
if(c1==1) x q[2];
```

We give a slightly different syntax from the above, and from the concrete syntax [6], as it will be more convenient and readable for our purposes. As is common in imperative languages, we leave some of the concrete syntactic classes of openQASM [6] separate in our formalization – since all operations in openQASM nominally have unit type, this allows terms with unitary and non-unitary *effects* to be distinguished, without relying on an effect system or

Identifier x
Index I ::= $i \in \mathbb{N}$
Expression E ::= $x \mid x[I]$
Unitary Stmt U ::= $\mathtt{cx}(E_1, E_2) \mid \mathtt{h}(E) \mid \mathtt{t}(E) \mid \mathtt{tdg}(E) \mid E(E_1, \ldots, E_n) \mid U_1 ;\ U_2$
Command C ::= $\mathtt{creg}\ x[I] \mid \mathtt{qreg}\ x[I] \mid \mathtt{gate}\ x(x_1, \ldots, x_n)\ \{\ U\ \}$
$\mid\ \mathtt{measure}\ E_1\ \texttt{->}\ E_2 \mid \mathtt{reset}\ E \mid U$
$\mid\ \mathtt{if}(E\texttt{==}I)\ \{\ U\ \} \mid C_1 ;\ C_2$

Location $l \in \mathbb{N}$
Value V ::= $(l_0, \ldots, l_{I-1}) \mid \lambda x_1, \ldots, x_n.U$

Fig. 2. openQASM (abstract) syntax

monadic types. In particular, terms of the class U of unitary statements represent computations with purely unitary effects, while commands C may have non-unitary effects, such as measurement. Statements of the form

$$E(E_1, \ldots, E_n)$$

represent the application of a unitary gate or named circuit E to the (quantum) arguments E_1 through E_n. While the openQASM specification includes built-in $\mathtt{cx}$ (controlled-NOT) and parametrized single qubit gates $\mathtt{U}$, we drop the parametrized $\mathtt{U}$ gate in favour of built-in Hadamard and $T/T^\dagger$ gates $\mathtt{h}$ and $\mathtt{t}/\mathtt{tdg}$, respectively (Fig. 2).

The commands $\mathtt{creg}$, $\mathtt{qreg}$ and $\mathtt{gate}$ declare classical registers, quantum registers, and unitary circuits, respectively. The $\mathtt{if}$ statement differs from the formal openQASM definition by testing the value of a *single* classical bit, rather than a classical register – this was done to simplify the semantics of the language. Locations l and values V do not appear directly in openQASM programs, but are used to define the semantics. In particular, values of the form $(l_0, \ldots, l_{I-1})$ denote registers and $\lambda x_1, \ldots, x_n.U$ denote unitary circuits. We leave out a number of features of openQASM which are orthogonal to the extensions we describe here, namely classical arithmetic and the $\mathtt{barrier}$ and $\mathtt{opaque}$ terms. We also write parentheses around arguments and parameters.

As no formal semantics of openQASM is given in [6], we define an operational semantics in Fig. 3. Our semantics is defined with respect to a *configuration* $\langle S, \sigma, \eta, |\psi\rangle \rangle$, which stores a term S taken from some syntactic class (e.g., C, U, E), an environment σ which maps variables to values, a classical heap η storing the value of the classical bits, and a quantum state $|\psi\rangle$. Gates applied to qubit l of a quantum state are written by added a subscript to the intended gate, e.g.,

$$H_l|\psi\rangle = (I^{\otimes l-1} \otimes H \otimes I^{\otimes n-l})|\psi\rangle$$

$\sigma[x \leftarrow v]$ denotes the environment mapping x to v or $\sigma(x)$ otherwise, and $S\{X/x\}$ denotes the substitution of X for x in S. We assume for convenience that no valid program will run out of classical memory or quantum bits. We say

$\langle S, \sigma, \eta, |\psi\rangle\rangle \Downarrow v$ if S reduces to v, where the form of v depends on the syntactic class of S – for instance, expressions evaluate to locations, arrays or circuits while commands produce a new environment, heap and quantum state. Note that we use a call-by-name evaluation strategy, as openQASM has only globally scoped variables.

Expressions:

$$\frac{x \in \mathsf{dom}(\sigma)}{\langle x, \sigma, \eta, |\psi\rangle\rangle \Downarrow \sigma(x)} \qquad \frac{\langle x, \sigma, \eta, |\psi\rangle\rangle \Downarrow (l_0, \ldots, l_{I'}) \quad I \leq I'}{\langle x[I], \sigma, \eta, |\psi\rangle\rangle \Downarrow l_I}$$

Unitary statements:

$$\frac{\langle E, \sigma, \eta, |\psi\rangle\rangle \Downarrow l}{\langle \mathtt{h}(E), \sigma, \eta, |\psi\rangle\rangle \Downarrow H_l |\psi\rangle} \qquad \frac{\langle E, \sigma, \eta, |\psi\rangle\rangle \Downarrow l}{\langle \mathtt{t}(E), \sigma, \eta, |\psi\rangle\rangle \Downarrow T_l |\psi\rangle} \qquad \frac{\langle E, \sigma, \eta, |\psi\rangle\rangle \Downarrow l}{\langle \mathtt{tdg}(E), \sigma, \eta, |\psi\rangle\rangle \Downarrow T_l^\dagger |\psi\rangle}$$

$$\frac{\langle E_1, \sigma, \eta, |\psi\rangle\rangle \Downarrow l_1 \quad \langle E_2, \sigma, \eta, |\psi\rangle\rangle \Downarrow l_2}{\langle \mathtt{cx}(E_1, E_2), \sigma, \eta, |\psi\rangle\rangle \Downarrow \mathrm{CNOT}_{l_1, l_2} |\psi\rangle} \qquad \frac{\langle E, \sigma, \eta, |\psi\rangle\rangle \Downarrow \lambda x_1, \ldots, x_n.U, \quad \langle U\{E_1/x_1, \ldots, E_n/x_n\}, \sigma, \eta, |\psi\rangle\rangle \Downarrow |\psi'\rangle}{\langle E(E_1, \ldots, E_n), \sigma, \eta, |\psi\rangle\rangle \Downarrow |\psi'\rangle}$$

$$\frac{\langle U_1, \sigma, \eta, |\psi\rangle\rangle \Downarrow |\psi'\rangle \quad \langle U_2, \sigma, \eta, |\psi'\rangle\rangle \Downarrow |\psi''\rangle}{\langle U_1 \,;\, U_2, \sigma, \eta, |\psi\rangle\rangle \Downarrow |\psi''\rangle}$$

Commands:

$$\frac{l_0, \ldots, l_{I-1} \text{ are fresh heap indices}}{\langle \mathtt{creg}\ x[I], \sigma, \eta, |\psi\rangle\rangle \Downarrow \langle \sigma[x \leftarrow (l_0, \ldots, l_{I-1})], \eta, |\psi\rangle\rangle}$$

$$\frac{l_0, \ldots, l_{I-1} \text{ are fresh qubit indices}}{\langle \mathtt{qreg}\ x[I], \sigma, \eta, |\psi\rangle\rangle \Downarrow \langle \sigma[x \leftarrow (l_0, \ldots, l_{I-1})], \eta, |\psi\rangle\rangle}$$

$$\overline{\langle \mathtt{gate}\ x(x_1, \ldots, x_n)\ \{\ U\ \}, \sigma, \eta, |\psi\rangle\rangle \Downarrow \langle \sigma[x \leftarrow \lambda x_1, \ldots, x_n.U], \eta, |\psi\rangle\rangle}$$

$$\frac{\langle E_1, \sigma, \eta, |\psi\rangle\rangle \Downarrow l_1 \quad \langle E_2, \sigma, \eta, |\psi\rangle\rangle \Downarrow l_2}{\langle \mathtt{measure}\ E_1\ \mathtt{\text{-}>}\ E_2, \sigma, \eta, |\psi\rangle\rangle \Downarrow \langle \sigma, \eta[l_2 \leftarrow 0], P_{l_1}^0 |\psi\rangle\rangle}$$

$$\frac{\langle E_1, \sigma, \eta, |\psi\rangle\rangle \Downarrow l_1 \quad \langle E_2, \sigma, \eta, |\psi\rangle\rangle \Downarrow l_2}{\langle \mathtt{measure}\ E_1\ \mathtt{\text{-}>}\ E_2, \sigma, \eta, |\psi\rangle\rangle \Downarrow \langle \sigma, \eta[l_2 \leftarrow 1], P_{l_1}^1 |\psi\rangle\rangle}$$

$$\frac{\langle E, \sigma, \eta, |\psi\rangle\rangle \Downarrow l}{\langle \mathtt{reset}\ E, \sigma, \eta, |\psi\rangle\rangle \Downarrow \langle \sigma, \eta, P_l^0 |\psi\rangle\rangle} \qquad \frac{\langle E, \sigma, \eta, |\psi\rangle\rangle \Downarrow l \quad \eta(l) \neq I}{\langle \mathtt{if}(E\mathtt{==}I)\ \{\ U\ \}, \sigma, \eta, |\psi\rangle\rangle \Downarrow \langle \sigma, \eta, |\psi\rangle\rangle}$$

$$\frac{\langle E, \sigma, \eta, |\psi\rangle\rangle \Downarrow l \quad \eta(l) = I \quad \langle U, \sigma, \eta, |\psi\rangle\rangle \Downarrow |\psi'\rangle}{\langle \mathtt{if}(E\mathtt{==}I)\ \{\ U\ \}, \sigma, \eta, |\psi\rangle\rangle \Downarrow \langle \sigma, \eta, |\psi'\rangle\rangle}$$

$$\frac{\langle C_1, \sigma, \eta, |\psi\rangle\rangle \Downarrow \langle \sigma', \eta', |\psi'\rangle\rangle \quad \langle C_2, \sigma', \eta', |\psi'\rangle\rangle \Downarrow \langle \sigma'', \eta'', |\psi''\rangle\rangle}{\langle C_1 \,;\, C_2, \sigma, \eta, |\psi\rangle\rangle \Downarrow \langle \sigma'', \eta'', |\psi''\rangle\rangle}$$

Fig. 3. openQASM semantics

Base types $\beta ::= \texttt{Bit} \mid \texttt{Qbit}$
Types $\tau ::= \beta \mid \beta[I] \mid \texttt{Circuit}(\tau_1, \ldots, \tau_n)$
Command $C ::= \ldots \mid \texttt{creg } x[I] \texttt{ in } \{ \ C \ \} \mid \texttt{qreg } x[I] \texttt{ in } \{ \ C \ \}$
$\mid \texttt{gate } x(x_1 : \tau_1, \ldots, x_n : \tau_n) \ \{ \ U \ \} \texttt{ in } \{ \ C \ \}$

Fig. 4. typedQASM specification

Rather than give a full probabilistic reduction system to account for measurement probabilities, it suffices for our purposes to make the semantics nondeterministic. In particular, rules are given for both of the possible measurement outcomes in $\texttt{measure } E_1 \texttt{ -> } E_2$, setting the classical bit to the result $c \in \{0, 1\}$ and non-destructively applying the projector $P^c = |c\rangle\langle c|$ (appropriately normalized) to the measured qubit.

4 Adding Types to QASM

Run-time errors may occur in syntactically valid openQASM programs in a number of ways – particularly when either an array access is out of bounds and the program halts, or a classical (resp. quantum) location is used in a context when a quantum (resp. classical) location is expected. In the official openQASM specification, the latter error is eliminated by the requirement that only (global) variables can be declared as quantum registers may be used as arguments to gates, for instance. In either case however, it is desirable to check that an openQASM program *will not go wrong*, as circuit simulations are frequently run on large, expensive supercomputers (e.g., [13]).

In this section we developed a typed variant of openQASM, called typedQASM, which provably rules out such runtime errors. Moreover, the type system uses *sized types* to eliminate out-of-bound accesses, which we later develop into the core of our metaprogramming type system. The use of a type system in this case actually allows *more* valid programs to be written than the standard openQASM specification, as the type system allows us to remove some syntactic distinctions and instead make them in the type system. In particular, our type system allows registers and circuits to be passed as functions to other circuits, whereas the formal specification restricts circuit arguments to only individual qubits.

Figure 4 gives the syntax of typedQASM. We only show the syntactic elements which are different from openQASM or otherwise new. To simplify our analysis, declarations are given explicit block scope, though we leave textual examples in the regular openQASM style of declaration. As the semantics of typedQASM is effectively identical, modulo the block scoping, to openQASM we don't explicitly give the semantics.

4.1   The Type System

Figure 5 gives the rules of our type system. As is standard, the judgement $\Gamma \vdash S : \tau$ states that in the context Γ consisting of pairs of identifiers and types, S can be assigned type τ. We overload $\vdash$ to allow environment judgements of the form $\vdash \sigma : \Gamma$ stating that the σ maps identifiers x to values of the type τ if $x : \tau \in \Gamma$.

Environment:

$$\frac{}{\vdash \cdot : \cdot} \qquad \frac{\vdash \sigma : \Gamma}{\vdash \sigma[x \leftarrow (l_0, \ldots, l_{I-1})] : \Gamma, x : \beta[I]}$$

$$\frac{\vdash \sigma : \Gamma \qquad \Gamma, x_1 : \tau_1, \ldots, x_n : \tau_n \vdash U : \mathtt{Unit}}{\vdash \sigma[x \leftarrow \lambda x_1 : \tau_1, \ldots, x_n : \tau_n.U] : \Gamma, x : \mathtt{Circuit}(\tau_1, \ldots, \tau_n)}$$

Expressions:

$$\frac{x : \tau \in \Gamma}{\Gamma \vdash x : \tau} \qquad \frac{\Gamma \vdash x : \beta[I'] \qquad I \leq I' - 1}{\Gamma \vdash x[I] : \beta} \qquad \frac{\Gamma \vdash E : \beta[I'] \qquad I \leq I'}{\Gamma \vdash E : \beta[I]}$$

Unitary statements:

$$\frac{\Gamma \vdash E_1 : \mathtt{Qbit} \qquad \Gamma \vdash E_2 : \mathtt{Qbit}}{\Gamma \vdash \mathtt{cx}(E_1, E_2) : \mathtt{Unit}} \qquad \frac{\Gamma \vdash E : \mathtt{Qbit} \qquad g \in \{\mathtt{h}, \mathtt{t}, \mathtt{tdg}\}}{\Gamma \vdash g(E) : \mathtt{Unit}}$$

$$\frac{\Gamma \vdash E : \mathtt{Circuit}(\tau_1, \ldots, \tau_n) \\ \Gamma \vdash E_1 : \tau_1 \quad \cdots \quad \Gamma \vdash E_n : \tau_n}{\Gamma \vdash E(E_1, \ldots, E_n) : \mathtt{Unit}} \qquad \frac{\Gamma \vdash U_1 : \mathtt{Unit} \qquad \Gamma \vdash U_2 : \mathtt{Unit}}{\Gamma \vdash U_1;\ U_2 : \mathtt{Unit}}$$

Commands:

$$\frac{\Gamma, x : \mathtt{Bit}[I] \vdash C : \mathtt{Unit}}{\Gamma \vdash \mathtt{creg}\ x[I]\ \mathtt{in}\ \{\ C\ \} : \mathtt{Unit}} \qquad \frac{\Gamma, x : \mathtt{Qbit}[I] \vdash C : \mathtt{Unit}}{\Gamma \vdash \mathtt{qreg}\ x[I]\ \mathtt{in}\ \{\ C\ \} : \mathtt{Unit}}$$

$$\frac{\Gamma, x_1 : \tau_1, \ldots, x_n : \tau_n \vdash U : \mathtt{Unit} \qquad \Gamma, x : \mathtt{Circuit}(\tau_1, \ldots, \tau_n) \vdash C : \mathtt{Unit}}{\Gamma \vdash \mathtt{gate}\ x(x_1 : \tau_1, \ldots, x_n : \tau_n)\ \{\ U\ \}\ \mathtt{in}\ \{\ C\ \} : \mathtt{Unit}}$$

$$\frac{\Gamma \vdash E_1 : \mathtt{Qbit} \qquad \Gamma \vdash E_2 : \mathtt{Bit}}{\Gamma \vdash \mathtt{measure}\ E_1\ \text{->}\ E_2 : \mathtt{Unit}} \qquad \frac{\Gamma \vdash E : \mathtt{Qbit}}{\Gamma \vdash \mathtt{reset}\ E : \mathtt{Unit}}$$

$$\frac{\Gamma \vdash E : \mathtt{Bit} \qquad \Gamma \vdash U : \mathtt{Unit}}{\Gamma \vdash \mathtt{if}(E{=}{=}I)\ \{\ U\ \} : \mathtt{Unit}} \qquad \frac{\Gamma \vdash C_1 : \mathtt{Unit} \qquad \Gamma \vdash C_2 : \mathtt{Unit}}{\Gamma \vdash C_1;\ C_2 : \mathtt{Unit}}$$

Fig. 5. typedQASM typing rules

The type system of typedQASM is mostly as expected, with the exception of static-length registers and register bounds checks in the typing rules for dereferences. To give the programmer flexibility to apply gates and circuits to just parts of a larger register – for instance, when performing an n-bit addition into a length $2n$ register as in binary multiplication – the type system also implicitly supports subtyping of static length registers. Specifically, any length I array can be used in a context requiring *at most* I cells. While this adds a great deal of flexibility on the side of the programmer, as a downside typedQASM typing derivations are not unique.

As an example of a well-typed QASM program, we show an implementation of the Toffoli circuit from Fig. 1 below:

```
gate toffoli(x:Qbit, y:Qbit, z:Qbit) {
    h(z);
    t(x); t(y); t(z);
    cx(x,y); cx(x,z);
    tdg(y); tdg(z);
    cx(y,z); cx(z,x);
    t(x); tdg(z);
    cx(z,x); cx(x,y); cx(y,z);
    h(z)
}
```

4.2 Type Safety

We now briefly sketch a proof of type safety for typedQASM. In particular, we show that typedQASM is strongly normalizing, as expected.

As is standard, we establish strong normalization by giving type preservation and progress lemmas. While type preservation is effectively implicit in the semantics of typedQASM due to the different syntactic classes, expressions may return different types of values and so we give a form of type preservation for such terms.

Lemma 1 (Preservation (expressions)). *If $\Gamma \vdash E : \tau$, $\vdash \sigma : \Gamma$ and $\langle E, \sigma, \eta, |\psi\rangle\rangle \Downarrow v$, then either*

- $\tau = \beta$ and $v = l$ for some base type β & location l,
- $\tau = \beta[I]$ and $v = (l_0, \ldots, l_{I'})$ where $I' \geq I$, or
- $\tau = \mathtt{Circuit}(\tau_1, \ldots, \tau_n)$ and $v = \lambda x_1 : \tau_1, \ldots, x_n : \tau_n.U$.

Proof. If $\tau = \beta$ then we must have $E = x[I]$, hence by the definition of $\Downarrow$, $v = l$. Likewise if $\tau = \beta[I]$ then we must have $E = x$ where $x : \beta[I'] \in \Gamma$ for some $I' \geq I$, and since $\vdash \sigma : \Gamma$ then $v = \sigma(x) = (l_0, \ldots, l_{I'})$. The case for $\tau = \mathtt{Circuit}(\tau_1, \ldots, \tau_n)$ is similar.

The following lemmas give progress properties – the fact that for a well-typed program, evaluation can always continue – for the different syntactic classes of typedQASM. Together with type preservation, the result is that any well-typed typedQASM program evaluates to a value, i.e. that typedQASM is strongly normalizing.

Lemma 2 (Progress (expressions)). *If $\Gamma \vdash E : \tau$ and $\vdash \sigma : \Gamma$, then for any $\eta, |\psi\rangle$, $\langle E, \sigma, \eta, |\psi\rangle \rangle \Downarrow v$.*

Proof. By case analysis on E. If $E = x$ the proof is trivial, as $x : \tau \in \Gamma$ by inversion and $\vdash \sigma : \Gamma$ implies $x \in \text{dom}(x)$. If on the other hand $E = x[I]$, we must have $x : \beta[I'] \in \Gamma$ for some $I' > I$. Then by preservation, $\langle x, \sigma, \eta, |\psi\rangle \rangle \Downarrow (l_0, \ldots, l_{I''})$ for some $I'' \geq I' - 1$, hence $\langle x, \sigma, \eta, |\psi\rangle \rangle \Downarrow l_I$.

Lemma 3 (Progress (unitary stmts)). *If $\Gamma \vdash U : \text{Unit}$ and $\vdash \sigma : \Gamma$, then for any $\eta, |\psi\rangle$, $\langle U, \sigma, \eta, |\psi\rangle \rangle \Downarrow |\psi'\rangle$.*

Proof. For the case $U = E(E_1, \ldots, E_n)$, by the typing derivation we have $\Gamma \vdash E : \text{Circuit}(\tau_1, \ldots, \tau_n)$ so by progress and preservation for expressions, $\langle E, \sigma, \eta, |\psi\rangle \rangle \Downarrow \lambda x_1 : \tau_1, \ldots, x_n : \tau_n.U$. By the substitution lemma below, $\Gamma \vdash U\{E_1/x_1, \ldots, E_n/x_n\} : \text{Unit}$ and hence we can structural induction to show that $\langle U, \sigma, \eta, |\psi\rangle \rangle \Downarrow |\psi'\rangle$.

Lemma 4 (Substitution). *If $\Gamma, x_1 : \tau_1, \ldots, x_n : \tau_n \vdash U : \text{Unit}$, and $\Gamma \vdash E_i : \tau_i$ for each $1 \leq i \leq n$ then $\Gamma \vdash U\{E_1/x_1, \ldots, E_n/x_n\} : \text{Unit}$.*

Lemma 5 (Progress (commands)). *If $\Gamma \vdash C : \text{Unit}$ and $\vdash \sigma : \Gamma$, then for any $\eta, |\psi\rangle$, $\langle C, \sigma, \eta, |\psi\rangle \rangle \Downarrow \langle \sigma', \eta', |\psi'\rangle \rangle$.*

Proof. Proof by induction on the structure of C. We show one case:

$$C = \text{gate } x(x_1 : \tau_1, \ldots, x_n : \tau_n) \ \{ \ U \ \} \text{ in } \{ \ C \ \}$$

We know that

$$\langle \text{gate } x(x_1 : \tau_1, \ldots, x_n : \tau_n) \ \{ \ U \ \}, \sigma, \eta, |\psi\rangle \rangle \Downarrow \langle \sigma[x \leftarrow \lambda x_1, \ldots, x_n.U], \eta, |\psi\rangle \rangle.$$

By the typing derivation, $\Gamma, x_1 : \tau_1, \ldots, x_n : \tau_n \vdash U : \text{Unit}$ and $\Gamma, x : \text{Circuit}(\tau_1, \ldots, \tau_n) \vdash C : \text{Unit}$. It then follows that

$$\vdash \sigma[x \leftarrow \lambda x_1 : \tau_1, \ldots, x_n : \tau_n.U] : \Gamma, x : \text{Circuit}(\tau_1, \ldots, \tau_n),$$

and hence we can apply the inductive hypothesis to complete the case.

The remaining cases are similar.

Theorem 1 (Strong normalization). *If $\vdash C : \text{Unit}$, then*

$$\langle C, \emptyset, \lambda l.0, |00 \cdots\rangle \rangle \Downarrow \langle \sigma, \eta, |\psi\rangle \rangle.$$

Proof. Direct consequence of Lemma 5.

5   MetaQASM

Now that we have a safe, array-bounds-checked, typed language, we can add metaprogramming features. In particular, we wish to support[2]

- circuit inversion/reversal, and
- circuits parametrized by sizes.

While the latter could be accomplished in an ad-hoc way, allowing *type-level* integers allows for more safety in that array bounds can be statically checked, and increases the readability of programs. Moreover, it enforces a clear separation between circuits and families of circuits, which naturally support different operations – for instance, a family of circuits can't easily be visualized diagrammatically, while a particular instance can [27].

$$
\begin{aligned}
\text{Types } \tau &::= \ldots \mid \texttt{Family}(y_1, \ldots, y_m)(\tau_1, \ldots, \tau_n) \\
\text{Index } I &::= \ldots \mid y \mid \infty \mid I_1 + I_2 \mid I_1 - I_2 \mid I_1 \cdot I_2 \\
\text{Range } \iota &::= [I_1, I_2] \\
\text{Expression } E &::= \ldots \mid \texttt{instance}(I_1, \ldots, I_m) \; E \\
\text{Unitary Stmt } U &::= \ldots \mid \texttt{reverse } U \mid \texttt{for } y = I_1..I_2 \texttt{ do } \{ \; U \; \} \\
\text{Command } C &::= \ldots \mid \texttt{family}(y_1, \ldots, y_m) \; x(x_1 : \tau_1, \ldots, x_n : \tau_n) \; \{ \; U \; \} \texttt{ in } \{ \; C \; \} \\
\text{Value } V &::= \ldots \mid \Pi y_1, \ldots, y_m.V
\end{aligned}
$$

Fig. 6. metaQASM syntax

Figure 6 gives the new syntax for metaQASM. Indices I are extended with index variables y and integer arithmetic, and a new syntactic form defining a family of quantum circuits parametrized over index variables is given. The index ∞ only exists in the process of type checking and is not valid syntax in source code. Intuitively, the declaration

$$
\texttt{family}(y_1, \ldots, y_m) \; x(x_1 : \tau_1, \ldots, x_n : \tau_n) \; \{ \; U \; \} \texttt{ in } \{ \; C \; \}
$$

introduces index variables $y_1, \ldots, y_m$ into the evaluation and type checking contexts for τ_i and U.

Figure 7 gives the semantics of the new syntax. Since index variables cannot be modified or captured, we use a substitution style of evaluation for circuit families. The **reverse** command introduces a new reduction relation $\langle U, \sigma, |\psi\rangle \rangle \Uparrow v$ for which reduction of U is inverted. We give a concrete semantics rather than an abstract rule such as

---

[2] Controlled circuits are another desirable metaprogramming feature found in many quantum circuit description languages. While metaQASM gates are in fact closed over qubit controls, they require *ancillae* to construct [21]. This complicates the inclusion of a control instruction in metaQASM, and further abstracts away from concrete, resource-driven nature of QASM.

$$\frac{\langle U, \sigma, \eta, |\psi'\rangle\rangle \Downarrow |\psi\rangle}{\langle \text{reverse } U, \sigma, \eta, |\psi\rangle\rangle \Downarrow |\psi'\rangle}$$

so that metaQASM has a concrete execution model. Inversion of circuits is straightforward in metaQASM, as in any closed context a unitary statement can be statically unrolled to a finite sequence of gates.

As an illustration of metaprogramming in metaQASM, Fig. 8 gives metaQASM code for a simple (non-garbage-cleaning) adder. Our syntax (and type system) also allows an instance of a family of circuits to accept other circuit families as arguments, a useful feature which allows circuit families to be parametric in the implementation of a sub-routine as shown below (using a minor syntax extension to allow array slicing).

```
family(n) mult(x:Qbit[n], y:Qbit[n], z:Qbit[2*n],
    anc:Qbit, ctrlAdd:Family(m)
        (x:Qbit, y:Qbit[m], z:Qbit[m], c:Qbit))
{
  for i=0..n-1 do {
    instance(n) ctrlAdd(x[i], y, z[i..i+n-1], anc)
  }
}
```

By extending our syntax with parametrized gates as in regular openQASM, we can also define a parametrized family of circuits computing the *quantum Fourier transform* as in [27].

```
include "cphase.qasm";
family(n) qft(x:Qbit[n]) {
    for i=0..n-1 do {
        h(x[i]);
        for j=i+1..n-1 do {
            cphase(j-1+1)(x[i], x[j])
        }
    }
}
```

5.1 Type System

The type system of metaQASM is inspired by Dependent ML [34]. Figure 9 gives the rules of our system. Type rules are defined over two contexts $\Delta; \Gamma$, where Δ contains interval constraints on index variables.

Indices:

$$\frac{}{\langle i, \sigma, \eta, |\psi\rangle\rangle \Downarrow i} \qquad \frac{\langle I_1, \sigma, \eta, |\psi\rangle\rangle \Downarrow i_1 \quad \langle I_2, \sigma, \eta, |\psi\rangle\rangle \Downarrow i_2 \quad \star \in \{+, -, \cdot\}}{\langle I_1 \star I_2, \sigma, \eta, |\psi\rangle\rangle \Downarrow i_1 \star i_2}$$

Expressions:

$$\frac{\langle E, \sigma, \eta, |\psi\rangle \Downarrow \Pi y_1, \ldots, y_m.\lambda x_1 : \tau_1, \ldots, x_n : \tau_n.U}{\langle \texttt{instance}(I_1, \ldots, I_m) \ E, \sigma, \eta, |\psi\rangle \Downarrow (\lambda x_1 : \tau_1, \ldots, x_n : \tau_n.U)\{I_1/y_1, \ldots, I_m/y_m\}}$$

Unitary statements:

$$\frac{\langle U, \sigma, \eta, |\psi\rangle\rangle \Uparrow |\psi'\rangle}{\langle \texttt{reverse}\ U, \sigma, \eta, |\psi\rangle\rangle \Downarrow |\psi'\rangle} \qquad \frac{\langle I_1, \sigma, \eta, |\psi\rangle\rangle \Downarrow i_1 \quad \langle I_2, \sigma, \eta, |\psi\rangle\rangle \Downarrow i_2 \quad i_1 > i_2}{\langle \texttt{for}\ y = I_1..I_2\ \texttt{do}\ \{\ U\ \}, \sigma, \eta, |\psi\rangle\rangle \Downarrow |\psi\rangle}$$

$$\frac{\langle I_1, \sigma, \eta, |\psi\rangle\rangle \Downarrow i_1 \quad \langle I_2, \sigma, \eta, |\psi\rangle\rangle \Downarrow i_2 \quad i_1 \leq i_2 \quad \langle U\{i_1/y\}, \sigma, \eta, |\psi\rangle\rangle \Downarrow |\psi'\rangle \quad \langle \texttt{for}\ y = i_1 + 1..i_2\ \texttt{do}\ \{\ U\ \}, \sigma, \eta, |\psi'\rangle\rangle \Downarrow |\psi''\rangle}{\langle \texttt{for}\ y = I_1..I_2\ \texttt{do}\ \{\ U\ \}, \sigma, \eta, |\psi\rangle\rangle \Downarrow |\psi''\rangle}$$

Reverse reduction:

$$\frac{\langle E, \sigma, \eta, |\psi\rangle\rangle \Downarrow l}{\langle \texttt{h}(E), \sigma, \eta, |\psi\rangle\rangle \Uparrow H_l|\psi\rangle} \qquad \frac{\langle E, \sigma, \eta, |\psi\rangle\rangle \Downarrow l}{\langle \texttt{t}(E), \sigma, \eta, |\psi\rangle\rangle \Uparrow T_l^\dagger|\psi\rangle} \qquad \frac{\langle E, \sigma, \eta, |\psi\rangle\rangle \Downarrow l}{\langle \texttt{tdg}(E), \sigma, \eta, |\psi\rangle\rangle \Uparrow T_l|\psi\rangle}$$

$$\frac{\langle E_1, \sigma, \eta, |\psi\rangle\rangle \Downarrow l_1 \quad \langle E_2, \sigma, \eta, |\psi\rangle\rangle \Downarrow l_2}{\langle \texttt{cx}(E_1, E_2), \sigma, \eta, |\psi\rangle\rangle \Uparrow \mathrm{CNOT}_{l_1, l_2}|\psi\rangle} \qquad \frac{\langle E, \sigma, \eta, |\psi\rangle\rangle \Downarrow \lambda x_1, \ldots, x_n.U, \quad \langle U\{E_1/x_1, \ldots, E_n/x_n\}, \sigma, \eta, |\psi\rangle\rangle \Uparrow |\psi'\rangle}{\langle E(E_1, \ldots, E_n), \sigma, \eta, |\psi\rangle\rangle \Uparrow |\psi'\rangle}$$

$$\frac{\langle U_2, \sigma, \eta, |\psi\rangle\rangle \Uparrow |\psi'\rangle \quad \langle U_1, \sigma, \eta, |\psi'\rangle\rangle \Uparrow |\psi''\rangle}{\langle U_1;\ U_2, \sigma, \eta, |\psi\rangle\rangle \Uparrow |\psi''\rangle}$$

$$\frac{\langle U, \sigma, \eta, |\psi\rangle\rangle \Downarrow |\psi'\rangle}{\langle \texttt{reverse}\ U, \sigma, \eta, |\psi\rangle\rangle \Uparrow |\psi'\rangle} \qquad \frac{\langle I_1, \sigma, \eta, |\psi\rangle\rangle \Downarrow i_1 \quad \langle I_2, \sigma, \eta, |\psi\rangle\rangle \Downarrow i_2 \quad i_2 > i_1}{\langle \texttt{for}\ y = I_1..I_2\ \texttt{do}\ \{\ U\ \}, \sigma, \eta, |\psi\rangle\rangle \Uparrow |\psi\rangle}$$

$$\frac{\langle I_1, \sigma, \eta, |\psi\rangle\rangle \Downarrow i_1 \quad \langle I_2, \sigma, \eta, |\psi\rangle\rangle \Downarrow i_2 \quad i_2 \geq i_1 \quad \langle U\{i_2/y\}, \sigma, \eta, |\psi\rangle\rangle \Uparrow |\psi'\rangle \quad \langle \texttt{for}\ y = i_1..i_2 - 1\ \texttt{do}\ \{\ U\ \}, \sigma, \eta, |\psi'\rangle\rangle \Uparrow |\psi''\rangle}{\langle \texttt{for}\ y = I_1..I_2\ \texttt{do}\ \{\ U\ \}, \sigma, \eta, |\psi\rangle\rangle \Uparrow |\psi''\rangle}$$

Commands:

$$\frac{\langle C, \sigma[x \leftarrow \Pi y_1, \ldots, y_m.\lambda x_1 : \tau_1, \ldots, x_n : \tau_n.U], \eta, |\psi\rangle\rangle \Downarrow \langle \sigma', \eta', |\psi'\rangle\rangle}{\langle \texttt{family}(y_1, \ldots, y_m)\ x(x_1 : \tau_1, \ldots, x_n : \tau_n)\ \{\ U\ \}\ \texttt{in}\ \{\ C\ \}, \sigma, \eta, |\psi\rangle\rangle \Downarrow \langle \sigma, \eta', |\psi'\rangle\rangle}$$

Fig. 7. metaQASM semantics

As with typedQASM, array bounds are checked and subtyping on array lengths is allowed. Integer expressions are assigned intervals which may be arbitrary (well-formed) integer expressions. The judgement $\Delta \models P$ which appears in the typing rules for integer expressions denotes that under the context Δ,

```
include "toffoli.qasm";
gate maj(a:Qbit, b:Qbit, c:Qbit, res:Qbit) {
    toffoli(b, c, res);
    cx(b, c);
    toffoli(a, c, res);
    cx(b, c)
}
family(n) add(a:Qbit[n], b:Qbit[n], c:Qbit[n], anc:Qbit[n]) {
    cx(a[0], c[0]);
    cx(b[0], c[0]);
    toffoli(a[0], b[0], anc[0]);
    for i=1..n-1 do {
        cx(a[i], c[i]);
        cx(b[i], c[i]);
        cx(anc[i-1], c[i]);
        maj(a[i], b[i], anc[i-1], anc[i])
    }
}
```

Fig. 8. metaQASM implementation of a carry-ripple adder.

the (in)equality P holds. We leave a particular constraint solver up to implementation. It remains an open question whether undecidable constraints can be generated by our type system, though in practice it appears most common constraints can be efficiently solved with off-the-shelf constraint solvers [34].

The type system of Fig. 9 also involves *kind* judgements of the form

$$\Delta \vdash \tau{::}*$$

stating that τ is a simple type in the index context Δ. While the rules of our kind system are not given here, it is straightforward to derive. In particular, τ has kind $*$ if τ does not reference any free index variables, and does not contain any registers of negative length.

Remark 1. The fact that metaQASM has no means of specifying and checking relational properties on indices causes some programs to require counter-intuitive type schemes. For instance, the following n-bit adder is not well-typed due to the statement toffoli(x[n-2], ctrl, y[n-1]), though it does not cause run-time errors when $n \geq 2$.

```
include "toffoli.qasm";
family(n) ctrlAdd(ctrl:Qbit, x:Qbit[n],
                  y:Qbit[n], c:Qbit) {
   toffoli(x[0], ctrl, y[0]);
   cx(x[0], c);
   toffoli(c, y[0], x[0]);
   for i=1..n-2 do {
       toffoli(x[i], ctrl, y[i]);
       cx(x[i-1], x[i]);
       toffoli(x[i-1], y[i], x[i])
   }
   toffoli(x[n-1], ctrl, y[n-1]);
   toffoli(x[n-2], ctrl, y[n-1]);
   for i=2..n-1 do {
       toffoli(x[n-i-1], y[n-i], x[n-i]);
       cx(x[n-i-1], x[n-i]);
       toffoli(x[n-i-1], ctrl, y[n-i])
   }
   toffoli(c, y[0], x[0]);
   cx(x[0], c);
   toffoli(c, ctrl, y[0])
}
```

The above adder can modified [7] to a well-typed program by using $m = n - 2$ as the parameter, effectively specifying the number of entries *greater than* 2 that the input registers contain. The program snippet below gives the declaration required to make the controlled Adder implementation (with appropriate re-indexing) well-typed.

```
family(m) ctrlAdd(ctrl:Qbit, x:Qbit[m+2],
                  y:Qbit[m+2], c:Qbit)
```

In most practical cases appropriate parameters can be given so as to allow a well-typed implementation of a circuit family. However, the family parameters can be counter-intuitive, and more egregiously it can be unclear as to how to generate an intended instance. We leave it as an avenue for future work to add specification and checking of bounds and relational properties to metaQASM.

5.2   Type Safety

As in the case of typedQASM, metaQASM is strongly normalizing, due to the lack of recursion and unbounded loops. Progress relies on the fact that during the course of evaluation, no free index variables are encountered – hence any term encountered by an interpreter is well-typed in the empty index context, and in particular indices can be evaluated to finite integers, as shown below.

Lemma 6. *If* $\cdot \vdash I : [I_1, I_2]$, *then* $\langle I, \sigma, \eta, |\psi\rangle \rangle \Downarrow i$.

Indices:

$$\frac{}{\Delta \vdash i : [i, i]} \qquad \frac{y : [I_1, I_2] \in \Delta}{\Delta \vdash y : [I_1, I_2]} \qquad \frac{\Delta \vdash I : [I_1, I_2] \quad \Delta \models I_1' \leq I_1 \quad \Delta \models I_2' \geq I_2}{\Delta \vdash I : [I_1', I_2']}$$

$$\frac{\Delta \vdash I : [I_1, I_2] \quad \Delta \vdash I' : [I_1', I_2']}{\Delta \vdash I + I' : [I_1 + I_1', I_2 + I_2']} \qquad \frac{\Delta \vdash I : [I_1, I_2] \quad \Delta \vdash I' : [I_1', I_2']}{\Delta \vdash I - I' : [I_1 - I_1', I_2 - I_2']}$$

$$\frac{\Delta \vdash I : [I_1, I_2] \quad \Delta \vdash I' : [I_1', I_2'] \quad \Delta \models I_1'' = \min(I_1 \cdot I_1', I_1 \cdot I_2', I_2 \cdot I_1', I_2 \cdot I_2') \quad \Delta \models I_2'' = \max(I_1 \cdot I_1', I_1 \cdot I_2', I_2 \cdot I_1', I_2 \cdot I_2')}{\Delta \vdash I \cdot I' : [I_1'', I_2'']}$$

Expressions:

$$\frac{\Delta; \Gamma \vdash x : \beta[I'] \quad \Delta \models 0 \leq I < I'}{\Delta; \Gamma \vdash x[I] : \beta}$$

$$\frac{\Delta; \Gamma \vdash E : \texttt{Family}(y_1, \ldots, y_m)(\tau_1, \ldots, \tau_n) \quad \Delta \vdash I_1 : [0, \infty] \quad \cdots \quad \Delta \vdash I_m : [0, \infty]}{\Delta; \Gamma \vdash \texttt{instance}(I_1, \ldots, I_m) \; E : \texttt{Circuit}(\tau_1\{I_1/y_1, \ldots, I_m/y_m\}, \ldots, \tau_n\{I_1/y_1, \ldots, I_m/y_m\})}$$

Unitary statements:

$$\frac{\Delta; \Gamma \vdash U : \texttt{Unit}}{\Delta; \Gamma \vdash \texttt{reverse} \; U : \texttt{Unit}} \qquad \frac{\Delta \vdash I : [I_1, I_2] \quad \Delta \vdash I' : [I_1', I_2'] \quad \Delta, y : [I_1, I_2']; \Gamma \vdash U : \texttt{Unit}}{\Delta; \Gamma \vdash \texttt{for} \; y = I..I' \; \texttt{do} \; \{ \; U \; \} : \texttt{Unit}}$$

Commands:

$$\frac{\Delta, y_1 : [0, \infty], \ldots, y_m : [0, \infty] \vdash \tau_1 :: * \quad \cdots \quad \Delta, y_1 : [0, \infty], \ldots, y_m : [0, \infty] \vdash \tau_n :: * \quad \Delta, y_1 : [0, \infty], \ldots, y_m : [0, \infty]; \Gamma, x_1 : \tau_1, \ldots, x_n : \tau_n \vdash U : \texttt{Unit}, \quad \Delta; \Gamma, x : \texttt{Family}(y_1, \ldots, y_m)(\tau_1, \ldots, \tau_n) \vdash C : \texttt{Unit}}{\Delta; \Gamma \vdash \texttt{family}(y_1, \ldots, y_m) \; x(x_1 : \tau_1, \ldots, x_n : \tau_n) \; \{ \; U \; \} \; \texttt{in} \; \{ \; C \; \} : \texttt{Unit}}$$

Fig. 9. metaQASM typing rules

Proof. Trivial since the judgement $\cdot \vdash I : [I_1, I_2]$ requires that I does not contain any variables. Note also that there is no derivation of a judgement of the form $\Delta \vdash \infty : [I_1, I_2]$ hence I cannot contain any infinite integers.

The remaining lemmas are extensions of results for typedQASM. Only the new or different cases are considered.

Lemma 7 (Preservation (expressions)). *If* $\cdot; \Gamma \vdash E : \tau$, $\vdash \sigma : \Gamma$ *and* $\langle E, \sigma, \eta, |\psi\rangle\rangle \Downarrow v$, *then either*

1. $\tau = \beta$ *and* $v = l$,
2. $\tau = \beta[I]$ *and* $v = (l_0, \ldots, l_{I'})$ *where* $I' \geq I$, *or*
3. $\tau = \texttt{Circuit}(\tau_1, \ldots, \tau_n)$ *and* $v = \lambda x_1 : \tau_1, \ldots, x_n : \tau_n.U$
4. $\tau = \texttt{Family}(y_1, \ldots, y_m)(\tau_1, \ldots, \tau_n)$ *and*

$$v = \Pi y_1, \ldots, y_m.\lambda x_1 : \tau_1, \ldots, x_n : \tau_n.U.$$

Proof. The new `Family` case is effectively identical to the `Circuit` case. For the case where $\tau = \beta$, it suffices to note that by Lemma 6, the expressions I and I' in the typing derivation reduce to integers i, i' and the proof concludes as in the typedQASM case.

Finally we have to revise the $\tau = \mathtt{Circuit}(\tau_1, \ldots, \tau_n)$ case as we now have two possible derivations. The new case $E = \mathtt{instance}(I_1, \ldots, I_m)\ E$ is also trivial as the only reduction produces a value of the form $\lambda x_1 : \tau_1, \ldots, x_n : \tau_n . U$. Note that the type τ in the derivation has I_i substituted for index variables y_i, as in the conclusion of the reduction rule.

Lemma 8 (Progress (expressions)). *If* $\cdot; \Gamma \vdash E : \tau$ *and* $\vdash \sigma : \Gamma$, *then for any* $\eta, |\psi\rangle$, $\langle E, \sigma, \eta, |\psi\rangle\rangle \Downarrow v$.

Proof. Again, the new case $E = \mathtt{instance}(I_1, \ldots, I_m)\ E$ needs consideration. By inversion we see that $E : \mathtt{Family}(y_1, \ldots, y_m)(\tau_1, \ldots, \tau_n)$. By structural induction and the preservation lemma, $\langle E', \sigma, \eta, |\psi\rangle\rangle \Downarrow \Pi y_1, \ldots, y_m . \lambda x_1 : \tau_1, \ldots, x_n : \tau_n . U$ and so $\langle E, \sigma, \eta, |\psi\rangle\rangle \Downarrow v$.

Lemma 9 (Progress (unitary stmts)). *If* $\cdot; \Gamma \vdash U : \mathtt{Unit}$ *and* $\vdash \sigma : \Gamma$, *then for any* $\eta, |\psi\rangle$, $\langle U, \sigma, \eta, |\psi\rangle\rangle \Downarrow |\psi'\rangle$.

Proof. The case $U = \mathtt{reverse}\ U$ requires a separate progress lemma for reverse reduction, which follows similar to progress for unitary statements.

For the remaining case $U = \mathtt{for}\ y = I_1 .. I_2\ \mathtt{do}\ \{\ U\ \}$, it suffices to observe that by inversion, $\cdot \vdash I_i : [I_i, I_i']$ and so both bounds reduce to integers. As each recursive call increases the lower bound I_1, and I_2 is necessarily finite, there can be no infinite chains of reductions. The only condition that needs checking is that $\langle U\{i_1/y\}, \sigma, \eta, |\psi\rangle\rangle \Downarrow |\psi'\rangle$, for which we need the following substitution lemma.

Lemma 10. *If* $\Delta, y : [I_1, I_2']; \Gamma \vdash U : \mathtt{Unit}$, *and* $\Delta \vdash i_1 : [I_1, I_2']$ *then* $\Delta; \Gamma \vdash U\{i_1/y\} : \mathtt{Unit}$

To complete the proof, another lemma is needed stating that the result of evaluating an integer expression is within the bounds of the expression's type. We leave this as an easy exercise.

Lemma 11 (Progress (commands)). *If* $\cdot; \Gamma \vdash C : \mathtt{Unit}$ *and* $\cdot; \cdot \vdash \sigma : \Gamma$, *then for any* $\eta, |\psi\rangle$, $\langle C, \sigma, \eta, |\psi\rangle\rangle \Downarrow \langle \sigma', \eta', |\psi'\rangle\rangle$.

Proof. We have one new command to check,

$$C = \mathtt{family}(y_1, \ldots, y_m)\ x(x_1 : \tau_1, \ldots, x_n : \tau_n)\ \{\ U\ \}\ \mathtt{in}\ \{\ C\ \}.$$

The proof in this case is effectively identical to regular gate declaration.

Theorem 2 (Strong normalization). *If* $\cdot; \cdot \vdash C : \mathtt{Unit}$, *then*

$$\langle C, \emptyset, \lambda l.0, |00\cdots\rangle\rangle \Downarrow \langle \sigma, \eta, |\psi\rangle\rangle.$$

Proof. Follows directly from Lemma 11.

6   Conclusion

We have described a typed extension to openQASM that supports static array bounds checking, higher-order circuits, and lightweight metaprogramming in the form of size-indexed families of circuits. The resulting language is powerful enough to use for writing libraries of general quantum circuit families, such as for reversible arithmetic, while low-level enough to be used wherever openQASM is used.

As this is preliminary work, much remains to be done to make metaQASM a practical language for quantum library development. In particular, a concrete implementation needs to be developed, as do more examples of practical circuit families. A major question which remains is whether a decision procedure for the simple, non-linear integer constraints generated by our type system exists.

Another interesting question for future work is whether *parametrized resource counts* for algorithms can be computed directly from metaQASM programs. In particular, a desirable feature would be to compute closed-form formulas for the number of qubits, gates, etc., in an arbitrary instance of a circuit family, so that different implementations of the same circuit family can be analytically compared *for any instance size*. Doing so would help not only with resource estimation, but also compilation by allowing compilers to automatically select the best implementation for a particular cost model.

Acknowledgements. The author wishes to thank Gregor Richards for motivating this project and Frank Fu for pointing out alternative ways of typing several examples in this manuscript. The author also wishes to thank the anonymous reviewers for their detailed comments which have vastly improved the presentation of this work.

References

1. Aharonov, D., Jones, V., Landau, Z.: A polynomial quantum algorithm for approximating the jones polynomial. In: Proceedings of the Thirty-Eighth Annual ACM Symposium on Theory of Computing, STOC, pp. 427–436 (2006). https://doi.org/10.1145/1132516.1132579
2. Altenkirch, T., Grattage, J.: A functional quantum programming language. In: 20th Annual IEEE Symposium on Logic in Computer Science, LICS, pp. 249–258 (2005). https://doi.org/10.1109/LICS.2005.1
3. Amy, M.: Feynman. https://github.com/meamy/feynman
4. Amy, M., Roetteler, M., Svore, K.M.: Verified compilation of space-efficient reversible circuits. In: Proceedings of the 29th International Conference on Computer Aided Verification, CAV, pp. 3–21 (2017). https://doi.org/10.1007/978-3-319-63390-9_1
5. Bello, L., et al.: Qiskit. https://github.com/Qiskit/qiskit-terra
6. Cross, A.W., Bishop, L.S., Smolin, J.A., Gambetta, J.M.: Open quantum assembly language. arXiv preprint (2017). http://arxiv.org/abs/1707.03429
7. Fu, P.: Private communication (2018)
8. Gay, S.J.: Quantum programming languages: survey and bibliography. Math. Struct. Comput. Sci. **16**(4), 581–600 (2006). https://doi.org/10.1017/S0960129506005378

9. Gheorghiu, V.: Quantum++: a modern C++ quantum computing library. PLoS ONE **13**(12), 1–27 (2018). https://doi.org/10.1371/journal.pone.0208073
10. Green, A.S., Lumsdaine, P.L.F., Ross, N.J., Selinger, P., Valiron, B.: An introduction to quantum programming in Quipper. In: Dueck, G.W., Miller, D.M. (eds.) RC 2013. LNCS, vol. 7948, pp. 110–124. Springer, Heidelberg (2013). https://doi.org/10.1007/978-3-642-38986-3_10
11. Green, A.S., Lumsdaine, P.L., Ross, N.J., Selinger, P., Valiron, B.: Quipper: a scalable quantum programming language. In: Proceedings of the 34th ACM SIGPLAN Conference on Programming Language Design and Implementation, PLDI 2013, pp. 333–342 (2013). https://doi.org/10.1145/2491956.2462177
12. Grover, L.K.: A fast quantum mechanical algorithm for database search. In: Proceedings of the Twenty-Eighth Annual ACM Symposium on Theory of Computing, STOC, pp. 212–219 (1996). https://doi.org/10.1145/237814.237866
13. Häner, T., Steiger, D.S.: 0.5 petabyte simulation of a 45-qubit quantum circuit. In: Proceedings of the International Conference for High Performance Computing, Networking, Storage and Analysis, SC, pp. 33:1–33:10 (2017). https://doi.org/10.1145/3126908.3126947
14. Häner, T., Steiger, D.S., Svore, K., Troyer, M.: A software methodology for compiling quantum programs. Quantum Sci. Technol. **3**(2), 020501 (2018). https://doi.org/10.1088/2058-9565/aaa5cc
15. Heyfron, L.E., Campbell, E.T.: An efficient quantum compiler that reduces T count. Quantum Sci. Technol. **4**(1), 015004 (2018). https://doi.org/10.1088/2058-9565/aad604
16. JavadiAbhari, A., et al.: ScaffCC: scalable compilation and analysis of quantum programs. Parallel Comput. **45**(C), 2–17 (2015). https://doi.org/10.1016/j.parco.2014.12.001
17. Khammassi, N., Ashraf, I., Fu, X., Almudever, C.G., Bertels, K.: QX: a high-performance quantum computer simulation platform. In: Proceedings of the 20th Design, Automation Test in Europe Conference Exhibition, DATE, pp. 464–469 (2017). https://doi.org/10.23919/DATE.2017.7927034
18. Khammassi, N., Guerreschi, G., Ashraf, I., Hogaboam, J.W., Almudever, C.G., Bertels, K.: cQASM v1.0: towards a common quantum assembly language. arXiv preprint (2018). http://arxiv.org/abs/1805.09607
19. Killoran, N., Izaac, J., Quesada, N., Bergholm, V., Amy, M., Weedbrook, C.: Strawberry fields: a software platform for photonic quantum computing. Quantum **3**, 129 (2019). https://doi.org/10.22331/q-2019-03-11-129
20. Kissinger, A., van de Wetering, J.: PyZX: large scale automated diagrammatic reasoning. arXiv preprint (2019). http://arxiv.org/abs/1904.04735
21. Kliuchnikov, V., Maslov, D., Mosca, M.: Fast and efficient exact synthesis of single-qubit unitaries generated by clifford and T gates. Quantum Inf. Comput. **13**(7–8), 607–630 (2013). https://doi.org/10.26421/QIC13.7-8
22. Liu, S., et al.: $Q|SI\rangle$: a quantum programming environment. arXiv preprint (2017). http://arxiv.org/abs/1710.09500
23. Lloyd, S.: Universal quantum simulators. Science **273**(5278), 1073–1078 (1996). https://doi.org/10.1126/science.273.5278.1073
24. Martonosi, M., Roetteler, M.: Next steps in quantum computing: computer science's role. Computing Community Consortium (CCC) workshop report (2019). http://arxiv.org/abs/1903.10541
25. Nielsen, M.A., Chuang, I.L.: Quantum Computation and Quantum Information. Cambridge Series on Information and the Natural Sciences. Cambridge University Press, Cambridge (2000)

26. Ömer, B.: Quantum programming in QCL. Master's thesis, Technical University of Vienna (2000). http://tph.tuwien.ac.at/~oemer/qcl.html
27. Paykin, J., Rand, R., Zdancewic, S.: QWIRE: a core language for quantum circuits. In: Proceedings of the 44th ACM SIGPLAN Symposium on Principles of Programming Languages, POPL, pp. 846–858 (2017). https://doi.org/10.1145/3009837.3009894
28. Preskill, J.: Quantum computing in the NISQ era and beyond. Quantum **2**, 79 (2018). https://doi.org/10.22331/q-2018-08-06-79
29. Shor, P.W.: Algorithms for quantum computation: discrete logarithms and factoring. In: Proceedings of the 35th Annual Symposium on Foundations of Computer Science, SFCS, pp. 124–134 (1994). https://doi.org/10.1109/SFCS.1994.365700
30. Smith, R.S., Curtis, M.J., Zeng, W.J.: A practical quantum instruction set architecture. arXiv preprint (2016). http://arxiv.org/abs/1608.03355
31. Soeken, M.: RevKit. https://msoeken.github.io/revkit.html
32. Steiger, D.S., Häner, T., Troyer, M.: ProjectQ: an open source software framework for quantum computing. Quantum **2**, 49 (2018). https://doi.org/10.22331/q-2018-01-31-49
33. Svore, K., et al.: Q#: enabling scalable quantum computing and development with a high-level DSL. In: Proceedings of the 3rd ACM International Workshop on Real World Domain Specific Languages, RWDSL, pp. 7:1–7:10 (2018). https://doi.org/10.1145/3183895.3183901
34. Xi, H.: Dependent types for program termination verification. In: Proceedings 16th Annual IEEE Symposium on Logic in Computer Science, LICS, pp. 231–242 (2001). https://doi.org/10.1109/LICS.2001.932500

Reversible Imperative Parallel Programs and Debugging

James Hoey[(✉)] and Irek Ulidowski

Department of Informatics, University of Leicester, Leicester, UK
{jbh11,iu3}@leicester.ac.uk

Abstract. We present a state-saving approach to reversible execution of imperative programs containing parallel composition. Given an original program, we produce an annotated version of the program that both performs forwards execution and all necessary state-saving of required reversal information. We further produce an inverted version of our program, capable of using this saved information to reverse the effects of each step of the forwards execution. We show that this process implements correct and garbage-free inversion. We give examples of how our implementation of reversible execution can be used for debugging, and demonstrate how a simulation tool we have developed for our approach can be used to examine the program state. Finally, we evaluate the performance and overheads associated with state-saving and inversion.

Keywords: Reversible computation · Debugging ·
Parallel composition · Imperative language · Inversion

1 Introduction

Reversible computation has been an area of increasing interest for many years. Reversible execution is the ability to undo the effects of running a program, and requires the majority of information to be preserved throughout the execution. This offers many benefits, including the suggestion within the Landauer principle [12] that not losing any information could lead to energy-efficient computation. Throughout this work we will explore the application to debugging.

An introduction into debugging and software bugs is provided by Zeller [28]. One common type of debugging, named *cyclic debugging*, is to run and re-run a program experiencing a bug. Each such run is used to observe different parts of the program state, typically using print operations. Doing so allows the first time an incorrect state occurs to be found, and can subsequently be repeated to find the original defect. This works well for deterministic sequential programs (i.e. no I/O etc.), since there is one possible execution path that must be followed each time. Parallel programs however do not share this property, as the random interleaving of two or more programs can produce several distinct execution paths. Interaction with shared memory by parallel programs may lead to *races*, where the components of a parallel compete to update shared memory locations.

© Springer Nature Switzerland AG 2019
M. K. Thomsen and M. Soeken (Eds.): RC 2019, LNCS 11497, pp. 108–127, 2019.
https://doi.org/10.1007/978-3-030-21500-2_7

As a result, it becomes much harder to reproduce the original failure, and introduces the potential for software bugs that appear and disappear among different execution paths (*Heisenbugs* [28]), *deadlocks* and *atomicity/order violations*.

With cyclic debugging not being suitable for parallel programs, other approaches have been developed. *Record replay debuggers* serialize a specific execution, and use this to force future runs to behave identically, meaning bugs can be reproduced [16]. *Reversible debugging* is described by Engblom [3], and is another alternative that has the ability to step backwards over an execution experiencing an error [1]. This avoids the issue of reproducing an error as no re-execution is required. Some approaches use forward execution from checkpoints to simulate moving backwards [4], while others, such as the Reverse C Compiler (RCC) [17] and our approach presented here, produce an inverted program that executes forwards but simulates reversal. Such approaches will typically reverse an execution in *backtracking* order, where steps of the execution are undone in exactly the inverted order of the forwards execution. Recently, some proposed solutions use *causal-consistent* reversibility [2,6,13], where a step of an execution can be reversed provided all steps that causally depend on it (consequences) have already been reversed. A recently proposed implementation of a causal-consistent reversible debugger is CauDEr [14].

We propose an approach to state-saving reversibility of imperative parallel programs, similar to RCC [17] and both the Backstroke framework [25] and works on it by Schordan [21,22]. We build on our previous work [10,11], and here discuss its application to debugging. We outline this proposal, beginning with the language that we support. We define the process of generating two versions of our original program, the *annotated version* that performs the forwards execution and the state-saving of all required information, and the *inverted version* that uses this saved data to simulate reverse execution. We describe a collection of environments representing our program state, and refer to three sets of small-step operational semantics defined previously [11].

Results that prove our approach to be correct are shown. Our first result shows that the process of state-saving does not alter the behaviour of the original program, as the final program state is unchanged. The second result states that given the inverted version starts in the final program state produced via the annotated execution, execution of this inverted version restores the program state to exactly as it was initially. This result is extended here to hold for all programs, including parallel composition and the challenges it introduces. Our results prove we achieve our aim of implementing correct reversal.

Three examples of common bug types are used to discuss the application of this state-saving reversibility to debugging. Each type of execution is defined in terms of small-step operational semantics, allowing us to advance through an execution one step at a time. This is highly desirable for debugging as intermediate program states can be viewed, allowing the initial effects of a bug to be seen. It also means that bugs leading to crashes can be viewed up to the point of the fatal error, as all previous small steps will have been performed. Similarly for the inverted version, the small-step semantics allow us to return to any intermediate position of our execution. We can also make use of the information saved during the forwards execution prior to its completion. For example, all values any variable has held up to this point will be saved.

We also introduce a simulation tool that implements our state-saving reversibility, specifically the three sets of small-step operational semantics referred to above. This allows the simulator to read and parse an original program, produce the two versions and perform all three types of execution. With the application to debugging being a consideration from the beginning of the development, we then discuss some of the key features that aid debugging. Such features include the ability to force a specific interleaving and the record mode.

Finally, we use this simulator to evaluate the performance of our approach to reversibility. We compare the execution times of programs with and without state-saving, producing an average overhead incurred. We likewise compare the execution times of forwards execution with that of the inverse execution, measuring the performance of reversal. Our main contributions are:

1. An overview of an approach for state-saving reversibility of imperative parallel programs proposed in [11]. A proof showing this holds for all valid programs of our language, extended here to include parallel composition.
2. The application of this method to debugging, explained using three examples of common bugs.
3. A simulator implementing our small-step semantics behind this method and how this is used for debugging.
4. The evaluation of the performance of our approach. This shows an acceptable overhead associated with both state-saving and inversion.

2   Our Approach

We begin with a state-saving approach to reversible execution of imperative parallel programs. A more in depth definition of this approach is available in our previous works [10,11]. Our discussion of this approach is split into the following five broad stages, each of which will be described below.

1. **Language and State.** We extend a typical while language with blocks, local variables, recursion-supported procedures (with no arguments) and parallel composition. We use 'parallel' in this context, but note that we could have used 'concurrent'. We introduce *construct identifiers* and *paths*, necessary to handle local variables and different scopes. The program state is represented as a collection of environments, each of which will be described later.
2. **Annotation.** This process introduces *identifier stacks* into the language syntax, necessary to record a particular run of the program. This produces an annotated version, that when executed saves *reversal information* required for inversion and captures the *non-deterministic interleaving order* via identifiers. This records the outcome of all races introduced by parallelism. All reversal information is stored within the *auxiliary data store*.

3. **Inversion.** This produces the corresponding inverted version of our original program, which itself is a forwards program capable of simulating the reverse execution. It is generated from the executed annotated version.
4. **Running Inverted Program.** Execution of the inverted version will then use both identifiers and the reversal information to simulate the undoing of the execution of the original program.
5. **Debugging.** The ability to execute step-by-step through the inverted version allows us to view the program state at any point. This can be used to compare the expected and actual program state, potentially helping us to find bugs.

Stage 1: Language and State. We begin with a typical imperative while language consisting of assignments, conditional statements and while loops. We extend this with blocks, local variables, procedures (with no arguments) capable of recursion, removal statements and the parallel composition operator **par**. This operator interleaves the execution of two (or more) programs randomly, while removal statements remove local variables or procedures at the end of a block. We refer informally to each argument program of a parallel statement as a *thread*.

Further to this, we also introduce *construct identifiers* and *paths*. Each conditional, loop, block, procedure declaration and procedure call is given a unique name, termed a construct identifier and represented as In, Wn, Bn, Pn and Cn respectively. These names are of the form `Unique name:Version number`. Each statement that requires evaluation will also contain a *path*, represented as pa. This is a sequence of the unique block names in which the specific statement resides, with λ representing an empty path (global). The syntax of this language is shown below, with paths and construct identifiers underlined here only to highlight them, and will be used henceforth without underlining. An example is shown in Fig. 1a, containing two assignments and a while loop performing six iterations. All paths are omitted as there are no blocks meaning all would be λ.

$$P ::= \varepsilon \mid S \mid P; \ P \mid par \ \{ \ P \ \} \ \{ \ P \ \}$$
$$S ::= skip \mid X = E \ \underline{pa} \mid if \ \underline{In} \ B \ then \ P \ else \ Q \ end \ \underline{pa} \mid$$
$$\qquad while \ \underline{Wn} \ B \ do \ P \ end \ \underline{pa} \mid begin \ \underline{Bn} \ DV \ DP \ P \ RP \ RV \ end \mid$$
$$\qquad call \ \underline{Cn} \ n \ \underline{pa} \mid runc \ \underline{Cn} \ P \ end$$
$$DV ::= \varepsilon \mid var \ X = v \ \underline{pa}; \ DV \qquad DP ::= \varepsilon \mid proc \ \underline{Pn} \ n \ is \ P \ end \ \underline{pa}; \ DP$$
$$RV ::= \varepsilon \mid remove \ X = v \ \underline{pa}; \ RV \qquad RP ::= \varepsilon \mid remove \ \underline{Pn} \ n \ is \ P \ end \ \underline{pa}; \ RP$$
$$E ::= Var \mid n \mid (E) \mid E \ Op \ E \qquad B ::= T \mid F \mid \neg B \mid (B) \mid E == E \mid E > E \mid B \wedge B$$

The program state is represented as a collection of environments. Firstly, the *data store* σ maps memory locations (**Loc**) to the value (**Num**) they currently hold ($\sigma : (\textbf{Loc} \mapsto \textbf{Num})$). Next, the *variable environment* γ maps variables (**V**) to memory locations. Before defining the variable environment, we note that the use of blocks mean that variables can be either global or local, and that a global variable can share its name with multiple local versions. Each such local version

```
1 X = 5;                          1 X = 5 [];
2 N = 0;                          2 N = 0 [];
3 while w1.0 (X >= N) do          3 while w1.0 (X >= N) do
4    X = X - 1;                   4    X = X - 1 [];
5    Y = Y + 1;                   5    Y = Y + 1 [];
6 end;                           6 end [];
```

(a) Original Loop Program   (b) Annotated Loop Program

Fig. 1. Small while loop example: forwards

will have been declared within a different scope, and specifically a different block. This means the unique block name in which a variable is declared is used within γ to differentiate multiple versions ($\gamma : (\mathbf{V} \times \mathbf{Bn}) \mapsto \mathbf{Loc}$). As a result of this, paths are used during variable evaluation to determine the block in which the variable was defined, with this then being used to access the correct memory location. The introduction of parallel composition and local variables mean that *data races* can occur, where the order in which two (or more) steps are performed directly affects the outcome. For example, two assignments to the same variable racing means the assignment performed last produces the final value.

Should the same code be executed in parallel, this approach to distinguishing versions of variables will not be sufficient. For example, consider two procedure calls to the same function on each side of a parallel that both declare a variable using the shared block name (as the same code is being used). In this case, both calls would use the same version of the declared variable, violating correct behaviour. Therefore any reused code, namely procedure and loop bodies, must be *renamed* prior to execution. Explained in [11], procedure bodies are renamed with all construct identifiers updated to begin with the unique call name (that will be different across a parallel). For example, a while loop w1.0 within a procedure call c1.0 becomes c1.0:w1.0. Loop bodies are renamed with all construct identifiers updated to their next version number. For example, the conditional i1.0 used in Fig. 5a will become i1.1 for the first iteration of the while loop. The renamed copies of procedure and loop bodies are stored within the *procedure environment* $\mu : (\mathbf{Pn} \cup \mathbf{Cn}) \mapsto (\mathbf{n} \times \mathbf{P})$ and *while environment* $\beta : \mathbf{Wn} \mapsto \mathbf{P}$ respectively. The *auxiliary data store* is discussed later.

The (forwards-only) execution of programs written in our language is defined in terms of a small-step operational semantics. We do not include this here as it is available in [11]. From here, we refer to each small step as a *transition* (or step) and consider an *execution* to be a sequence of transitions (or steps).

Stage 2: Annotation. Similarly to the Reverse C Compiler (RCC) [17], we produce two versions of an original program. The process of annotation produces the first of our versions, specifically the *annotated version* capable of recording the specific execution. This is implemented via the function $ann()$, shown in [11]. Recording a run of a program can be split into two main tasks, namely

1. Recording required data lost during forward execution (reversal information)

2. Capturing the non-deterministic execution order (due to having `par`).

Firstly, all reversal information is saved during the execution of the annotated program via the operational semantics [11]. This matches closely with the semantics of forwards-only execution, differing only on the state-saving. Such examples of this information include old values overwritten (and lost) as a result of destructive assignments, a boolean value indicating which branch of each conditional was executed, and a sequence of boolean values capturing the number of iterations of each loop. Further, the final value held by a local variable, and any identifiers assigned to a loop/procedure copy (*annotation information*), are saved prior to their deletion via removal statements.

This information is saved in the auxiliary data store δ, keeping all reversal information separate to the program state. This is a collection of stacks, with one for each variable name. All versions of a variable name use a single stack, storing overwritten or final values they held. Using a single stack helps to determine the outcome of races. There is a single stack B that holds boolean values for conditionals, and similarly W for loops. Finally, the stacks WI and Pr hold annotation information from loop or procedure body copies prior to removal.

Secondly, the non-deterministic execution order is captured via the use of identifiers. Sequential programs have a single path that can be followed in both directions. Parallel programs have many possible paths, with correct inversion dependent on following the correct inverted path of execution. Not doing so can lead to a state that was not reachable during forwards execution. To avoid this, as each statement of a program is executed, the next available identifier (used in ascending order) is assigned to that statement. In doing so, the overall statement order (interleaving) is recorded as required to ensure correct reversal. The syntax of each statement that requires identifiers to be saved will therefore have a stack for these, represented using A. Each identifier is also used to index any reversal information saved for that statement in δ, with all stacks on δ consisting of pairs. Within our operational semantics, any transition that uses an identifier is labelled with it, while those that do not are unlabelled and referred to as *skip steps*. The three types of skip steps are the removal of skip statements as a result of sequential or parallel composition and the closure of a block or loop iteration. The following is the updated syntax for annotated programs, where P and S are now used to represent annotated programs and statements respectively, and our additional stacks are highlighted via underlining. As with paths and construct identifiers before, these stacks will not be underlined from this point. We omit program expression definitions as they are unchanged.

$$
\begin{aligned}
&\text{S ::= skip I | X = E (pa,\underline{A}) | if In B then P else Q end (pa,\underline{A}) |}\\
&\quad\quad \text{while Wn B do P end (pa,\underline{A}) | begin Bn DV DP P RP RV end |}\\
&\quad\quad \text{call Cn n (pa,\underline{A}) | runc Cn P end}\\
&\text{DV ::= } \varepsilon \text{ | var X = v (pa,\underline{A}); DV} \quad\quad \text{DP ::= } \varepsilon \text{ | proc Pn n is P end (pa,\underline{A}); DP}\\
&\text{RV ::= } \varepsilon \text{ | remove X = v (pa,\underline{A}); RV} \quad \text{RP ::= } \varepsilon \text{ | remove Pn n is P end (pa,\underline{A}); RP}
\end{aligned}
$$

As shown in the syntax above, the only difference between an original program and the corresponding annotated version is the presence of identifier stacks within certain statements. Returning to our while loop example shown in Fig. 1a, the corresponding annotated version is shown in Fig. 1b. Execution of the annotated program will populate these identifier stacks with identifiers capturing the execution order. The corresponding executed annotated version containing populated identifier stacks is shown in Fig. 2a.

```
1 X = 5 [0];
2 N = 0 [1];
3 while w1.0 (X >= N) do
4   X = X - 1 [3,6,9,12,15,18];
5   Y = Y + 1 [4,7,10,13,16,19];
6 end [2,5,8,11,14,17,20];
```

(a) Executed Annotated Program

```
1 while w1.0 (X >= N) do
2   Y = Y + 1 [4,7,10,13,16,19];
3   X = X - 1 [3,6,9,12,15,18];
4 end [2,5,8,11,14,17,20];
5 N = 0 [1];
6 X = 5 [0];
```

(b) Inverted Loop Program

Fig. 2. Small while loop example: inversion

Stage 3: Inversion. After defining annotated execution, the next step is to produce the inverted version via the function $inv()$ and execute it via our small-step operational semantics [11]. This version executes forwards as expected, and is produced based on the executed version of the annotated program, meaning all stacks are populated appropriately. The overall statement order is inverted, as well as each declaration statement becoming an equivalent removal statement and vice versa. We use the same syntax for both the annotated and inverted versions, but with P and S for inverted programs and statements respectively. Returning to our small while loop example discussed throughout previous stages, the inverted version of this program is shown in Fig. 2b. The difference between this and the executed annotated version is the statement order is inverted.

Stage 4: Inverse Execution. Starting in the final program state produced via annotated forwards execution, the inverted version will restore the program state to as it was prior to forwards execution (see results below). The order in which the program executes is determined by the identifiers associated with its inverted statements, with only the statement that has the highest identifier eligible to be executed next. This means we follow backtracking order, where statements are undone in exactly the inverted order of the forwards execution. Backtracking order is necessary to ensure races are reversed correctly. There is however potential for limited causal consistent reversibility, where skip steps and block closures can be executed in any order. A small example of how identifiers capture the execution order and can be used for inversion is shown in [10].

When the choice of the next statement to invert has been made, the reversal information and identifiers saved via annotation are then used to undo the effects of that statement. Specifically this includes the old value of a variable to be restored during a destructive assignment, and boolean values to govern inverse control flow of conditionals or loops. The final value held by local variables will have been saved prior to its removal and so is used to initialise the inverted version, as well as the annotation information that must be used to repopulate all stacks within copies of reused code.

Stage 5: Debugging. In Sect. 4, we will discuss using our approach for debugging and present three examples of identifying common bug types. In Sect. 5, we introduce a simulation tool implementing the process described above, and show how its abilities further aid debugging.

3 Correctness of Our Approach

One motivation for this work is to have an approach to reversible execution of imperative parallel programs that is proved to be correct. Therefore we have proved two properties related to our approach. Prior to discussing these properties, we first provide several definitions and explain important notation.

We begin with defining equivalence. Firstly, two states $\Box = \{\sigma,\gamma,\mu,\beta\}$ and $\Box' = \{\sigma',\gamma',\mu',\beta'\}$ are equivalent, written $\Box \approx \Box'$, provided each pair of matching environments are not necessarily identical, but semantically equivalent. Secondly, two auxiliary stores δ and δ' are equivalent, written $\delta \approx_A \delta'$, provided the two stores are semantically equivalent. For example, actual memory locations used within the matching environments may differ, but the 'meaning' is the same. Finally, we define equivalence between a program execution and its corresponding *uniform version*. A uniform execution is a version of an original execution where all skip steps are performed as soon as they are available. Performing skip steps immediately does not alter the behaviour of the program as each such transition does not alter the program state. Therefore a program and its uniform version are equivalent as the program states produced are equal, since the order of transitions using identifiers is unchanged.

We shall use the following notation. A step of forwards only execution is represented using $\hookrightarrow$, while a step of both annotated and inverted execution are represented using $\xrightarrow{\circ}$ and $\xrightarrow{\circ}$ respectively, where $\circ$ represents the possible use of an identifier. For example, a destructive assignment is performed to skip via a transition that uses an identifier, while the skip operation is then removed via a transition without an identifier. Uniform versions of both an annotated and inverted execution are represented as $\xrightarrow{\circ}_U$ and $\xrightarrow{\circ}_U$ respectively.

Theorem 1 states an original program and its annotated version behave identically (under the same interleaving) with respect to all environments, except the auxiliary store. This shows annotation has no unwanted side effects.

Theorem 1. *Let* P *be an original program,* $\Box$ *be the set* $\{\sigma,\gamma,\mu,\beta\}$ *of all environments,* $\Box_1$ *be the set* $\{\sigma_1,\gamma_1,\mu_1,\beta_1\}$ *of annotated environments such that* $\Box \approx \Box_1$ *and* δ *be the auxiliary store. If* $(\mathrm{P} \mid \Box,\delta) \hookrightarrow^* (\mathrm{skip} \mid \Box',\delta)$, *for some* $\Box'$, *then there exists an execution* $(ann(\mathrm{P}) \mid \Box_1,\delta) \xrightarrow{\circ}^* (\mathrm{skip\ I} \mid \Box'_1,\delta')$, *for some* I, $\Box'_1$ *and* δ', *such that* $\Box' \approx \Box'_1$.

$$(P \mid \Box) \xrightarrow{\circ}^{*} (\text{skip I} \mid \Box') \implies (P \mid \Box) \xrightarrow{\circ}_{U}^{*} (\text{skip I} \mid \Box')$$

$$? \downarrow \qquad\qquad \Downarrow$$

$$(P^{-1} \mid \Box_1') \xrightsquigarrow{\circ}^{*} (\text{skip I'} \mid \Box_1) \impliedby (P^{-1} \mid \Box_1') \xrightsquigarrow{\circ}_{U}^{*} (\text{skip I'} \mid \Box_1)$$

Fig. 3. Diagram representation of proof outline

Theorem 2 states that given an original execution and its annotated equivalent, there exists an inverted execution that starts with the final program state, and restores this to exactly as initially. Shown in [11] to hold for sequential programs only, we note here that it now also holds for parallel programs. As a result, our approach is garbage free, as the auxiliary store is also restored.

Theorem 2. *Let* P *be a program and* AP *be* ann(P)*. Further let* $\Box$ *be the set* $\{\sigma,\gamma,\mu,\beta\}$ *of all environments,* $\Box_1$ *be the set* $\{\sigma_1,\gamma_1,\mu_1,\beta_1\}$ *of annotated environments such that* $\Box \approx \Box_1$*,* $\Box_1'$ *be the set* $\{\sigma_1',\gamma_1',\mu_1',\beta_1'\}$ *of final annotated environments,* $\Box_2$ *be the set* $\{\sigma_2,\gamma_2,\mu_2,\beta_2\}$ *of inverted environments such that* $\Box_2 \approx \Box_1'$*,* δ *be the auxiliary store,* δ' *be the final auxiliary store and* δ_2 *be the inverted auxiliary store such that* $\delta_2 \approx_A \delta'$*.*

If $(P \mid \Box,\delta) \hookrightarrow^{*} (\text{skip} \mid \Box',\delta)$*, for some* $\Box'$*, and there exists an annotated execution* $(\text{AP} \mid \Box_1,\delta) \xrightarrow{\circ}^{*} (\text{skip I} \mid \Box_1',\delta')$*, for some* I*,* $\Box_1'$ *and* δ'*, such that* $\Box' \approx \Box_1'$ *and that the executed annotated version of* AP *produced by its execution is* AP'*, then there also exists* $(\text{IP} \mid \Box_2,\delta_2) \xrightsquigarrow{\circ}^{*} (\text{skip I'} \mid \Box_2',\delta_2')$*, for* $\text{IP} = inv(\text{AP}')$ *and some* I'*,* $\Box_2'$ *and* δ_2'*, such that* $\Box_2' \approx \Box$ *and* $\delta_2' \approx_A \delta$*.*

Proof. The diagram shown in Fig. 3 outlines the proof omitted here due to space constraints. From this diagram, we aim to prove the correctness of the arrow labelled with a question mark, and we do so with the three step approach indicated with double arrows. We begin with an arbitrary execution of an annotated program P (top left of Fig. 3), and transform this into an equivalent uniform execution (top right of Fig. 3). Recall the definitions of uniform execution and equivalence above. This transformation consists of moving all skip steps (transitions that do not use identifiers) as close to the beginning of the execution as possible, ensuring all dependencies are maintained. An example is a destructive assignment that executes to skip, before this skip is eventually (with other steps potentially interleaved) removed. In a uniform execution, these two steps happen consecutively, with no interleaving of other statements in between.

From this equivalent uniform execution, we then prove two properties by mutual induction on the length of the execution. The first property is similar to that of Theorem 2 and concerns entire executions. This shows that if a uniform annotated program P executes to skip, then there exists a uniform inverse execution that, when beginning in the final state equivalent to that produced by forwards execution, also completes producing a program state equivalent to that of prior to the forwards execution. The second property is similar, but concerns only the execution of statements S. Since many statements contain complex subprograms, the first property is used by induction here (hence mutual induction). We consider each base case of both properties, and each (mutual) induction case. Using these properties, we obtain the corresponding uniform inverse execution (bottom right of Fig. 3), where $\square_1' \approx \square'$ and $\square \approx \square_1$.

The final step is to relax this uniform inverse execution into a non-uniform equivalent. This process is the opposite of that described for producing a uniform execution, and allows skip steps to be moved appropriately within the execution. Therefore we have shown the arrow from Fig. 3 to be valid, as required.

4   Debugging

This section describes the application of our approach to debugging. Some important aspects of this are:

1. Small-step semantics allow the execution to be paused at any point. Intermediate program states can be viewed, and compared with the expected state. This includes current position and current values of variables.
2. All reversal information saved up to a specific point can also be viewed. This can display the current number of loop iterations, all previous values of a variable and all results of evaluating conditional statements.
3. Program state is accessible in intermediate states, and can be changed to test things including temporary bug fixes.
4. Inversion can be started at any point, allowing debugging of fatal errors.

We now discuss three examples of common bug types, and how our approach to reversibility can be used to aid the process of identifying the underlying cause. We omit all paths and programs within procedure removal statements from all examples, all of which can easily be read from the remaining code.

4.1   Incorrect Logic Bug

We first consider a logic error, typically made by inexperienced programmers. The program in Fig. 2a is intended to have five iterations, however this specific run performs six (as Y = 6 after execution). The inverted program is shown in Fig. 2b. Beginning in the final program state, the inverted program can be executed forwards for four steps. This involves opening the loop (identifier 20), inverting the final iteration of the loop (identifiers 19 and 18) and finally inverting the second to last condition evaluation (identifier 17). This state, shown in Fig. 2b where all underlined identifiers have been removed and the arrow $\Longleftarrow$ indicates the current position, is now identical to that of the second to last time the condition was evaluated during forwards execution. Using the current program state, we then see that the condition 0 >= 0 holds true, when we expected false. We can see the logic is incorrect, and that replacing the logic symbol within the condition with > fixes this bug.

4.2   Parallel - Slow Write

Our second example is of an atomicity violation bug. With a write operation often being slower than a read, we use the program shown in Fig. 4a to simulate this. This contains a race between a read and write of the same variable in parallel. In order to mimic the write operation being slow but atomic, our write is implemented via the procedure update that actually performs two assignments, which we assume are performed one after another (with no statements interleaved). This is like saying the write is both slow and atomic. This means the execution will produce one of two possible outcomes. Firstly, the read (line 8) is followed by the write (line 9), meaning result = 10 and X = 12 (Outcome 1). Secondly, the write (line 9) is followed by the read (line 8), meaning result = 12 and X = 12 (Outcome 2). However, the interleaving shown in Fig. 4a produces an incorrect third state, where result = 11 and X = 12.

The inverted version of our program is shown in Fig. 4b (recall that this is a normal, forwards executing program). Beginning in our incorrect final state described above, the inverse execution first opens the block, re-declares the local variable X to the value 12 retrieved from the stack (line 4 using identifier 7), and then re-declares the procedure update (lines 5–8 using identifier 6). Next, the parallel statement starts by beginning the inverted procedure call (line 11 using identifier 5). This implies that the write finished last during forwards execution, meaning we should have expected Outcome 1. Then the inverse execution performs the destructive assignment (line 6 using identifier 4). At this point, the only available step is to undo the read now (line 10 using identifier 3). This state, shown in Fig. 4b with all underlined identifiers having been removed, shows that interleaving has occurred, with the arrows indicating current options (at this point in the forwards execution). From this, we observe that interleaving has occurred that directly conflicts our atomicity assumption. Further to this, if we were to continue the inverse execution we would complete the procedure call last, implying the write happened first during forwards execution meaning we should have seen Outcome 2. This inconsistency and the interleaving shown reassures us that we have found the bug. Such a bug can now be fixed, for example, by using an atomic construct (which can be easily added to our language).

4.3   Parallel - Race - Airline Example

Our final example is a program implementing a model of an airline that sells tickets via two agents. Each agent remains open and able to sell tickets until there are no remaining free seats. This program is shown in Fig. 5a, where the number of initially free seats is 3, and the number of agents is 2, in order to keep the execution and accompanying environments concise enough for discussion here. We return later to this example and increase both of these when evaluating the

```
 1 begin b1.0
 2     var X = 10 [0];
 3     proc p1.0 update is
 4         X = X + 1 [2];
 5         X = X + 1 [4];
 6     end [1];
 7
 8     par { result = X [3]; }
 9         { call c1.0 update [5]; }
10     remove proc p1.0 update end [6];
11     remove var X = 10 [7];
12 end
13 //Finishes with result = 11 and
14 //X = 12
```

(a) Executed Annotated Program

```
 1 //Initial value of result should
 2 //be 12 or 10
 3 begin b1
 4     var X = 10 [7];
 5     proc p1.0 update is
 6         X = (X + 1) [4];
 7         X = (X + 1) [2];      ⇐
 8     end [6];
 9
10     par { result = X [3]; ⇐ }
11         { call c1.0 update [5]; }
12     remove proc p1.0 update end [1];
13     remove var X = 10 [0];
14 end
```

(b) Inverted Program

Fig. 4. Slow write example

performance. The specific execution captured in Fig. 5a incorrectly results in 4 tickets being sold, as the final number of free seats is -1 (seats = -1).

The inverted version of this program is shown in Fig. 5b. Beginning in the incorrect final state, the inverse execution will begin by opening the block and re-declaring the local variables and the procedure. Next, the parallel statement is started, with each while loop executing an entire iteration (to simulate the inversion of the closure of each agent) using identifiers 33–24. From here, we now begin the inversion of the penultimate iterations of each while loop. The identifiers 23–14 are used to govern the interleaving across the two threads. The state reached is shown in Fig. 5b where all underlined identifiers have been removed, with the arrows indicating the current position. As this shows, the choice of next step is between the closing of two inverse conditionals. Closing an inverse conditional will reverse the opening of the forwards version, implying that both were open (during the forwards execution) at the same time (consecutive identifiers). Considering each conditional statement as the *critical section* of each thread, we see the mutual exclusion of these sections has been violated. Crucially, when there is a single seat left, if each conditional statement is evaluated consecutively, both conditions will be true. From here, the two calls from each of the true branches will be executed, allocating two seats when only one remains free. Therefore we see there is a race between the read of (conditional evaluation) and write (line 6) to the shared variable seats. One solution is to implement the mutual exclusion of the critical sections of each thread (agent).

5   Evaluation of Our Approach

An important next step of our work is to evaluate the performance of this approach. Prior to evaluation, we note that our focus so far has been on proving

```
 1 seats = 3 [0];
 2 begin b1.0
 3   var agent1 = 1 [1];
 4   var agent2 = 1 [2];
 5   proc p1.0 sell is
 6     seats = seats - 1 [6,11,18,19];
 7   end [3];
 8
 9   par {
10     while w1.0 (agent1 == 1) do
11       if i1.0 (seats > 0) then
12         call c1.0 sell [7,20];
13       else
14         agent1 = 0 [27];
15       end [5,8,16,22,26,28];
16     end [4,15,25,29];
17   } {
18     while w2.0 (agent2 == 1) do
19       if i2.0 (seats > 0) then
20         call c2.0 sell [12,21];
21       else
22         agent2 = 0 [31];
23       end [10,13,17,23,30,32];
24     end [9,14,24,33];
25   }
26   remove proc p1.0 sell end [34];
27   remove var agent2 = 1 [35];
28   remove var agent1 = 1 [36];
29 end
30 //Finishes with seats = -1
```

```
 1 //Expect seats = 0, not seats = -1
 2 begin b1.0
 3   var agent1 = 1 [36];
 4   var agent2 = 1 [35];
 5   proc p1.0 sell is
 6     seats = seats - 1 [6,11,18,19];
 7   end [34];
 8
 9   par {
10     while w1.0 (agent1 == 1) do
11       if i1.0 (seats > 0) then
12         call c1.0 sell [7,20];
13       else
14         agent1 = 0 [27];
15       end [5,8,16,22,26,28];    ⟸
16     end [4,15,25,29];
17   } {
18     while w2.0 (agent2 == 1) do
19       if i2.0 (seats > 0) then
20         call c2.0 sell [12,21];
21       else
22         agent2 = 0 [31];
23       end [10,13,17,23,30,32];    ⟸
24     end [9,14,24,33];
25   }
26   remove proc p1.0 sell end [3];
27   remove var agent2 = 1 [2];
28   remove var agent1 = 1 [1];
29 end
30 seats = 3 [0];
```

(a) Executed Annotated Program   (b) Inverted Program

Fig. 5. Airline example

this approach to be correct. Identifiers are saved into stacks contained within the syntax, and all reversal information is contained within the additional stacks. Multiple stacks are used as this separation aids the proof, while not necessarily being the most efficient approach. Therefore we remark that all results displayed within this section are produced without any optimization techniques applied.

To aid evaluation, a simulation tool implementing our approach has been developed. An overview and description of key features is shown below. This is used to examine the performance of two keys aspects, namely the overheads or reductions associated with both annotation and inversion.

5.1   Simulation Tool

We have developed a simulator that implements the small-step semantics of our approach [11]. It is capable of reading an original program written in our language from a text file, and parsing this into a linked list structure. This structure can be analysed and used to correctly initialise all of the required environments (including global variables).

The simulator has the ability to simulate all three possible executions, namely traditional forwards only with no state-saving, annotated forwards with state-saving, and inverse. All three executions can be either step-by-step or from start-to-finish. The current program state is viewable at each stage. Annotation and inversion are implemented, transforming an original program into the corresponding annotated and inverse version respectively. The execution of the inverse version follows backtracking in the majority of cases (as discussed above), while also supporting a limited form of causal-consistent reversibility.

The interface of the simulator is currently through the command line. A more user-friendly, graphical user interface (GUI) is currently under development. The following are some of the key features of the simulator.

Auto-generation of Modified Syntax. In order to remove the burden on the programmer, some of the additional parts of the syntax can be automatically generated. This includes the insertion of all unique construct identifiers, paths and removal statements at the end of blocks.

Random or User-defined Interleaving. Any interleaving of programs can either be determined randomly (via random number generation) or by the user at runtime, allowing testing of unlikely executions. This can be switched on/off at runtime, allowing a user to only determine the parts they require.

Record Mode. History logs can be recorded. Firstly, the entire sequence of small-step transitions can be saved. Secondly, for each interleaving decision, all possible choices and an indication of which was chosen can be saved.

5.2   Evaluation

In this section, we consider the following two aspects of our approach.

1. Costs/overheads associated with annotation and state-saving (**Annotation**)
2. Costs/benefits associated with inversion (no evaluation etc.) (**Inversion**)

Evaluation of these aspects consists of timing the executions of three programs written in our language. An average execution time is computed from 100 runs for two execution lengths (e.g. more loop iterations). One aim is to show that any overhead is consistent and does not increase exponentially. All experiments were ran on an Intel Core i5 quad core 3.2 GHz computer with 7.7 Gb memory, running Linux Ubuntu 16.04. Table 1 shows our results, with all times in seconds.

Annotation. Firstly, we consider while loops. The programs **Loop 1** and **Loop 2** (see Appendix A) each contain a while loop with 100 iterations, and a nested while loop with 1,000 and 10,000 iterations respectively. Each of these loops contain a single destructive assignment, meaning 100,000 (Loop 1) and 1,000,000 (Loop 2) of these are performed. Table 1 shows the average overhead introduced as a result of state-saving is 8.3% (Loop 1) and 7.9% (Loop 2).

Next we return to our airline example in Fig. 5a, and extend it with multiple agents (see Appendix B). The programs **Airline 1** and **Airline 2** each have 1000 initially free seats, and contain three and four agents respectively. Table 1 shows the average overhead is 4.6% (Airline 1) and 4.2% (Airline 2).

Finally, we consider all constructs of our language. The programs **General 1** and **General 2** (see Appendix C) each contain two while loops in parallel with 25 and 50 iterations respectively. Each loop contains an assignment and a procedure call, which uses a conditional statement to determine 5 recursive calls. Table 1 shows the average overhead is 13.2% (General 1) and 13.4% (General 2).

Therefore our results show the overhead of annotation for these specific programs to be within the range of 4.2–13.4%. We believe this is reasonable as it does not increase exponentially and given no optimization has been performed. A potential cause of this overhead is the unoptimized process of saving annotation information from copies of loop or procedure bodies prior to the removal of these. Our airline example results also show that increasing the number of programs in parallel does not seem to result in an increased overhead.

Table 1. Performance evaluation of our approach

Program	Original	Annotated	Change from Orig	Inverse	Change from Ann	Change from Orig
Loop 1	0.346	0.375	1.083	0.321	0.855	0.926
Loop 2	3.446	3.717	1.079	3.172	0.853	0.920
Airline 1	0.098	0.103	1.046	0.104	1.013	1.060
Airline 2	0.138	0.144	1.042	0.147	1.019	1.063
General 1	0.033	0.037	1.132	0.037	1.008	1.141
General 2	0.064	0.072	1.134	0.073	1.012	1.147

Inversion. Firstly, we consider the inverse execution time of programs **Loop 1** and **Loop 2**. Table 1 indicates a 7.4% (Loop 1) and 8% (Loop 2) reduction compared to the original execution, and a 14.5% (Loop 1) and 14.7% (Loop 2) reduction compared to the annotated execution.

The inverted executions of the programs **Airline 1** and **Airline 2** are now analysed. Table 1 shows a 6.0% (Airline 1) and 6.3% (Airline 2) increase on the original execution, and a 1.3% (Airline 1) and 1.9% (Airline 2) increase when compared to the annotated execution.

Finally, the programs **General 1** and **General 2** are inverted. Table 1 shows an increase of 14.1% (General 1) and 14.7% (General 2) on the original execution, and 0.8% (General 1) and 1.2% (General) on the annotated execution.

Therefore our results show that for these specific programs running on our unoptimized simulator, the inverse execution time ranges from a 14.7% decrease to a 1.9% increase compared to the annotated execution. A reduction is largely a result of the program containing large amounts of condition/expression evaluation during forwards execution, which is then not required during reversal as appropriate values are retrieved from the auxiliary store. Programs that do not contain large amounts of evaluation may not achieve this reduction, and may be slightly slower. A possible cause is the currently unoptimized process of checking the first identifier of each possible statement to determine the next step.

Though not perfect for comparison since it focuses on Parallel Discrete Event Simulation and distributed systems, the Backstroke framework [25] and work using it by Schordan [21,22] have also been evaluated. In [21], original execution of 100,000 events with a varying number of operations per events was compared to the forwards execution with instrumentation, showing a penalty factor of between 2 and 3 (Mode B). Both the reverse and commit versions are shown to typically be slightly faster than the original execution.

5.3   Related Work

Reversible computation can be applied to Parallel Discrete Event Simulation (PDES) [5], including the Backstroke framework [25] and works by Schordan et al. [21,22]. Backstroke implements a similar approach to that described here, but is capable of handling all of C++ efficiently. To the best of our knowledge, there is no proof of correctness for this framework. Other work focuses on reversible languages, including the imperative languages Janus [26,27], R-CORE [8] and R-WHILE [7], and the object-oriented languages Joule [23] and ROOPL [9]. We employ *identifiers* very much like in the work by Phillips and Ulidowski [18,20]. Causal consistent reversibility of programming languages have been studied, including the recent work on reversible Erlang [14,15], and μOz [6].

6   Conclusion

We have shown a state-saving approach to reversibility of imperative programs containing parallel composition. Our results displayed here prove this method implements correct and garbage free inversion. We have shown there is the possibility of using our approach for debugging, overcoming issues introduced by parallelism, including data races and randomly interleaved execution paths. We have proposed a simulator implementing our reversibility and used it to evaluate the performance. Our experiments show that the overhead incurred as a result of both state-saving and inversion is reasonable. Future work will focus on optimising the simulator, and extending our underlying approach with more constructs to increase the language complexity. We aim to support all constructs of an actual programming language, and potentially to apply our framework to an existing programming language. Extending our limited form of causal-consistent reversibility to allow undoing of more forms of causally independent steps could be also interesting, where we could follow approaches to reversing prime event structures as in [19,24], work on μOz [6], and reversing Erlang as in [14,15].

Acknowledgements. We are grateful to the referees for their detailed and helpful comments. We also thank Shoji Yuen for stimulating discussions on reversing programs for debugging. The authors acknowledge partial support of COST Action IC1405 on Reversible Computation - Extending Horizons of Computing.

A   Loop Program

All paths and identifier stacks are omitted as these are automatically inserted by the simulator.

Loop 1. Program used to test performance of while loops

```
1: X = 100;
2: while w1.0 (X > 0) do
3:    Y = 1000;
4:    while w2.0 (Y > 0) do
5:       Y = Y - 1;
6:    end;
7:    X = X - 1;
8: end;
```

B   Extended Airline

All paths, identifier stacks and removal statements are omitted as these are automatically inserted by the simulator.

Airline 1. Airline model extended with three agents

```
1: numOfSeats = 1000;
2: begin b1.0
3:    var agent1Open = 1;
4:    var agent2Open = 1;
5:    var agent3Open = 1;
6:    proc p1.0 sellTicket is numOfSeats = (numOfSeats - 1); end;
7:    par {
8:       par {
9:          while w1.0 (agent1Open == 1) do
10:             if i1.0 (numOfSeats > 0) then
11:                call c1.0 sellTicket;
12:             else
13:                agent1Open = 0;
14:             end
15:          end;
16:       } {
17:          while w3.0 (agent3Open == 1) do
18:             if i3.0 (numOfSeats > 0) then
19:                call c3.0 sellTicket;
20:             else
21:                agent3Open = 0;
22:             end
23:          end;
24:       }
25:    } {
26:       while w2.0 (agent2Open == 1) do
27:          if i2.0 (numOfSeats > 0) then
28:             call c2.0 sellTicket;
29:          else
30:             agent2Open = 0;
31:          end
32:       end;
33:    }
34: end
```

C   General Program

All paths, identifier stacks and removal statements are omitted as these are automatically inserted by the simulator.

General 1. Program used to test overall performance of our approach

```
 1: begin b1.0
 2:    var left = 25;
 3:    var right = 25;
 4:    var loop1Count = 10;
 5:    var loop2Count = 10;
 6:    proc p1.0 fun1 is
 7:       begin b2.0
 8:          var other = 0;
 9:          if i3.0 (loop1Count > 5) then
10:             loop1Count = (loop1Count - 1);
11:             call c1.0 fun1;
12:          else
13:             loop1Count = (loop1Count - 1);
14:             other = other + 1;
15:          end
16:       end
17:    end;
18:    proc p2.0 fun2 is
19:       begin b3.0
20:          var other = 0;
21:          if i4.0 (loop3Count > 5) then
22:             loop2Count = (loop2Count - 1);
23:             call c2.0 fun1;
24:          else
25:             loop2Count = (loop2Count - 1);
26:             other = other + 1;
27:          end
28:       end
29:    end;
30:    par {
31:       while w2.0 (left > 0) do
32:          left = left - 1;
33:          call c2.0 fun1;
34:          loop1Count = 10;
35:       end;
36:    } {
37:       while w3.0 (right > 0) do
38:          right = right - 1;
39:          call c3.0 fun2;
40:          loop2Count = 10;
41:       end;
42:    }
43: end
```

References

1. Chen, S., Fuchs, W.K., Chung, J.: Reversible debugging using program instrumentation. IEEE Trans. Softw. Eng. **27**(8), 715–727 (2001). https://doi.org/10.1109/32.940726
2. Danos, V., Krivine, J.: Reversible communicating systems. In: Gardner, P., Yoshida, N. (eds.) CONCUR 2004. LNCS, vol. 3170, pp. 292–307. Springer, Heidelberg (2004). https://doi.org/10.1007/978-3-540-28644-8_19
3. Engblom, J.: A review of reverse debugging. In: Proceedings of the 2012 System, Software, SoC and Silicon Debug Conference (2012)
4. Feldman, S.I., Brown, C.B.: Igor: a system for program debugging via reversible execution. In: Workshop on Parallel and Distributed Debugging, pp. 112–123. ACM (1988). https://doi.org/10.1145/68210.69226
5. Fujimoto, R.: Parallel discrete event simulation. Commun. ACM **33**(10), 30–53 (1990). https://doi.org/10.1145/84537.84545
6. Giachino, E., Lanese, I., Mezzina, C.A.: Causal-consistent reversible debugging. In: Gnesi, S., Rensink, A. (eds.) FASE 2014. LNCS, vol. 8411, pp. 370–384. Springer, Heidelberg (2014). https://doi.org/10.1007/978-3-642-54804-8_26
7. Glück, R., Yokoyama, T.: A linear-time self-interpreter of a reversible imperative language. Comput. Softw. **33**(3) (2016). https://doi.org/10.11309/jssst.33.3_108
8. Glück, R., Yokoyama, T.: A minimalist's reversible while language. IEICE Trans. **100–D**(5), 1026–1034 (2017). https://doi.org/10.1587/transinf.2016EDP7274
9. Haulund, T.: Design and implementation of a reversible object-oriented programming language. CoRR abs/1707.07845 (2017)
10. Hoey, J., Ulidowski, I., Yuen, S.: Reversing imperative parallel programs. In: Combined Proceedings of EXPRESS/SOS 2017, EPTCS, vol. 255, pp. 51–66 (2017). https://doi.org/10.4204/EPTCS.255.4
11. Hoey, J., Ulidowski, I., Yuen, S.: Reversing parallel programs with blocks and procedures. In: Combined Proceedings of EXPRESS/SOS 2018, EPTCS, vol. 276, pp. 69–86 (2018). https://doi.org/10.4204/EPTCS.276.7
12. Landauer, R.: Irreversibility and heat generation in the computing process. IBM J. Res. Dev. **5**(3), 183–191 (1961). https://doi.org/10.1147/rd.53.0183
13. Lanese, I., Mezzina, C.A., Tiezzi, F.: Causal-consistent reversibility. Bull. EATCS **3**, 114 (2014)
14. Lanese, I., Nishida, N., Palacios, A., Vidal, G.: CauDEr: a causal-consistent reversible debugger for Erlang. In: Gallagher, J.P., Sulzmann, M. (eds.) FLOPS 2018. LNCS, vol. 10818, pp. 247–263. Springer, Cham (2018). https://doi.org/10.1007/978-3-319-90686-7_16
15. Lanese, I., Nishida, N., Palacios, A., Vidal, G.: A theory of reversibility for Erlang. J. Log. Algebr. Methods Program. **100**, 71–97 (2018). https://doi.org/10.1016/j.jlamp.2018.06.004
16. LeBlanc, T.J., Mellor-Crummey, J.M.: Debugging parallel programs with instant replay. IEEE Trans. Comput. **36**(4), 471–482 (1987). https://doi.org/10.1109/TC.1987.1676929
17. Perumalla, K.: Introduction to Reversible Computing. CRC Press, Boca Raton (2014)
18. Phillips, I., Ulidowski, I.: Reversing algebraic process calculi. J. Log. Algebr. Methods Program. **73**(1–2), 70–96 (2007). https://doi.org/10.1016/j.jlap.2006.11.002
19. Phillips, I., Ulidowski, I.: Reversibility and asymmetric conflict in event structures. J. Log. Algebr. Methods Program. **84**(6), 781–805 (2015). https://doi.org/10.1016/j.jlamp.2015.07.004

20. Phillips, I., Ulidowski, I., Yuen, S.: A reversible process calculus and the modelling of the ERK signalling pathway. In: Glück, R., Yokoyama, T. (eds.) RC 2012. LNCS, vol. 7581, pp. 218–232. Springer, Heidelberg (2013). https://doi.org/10.1007/978-3-642-36315-3_18

21. Schordan, M., Jefferson, D., Barnes, P., Oppelstrup, T., Quinlan, D.: Reverse code generation for parallel discrete event simulation. In: Krivine, J., Stefani, J.-B. (eds.) RC 2015. LNCS, vol. 9138, pp. 95–110. Springer, Cham (2015). https://doi.org/10.1007/978-3-319-20860-2_6

22. Schordan, M., Oppelstrup, T., Jefferson, D., Barnes, Jr, P.D., Quinlan, D.J.: Automatic generation of reversible C++ code and its performance in a scalable kinetic Monte-Carlo application. In: Proceedings of SIGSIM-PADS 2016, pp. 111–122. ACM (2016). https://doi.org/10.1145/2901378.2901394

23. Schultz, U.P., Axelsen, H.B.: Elements of a reversible object-oriented language. In: Devitt, S., Lanese, I. (eds.) RC 2016. LNCS, vol. 9720, pp. 153–159. Springer, Cham (2016). https://doi.org/10.1007/978-3-319-40578-0_10

24. Ulidowski, I., Phillips, I., Yuen, S.: Reversing event structures. New Gener. Comput. **36**(3), 281–306 (2018). https://doi.org/10.1007/s00354-018-0040-8

25. Vulov, G., Hou, C., Vuduc, R.W., Fujimoto, R., Quinlan, D.J., Jefferson, D.R.: The backstroke framework for source level reverse computation applied to parallel discrete event simulation. In: Proceedings of WSC 2011, pp. 2965–2979. IEEE (2011). https://doi.org/10.1109/WSC.2011.6147998

26. Yokoyama, T., Axelsen, H., Glück, R.: Principles of a reversible programming language. In: Proceedings of Computing Frontiers, pp. 43–54. ACM (2008). https://doi.org/10.1145/1366230.1366239

27. Yokoyama, T., Glück, R.: A reversible programming language and its invertible self-interpreter. In: Proceedings of PEPM 2007, pp. 144–153. ACM (2007). https://doi.org/10.1145/1244381.1244404

28. Zeller, A.: Why Programs Fail: A Guide to Systematic Debugging, 2nd edn. Academic Press, Cambridge (2009)

Circuit Synthesis

Efficient Realization of Toffoli and NCV Circuits for IBM QX Architectures

Alexandre A. A. de Almeida[1(✉)], Gerhard W. Dueck[2],
and Alexandre César Rodrigues da Silva[1]

[1] Department of Electrical Engineering, FEIS - Univ Estadual Paulista,
Ilha Solteira, Brazil
{alexandre.amaral,alexandre.cr.silva}@unesp.br
[2] Faculty of Computer Science, University of New Brunswick,
Fredericton, Canada
gdueck@unb.ca

Abstract. The quantum computers available from IBM's QX project, implement circuits with Clifford+T gates. In order to implement Toffoli or NCV circuits in such architectures, they need to be mapped to Clifford+T gates. Another challenge is that some CNOT gates cannot be directly implemented in the IBM quantum computers and must be changed to comply with the specific architecture constrains. In this paper we propose a methodology to map Toffoli and NCV circuits such that they are compliant with a given IBM architecture. The proposed approach to accomplish this, is to find a set of low cost mappings for NCV and Toffoli circuits targeting IBM's architecture constraints. With this approach, the number of CNOT that need to be changed will be reduced, resulting in a smaller circuit regarding the number of gates. To evaluate the proposed approach, Toffoli circuits were mapped to Clifford+T and then realized on IBM's QX4 architecture. The benchmarks were compared with Toffoli circuits mapped without the methodology proposed in this paper and implemented on IBM QX4 using two different approaches. The results show that the proposed approach resulted in circuits with up to 67% fewer gates compared with Qiskit and with up to 50% fewer gates compared to a Clifford+T mapping algorithm.

Keywords: IBM QX architectures · Toffoli circuits · NCV circuits

1 Introduction

The interest in quantum computing has increased, as more quantum devices become available. It is well know that the quantum computers can perform some tasks faster than the classical computers [14]. IBM has a project that offers quantum computers that can be used to perform experiments [18]. Several different architectures are available. However, all of them implement gates from the Clifford+T gate library. The only restriction is, that not all CNOT gates are implemented.

© Springer Nature Switzerland AG 2019
M. K. Thomsen and M. Soeken (Eds.): RC 2019, LNCS 11497, pp. 131–145, 2019.
https://doi.org/10.1007/978-3-030-21500-2_8

When designing quantum circuits the gate library of the target computer must be considered. Mapping Clifford+T circuits into IBM architectures has been considered in [3,21]. Traditionally, quantum circuits have often been expressed with Toffoli gates [19]. An approach to map mixed polarity multiple controlled Toffoli gates into Clifford+T quantum circuits has also been proposed [1,5].

In this paper we propose an approach to map Toffoli and NCV circuits into IBM architectures. This approach aims to find an optimized mapping, since it has already been shown that the size of the circuit can reduce the fidelity of the output state [15]. In order to achieve that, NCV and Toffoli circuits are mapped to Clifford+T targeting IBM architecture restrictions, reducing the cost of the mapping.

The paper is structured as follows. In the next section the basic background is presented followed by Sect. 3 describing the IBM architectures. Section 4 explains the proposed approach to map the NCV and Toffoli circuits into the quantum computers. The results are shown in Sect. 5 and conclusions are presented in Sect. 6.

2   Background

2.1   Reversible Circuits

Reversible functions are bijective, i. e. each input results in a unique output pattern. Reversible circuits are composed of cascades of reversible gates. Reversible gates are described by a *target*, represented by the symbol $\oplus$ and *controls* represented by the symbols ● (positive control) or ○ (negative control). Basic reversible logic gates are NOT, CNOT, and Toffoli. Sample gates are shown in Fig. 1.

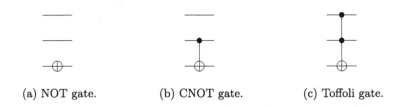

(a) NOT gate.   (b) CNOT gate.   (c) Toffoli gate.

Fig. 1. Reversible gates.

The NOT gate is only reversible gate that has no control. The *target* of the NOT gate will always be inverted. In the gates with controls, the *target* will only invert the logic value if the controls are true. For example, the *target* of a Toffoli gate will only invert if the value both controls are true ("1"). For negative controls, the control will be true with the value "0". When a set of reversible gates are used in sequence, it forms a reversible circuit. An example of a reversible circuit is shown in Fig. 2.

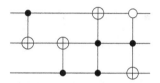

Fig. 2. Toffoli circuit.

2.2   Quantum Circuits

Quantum computation uses quantum bits (qubit) instead of classical binary bits. The main difference is that a qubit can represent the superposition of two states [12]. For quantum computation, different gates libraries exist; such as the NCV library [13] or the Clifford+T library [1]. The NCV library is composed of the gates NOT, CNOT, V and $V^\dagger$. The Clifford+T library is composed of the gates NOT, CNOT, H (Hadamard), S, $S^\dagger$, T, and $T\dagger$. Table 1 shows the gates of both libraries and the matrix representation for each gate.

Table 1. Clifford+T and NCV quantum library.

Gate	Matrix	Representation	Gate	Matrix	Representation
NOT	$\begin{pmatrix} 0 & 1 \\ 1 & 0 \end{pmatrix}$	—⊕—	CNOT	$\begin{pmatrix} 1&0&0&0 \\ 0&1&0&0 \\ 0&0&0&1 \\ 0&0&1&0 \end{pmatrix}$	
V	$\begin{pmatrix} 1&0&0&0 \\ 0&1&0&0 \\ 0&0&\frac{1+i}{2}&\frac{1-i}{2} \\ 0&0&\frac{1-i}{2}&\frac{1+i}{2} \end{pmatrix}$	$-\boxed{V}-$	$V^\dagger$	$\begin{pmatrix} 1&0&0&0 \\ 0&1&0&0 \\ 0&0&\frac{1-i}{2}&\frac{1+i}{2} \\ 0&0&\frac{1+i}{2}&\frac{1-i}{2} \end{pmatrix}$	$-\boxed{V^\dagger}-$
T	$\begin{pmatrix} 1 & 0 \\ 0 & e^{\frac{i\pi}{4}} \end{pmatrix}$	$-\boxed{T}-$	$T^\dagger$	$\begin{pmatrix} 1 & 0 \\ 0 & e^{\frac{-i\pi}{4}} \end{pmatrix}$	$-\boxed{T^\dagger}-$
S	$\begin{pmatrix} 1 & 0 \\ 0 & i \end{pmatrix}$	$-\boxed{S}-$	$S^\dagger$	$\begin{pmatrix} 1 & 0 \\ 0 & -i \end{pmatrix}$	$-\boxed{S^\dagger}-$
H	$\frac{1}{\sqrt{2}}\begin{pmatrix} 1 & 1 \\ 1 & -1 \end{pmatrix}$	$-\boxed{H}-$			

A quantum circuit can be generated with a cascade of quantum gates. An example of a quantum circuit using the Clifford+T library is shown in Fig. 3.

In the rest of the paper a Clifford+T circuit is a quantum circuit composed of gates from the Clifford+T library. A NCV circuit is a quantum circuit composed of gates from the NCV library and a Toffoli circuit is a reversible circuit composed by the gates NOT, CNOT and Toffoli.

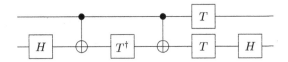

Fig. 3. Clifford+T circuit.

3 IBM Architectures

IBM's Q project [7] makes quantum computers available to researchers. The goal of the project is to facilitate experimentation with quantum circuits. Quantum computers with 5 [9] and 16 qubits [8] can be accessed to via cloud services. Along with the difference in the number of qubits, these quantum computers also differ in their architectures.

The main characteristic of these quantum computers is that only a specific set of gates can be used. All architectures accept the Pauli X, Y, and Z gates, along with the quantum gates from the Clifford+T library, which consists of NOT, CNOT, H, S, $S^{\dagger}$, T, and $T^{\dagger}$ gates. Besides the specific set of gates that can be used, IBM quantum computers also have another restriction regarding the CNOT gates. Each architecture has a specific set of CNOT gates that are implemented. For example, Fig. 4 shows the 5 qubit IBM QX4 architecture [9].

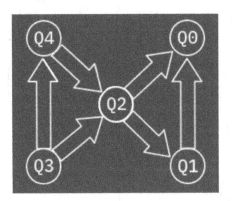

Fig. 4. IBM QX4 architecture.

The circles in Fig. 4 represent the qubits $(Q_0, Q_1, Q_2, Q_3, Q_4)$ and each arrow represents a CNOT that is available. The base of the arrow is the control qubit of the CNOT and the tip of the arrow is the target qubit. So, in this architecture with 5 qubits has only 6 (out of 20) CNOT gates. For example, a CNOT that can be implemented in the IBM QX4 architecture is the CNOT(Q_2, Q_0), *i.e.* the control in the qubit Q_2 and the target in the qubit Q_0. However, to realize the CNOT(Q_0, Q_2) a sequence of gates is needed. One possible way to realize it, is to invert the direction of the CNOT by adding 4 Hadamard gates. For each

CNOT that is not provided by the architecture, more gates must be added to the circuit, increasing its size.

The goal of this work is to find ways to map Toffoli and NCV circuits to a given IBM QX architecture with the fewest number of added gates. In the next section different types of mappings will be discussed in order to accomplish this.

4 Mappings

In order to implement a Toffoli or NCV circuit using an IBM architecture, the circuit must first be transformed to Clifford+T. Additional transformations may be required to overcome the absence of some CNOT gates. These transformations can be found in [3]. With these mappings it is possible to obtain a matrix with the cost of each CNOT gate in the target architecture. This costs are determined by the number of gates that must be added in the circuit in order to map the desire CNOT. The matrix with the costs of each CNOT for the IBM QX4 architecture from Fig. 4 is shown in Fig. 5.

$$\begin{bmatrix} - & 4 & 4 & 7 & 7 \\ 0 & - & 4 & 7 & 7 \\ 0 & 0 & - & 4 & 4 \\ 3 & 3 & 0 & - & 0 \\ 3 & 3 & 0 & 4 & - \end{bmatrix}$$

Fig. 5. Cost of each CNOT realization for the IBM QX4 architecture.

Each cell in the matrix represents the CNOT cost to be realized in the QX4 architecture. A "−" means that this CNOT does not exist. For example, the CNOT(Q_1, Q_0) has 0 cost, since it is available in the QX4 architecture. However, the CNOT(Q_0, Q_1) needs to be changed and the number of gates that must be added to the circuit in order to accomplish that (cost) is 4. The CNOT with cost 7 does not come from [3]. This mapping is a combination of the movement with cost 3 from [6] and 4 Hadamards. Figure 6 shows an example of how the CNOT with cost 7 is mapped using the CNOT(Q_0, Q_3) in the IBM QX4. The final mapping of the CNOT(Q_0, Q_3) has 8 gates, *i.e.* the circuit increased by 7 gates.

The matrix with the CNOT costs is used to find a good mapping of NCV circuits to Clifford+T.

4.1 NCV Circuit to Clifford+T

The NCV gate library is comprised of NOT, CNOT, V, and $V^\dagger$ gates. The NOT gate can be realized on the IBM QX architectures, the V and $V^\dagger$ need to be mapped. Some CNOT gates need to be mapped due to the architecture constraints. The mappings of the controlled-V and $V^\dagger$ [16] gates are shown in Fig. 7.

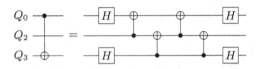

Fig. 6. CNOT(Q_0, Q_3) mapped on IBM QX4 with cost 7.

Fig. 7. Controlled-V and $V^\dagger$ gate realized with Clifford+T library.

Both mappings require 7 gates and the only difference is that the T and $T^\dagger$ gates are interchanged. As the restriction in the IBM Q architectures are the CNOT gates, the cost of this mapping is the cost of the CNOTs, e. g., if the V gate has the control in qubit Q_0 and the target in qubit Q_2 with a cost of 8. A property from [10] can be used in order to reduce this cost. This property is shown in Fig. 8.

Fig. 8. Property of CNOT with T and $T^\dagger$ gates.

With this property the V and $V^\dagger$ gates can be mapped with CNOTs in either directions without added cost, that means that the mapping can be done using the CNOT with lower cost. For example, consider a V gate with control in qubit Q_0 and the target in Q_2 in the architecture QX4. Note that this V gate can be mapped without additional cost, since the CNOT gates in the mapping can be swapped using the property presented in Fig. 8. Therefore, a matrix with the cost of each V and $V^\dagger$ gates (both having the same cost, since the CNOT gates are the same in both mappings), can be generated. This matrix is shown in Fig. 9 and only takes in account the cost of the additional CNOTs. The matrix with the cost of each V and $V^\dagger$ mapping can be used to map a NCV circuit with lower cost into IBM Q architectures.

$$\begin{bmatrix} - & 0 & 0 & 6 & 6 \\ 0 & - & 0 & 6 & 6 \\ 0 & 0 & - & 0 & 0 \\ 6 & 6 & 0 & - & 0 \\ 6 & 6 & 0 & 0 & - \end{bmatrix}$$

Fig. 9. Cost of each V and $V^\dagger$ mapping for the IBM QX4 architecture.

4.2 Toffoli to Clifford+T

In order to use Toffoli circuits in the IBM architectures they must be mapped to Clifford+T circuits. There are different alternatives to map Toffoli to a Clifford+T circuits. A possible mapping with 17 gates [10] is shown in Fig. 10.

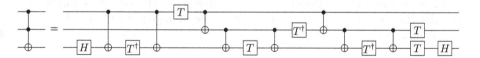

Fig. 10. Toffoli implementation with Clifford+T gates using 17 gates.

Since the CNOT gates used in the circuit must comply with the target IBM architecture, the property from Fig. 8 to swap the control and target qubits of the CNOT, without additional cost, can be used. Also, the control qubits can be swapped in order to reduce the need for CNOT transformations. Applying some optimization rules [17] to this mapping are possible.

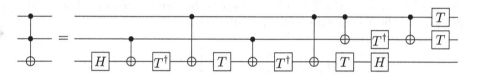

Fig. 11. Toffoli implementation with Clifford+T gates using 15 gates.

Figure 11 shows the optimized mapping presented in [11]. The mapping has 15 gates (six CNOTs), two fewer compared with the previous mapping. That means that the mapped circuit complying with IBM architectures will be smaller. However, that is not true due the characteristics of the mapping. Note that swapping the control qubits of the Toffoli will have the same structure. Thus, it has less chance for the CNOT gates be placed in the IBM architecture without additional cost. This has been verified experimentally. To solve this problem, another possible optimization for the mapping from Fig. 10 can be used. The optimized mapping was proposed in [4].

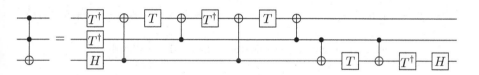

Fig. 12. Toffoli implementation with target qubit swapped.

This mapping has 15 gates (six CNOTs) with different characteristic from the previous mapping. In this case, swapping the controls qubits of the Toffoli can reduce the need of additional gates in the circuit. Therefore, this is the mapping that will be used to target Toffoli circuits to IBM architectures. The next step is to find mappings with the same structure for the Toffoli where negative controls are permitted (Fig. 12).

In order to find the mapping with the same structure for Toffoli gates with mixed polarities the T and $T^\dagger$ gates must be changed. Figure 13 shows the mapping.

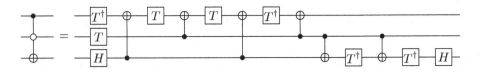

Fig. 13. Mixed control Toffoli mapped to Clifford+T.

In the mapping of Toffoli with mixed polarities swapping the controls will result in a different circuit. To solve this problem, the mapping of Toffoli with mixed polarities swapped must be found. Again, to keep the structure of the mapping unchanged, the T and $T^\dagger$ gates must be changed. Figure 14 shows the mapping of the Toffoli with mixed polarities swapped.

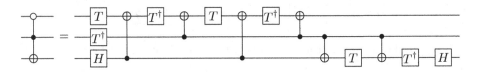

Fig. 14. Mixed control Toffoli realized with Clifford+T gates.

With both circuits of the Toffoli with mixed polarities is possible to swap the controls in order to reduce the need of additional gates. The remaining Toffoli is the one with both negative controls. As the goal is to keep the same structure and the number of gates, another combination of the T and $T^\dagger$ gates can be found to realize this Toffoli. This realization is shown in Fig. 15.

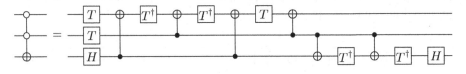

Fig. 15. Negative controls Toffoli mapped to Clifford+T.

With the mapping of each Toffoli and the costs of each CNOT, the next problem is to find the best permutation of qubits in a way that the lowest number of CNOTs must be changed in order to implement the circuit in a IBM Q architecture. For now, as the IBM QX4 has 5 qubits, it is feasible to find the best permutation by exhaustive enumeration, *i.e.* trying all 120 possible permutations and select the one with lowest cost. To scale this approach, a different way needs to be developed. After the mapping, some optimizations can be done to the Clifford+T circuits.

4.3   Optimization

Some equivalences can be used after the mapping to optimize the circuit. Since the gates T, $T^\dagger$, S, $S^\dagger$, and Z can commute with each other, the goal is to move these gates together and remove them whenever possible. Figure 16 shows some identities that can be used to remove two adjacent gates.

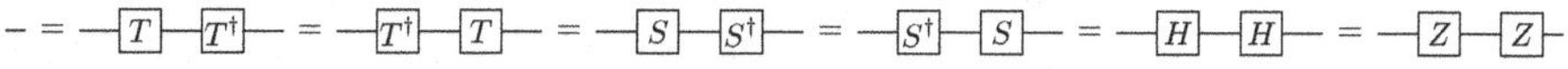

Fig. 16. Some identities used in this work.

Another possible optimization is to replace a set of gates with an equivalent one with fewer gates. Some of these equivalences used in this work are presented in Fig. 17.

The tests and benchmarks done to evaluate this methodology are presented in the next section.

5   Results

In order to evaluate the proposed methods, a series of tests were performed. For the tests the IBM QX4 architecture with 5 qubits (Fig. 4) was used to implement

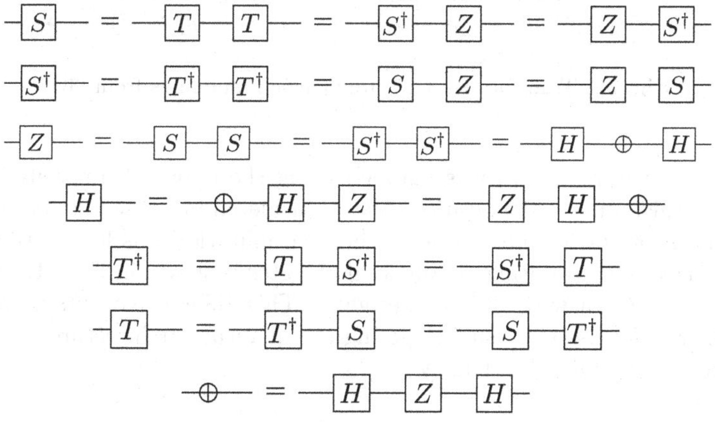

Fig. 17. Equivalences used to optimize the circuits.

the mapped circuits. The first test was the circuit 3_17 from [10]. This is a NCV circuit with 10 gates is shown in Fig. 18. The goal of this test is to check if a mapping using the approach presented in [10] combined with the CNOT mappings from [3] will result in a circuit with fewer gates than the approach presented in this paper. In [10] the authors transformed the circuit of Fig. 18 to Clifford+T without taking architectural constraints into account. The transformed circuit with 32 gates is shown in Fig. 19.

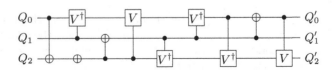

Fig. 18. Circuit 3_17a from [10].

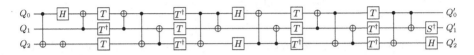

Fig. 19. Circuit 3_17e from [10].

Some of the CNOTs from Fig. 19 must be changed to comply with the IBM's QX4 constraints. Applying the CNOT mappings in the circuit and then optimizing it with the equivalences previously presented, results in a circuit with 40 gates (see Fig. 20).

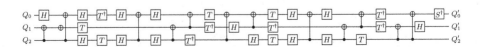

Fig. 20. Transformed 3_17 circuit using mappings from [3].

The circuit from Fig. 18 was mapped using the approach presented in this paper. For this, all the permutations were considered in order to select the best permutation for this circuit. After the best permutation was found, the circuit was optimized. The resulting circuit with 35 gates is shown in Fig. 21. Our approach found a circuit with 12.5% fewer gates. This difference occurs because our approach transforms the circuit targeting the quantum architecture, generating fewer CNOT that must be changed.

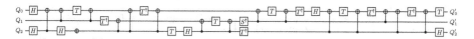

Fig. 21. Transformed 3_17 circuit using our approach.

Fig. 22. Circuit a2x_a from [10].

As a second test, a Toffoli circuit was considered. The circuit used for this test is a2x from [10]. This circuit has 2 Toffoli gates as shown in Fig. 22. Mapping the circuit using the approach from [10] result in the circuit with 30 gates that is shown in Fig. 23. Some of the CNOT must be changed to comply with the IBM QX4 constraints.

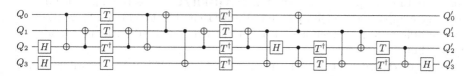

Fig. 23. Circuit a2x_e from [10].

To find the best permutation of the circuit from Fig. 23, all possible permutations with the CNOT mappings from [3] were performed and the best one was selected. The mapping for this circuit has 48 gates. Figure 24 shows the circuit. Note that the lines Q_0 and Q_3 were swapped.

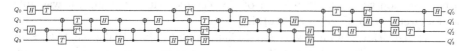

Fig. 24. Circuit a2x transformed with [10] and [3].

Applying our approach to the circuit from Fig. 22 result in the circuit presented in Fig. 25. The circuit has 36 gates, *i.e.* a reduction of 25% in the number of gates. The approach used to find this circuit was to map the Toffoli circuit to Clifford+T using the lower cost mappings for the IBM QX4 architecture. This was done for each permutation and the best one was selected.

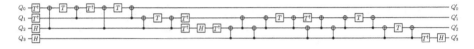

Fig. 25. Circuit a2x transformed with proposed approach.

The third test was to compare our approach with the mapping algorithms from [21] and Qiskit [2]. For this, a set of reversible circuits were used as benchmarks [20]. Since both algorithms only work with Clifford+T circuits, the reversible circuits were transformed using the Toffoli equivalences presented in Sect. 4.2. Then, the mapped circuits were realized on IBM QX4 using each algorithm. In our approach, this mapping was not necessary. The benchmarks results are shown in Table 2. The first column, **Circuit**, is the name of the benchmark. The column **#Rev** is the number of gates of the original circuit and the column **#Clif+T** is the number of gates of the Clifford+T circuit after the mapping from the reversible circuit. The column **#Std** is the number of gates using the mapping algorithm from [21] and optimized with Qiskit. The fourth column, **#Qiskit**, is the number of gates of the mapped circuit using Qiskit. The column **#Our** is the number of gates of the mapped circuit using the approach presented in this paper. The column, **%(Qiskit/Our)**, is the difference in percentage comparing the Qiskit with our approach. The las column **%(Std/Our)** is the difference in percentage of our approach compared with the Standalone algorithm optimized.

Due to the efficient Toffoli mappings to Clifford+T, it was possible to find permutations that resulted in good cost mappings. Our approach was able to find permutations with lower costs by mapping the Toffoli gates to Clifford+T circuit targeting the IBM QX4 architecture constraints. Circuits with up to 67% fewer gates compared to the Qiskit mapping have been obtained and compared with the Standalone algorithm, circuits with up to 50% fewer gates. For example, the circuit *mod5d2_70* with 8 gates has two Toffoli gates. After mapping this circuit to Clifford+T it resulted in a circuit with 36 gates (column **#Clif+T**). The gate count may increase, since this mapping did not consider any constraints of the IBM QX4. However, our approach permutes the qubits in order to find a permutation with a lower number of CNOTs requiring mappings, it was able find a circuit with 45 gates after optimization.

Our algorithm obtained very good results due the fact that it calculates all possible permutations of a circuit and selects the best one. For this approach to work with an architecture with more qubits, an algorithm to find a "good" permutation must be developed. It is not tractable to find the "best" permutation. So, the next step of this work is to develop algorithms to find a good permutation in order to obtain low cost mappings for Toffoli and NCV circuits with more qubits.

Table 2. Reversible benchmark circuits mapped to IBM QX4.

Circuit	#Rev	#Clif+T	#Std	#Qiskit	#Our	%(Qiskit/Our)	%(Std/Our)
mod5d2_70	8	36	90	124	45	63.71	50.00
alu-v0_26	9	79	146	172	76	55.81	47.95
4mod5-v1_22	5	19	44	65	23	64.62	47.73
one-two-three-v2_100	8	64	111	177	63	64.41	43.24
alu-v1_28	7	35	70	100	40	60.00	42.86
alu-v3_35	7	35	66	112	40	64.29	39.39
alu-v4_37	7	35	66	87	40	54.02	39.39
mod5d1_63	7	21	46	52	28	46.15	39.13
alu-v3_34	7	49	79	111	49	55.86	37.97
4mod5-v0_18	9	65	116	174	73	58.05	37.07
mod5mils_65	5	33	64	76	41	46.05	35.94
4mod5-v0_19	5	33	63	52	41	21.15	34.92
alu-v0_27	6	34	66	88	43	51.14	34.85
4mod5-v1_23	8	64	112	155	74	52.26	33.93
alu-v1_29	7	35	66	136	44	67.65	33.33
4mod7-v1_96	13	153	255	384	171	55.47	32.94
4mod7-v0_95	12	152	255	287	171	40.42	32.94
one-two-three-v3_101	8	64	115	122	78	36.07	32.17
rd32_272	6	48	90	112	62	44.64	31.11
mod5mils_71	5	33	59	69	41	40.58	30.51
mini-alu_167	18	270	425	528	296	43.94	30.35
4_49_17	12	82	148	167	104	37.72	29.73
4gt11_82	12	26	70	54	50	7.41	28.57
decod24-v0_38	6	48	72	133	52	60.90	27.78
4gt11_83	8	22	51	51	37	27.45	27.45
4gt11_84	3	17	27	29	20	31.03	25.93
alu-v2_33	7	35	51	85	38	55.29	25.49
rd32_271	9	79	118	181	88	51.38	25.42
4gt13_92	6	62	73	61	55	9.84	24.66
aj-e11_165	16	142	234	376	178	52.66	23.93
one-two-three-v0_98	11	137	215	234	164	29.91	23.72
mod5d2_64	8	50	84	116	65	43.97	22.62
decod24-v2_43	6	48	63	105	49	53.33	22.22
4gt11-v1_85	4	18	24	22	19	13.64	20.83
decod24-v3_45	13	139	197	326	157	51.84	20.30
4gt13-v1_93	7	63	69	170	55	67.65	20.29
4gt5_77	10	122	166	232	133	42.67	19.88
hwb5_55	39	389	544	529	437	17.39	19.67
ham3_103	4	18	21	22	17	22.73	19.05
hwb4_49	23	219	342	371	280	24.53	18.13
mod10_171	19	229	319	441	262	40.59	17.87
sf_275	17	185	269	310	221	28.71	17.84
4gt5_75	8	78	106	176	88	50.00	16.98
alu-v2_31	31	423	585	843	488	42.11	16.58
decod24-v1_41	9	79	109	260	91	65.00	16.51
4mod7-v0_94	12	152	204	233	171	26.61	16.18
hwb4_52	11	53	94	109	79	27.52	15.96
one-two-three-v1_99	11	123	171	215	144	33.02	15.79
mod10_176	13	167	238	359	205	42.90	13.87
3_17_14	6	34	35	40	31	22.50	11.43
rd32-v1_68	5	33	39	67	35	47.76	10.26

6   Conclusions

To implement Toffoli and NCV circuits in a IBM QX architecture, they need to be mapped to a Clifford+T circuits. This is due to the fact that quantum computers available from IBM Q project only implement circuits with Clifford+T gates. Along with that, some CNOTs cannot be directly implemented and must be changed to comply with the architecture constraints.

Therefore, in this paper we present a methodology to map Toffoli and NCV circuits to IBM Q architectures. This methodology consists in finding a low cost mapping of NCV and Toffoli circuits to quantum computers and use it to map the circuits.

To evaluate the proposed approach we used the IBM QX4 architecture with five qubits and a set of reversible circuits. The reversible circuits were mapped to a Clifford+T circuit and then applied in two different mapping strategies in order to be compared with our approach. Experimental results show that the proposed approach can find circuits with up to 67% fewer gates than the ones mapped to Clifford+T and applied in Qiskit. Also, compared with the algorithm Standalone from [21] then applied into Qiskit for optimizations, our approach found circuits with up to 49% fewer gates. These results were possible because the permutation with lower mapping cost were found. The next step is to develop an algorithm to find a good (not necessarily best) permutation without the need to inspect all of them. The key is to find good heuristics to guide the search. With such an algorithm the proposed approach can be used to map Toffoli and NCV circuits to architectures with more qubits.

Acknowledgment. The authors would like to thank the anonymous reviewers for the directions to improve the quality of this paper. The authors are grateful for the support of CAPES PDSE process $n°$ 88881.189547/2018-01, CNPq process $n°$ 309193/2015-0, and NSERC. The authors also thanks the Department of Electrical Engineering of São Paulo State University (Unesp), School of Engineering of Ilha Solteira. This study was financed in part by the Coordenação de Aperfeiçoamento de Pessoal de Nível Superior - Brasil (CAPES) - Finance Code 001.

References

1. Abdessaied, N., Amy, M., Soeken, M., Drechsler, R.: Technology mapping of reversible circuits to clifford+t quantum circuits. In: 2016 IEEE 46th International Symposium on Multiple-Valued Logic (ISMVL), pp. 150–155, May 2016. https://doi.org/10.1109/ISMVL.2016.33
2. Aleksandrowicz, G., et al.: Qiskit: An open-source framework for quantum computing (2019). https://doi.org/10.5281/zenodo.2562110
3. de Almeida, A.A.A., Dueck, G.W., da Silva, A.C.R.: Efficient realizations of CNOT gates in IBM's quantum computers. In: Eighth International Symposium on Embedded Computing and System Design (ISED), Kochi, India, December 2018
4. Amy, M., Maslov, D., Mosca, M., Roetteler, M.: A meet-in-the-middle algorithm for fast synthesis of depth-optimal quantum circuits. IEEE Trans. Comput.-Aided Des. Integr. Circuits Syst. **32**(6), 818–830 (2013). https://doi.org/10.1109/TCAD.2013.2244643

5. Biswal, L., Bandyopadhyay, C., Chattopadhyay, A., Wille, R., Drechsler, R., Rahaman, H.: Nearest-neighbor and fault-tolerant quantum circuit implementation. In: 2016 IEEE 46th International Symposium on Multiple-Valued Logic (ISMVL), pp. 156–161, May 2016. https://doi.org/10.1109/ISMVL.2016.48
6. Dueck, G.W., Pathak, A., Rahman, M.M., Shukla, A., Banerjee, A.: Optimization of circuits for IBM's five-qubit quantum computers. In: Euromicro Conference on Digital System Design, Prague, Czech Republic, pp. 680–684, August 2018
7. IBM: IBM Q. https://www.research.ibm.com/ibm-q/. Accessed 10 Feb 2019
8. IBM: IBM Q16 Rueschlikon. https://github.com/QISKit/qiskit-backend-information/blob/master/backends/rueschlikon/V1/README.md. Accessed 15 Feb 2019
9. IBM: IBM Q5 Tenerife. https://github.com/Qiskit/ibmq-device-information/tree/master/backends/tenerife/V1. Accessed 28 Jan 2019
10. Miller, D.M., Soeken, M., Drechsler, R.: Mapping NCV circuits to optimized Clifford+T circuits. In: Yamashita, S., Minato, S. (eds.) RC 2014. LNCS, vol. 8507, pp. 163–175. Springer, Cham (2014). https://doi.org/10.1007/978-3-319-08494-7_13
11. Nam, Y., Ross, N.J., Su, Y., Childs, A.M., Maslov, D.: Automated optimization of large quantum circuits with continuous parameters. npj Quantum Inf. **4**(1), 23 (2018). https://doi.org/10.1038/s41534-018-0072-4
12. Nielsen, M.A., Chuang, I.L.: Quantum Computation and Quantum Information: 10th Anniversary Edition, 10th edn. Cambridge University Press, New York (2011)
13. Sasanian, Z., Miller, D.M.: NCV realization of MCT gates with mixed controls. In: Proceedings of 2011 IEEE Pacific Rim Conference on Communications, Computers and Signal Processing, pp. 567–571, August 2011. https://doi.org/10.1109/PACRIM.2011.6032956
14. Shor, P.W.: Polynomial-time algorithms for prime factorization and discrete logarithms on a quantum computer. SIAM J. Comput. **26**(5), 1484–1509 (1997)
15. Sisodia, M., Shukla, A., Pathak, A.: Experimental realization of nondestructive discrimination of Bell states using a five-qubit quantum computer. Phys. Lett. A **381**(46), 3860–3874 (2017)
16. Soeken, M., Miller, D.M., Drechsler, R.: Quantum circuits employing roots of the Pauli matrices. Phys. Rev. A **88**, 042322 (2013). https://doi.org/10.1103/PhysRevA.88.042322
17. Soeken, M., Thomsen, M.K.: White dots do matter: rewriting reversible logic circuits. In: Dueck, G.W., Miller, D.M. (eds.) RC 2013. LNCS, vol. 7948, pp. 196–208. Springer, Heidelberg (2013). https://doi.org/10.1007/978-3-642-38986-3_16
18. Spišiak, M., Kollár, J.: Quantum programming: a review. In: 2017 IEEE 14th International Scientific Conference on Informatics, pp. 353–358, November 2017. https://doi.org/10.1109/INFORMATICS.2017.8327274
19. Toffoli, T.: Reversible computing. Tech memo MIT/LCS/TM-151, MIT Lab for Comp. Sci (1980)
20. Wille, R., Große, D., Teuber, L., Dueck, G.W., Drechsler, R.: RevLib: An online resource for reversible functions and reversible circuits. In: International Symposium on Multiple Valued Logic, pp. 220–225 (2008). http://www.revlib.org
21. Zulehner, A., Paler, A., Wille, R.: Efficient mapping of quantum circuits to the IBM QX architectures. In: Design Automation and Test in Europe (2018)

Automatically Translating Quantum Programs from a Subset of Common Gates to an Adiabatic Representation

Malcolm Regan, Brody Eastwood, Mahita Nagabhiru, and Frank Mueller[✉] [iD]

Department of Computer Science, North Carolina State University, Raleigh, USA
mueller@cs.ncsu.edu

Abstract. Adiabatic computing with two degrees of freedom of 2-local Hamiltonians has been theoretically shown to be equivalent to the gate model of universal quantum computing. But today's quantum annealers, namely D-Wave's 2000Q platform, only provide a 2-local Ising Hamiltonian abstraction with a single degree of freedom. This raises the question what subset of gate programs can be expressed as quadratic unconstrained binary problems (QUBOs) on the D-Wave. The problem is of interest because gate-based quantum platforms are currently limited to 20 qubits while D-Wave provides 2,000 qubits. However, when transforming entire gate circuits into QUBOs, additional qubits will be required.

The objective of this work is to determine a subset of quantum gates suitable for transformation into single-degree 2-local Ising Hamiltonians under a common qubit base representation such that they comprise a compound circuit suitable for pure quantum computation, i.e., without having to switch between classical and quantum computing for different bases. To this end, this work contributes, for the first time, a fully automated method to translate quantum gate circuits comprised of a subset of common gates expressed as an IBM Qiskit program to single-degree 2-local Ising Hamiltonians, which are subsequently embedded in the D-Wave 2000Q chimera graph. These gate elements are placed in the chimera graph and augmented by constraints that enforce inter-gate logical relationships, resulting in an annealer embedding that completely characterizes the overall gate circuit. Annealer embeddings for several example quantum gate circuits are then evaluated on D-Wave 2000Q hardware.

Keywords: Quantum computation · Quantum annealing · Quantum gate circuits · Adiabatic computation

1 Introduction

Recent advances in quantum hardware have resulted in the first systems becoming publicly available. On one hand, gate-based quantum computers have been

This work was funded in part by NSF grants 1525609 and 1813004.

© Springer Nature Switzerland AG 2019
M. K. Thomsen and M. Soeken (Eds.): RC 2019, LNCS 11497, pp. 146–161, 2019.
https://doi.org/10.1007/978-3-030-21500-2_9

designed, such as the IBM Q, Rigetti's Aspen, or IonQ's systems using using superconducting transmons or ion tubes [2,11]. On the other hand, quantum annealing has been promoted by D-Wave's RF-Squids [6]. Both types of systems are available in the cloud and can be programmed using Python, e.g., via IBM's Qiskit in the IBM Q Experience [1], Rigetti's Forest DSK in their Quantum Cloud Services [2], and D-wave's Ocean Software [9] accessible via the cloud through D-Wave Leap [8].

It was shown that adiabatic quantum computing can solve the same problems as gate-based (universal) quantum computing given at least two degrees of freedom for 2-local Hamiltonian [3,5,10]. D-Wave supports a 2-local Ising Hamiltonian with a single degree of freedom in their 2000Q system, which is why it is believed to only solve a subset of the problems that can be expressed by gate-based (universal) quantum machines. In fact, D-Wave's programming abstraction is specifically catering to optimization problems while gate-based abstractions map to quantum gates, e.g., by expressing programs as circuits of gates in OpenQASM [7].

In 2014, Warren outlined how a set of universal quantum gates could be realized in adiabatic form using D-Wave's annealing abstraction [12]. This is demonstrated, among others, for C-NOT, Toffoli (CC-NOT), Swap and C-Swap (Fredkin) gates in a $\{0,1\}$ base of qubit states, and for the Hadamard gate in a two-vector $\{|0\rangle, |1\rangle\}$ base.

In this paper, we contribute a framework to automatically translate gate-based circuits into adiabatic single-degree 2-local Hamiltonians expressed as quadratic unconstrained binary optimization problems (QUBOs). We constrain ourselves to a subset of quantum gates in the common $\{0,1\}$ base so that an entire circuit can be expressed as a single QUBO. This allows us, given a Qiskit program suitable for IBM Q execution, to generate an equivalent Ocean program that can execute on a D-Wave machine. Such a translation is significant since today's gate computers are constrained to 20 qubits for IBM Q (or 19 qubits for Rigetti's available platform), while D-Wave supports around 2,000 qubits on their latest publicly available platform, which enables experimentation at a different scale.

The objectives of this work are (1) to identify a subset of gates suitable for translation, (2) to demonstrate the feasibility of auto-translating entire circuits of these quantum gates to adiabatic programs, (3) to assess the cost of ancilla qubits required to express gates in QUBOs, (4) to find an embedding into D-Wave's Chimera graph for a circuit and assess its cost in extra qubits and circuit lines/wires, and (5) to compare hardware experimentation results with the expected ground state to determine the annealer's ability identify coherent solutions for circuit embedding. We contribute an automated method for encoding quantum gate circuits comprising X, C-NOT, Toffoli, Swap and C-Swap (Fredkin) gates as single-degree 2-local Ising Hamiltonians (QUBOs) and embed the resulting representation in the D-Wave 2000Q chimera graph. We provide the single-degree 2-local Ising QUBOs with $K_{4,4}$ connectivity, a compete bipartite graph with 8 vertices corresponding to D-Wave's unit cell, for which ground state configurations logically characterize quantum X, C-NOT, Toffoli, and Swap gates. Notice that we do not provide a translation for the Hadamard gate, H, as it requires a different base of qubit states than the above, i.e., one cannot directly embed H in the same circuit. Instead, one would have to transition between quantum and classical programs, which collapses the quantum state and thus defeats the purpose of quantum computing in first place. These gates supported by our translation constitute building blocks that are placed in the chimera graph and augmented by constraints that enforce inter-gate logical relationships. The resulting annealer embedding is equivalent to the corresponding gate circuit in terms of its computational functionality. In experimental results, we evaluate annealer embeddings for several sample quantum gate circuits on D-Wave hardware.

2   Design and Implementation

In adiabatic computing, the comprehensive state of qubits is annealed via a combination of tunneling and entanglement toward a ground (energy) state. There may be more than one such state, and tunneling aids in not getting stuck in local minima but rather find other ground states, subject to practical considerations of adiabatic computing, such as experienced by near absolute zero Kelvin operation and hardware-induced errors in any practical quantum devices. To this end, D-Wave supports a single-degree 2-local Ising Hamiltonian

$$\mathcal{H}(t) = -\sum\nolimits_{i=0}^{N-2} \sum\nolimits_{j=0}^{N-1} J_{i,j}\sigma_i\sigma_j - \sum\nolimits_{i=0}^{N-1} S_i\sigma_i - \Gamma(t)\sum\nolimits_{i=0}^{N-1} \sigma_i$$

with N qubits $\sigma_i \in \{-1,1\}$ as vertices, coupler strengths $J_{ij} \in \{-2,2\}$ that connect σ_i, σ_j and biases (weights) S_i per qubit such that the amplitude, $\Gamma(t)$, of the third term, the traverse field is gradually decreased to drive the aggregate of the first and second term into a ground state, $\mathcal{H}_0$.

A 2-local Hamiltonian is expressed as quadratic unconstrained binary optimization problem (QUBO) that describes a ground state and is subsequently mapped onto D-Wave's 2000Q embedding of qubits respecting the connectivity of qubit pairs. Specifically, D-Wave's inner cell is a $K_{4,4}$ bipartite graph to which we map quantum gates. This embedding of a gate is described in Sect. 2.1.

The $K_{4,4}$ unit cells are arranged in a 2-dimensional 16×16 grid in a Chimera graph with sparse horizontal and vertical couplings between equivalent qubits of neighboring unit cells. The Chimera graph provides the means to connect unit cells representing a quantum gate with each other to create the desired quantum circuit of a given gate-based quantum program, which is described in Sect. 2.2.

We then develop an automatic transition from Qiskit programs representing circuits of quantum gates to an equivalent adiabatic representation in a systematic manner in Sect. 2.3. This translator leverages the class and file structure of IBM's open-source Qiskit API for definitions of quantum gate circuits due to its familiarity and ease-of-use. Specifically, a Qiskit translator was created so that any Qiskit script defining a quantum gate circuit could be used to generate and run a corresponding annealer embedding.

2.1   2-Local Ising Hamiltonians for $K_{4,4}$ Embeddings of Quantum Gates

Gate embeddings for a $\sigma_i \in \{0, 1\}$ base, depicted in Fig. 4, were designed to have a ground state characterizing the corresponding quantum gate's logical function. The process by which the gate embeddings used in this project were determined is described below in terms of the C-NOT gate as an example.

The C-NOT gate operates on 2 qubits, a control qubit and a target qubit. Because the target qubit is potentially altered by the C-NOT operation, its value after the C-NOT operation must be considered distinctly. Accordingly, the 8 possible configurations of 3 binary variables—q_0, q_1, and q_2—are shown in the truth table on the left of Fig. 1. Arbitrarily, these variables are designated to represent the control qubit value, the value of the target qubit before the C-NOT operation, and the value of the target qubit after the C-NOT operation, respectively.

ctl q_0	targ q_1	out q_2	
0	0	0	$0 = G$
0	0	1	$S_2 > G$
0	1	0	$S_1 > G$
0	1	1	$S_1 + S_2 + J_{12} = G$
1	0	0	$S_0 > G$
1	0	1	$S_0 + S_2 + J_{02} = G$
1	1	0	$S_0 + S_1 + J_{01} = G$
1	1	1	$S_0 + S_1 + S_2 + J_{01} + J_{02} + J_{12} > G$

Fig. 1. Truth table showing all possible logical combinations of 3 binary variables and the corresponding Ising Hamiltonian constraints for a C-NOT operation. Ground state configurations are highlighted in green. (Color figure online)

Of the 8 possible configurations, only 4 correspond to a qubit transformation performed by a C-NOT gate. As such, it is these configurations that we require to correspond to the lowest energy of the Ising Hamiltonian. This results in a set of constraints—one for each row of the truth table shown in Fig. 1—in terms of 2-local Ising Hamiltonian variables, S_i and J_{ij}, and ground state energy, G. These constraints are shown on the right of Fig. 1. S_i and J_{ij} are referred to as qubit biases and coupler strengths, respectively.

These inequalities were then solved under the constraint that the solution comprised only integer values between -10 and 10. (Notice that this range is later mapped to some $S_i \in \{-2, 2\}$ to meet the D-Wave embedding constraints.) If a given set of constraints had no solution, as in the case of the C-NOT, an ancilla variable was added as shown in Fig. 2 and a system of constraints was again generated and a solution was sought.

The graph of the resulting C-NOT Ising Hamiltonian is shown on the left of Fig. 3. This graph however, is not compatible to D-Wave's chimera graph. Recall

ctl q_0	targ q_1	out q_2	anc q_a	
0	0	0	0	$0 = G$
0	0	0	1	$S_a > G$
0	0	1	0	$S_2 > G$
0	0	1	1	$S_2 + S_a + J_{2a} > G$
0	1	0	0	$S_1 > G$
0	1	0	1	$S_1 + S_a + J_{1a} > G$
0	1	1	0	$S_1 + S_2 + J_{12} = G$
0	1	1	1	$S_1 + S_2 + S_a + J_{12} + J_{1a} + J_{2a} > G$
1	0	0	0	$S_0 > G$
1	0	0	1	$S_0 + S_a + J_{0a} > G$
1	0	1	0	$S_0 + S_2 + J_{02} = G$
1	0	1	1	$S_0 + S_2 + S_a + J_{02} + J_{0a} + J_{2a} > G$
1	1	0	0	$S_0 + S_1 + J_{01} > G$
1	1	0	1	$S_0 + S_1 + S_a + J_{01} + J_{0a} + J_{1a} = G$
1	1	1	0	$S_0 + S_1 + S_2 + J_{01} + J_{02} + J_{12} > G$
1	1	1	1	$S_0 + S_1 + S_2 + S_a + J_{01} + J_{02} + J_{12} + J_{0a} + J_{1a} + J_{2a} > G$

Fig. 2. Truth table showing all possible logical combinations of binary variables after an ancilla variable is added and the corresponding Ising Hamiltonian constraints for a C-NOT operation. Ground state configurations are highlighted in green. (Color figure online)

that the chimera graph is a 16 by 16 array of $K_{4,4}$ unit cells whose right-hand nodes are connected horizontally and left-hand nodes are connected vertically. Therefore, the graphs obtained by solving the system of constraints were modified into logically equivalent graphs conforming to the $K_{4,4}$ connectivity of a unit cell. This was done by splitting qubits requiring connections having no corresponding coupler in the chimera graph. For example, as shown on the left of Fig. 3, the vertical connections, J_{1a} and J_{02}, have no physical counterpart in the chimera graph. To remedy this, one of the logical qubits being coupled through these connectors can be represented by two physical qubits, one on each side of the graph, rendering the all the connections physically realizable. On the right of Fig. 3 is the graph that results from splitting q_a into q_a and $q_{a'}$ and q_2 into q_2 and $q_{2'}$. Qubit biases for these new qubits are increased from their original value by a positive offset, δ, and the coupling strength between them is set to the negative of the bias of the original qubit minus 2δ. This ensures that, when both physical qubits are in sync, the embedding is equivalent to the corresponding configuration in the unmodified graph. For example, referring to the graph on the right of Fig. 3, when both q_a and $q_{a'}$ are equal to 1, an energy of

$$(S_a + \delta) + (S_a + \delta) + (-S_a - 2\delta) = S_a$$

is contributed to the system. This is the same energy contribution made to the system represented by the graph on the left of Fig. 3 when q_a is equal to 1. Further, splitting qubits in this way ensures that the energy of any new logical configurations introduced by the new qubits are above the ground state by at least δ. In this work, δ was set to 5.

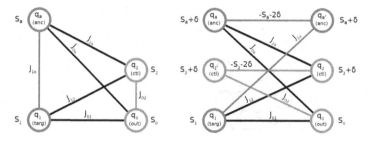

Fig. 3. (Left) Ising Hamiltonian graph obtained from system of constraints. Sections highlighted in green and orange are not compatible with D-Wave's chimera graph. (Right) Logically equivalent graph modified to conform to chimera graph unit cell connectivity. Sections highlighted in green and orange indicate the modifications to the graph. (Color figure online)

Finally, to ease the process of embedding the overall gate circuit (described in Sect. 2.2), we also required that any qubit representing a gate input be on one side of the graph and any qubit that could be used as an input to a later gate be on the opposite side of the graph. For example, the Toffoli gate pictured in Fig. 4(c) has 3 inputs (Target, Control 1, and Control 2) and 3 outputs (Out, Control 1, and Control 2). The value of the Control qubits are not transformed by the gate and as such must be present on both sides of the graph. This ensures that the most recent state of these qubits are easily accessible to other, later gates. The value of the Target qubit is transformed by the gate into the value of the Out qubit. As such, the Target qubit is required to be present on the input side of the gate embedding and the Out qubit is required to be on the output side of the gate embedding. In the Toffoli embedding, the Out qubit also happens to be present on the input side, but this is for the purpose of making the connections needed to form a valid gate embedding.

The above process was carried out to determine embeddings for X, Toffoli, and Swap gates. A 2-local Ising Hamiltonian assuming full graph connectivity for the C-NOT gate was sufficiently determined in a previous work [12]. This Ising Hamiltonian was used as a starting point and modified to conform to the criteria described above. A 2-local Ising Hamiltonian assuming full graph connectivity for the C-Swap function was also determined in this work. However, the graph of this Hamiltonian could not be modified into a form meeting the criteria described above. Specifically, configuring the connections comprising the full connectivity graph to conform to chimera graph connectivity requires at least 2 unit cells. Also, satisfying our requirement that gate inputs and outputs be present on certain sides of a cell requires the use of more resources, and further removes the symmetries that the circuit embedding algorithm relies on. Due to these problems, the C-Swap gate was implemented with 2 C-NOT embeddings and a Toffoli embedding, connected as illustrated on the right of Fig. 5.

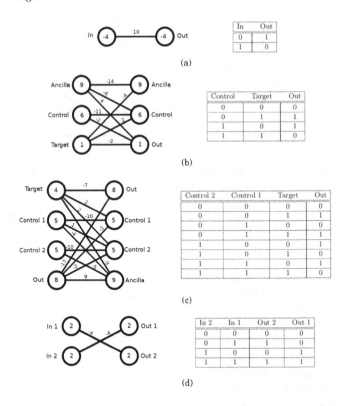

(a)

In	Out
0	1
1	0

(b)

Control	Target	Out
0	0	0
0	1	1
1	0	1
1	1	0

(c)

Control 2	Control 1	Target	Out
0	0	0	0
0	0	1	1
0	1	0	0
0	1	1	1
1	0	0	1
1	0	1	0
1	1	0	1
1	1	1	0

(d)

In 2	In 1	Out 2	Out 1
0	0	0	0
0	1	1	0
1	0	0	1
1	1	1	1

Fig. 4. (Left) Embeddings for (a) X, (b) C-NOT, (c) Toffoli, and (d) Swap gates illustrated to show qubit names, qubit biases, and coupler strengths. (Right) Ground state configurations of logical variables.

Fig. 5. (Left) C-Swap gate symbol with qubit names indicated (Right) Functionally equivalent circuit used to implement C-Swap gate.

2.2 Embedding the Problem in the Chimera Graph

Determining an optimal embedding for an arbitrary annealer problem is NP-complete and the heuristics commonly used to determine working embeddings can often fail when the problem is complex. We implement a process that exploits properties of quantum gate circuits and the symmetries of the gate embeddings determined above to reliably construct working embeddings for gate circuits.

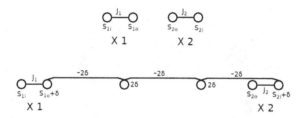

Fig. 6. Chaining example. (Top) Illustration of gate elements X1 and X2 showing names of qubit biases and coupler strengths. Qubits whose biases are denoted with the letter "i" are input qubits and those denoted with the letter "o" are output qubits. (Bottom) An embedding of the identity function resulting from chaining the output of X1 to the input of X2.

Chaining. Logical connections between gate embeddings are made via "chains" of qubits that encode a single logical qubit. A chain is created by assigning the biases of the qubits that comprise the chain and the strengths of the couplers between them similarly to how they were assigned when splitting a logical qubit (Fig. 3). Specifically, each section of the chain is constructed by offsetting the biases of the qubits being connected by δ and assigning to the corresponding coupler a strength of -2δ. This is done one section at a time, from the earlier gate to the later gate. An example of the resulting chain is shown in Fig. 6 for the case of two X gates connected by an identity function.

Chimera Graph Cell Designations. The "signal flow" of a gate circuit naturally lends itself as an organizing principle for the problem embedding. To best translate the notion of a signal flow to the Chimera graph, gate embeddings are placed as shown in Fig. 7. The connectivity between adjacent gate embeddings is highlighted and cell designations are indicated. Each gate embedding has corresponding sections of the graph designated for delivering chains to non-adjacent gates (chain output column) and assembling its inputs (input assembly cell) denoted in Fig. 7 as CO and IA, respectively.

Gate embeddings, designed to have inputs and outputs on either side of a single bipartite cell, are reflected depending on whether the gate number is even or odd. Specifically, if the gate number is even, the output column of the gate embedding is on the left and the input column is on the right. If the gate number is odd, the input column is on the left and the output column is on the right.

If an input of a given gate is dependent on an output of a previous adjacent gate, the rows of the new gate embedding are permuted to align its input with the previous output and a chain is made through its input assembly cell. Rows of unit cells can be permuted without change to the network topology of the gate embedding, which makes connections between adjacent gates trivial.

If an input of a gate is dependent on an output of a previous non-adjacent gate, a chain is routed from the chain output column of the earlier gate through empty positions on the Chimera graph to the input assembly cell of the new

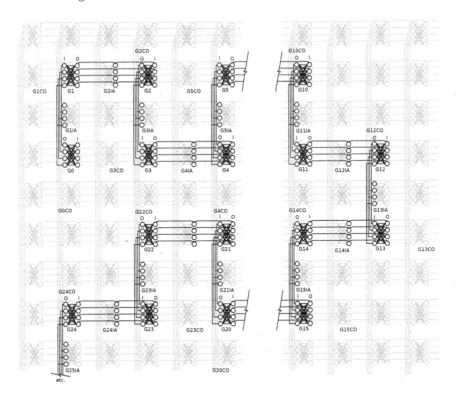

Fig. 7. Chimera graph cell designations for gate circuit embeddings. G1, G2, etc. = Gate 1, Gate 2, etc.; IA = Input assembly cell; CO = Chain out column; I/O = Input/Output column

gate. The role of chain out column and input assembly cell designations in chain routing are illustrated in Fig. 8. New gates first align their rows with connections to adjacent gates, then non-adjacent gates. Rows with no dependencies are assigned a position in the bipartite cell last.

2.3   Implementing the Qiskit to D-Wave Ocean Translator

Qiskit is an open-source Python API developed for the implementation and execution (or simulation) of quantum gate circuits on IBM quantum computers [1]. As this API provides a convenient and intuitive framework with which quantum gate circuits can be defined, this translator project was built within its class structure. This was achieved with the objective that any Qiskit script defining a quantum gate circuit could be used to generate and run a corresponding annealer embedding. Our approach allows a gate circuit in Qiskit to be executed (a) on IBM Q quantum hardware, (b) in simulation using IBM's APIs, or, after translation, (c) on D-Wave's quantum annealer hardware. Given IBM Q's constraint to at most 20 qubits at this time, Qiskit programs requiring more than 20 qubits,

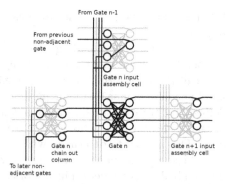

From Gate n-1

From previous
non-adjacent
gate

Gate n input
assembly cell

Gate n
chain out
column

Gate n

Gate n+1 input
assembly cell

To later non-
adjacent gates

Fig. 8. Detail illustrating role of input assembly cells and chain out columns in making inter-gate connections

which may be very slow in simulation, can be executed on D-Wave hardware in a fraction of the corresponding simulation time.

Our translator is implemented as new backend to the Qiskit source code in terms of the AnnealerGraph class, whose methods handle the configuration, placement, and chaining together of gate embeddings. An instance of AnnealerGraph was added as an attribute to Qiskit's QuantumCircuit class, which is a central object in the Qiskit framework, whose attributes are operated on or used by every Qiskit function relevant to this project.

In a Qiskit script, an instance of QuantumCircuit is initialized as a collection of QuantumRegister and ClassicalRegister instances. A gate circuit is then defined via QuantumCircuit methods that operate on QuantumRegister objects.

Our translator thus implements a modified version of Qiskit, where an AnnealerGraph instance is initialized in the QuantumCircuit initialization function and builds data structures needed to construct an annealer embedding from Qiskit instructions. AnnealerGraph has a dictionary attribute, qubits, in which each qubit in the gate circuit, assigned a name in the initialization function of QuantumCircuit, has a corresponding entry (with keys corresponding to Qiskit register names). This dictionary keeps track of which annealer graph nodes are assigned to a given logical qubit, in what order these nodes were assigned, and whether or not the final state of this qubit is considered an output (i.e., whether the measure function was used on this qubit). There is also an entry in qubits that keeps track of annealer graph nodes that do not correspond to logical qubits.

Annealer graph nodes, identified by D-Wave Ocean as numbers, are added to the lists comprising the qubits dictionary as gates and chains between gates are added to the graph. Dictionary objects used as the input arguments to the D-Wave Ocean embedding compilation function, qubitbiases and couplerstrengths, are also built as gates and chains are assigned to the graph. The qubitbiases dictionary contains as keys a number identifying a given node in the chimera graph. The value associated with a given key is the bias itself. The couplerstrengths dictionary contains as keys a tuple identifying the two qubits being coupled (smaller number first). The value associated with a given key is the coupler strength.

AnnealerGraph contains methods for adding the circuit's gate elements (addX, addCNOT, etc.). Therefore, Qiskit functions for adding gates to a quantum circuit were modified to call the appropriate AnnealerGraph method in lieu of the original Qiskit code. In general, AnnealerGraph methods for adding gate elements to the circuit embedding are structured as follows. AnnealerGraph has as an attribute a counter that indicates how many gates have already been placed in the circuit embedding. This is used to determine where in the graph the new gate is placed per the cell designations described in Sect. 2.2. Next, connections to previously placed gate embeddings are determined. For each input in the gate, the last element in the qubit dictionary entry for the corresponding gate circuit qubit indicates the most recent state of that of that qubit and its position. If its position is in an adjacent gate, the row containing the corresponding input of the new gate is placed in the unit cell to align it with its connection in the previous gate. These qubits are then connected with a chain through the new gate embedding's input assembly cell. If the new gate requires a connection from a non-adjacent gate, a chain is made from the last instance of the qubit to the input assembly cell of the new gate. The input of the new gate is then assigned a position in the gate cell aligned with the position of its connection. Once gate qubits with dependencies are placed in the gate cell, qubits with no dependencies are placed in remaining positions.

The last significant modification to Qiskit was to its execute function, which was modified to make final adjustments to the circuit embedding, execute the embedding on D-Wave hardware, and report the results. In our code, when execute is called, the user is prompted, for each qubit in the gate circuit, to answer whether the initial state of the qubit should be constrained to a value of zero. If the user answers that it should be and it was not earlier identified as a circuit output by the measure command, it is assumed this qubit is an ancilla and as such is not reported in the results. If the user answers that it should be constrained to zero and it has been identified as a circuit output by the measure command, the output values are still reported, but the input values are not. The initial state of a logical qubit is constrained to a value of zero by adding 5 to the bias of the first physical qubit associated with it. Results are reported with input variable values on the left and output variable values on the right.

3   Experimental Results

An upper bound on the resource requirements on both ends can be given as follows. Given an n-gate quantum circuit (in our case specified as a Qiskit program), a translation to an adiabatic form is provided in no more than $32n$ adiabatic qubits on the D-Wave 2000Q. The factor is comprised of 8 qubits for the $K_{4,4}$ representation of a gate, the remaining 24 qubits are used as wiring to the left and below that gate-equivalent $K_{4,4}$ graph (cf. the example below and Sect. 3.1).

Notice that an increase by 32X still increases the capabilities by mapping to D-Wave, if possible, since the IBM/D-Wave gap is 100X now, and problems can often be mapped more efficiently.

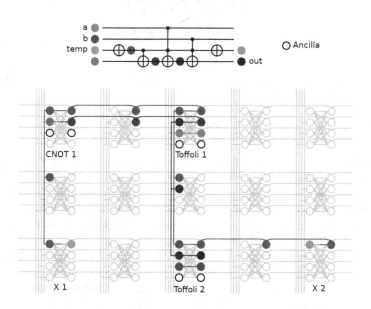

Fig. 9. Embedding of equivalence check circuit for 1-qubit numbers. Colors indicate logical qubits. (Color figure online)

3.1 Circuit for Comparison of 1-Qubit Numbers

Shown at the top of Fig. 9 is a quantum circuit whose output is $|1\rangle$ if its two input qubits, $|a\rangle$ and $|b\rangle$, are in the same logical state and $|0\rangle$ if they are not. The temporary qubit is not necessary for a 1-qubit equivalence circuit such as this but temporary registers are needed for similar circuits when comparing multi-bit inputs. The temporary register is included here to make this example more interesting. The main illustration in Fig. 9 shows the embedding automatically generated from a Qiskit program that defines the circuit depicted. This embedding anneals as expected. If the initial states of the output and temporary qubits are constrained to be zero there are 4 valid results. All 4 results are reliably obtained within 100 samples. The embedding uses 32 physical qubits and 48 couplers, 12 of which are used for inter-gate connections. This embedding is clearly not optimal. An optimal graph for a circuit of this size and functionality is easily obtained using the process by which the gate embeddings were determined (Sect. 2.1). An optimal graph for this circuit's function (XNOR) is shown in Fig. 10. It uses 6 qubits and 8 couplers and is contained within a single $K_{4,4}$ cell. Therefore, the generated circuit uses about 6 times more resources than is optimal.

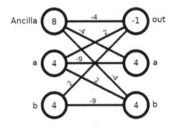

Fig. 10. An optimal XNOR graph with matching functionally to the generated 1-qubit equivalence circuit embedding

3.2   Circuit for Comparison of 5-Qubit Numbers

The 1-qubit equivalence circuit was expanded into a circuit for comparison of 5-qubit numbers. The current chain routing algorithm caused the embedding for this circuit to become congested when routing temporary qubits from earlier in the circuit to be uncomputed at the end of the circuit, which resulted in a graph that did not map to the chimera graph. Specifically, the current chain routing algorithm does not yet implement any precautions against routing chains into graph positions from which there are no further available connections. When this occurs, the algorithm is forced to assign a connection via a nonexistent coupler. Due to this, gates used for uncomputing the temporary qubits were not included in the circuit, and without them, the resulting embedding conformed to chimera graph connectivity and was able to be annealed on D-Wave 2000Q hardware.

The embedding generated for the 5-qubit equivalence circuit uses 156 physical qubits and 240 couplers, 68 of which are used in chains between gates. These values are also about 5 times larger than those of the 1-qubit equivalence circuit, as expected. However, this embedding does not anneal as effectively as the 1-qubit equivalence circuit. Only about 20 of the 1,024 valid results are obtained within 10,000 samples.

3.3   Adder for 1-Qubit Numbers

The top of Fig. 11 shows a quantum circuit implementing a full adder function. The main illustration in this figure shows the embedding generated from a Qiskit script defining this circuit. This embedding is composed of 79 physical qubits and 110 couplers, 47 of which are used for inter-gate connections. Several improvements that could be made to this embedding are apparent. Most obviously, the chains connecting gates could be routed more efficiently. An optimal full adder annealer embedding uses 8 qubits and 13 couplers and fits within a single $K_{4,4}$ cell [4]. So, in terms of bipartite cell embeddings used, the generated full adder embedding is 6 times larger than the optimal case. Considering resources used to connect gates, the generated embedding is about 11 times larger.

The generated full adder embedding anneals as expected. There are 8 valid results if the initial states of sum and carry-out qubits are constrained to be zero. All 8 results are reliably obtained within 400 samples.

3.4 Adder for 4-Qubit Numbers

The 1-qubit adder was expanded to implement a 4-qubit adder. The corresponding embedding used 322 physical qubits and 430 couplers, 212 of which were used for inter-gate connections. Qubits in gate cells G9, G10, and G17 were down on the D-Wave machine, and as such these cells were not used. Due to having to route around these cells, extra qubits and couplers were included in the embedding. Nonetheless, the number of qubits and couplers used in the generated embedding are still approximately 4 times that of the 1-qubit adder embedding.

This embedding does not anneal as effectively as the 1-qubit adder. There are 256 valid ground states when the initial state of the output qubits are constrained to zero. Only 16 of these are ground states are found within 10,000 samples.

3.5 Multiplication Circuit for 2-Qubit Numbers

The quantum circuit pictured in Fig. 12 takes 2-qubit numbers, a_1a_0 and b_1b_0, as input and computes their product $p_3p_2p_1p_0$. The embedding generated from a Qiskit script defining this quantum circuit comprises 200 physical qubits and 262 couplers, 142 of which were used for inter-gate connections. In related work, an

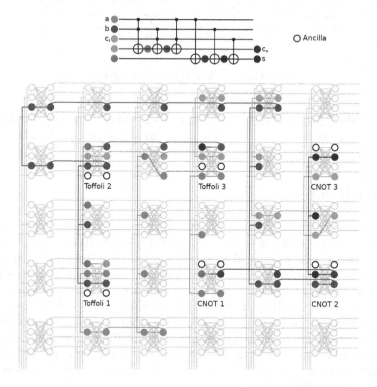

Fig. 11. Embedding of adder for 1-qubit numbers. Colors indicate logical qubits. (Color figure online)

embedding for a 3-bit multiplication function was implemented by making appropriate connections between single cell embeddings for full adder, half adder, and AND functions [4]. An embedding for a 2-bit multiplication function constructed in this way would comprise 4 AND embeddings and 2 half adder embeddings, which require 28 qubits and 32 couplers between them. Assuming a similar chaining scheme, about 16 qubits and 23 couplers would be required to connect the minor embeddings. Therefore, the embedding would require approximately 44 qubits and 55 couplers. Compared to this embedding, the embedding generated here uses about 6 times the amount of qubits, and about 3 times the number of couplers. Note that, as in the case of the 4-qubit adder, qubits in gate cells G9, G10, and G17 were down on the D-Wave machine, and so these cells were not used. This resulted in extra qubits and couplers being included in the generated embedding.

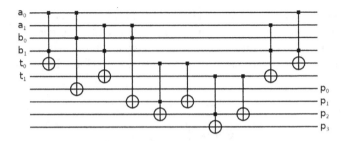

Fig. 12. 2-qubit multiplication circuit

This embedding anneals as expected. If the initial state of output qubits and temporary qubits, t_0 and t_1, are constrained to zero there are 16 valid results. All 16 results have been obtained in 10,000 samples.

4   Conclusion

We contributed an automatic translation scheme from a set of quantum gates, expressed as a Qiskit circuit suitable for execution on the IBM Q platform, to an adiabatic circuit with an equivalent single-degree 2-local Ising Hamiltonian that is embedded on a chimera graph and expressed as an Ocean program suitable for D-Wave 2000Q execution. Experiments indicated that the generated target circuits were using six times more qubits and three times more couplers than the source circuits. In future work, we plan to develop optimization techniques to reduce the number of resources required by exploiting inter-gate embeddings within unused couplers of a cell representing a gate and by reducing qubits by fusing gates together. We also intend to further extend the set of gates suitable for adiabatic transformation in circuits.

References

1. Ibm qiskit (2018). https://github.com/Qiskit/qiskit-terra
2. Rigetti forest (2018). https://www.rigetti.com/forest
3. Aharonov, D., van Dam, W., Kempe, J., Landau, Z., Lloyd, S., Regev, O.: Adiabatic quantum computation is equivalent to standard quantum computation. SIAM J. Comput. **37**(1), 166–194 (2007). https://doi.org/10.1137/S0097539705447323
4. Andriyash, E., et al.: Boosting integer factoring performance via quantum annealing offsets. Technical report (2016)
5. Bacon, D., Flammia, S.T., Crosswhite, G.M.: Adiabatic quantum transistors (2012). https://doi.org/10.1103/PhysRevX.3.021015
6. Boixo, S., Albash, T., Spedalieri, F.M., Chancellor, N., Lidar, D.A.: Experimental signature of programmable quantum annealing. arXiv:1212.1739 (2012)
7. Cross, A.W., Bishop, L.S., Smolin, J.A., Gambetta, J.M.: Open quantum assembly language. arXiv:1707.03429 (2017)
8. D-Wave: D-wave leap. https://www.dwavesys.com/take-leap
9. D-Wave: D-wave's ocean software. https://ocean.dwavesys.com/
10. Aharonov, D., van Dam, W., Kempe, J., Landau, Z., Lloyd, S., Regev, O.: Adiabatic quantum computation is equivalent to standard quantum computation. ArXiv e-prints, May 2004. https://arxiv.org/abs/quant-ph/0405098
11. IBM: IBM Q Experience. https://quantumexperience.ng.bluemix.net/qx
12. Warren, R.H.: Gates for adiabatic quantum computing. ArXiv e-prints, August 2014. https://arxiv.org/abs/1405.2354

An Efficient Method for Quantum Circuit Placement Problem on a 2-D Grid

Atsushi Matsuo[1] and Shigeru Yamashita[2(✉)]

[1] IBM Research, Tokyo, Japan
[2] Ritsumeikan University, Kusatsu, Japan
ger@cs.ritsumei.ac.jp

Abstract. This work-in-progress report proposes an efficient method to solve "quantum circuit placement problems" which are considered explicitly or implicitly when we convert an arbitrary quantum circuit into a nearest neighbor (NN) compliant circuit. A quantum circuit placement problem is to find as few SWAP gates as possible to convert a given initial qubit placement into a desired qubit placement. In the existing methods, the problem is solved by an ILP formulation or an A* search algorithm; the existing approaches may not be scalable for large quantum circuits. Thus, we are considering a more efficient method to solve the problem; our method tries to apply only SWAP gates such that do not have any bad effect on the desired movement of all the qubits. We also report a preliminary experimental result to show how our method improve the A* search algorithm which is used to generate NN compliant circuits.

Keywords: Quantum circuit placement problem · Nearest neighbor · SWAP gate

1 Introduction

Recently many companies (e.g., IBM, Intel, Rigetti, and Google) has been competing to develop quantum computers which are called Noisy Intermediate-Scale Quantum Computers (NISQCs). From these researches, it would be natural to consider that the future quantum circuits can support only operations between *nearest neighbor* two qubits. Therefore, we need to convert a desired quantum circuit into so called a *nearest neighbor (NN) compliant circuit* which consists of only one-qubit operations and two-qubit operations on adjacent pairs of qubits.

Therefore, it has been studied intensively to convert a quantum circuit into an NN compliant circuit [1–4]. These existing methods convert any circuits into NN compliant circuits by inserting *SWAP gates*. They should work well for the circuits used in the current NISQCs, but they may not be applicable to very large quantum circuits in the future. In such a case, as the case of classical circuit design, we can divide a given large circuit into small sub-circuits, convert each sub-circuits into NN compliant circuits, and then combine them. Also, we may want to reuse already optimized small NN compliant components (such

© Springer Nature Switzerland AG 2019
M. K. Thomsen and M. Soeken (Eds.): RC 2019, LNCS 11497, pp. 162–168, 2019.
https://doi.org/10.1007/978-3-030-21500-2_10

as, adders, multipliers, error-correcting circuits, etc.) when we construct a large quantum circuit. In these design procedures, we need to combine each NN compliant circuit.

When we combine two NN compliant circuits, we may need to change the qubit placement between the two circuits because each circuit may assume different qubit placements to be NN compliant. More precisely, we need to consider how to insert SWAP gates between two sub-circuits to change the qubit placement for the first circuit into the one for the second circuit. We call this problem "quantum circuit placement problems" in this work-in-progress report.

Indeed, the problem is considered in the existing methods to design NN compliant circuits explicitly [1] or implicitly [2–4]. In the existing methods, the problem is solved by an ILP formulation [1] or an A* search algorithm [2,3], which may not be scalable for large quantum circuits. The existing heuristic [4] is very simple, and seems not to be so efficient. Thus, we are considering a more scalable and better heuristic to solve the problem on a 2-D grid. Our method tries to apply only SWAP gates that do not have any bad effect on the desired movement of all the qubits. To do so, we introduce a notion of *"desired direction,"* which is natural and useful for our purpose. We report a preliminary experimental result to show how our method improve the A* search algorithm which is used to generate NN compliant circuits.

2 The Proposed Heuristic Method

In this section, we explain the problem definition of quantum circuit placement problem on a 2-D grid and our proposed heuristic method to solve the problem efficiently.

2.1 Problem Definition

The problem of converting a given initial qubit placement into a desired qubit placement is formulated as follows:

Quantum Circuit Placement Problem on a 2-D Grid
Given two qubit placements on a 2D grid, one is an initial qubit placement and the other one is a desired qubit placement, the problem is to convert the initial qubit placement into a desired qubit placement with the minimum number of adjacent transpositions (which can be done by SWAP gates) on a 2D grid.

The input/output of the problem can be stated formally as follows:

Input: an initial qubit placement q^i, a desired qubit placement q^d, a 2D grid graph G.
Output: products of adjacent transpositions.

In the following, we denote qubits as $q_1, q_2, \cdots$ and q_1^i in Fig. 1(a) means the initial qubit placement of q_1. Similarly, q_2^d in Fig. 1(b) means the desired qubit placement of q_2. We assume that qubits are placed in one node which is placed

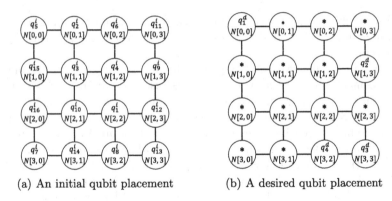

(a) An initial qubit placement   (b) A desired qubit placement

Fig. 1. An example of an initial qubit placement and a desired qubit placement

in a 2D grid as shown in Fig. 1(a). We denote the node locations in the grid as $N[i, j]$ where $N[0, 0]$ means the top-left in Fig. 1. For example, node locations of q_1^i and q_2^i in Fig. 1(a) are represented as $N[2, 2]$ and $N[0, 1]$, respectively.

An example of a problem input is as shown in Fig. 1. Figures 1(a) and (b) are examples of an initial qubit placement and a desired qubit placement, respectively. Note that some qubits are not used in some sub-circuits. We do not care their node locations while solving a problem. A symbol $*$ (as shown in Fig. 1(b)) indicates such a *don't care* node. we can place any qubit on a don't care node if the qubit is not specified to be placed in another node.

2.2   The Proposed Heuristic Method

We explain our heuristic method in this section. To begin with, we introduce a notion of *"desired direction,"* which is natural and useful. As shown in Fig. 1, q_1 in q^i needs to move to $N[0, 0]$ from $N[2, 2]$ by using adjacent transpositions on the 2D grid. A direction from $N[2, 2]$ to $N[0, 0]$ is upper-left. Since using only adjacent transpositions on the 2D grid, the upper-left direction is decomposed into left and up directions for implementation. These decomposed directions are called desired directions of node q_1. Each node which is not a don't care node has one or two desired directions if the node is not at its desired placement. We call an out-going edge from a node as a *desired direction edge* of the node when the edge goes to the desired direction from the node. For example, if the desired directions of a node is upper and left, the two edges which goes upper and left from the node are called desired direction edge of the node. Desired direction edges of q_1 are shown as red arrows in Fig. 2. Desired direction edges of q_2, q_3, and q_4 are as shown in Fig. 2 as well.

For our purpose, we consider the following three situations for an adjacent pair of nodes as shown in Fig. 3. When an edge is a desired direction edge for the both of nodes, we call the edge between the such two nodes as a *Type-2* edge. If we swap two qubits that are connected by a Type-2 edge, the both of qubits moves closer to their desired qubit locations. When an edge is a desired

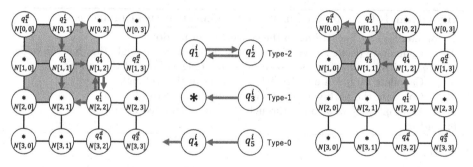

Fig. 2. Desired directions of q_1, q_2, q_3 and q_4 in the problem (Color figure online)

Fig. 3. Types of edges with desired directions

Fig. 4. A path with the highest score (Color figure online)

direction edge for one of qubits and the other qubit is a don't care qubit, we call the edge between such the two nodes as a *Type-1* edge. When an edge is a desired direction edge of one of qubits but not a desired direction edge of the other node (which is not a don't care node), we call the edge between the such two nodes as a *Type-0* edge.

Our Observation

Let us consider to swap the locations of an adjacent pair of node by inserting a SWAP gate. If the edge between the two nodes is Type-2, both the two nodes move closer to their goals. If the edge is Type-1, only one node moves closer to its goal because the other node is a don't care node. If the edge is Type-0, one node moves closer to its goal, but the other node moves in the opposite direction to its goal. Our observation is that the conversion should be optimal if we can choose only Type-2 edges to swap two qubits. Of course, we cannot choose all Type-2 edges during the conversion generally. Nevertheless we consider that it is better to choose Type-2 or Type-1 edges as much as possible.

Based on the above observation, we try to swap adjacent pairs of nodes that are connected by Type-2 edges as many as possible (and then Type-1 edges). To do so, we consider that Type-2, Type-1 and Type-0 edges have score $+1$, 0 and -1, respectively, and we choose a path whose total score becomes the largest in the following our heuristic.

Now we are ready to explain our heuristic method. In our method, we consider to move a qubit to its desired location one by one. In our current implementation, the order of qubits is fixed in advance, but we can consider another way as we will mention later.

When we move q_k from its initial location q_k^i to its desired location q_k^d, we consider a *possibly best* path from q_k^i to q_k^d, and we swap adjacent pairs of qubits one by one along the path. To do so, first we calculate the types of all the edges

---

Algorithm 1. Our proposed heuristic for qubit placement problems

---

1: **for each** $q_k^d \in q^d$ according to the converting order **do**
2:     Enumerate desired directions for each qubits in a rectangle that has the node
    of q_k^i and the node of q_k^d as two vertices on a diagonal line of the rectangle.
3:     Calculate a type of an edge for each edges in the rectangle.
4:     Compute the path with the highest score from q_k^i to q_k^d.
5:     Move q_k to q_k^d in q^d on G through the path computed in Step 4.
6: **end for**

---

in a rectangle whose diagonal line is q_k^i to q_k^d. Then, we choose a path from q_k^i to q_k^d with the highest score.

In our example, when we move q_1 from $N[2,2]$ (q_1^i) to $N[0,0]$ (q_1^d), we choose a path from $N[2,2]$ to $N[0,0]$ with the highest score in the blue rectangle as shown in Fig. 2. In this example, we choose the path with the highest score which is: $N[2,2] \to N[1,2] \to N[1,1] \to N[0,1] \to N[0,0]$ as shown in Fig. 4.

We repeat the procedure explained in the above for all qubits in q^d one by one. In our current implementation, the order to move qubits is from the most upper-left node (i.e., $N[0,0]$) to the right nodes in q^d. If we reach to the most right node in the row, we choose the most left node in the next row. We can consider much more efficient order, which we will discuss in the last section.

The formal algorithm description is as shown in Algorithm 1.

3   Preliminary Experimental Results

We implemented our proposed heuristic method in Python and an A* search algorithm in C++ to evaluate the performance of our proposed heuristic method. To evaluate our heuristic method, we divided a quantum circuit into a series of NN compliant sub-circuits by the method [2]. Then we used the qubit placements of these NN compliant sub-circuits for initial qubit placements and desired qubit placements. We solved the qubit placement problem between the two sub-circuits, and reported the total numbers of SWAP gates with the A* search and our heuristic in Table 1. Note that "-" in Table 1 means that the execution time exceeded thousand seconds.

For circuits with 64 or more qubits, the A* search cannot find the answer within thousand seconds, but our heuristic method can find a solution within less than one second; As expected, our heuristic seems to be very scalable. The quality of the solutions seems to be slightly worse than the A* search with our current naive algorithm. However, we expect the quality would become better if we implement the dynamic order of qubits to be selected in our algorithm, which will be mentioned in the next section.

Table 1. The total number of SWAP gates for quantum circuit placement problems by an A* search and our proposed method.

Circuits	A* search	Our heuristic	CPU time (ms)
3 × 3 (qft8)	28	26	4.02
3 × 3 (qft9)	40	42	5.92
4 × 5 (adder8)	44	50	7.97
6 × 6 (adder16)	112	124	27.8
8 × 8 (random)	–	892	155
8 × 8 (random)	–	914	164
9 × 9 (random)	–	938	175
9 × 9 (random)	–	968	173
10 × 10 (random)	–	1350	292
10 × 10 (random)	–	1624	347

4   Discussion and Future Work

This work-in-progress report proposed a scalable heuristic to solve so called quantum circuit placement problems, which should be important when we need to design very large NN compliant quantum circuits in the future. As we mentioned in the previous section, our current algorithm seems to have room to improve; we found one of the reasons why our algorithm cannot find a better solution than the A* search is the order of qubits to move in our algorithm. Indeed, our current algorithm fixes the order of qubits to move such that the top left qubit in the desired placement will be moved first. This strategy is obviously naive, and we should be able to improve in many ways.

As we observed, if we swap two qubits which are connected by a Type-2 edge, the swap operation should be very beneficial. However, if we move qubits in the fixed order, we may need to choose many Type-1 or Type-0 edges during the process. So, the following heuristic should work better than our current algorithm.

Step 1 During the conversion, we swap all the pairs of two qubits which are connected by a Type-2 edge until there is no Type-2 edge.

Step 2 When there is no Type-2 edge, choose Type-1 edge (if there is no Type-1, then Type-0) which is connected to the current target qubit to be moved. The order of target qubits may be similar to our current strategy, but we may choose the target qubit such that the movement of the target qubit increases the number of Type-2 edges; after that we can go back to the above Step 1.

By implementing the above algorithm, we expect our approach should improve the existing result [2] even for the small cases.

Acknowledgments. This work was supported by JSPS KAKENHI Grant Number 15H01677 and 18K19790, and by the Asahi Glass Foundation.

References

1. Bhattacharjee, D., Chattopadhyay, A.: Depth-optimal quantum circuit placement for arbitrary topologies. *arXiv preprint* arXiv:1703.08540 (2017)
2. Hattori, W., Yamashita, S.: Quantum circuit optimization by changing the gate order for 2D nearest neighbor architectures. Proc. Revers. Comput. **2018**, 228–243 (2018)
3. Zulehner, A., Wille, R.: Compiling SU(4) quantum circuits to IBM QX architectures. Proc. ASPDAC **2019**, 185–190 (2019)
4. Shafaei, A., Saeedi, M., Pedram, M.: Qubit placement to minimize communication overhead in 2D quantum architectures. Proc. ASPDAC **2014**, 495–500 (2014)

Evaluation of Circuit Synthesis

Evaluating the Flexibility of A* for Mapping Quantum Circuits

Alwin Zulehner[✉], Hartwig Bauer, and Robert Wille

Johannes Kepler University Linz, Linz, Austria
{alwin.zulehner,hartwig.bauer,robert.wille}@jku.at

Abstract. Mapping quantum circuits to real quantum architectures (while keeping the respectively considered cost as small as possible) has become an important research task since it is required to execute algorithms on real devices. Since the underlying problem is NP-complete, several heuristic approaches have been proposed. Recently, approaches utilizing A^* search to map quantum circuits to, e.g., Nearest Neighbor architectures or IBM QX architectures have gained substantial interest. However, their performance usually has only been evaluated in a rather narrow context, i.e., for single architectures and objectives only. In this work, we evaluate the flexibility of A^* in the context of mapping quantum circuits to physical devices. To this end, we review the underlying concepts and show its flexibility with respect to the considered architecture. Furthermore, we demonstrate how easy such solutions can be adjusted towards optimizing different design objectives or cost metrics by providing a generalized and parameterizable cost function for the A^* search that can also be easily extended to support future cost metrics.

1 Introduction

Quantum computing [1] utilizes quantum mechanical effects like superposition and entanglement to allow for significant (in many cases exponential) speedups compared to current devices for applications like integer factorization [2], database search [3], or simulation of physical systems [4]. In the recent years, there has been a significant progress in the physical realizations of real quantum hardware. Arising from academic proof-of-concept realizations [5,6], nowadays publicly available quantum computers are made accessible, e.g., by IBM through a cloud interface [7] and a first prototype for commercial use is available as well [8]. Moreover, architectures are envisioned to manage the step from current *Noisy Intermediate Scale Quantum* (NISQ [9]) devices to fault-tolerant ones composed of thousands of qubits [10,11].

However, to run quantum algorithms on such real devices, the respective high-level operations have to be broken down into elementary operations (acting on one or two qubits only) supported by the hardware (e.g., using approaches such as [12–14]) and the logical qubits of the quantum algorithm have to be mapped to physical ones of the quantum device. Especially the mapping part

© Springer Nature Switzerland AG 2019
M. K. Thomsen and M. Soeken (Eds.): RC 2019, LNCS 11497, pp. 171–190, 2019.
https://doi.org/10.1007/978-3-030-21500-2_11

constitutes a tough challenge since further physical constraints have to be considered. In fact, not all pairs of qubits may interact with each other due to so-called coupling-constraints. Hence, the mapping usually has to change dynamically throughout the execution of a quantum computation. This is achieved by adding so-called SWAP operations that exchange the state of two physical qubits and, by this, "move around" the logical qubits on the hardware. This overhead shall obviously be kept as small as possible since each additional operation increases the execution time and the possibility of an unreliable result (since quantum computing is error prone yet)—resulting in a task that has recently been proven to be NP-complete [15, 16].

In the last decade, several solutions for this mapping problem have been proposed. First solutions focused on *Nearest Neighbor* (NN) architectures where the qubits are located in a 1- or 2-dimensional grid and only neighboring qubits may interact with each other [17–20]. With the appearance of publicly available quantum computers, researchers also started to focus on the mapping problem for IBM QX architectures—leading to further solutions dedicated for these architectures [21–26]. Many of the proposed approaches—for NN as well as for IBM QX architectures—have in common that they utilize the A* search algorithm. However, their performance usually has only been evaluated in a rather narrow context, i.e., for single architectures and objectives.

In this work, we investigate the flexibility of A*-based mapping and propose a generic approach that allows for an efficient mapping to NN as well as to IBM QX architectures while optimizing different design objectives. This is achieved by exploiting the fact that the constraints of different architectures can be modeled by coupling maps and by using a generic and parameterizable cost function. Given the coupling-constraints of any envisioned new architecture as well as appropriate parameters for the cost function, the proposed solution inherently provides a customized mapping algorithm without writing any code. Moreover, by slightly adjusting the cost function, future design objectives can be easily incorporated as well.

Our evaluations show that the resulting approach, although being generic and flexible with respective to different architectures and objectives, remains competitive even against state-of-the-art solutions which have been optimized over the last ten years and to a single architecture and a single objective. Moreover, the evaluations demonstrate that simply changing some few parameters (rather than developing new dedicated algorithms) allows to optimize for various design objectives like gate count, circuit depth, or an equally distributed workload for the qubits. Overall, this shows the flexibility of A*-based mapping of quantum circuits.

This paper is structured as follows. In Sect. 2, we review quantum circuits and quantum architectures including a description of the considered mapping problem. Section 3 discusses the A*-based mapping in general as well as its flexibility. Eventually, the proposed resulting generic approach is evaluated in Sect. 4, while Sect. 5 concludes the paper.

2   Quantum Circuits and Quantum Architectures

To keep the paper self-contained, this section briefly recapitulates quantum circuits as well as currently considered quantum architectures.

2.1   Quantum Circuits

In contrast to conventional computations, *quantum computations* [1] operate on qubits instead of bits. A *qubit* is a two-state quantum system, with basis states $|0\rangle \equiv \binom{1}{0}$ and $|1\rangle \equiv \binom{0}{1}$ (representing Boolean values 0 and 1, respectively). Furthermore, a qubit can be in a superposition of these basis states, i.e., $|x\rangle = \alpha\,|0\rangle + \beta\,|1\rangle$, where the complex amplitudes α and β satisfy $|\alpha|^2 + |\beta|^2 = 1$. The state of a qubit can be modified by applying quantum operations, whose functionality can be described by 2×2-dimensional unitary matrices. Commonly used 1-qubit gates are

$$NOT = X = \begin{bmatrix} 0 & 1 \\ 1 & 0 \end{bmatrix}, \quad H = \frac{1}{\sqrt{2}} \begin{bmatrix} 1 & 1 \\ 1 & -1 \end{bmatrix}, \text{ and } \quad T = \begin{bmatrix} 1 & 0 \\ 0 & \frac{1+i}{2} \end{bmatrix},$$

which invert the state of a qubit, sets it into a superposition, or conducts a phase shift by $\frac{1+i}{\sqrt{2}}$, respectively.[1] The state of a qubit cannot be directly observed. Instead, measurement collapses the qubit into one of the two basis states $|0\rangle$ or $|1\rangle$. More precisely, the qubit collapses to basis state $|0\rangle$ with probability $|\alpha|^2$ and to basis state $|1\rangle$ with probability $|\beta|^2$.

The above extends to quantum systems composed of n qubits. Here, due to a quantum mechanical effect called *entanglement*, the state of a qubit might additionally be influenced by other qubits.[2] Hence, the qubits can not be considered individually, rather as complete system with 2^n basis states and corresponding amplitudes. The state of such a system is then accordingly manipulated by a $2^n \times 2^n$-dimensional unitary matrix. Since such operations acting on all qubits can not be realized physically, they are usually decomposed into a sequence of operations that act on one or two qubits only (other qubits are not affected). For example, it has been shown that—besides arbitrary single-qubit operations—having a controlled *NOT* (i.e., CNOT) operation

$$CNOT = CX = \begin{bmatrix} 1 & 0 & 0 & 0 \\ 0 & 1 & 0 & 0 \\ 0 & 0 & 0 & 1 \\ 0 & 0 & 1 & 0 \end{bmatrix},$$

---

[1] The new state of the qubit is determined by multiplying the corresponding state vector and the unitary matrix [27].

[2] Albert Einstein referred to this effect as *spooky action at a distance*.

where the state of the *target qubit* is inverted if the *control qubit* is in its basis state $|1\rangle$, is sufficient to allow for universal quantum computing. Hence, any $2^n \times 2^n$ unitary matrix can be decomposed into a sequence composed of 1-qubit operations and CNOTs.

A commonly used representation for quantum computations are *quantum circuits*. Here, the respective qubits are denoted by horizontal *circuit lines*. Operations are represented by *quantum gates*. Boxes labeled with the respective functionality denote 1-qubit gates, whereas • and ⊕ denote the control and target qubit of a CNOT gate, respectively. Overall, this yields a representation of a quantum circuit as a cascade $G = g_1 g_2 \ldots g_{|G|}$ of gates (drawn from left to right), where $|G|$ denotes the total number of gates. The number of qubits and, thus, the number of circuit lines is denoted by n.

Example 1. *Figure 1 shows a quantum circuit composed of $|G| = 22$ gates and $n = 5$ circuit lines. Each circuit line represents a qubit $q_0 - q_4$. The first (leftmost) gate describes a CNOT operation with control line q_1 and target line q_0. The U blocks represent single qubit operations.*[3]

Since there are various ways to realize certain quantum functionality by means of a quantum circuit, one has to define cost metrics that allow designers to chose the best realization. Commonly used cost metrics are:

- *Gate count gc(G):* The gate count of a circuit G is its number of elementary gates. When using weights for each gate type, this also allows to estimate the fidelity of the overall circuit.
- *Circuit Depth cd(G):* The depth of a circuit G describes the minimal number of time-steps required to execute all gates. In this work, we assume that all elementary operations require one time-step and that operations acting on disjoint sets of qubits can be executed in parallel. However, these assumptions can be easily adjusted if desired.

Besides these established cost metrics, we define another (artificial) cost metric to demonstrate the flexibility of A*-based mapping of quantum circuits, e.g., when extending the cost function to take qubit fidelity [28] into account in the future.

- *Workload Distribution wd(G):* The workload $wd'(q_i)$ of a qubit q_i is determined by the number of gates that act on q_i (or use it as a control). Workload distribution of a circuit G is then defined as standard deviation of the workload for each qubit (that is affected by at least one gate), i.e.,

$$wd(G) = \sqrt{\frac{1}{n} \sum_{i=0}^{n} (wd'(q_i) - wd_{avg})^2}.$$

---

[3] Note that we do not further specify the functionality of the single qubit gates since it is irrelevant for the mapping process.

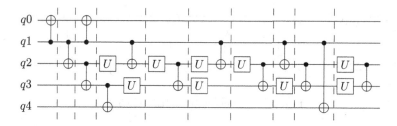

Fig. 1. Quantum circuit

Example 1 (continued). *As stated above, the gate count of the circuit* G *shown in Fig. 1 is* $gc(G) = 22$. *The depth of this circuit* $cd(G) = 15$. *For example, the CNOT with control* q_1 *and target* q_0 *(i.e.,* $CNOT(q_1, q_0)$*) can be applied simultaneously with the gate* $CNOT(q_2, q_3)$. *The gate* $CNOT(q_3, q_4)$ *has to be applied later because it operates also on* q_3. *Finally, the workload distribution is* $wd(G) = \sqrt{\frac{108}{5}} = 4.65$.

2.2 Mapping Quantum Circuits to Quantum Architectures

In the recent years, there has been a significant progress in the physical realization of real quantum hardware. Arising from academic proof-of-concept realizations [5,6], there are already publicly available quantum computers made accessible by IBM through a cloud interface [7] as well as first commercially available ones [8]. Moreover, architectures are envisioned to manage the step from current *Noisy Intermediate Scale Quantum* (NISQ [9]) devices to fault-tolerant ones composed of thousands of qubits [10,11]. However, all these architectures come with certain restrictions regarding (1) the available elementary quantum operations and (2) the allowed qubit connectivity (i.e., which pairs of qubits may interact with each other by means of two-qubit gates). These restrictions have to be considered when executing quantum circuits on them.

Since decomposition into different gate libraries is already well covered by literature (see, e.g., [12–14]), we focus on the connectivity constraints of the architectures in the following. Before real quantum computers became available, researchers considered so-called *Nearest Neighbor* (NN) architectures, where the qubits are arranged in a 1- or 2-dimensional grid and interactions are only possible between neighboring qubits.[4] However, IBM's QX architectures—the first quantum computers made publicly available—employ slightly different constraints. While interactions are also only possible between certain pairs of qubits, their layout is not necessarily as regular as a 1- or 2-dimensional grid and it is additionally given which qubit may act as control and which qubit may act as target (i.e., the *direction* of the CNOT is fixed). These constraints are defined

---

[4] Note that this constraint is still valid for many recent architectures, e.g., Google's *Bristlecone* relies on such a 2D architecture [29].

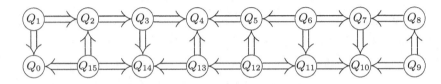

Fig. 2. Coupling map for IBM QX5 [30]

by so-called *coupling maps* (i.e., a directed graph), where the m *physical qubits* $Q_0, Q_1, \ldots Q_{m-1}$ are represented by vertices and an arrow from Q_i to Q_j indicates that a CNOT with control qubit Q_i and target qubit Q_j can be executed (these constraints are denoted *coupling-constraints* in the following). In the following, we consider architectures specified by coupling maps, since this approach is more general (constraints of NN architectures can be easily modeled by an according coupling map as well).

Example 2. *Figure 2 shows the coupling map of IBM's QX5 [30] architecture. As described above, the arrow from Q_1 to Q_2 represents that CNOTs with control Q_1 and target Q_2 can be applied. It also means that a CNOT with control Q_2 and target Q_1 is not possible. Since there is also no arrow connecting Q_1 and Q_3, a CNOT cannot be applied on these two qubits (independent of its direction).*

In order to execute quantum circuits on architectures as described above, two steps are conducted. First, the quantum gates of the circuit are decomposed into elementary operations available on the hardware. Since this step is already well covered in the literature [12–14], we assume that is has already been conducted. The second step—mapping the n logical qubits $q_0, q_1, \ldots q_{n-1}$ of a quantum circuit to the m physical qubits $Q_0, Q_1, \ldots Q_{m-1}$ of a quantum computer while satisfying all *coupling-constraints*—constitutes a tougher challenge. Usually it is not possible to find a mapping that satisfies the constraints throughout the whole circuit. This becomes immediately clear by considering a circuit where one qubit interacts with more other qubits than the maximal degree of a coupling map. Assuming an initial mapping, the following problems may occur:

- A CNOT shall be applied where the control and the target qubit are mapped to physical qubits that are not connected in the coupling map.
- A CNOT shall be applied where the control and the target qubit are mapped to physical qubits that are connected in the coupling map, but there is only a connection in the "wrong" direction.

To overcome these issues, the mapping procedure has to change the mapping dynamically by inserting additional operations. The most established technique is to insert so-called SWAP operations that exchange the state of two physical qubits and, thus, move around the logical qubits—changing their mapping dynamically.[5]

---

[5] Note that there also exist other methods to overcome the problems [25], but they tend to generate larger overhead for bigger circuits.

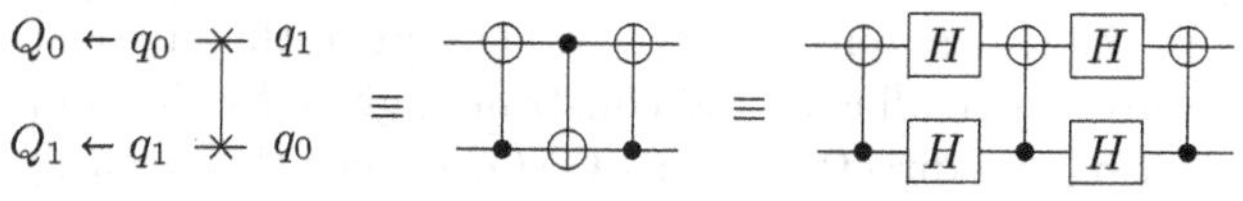

$$Q_0 \leftarrow q_0 \quad Q_1$$
$$Q_1 \leftarrow q_1 \quad q_0$$

Fig. 3. SWAP operation

Example 3. *Figure 3 shows a SWAP operation that swaps the state of the physical qubits Q_0 and Q_1 of IBM QX5. Since the logical qubits q_0 and q_1 are mapped to Q_0 and Q_1 initially, the SWAP operations changes the mapping such that q_0 and q_1 are mapped to Q_1 and Q_0 afterwards. The SWAP operation is decomposed into three CNOTs as shown in the middle of Fig. 3. Since only CNOTs with control Q_1 and target Q_0 are possible (cf. Fig. 2), the direction of the middle CNOT has to be switched. This is achieved by inserting Hadamard gates before and after this CNOT.*

While SWAP operations are sufficient to overcome both issues listed above, the second one can be handled with fewer overhead. Like in the decomposition of a SWAP operation shown in Example 3, the direction of a CNOT can be switched by inserting four Hadamard operations. Minimizing the overhead (e.g., regarding one of the cost metrics defined in Sect. 2.1) caused by satisfying the coupling-constraints has recently been proven to be an NP-complete problem [15,16].

Since the mapping problem is NP-complete, several heuristic approaches have been proposed. These include dedicated solutions for NN architectures [17–20] or for real ones [21–26] (e.g., IBM's QX architectures) that are specified by coupling maps and usually focus on optimizing the gate count of the mapped circuit. Since many of these algorithms are based on an A* search, we analyze and evaluate the flexibility of an A*-based mapping in this work.

3 Mapping Quantum Circuits Using A*

This section discusses the flexibility of A*-based search methods for mapping quantum circuits to quantum architectures. To this end, we first sketch the general idea and, afterwards, provide the details of the A*-based mapping algorithm. Based on that, we discuss how easily the approach can be extended for different architectures and objectives.

3.1 General Idea

This section briefly lines out the general idea of mapping quantum circuits to real architectures using the A* search algorithm. Since solving the problem in an exact fashion (i.e., with minimal overhead) has been proven to be NP-complete [15,16], we aim for a heuristic approach to provide a solution within reasonable time.

The general idea is to partition the circuit to be mapped into k sub-circuits $G_0, G_1, \ldots G_{k-1}$. These sub-circuits are formed in a way, such that there exists a mapping from the logical qubits of the sub-circuit to the physical qubits of the target architecture where all coupling-constraints given by the coupling map are satisfied (neglecting the direction of the CNOTs since this is easily adjusted by inserting four Hadamard operations). Having that, no SWAP operations have to be inserted inside the sub-circuits (only H operations may be required). In between the sub-circuits, *permutation sub-circuits* composed of SWAP operations are inserted that change the mapping of logical qubits to physical ones dynamically. Determining the cheapest permutation circuit (with respect to a given cost function) such that all coupling-constraints are satisfied for the next sub-circuit to be mapped (again, neglecting the direction of the connections between physical qubits) is conducted using an A^* search. Hereby it is notable that the cost function might include a look-ahead for future sub-circuits such that the overall cost are subject to be optimized rather than utilizing locally-optimal permutations (which often leads to an increase of the overall cost [22]).

One flexibility of the proposed mapping algorithm is how to form the sub-circuits. In the literature, there exist approaches using different strategies. The most straightforward and naive version is to treat each gate as its own sub-circuit. Then, the A^* search algorithm is called once for each gate (except for the first one). To reduce the number of calls to the search algorithm and to optimize the overall cost by explicitly considering multiple gates, sub-circuit composed of several gates are usually considered. One commonly used possibility is to group all gates that act on disjoint qubits into a sub-circuit [21,22].[6] Alternatively, it is also possible to group as many gates into a sub-circuit such that a satisfying mapping can still be found for the sub-circuit (e.g., using SAT solvers as done in [20,26]). Finally, it is also possible leave the decision of determining the sub-circuits open for the A^* search as done in [23]. Here, a set of possible gates to be grouped are passed to the search algorithm, which inherently chooses a subset of these gates to be included in the next sub-circuit according to its objective function.[7]

Example 4. *Considering the circuit shown in Fig. 1, the partitioning into sub-circuits based gates acting on disjoint qubits [21,22] is conducted as follows when ignoring 1-qubit gates. The first sub-circuit G_0 contains the CNOT gate with control q_1 and target q_0, i.e., $CNOT(q_1, q_0)$. The second gate of the circuit $CNOT(q_1, q_2)$ has to be placed in a new sub-circuit G_1, since it also acts on qubit q_1. The third sub-circuit G_3 contains two gates, i.e., $CNOT(q_1, q_0)$ and $CNOT(q_2, q_3)$, since they act on disjoint sets of qubits. Continuing this procedure results in $k = 10$ sub-circuits. That are indicated by dashed lines in Fig. 1.*

In the following, we discuss how the A^* search algorithm is used to determine the "best" permutation (with respect to a certain cost metric) in between two sub-circuits to be mapped. Note that no such call of the algorithm is required for

---

[6] Note that 1-qubit gates can be neglected when forming the sub-circuits.

[7] Note that a similar strategy is used in [24] (even though the permutation is not found using A^* search).

the first sub-circuit since the effect of these SWAP gates are directly incorporated into the initial mapping of the logical qubits.

3.2   A* Search

How to conduct mapping of quantum circuits using A* search algorithms is described in two steps. First, we review how A* search works in general. Afterwards, its utilization in the considered problem is described.

General Algorithm. The A* algorithm is a state-space search algorithm. To this end, (sub-)solutions of the considered problem are represented by state nodes. Nodes that represent a solution are called *goal nodes* (multiple goal nodes may exist). The main idea is to determine the cheapest path (i.e., the path with the lowest cost) from the root node to a goal node. Since the search space is typically exponential, sophisticated mechanisms are employed in order to consider as few paths as possible.

All state-space search algorithms are similar in the way that they start with a root node (representing an initial state) which is iteratively expanded towards a goal node (i.e., one of the desired solutions). How to choose the node that shall be expanded next depends on the actual search algorithm. For A* search, we determine the cost of each leaf-node of the search tree. Then, the node with the lowest cost is chosen to be expanded next. The cost of a node x is given by $f(x) = g(x) + h(x)$. The first part, $g(x)$, describes the *path cost* of the current state (i.e., the cost of the path from the root to x). The second part provides an approximation of the remaining cost (i.e., the path cost from x to a goal node), which is estimated by a *heuristic cost* function $h(x)$. Since the node with the lowest cost is expanded, some parts of the search space (those leading to expensive solutions) are never expanded.

Example 5. *Consider the search tree shown in Fig. 4. This tree represents the part of the search space that has already been explored for a certain search problem. The nodes that are candidates to be expanded in the next iteration of the A* algorithm are highlighted in blue. For all these nodes, we determine the cost $f(x) = g(x) + h(x)$. This sum is composed by the cost of the path cost from the root to x (i.e., the sum of the cost annotated at the respective edges) and the estimated path cost from x to a goal node (highlighted in red). Consider the node labeled E. This node has cost $f(E) = (40 + 60) + 200 = 300$. The other candidates labeled B, C, and F have cost $f(B) = 580$, $f(C) = 360$, and $f(F) = 320$, respectively. Since the node labeled E has the fewest expected cost, it is expanded next.*

Obviously, the heuristic cost should be as accurate as possible, to expand as few nodes as possible. If $h(x)$ always provides the correct minimal remaining cost, only the nodes along the cheapest path from the root node to a goal node would be expanded. But since the minimal costs are usually not known (otherwise, the search problem would be trivial to solve), estimations are employed. However,

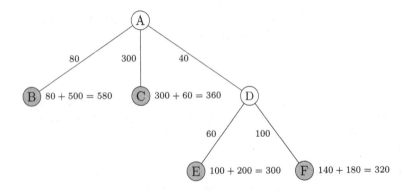

Fig. 4. A* search algorithm (Color figure online)

to ensure an optimal solution, $h(x)$ has to be *admissible*, i.e., $h(x)$ must not overestimate the cost of the cheapest path from x to a goal node. This ensures that no goal node is expanded (which terminates the search algorithm) until all nodes that have the potential to lead to a cheaper solution are expanded.

Example 5 (continued). *Consider again the node labeled E. If $h(x)$ is admissible, the true cost of each path from this node to a goal node is greater than or equal to 200.*

Using A* for Mapping. To utilize the A* algorithm recapitulated above for searching for the "best" permutation in between two sub-circuits of the circuit to be mapped, we have to define (1) the semantics of a node, (2) an expansion strategy for the nodes, and (3) a cost function to determine which node is expanded next.

Semantics of the Nodes: Each node in the A* search adaption for the quantum-circuit mapping problem represents a mapping of the logical qubits of the quantum circuit to the physical ones of the quantum hardware. The root node for our search represents the mapping found by the last call of the search algorithm (or the initial mapping when searching for the permutation after the first sub-circuit G_0). Each node that represents a mapping that satisfies all coupling-constraints for the gates in the currently considered sub-circuit is a goal node.

Expansion Strategy: As discussed in Sect. 2.2, the mapping is changed dynamically by inserting SWAP operations. Hence, a node is expanded by adding one node with a correspondingly modified mapping for each possible SWAP operation (according to the coupling map). To reduce the search space, we consider only SWAP operations that affect physical qubits to which a logical qubit is mapped that also occurs as control or target in a CNOT gate of the currently considered sub-circuit.

Example 6. *Considering again the quantum circuit shown in Fig. 1 and assuming that the logical qubits q_0, q_1, q_2, q_3, and q_4 are mapped to the physical qubits Q_0, Q_1, Q_2, Q_3, and Q_4 (cf. Figure 2), respectively. A permutation has to be inserted before sub-circuit $G_8 = \{CNOT(q_2, q_3), CNOT(q_1, q_4)\}$ since the coupling-constraints are not satisfied for $CNOT(q_1, q_4)$—there is no arrow between Q_1 and Q_4 in the coupling map. A* search is applied to determine the best permutation circuit. Expanding the root node of the search tree (i.e., the node representing the current mapping) causes 8 successors (instead of 22) since there exist eight connections in the coupling map that affect the physical qubits Q_0, Q_1, Q_2, Q_3, or Q_4.*

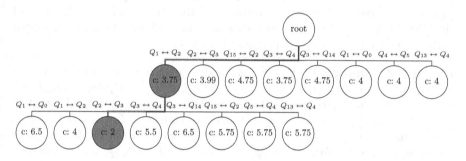

Fig. 5. First two expansion steps

Cost Function: Eventually, we need to specify a cost function for the nodes in the search tree to determine which node has to be expanded next. For demonstration purposes, we describe the cost function for optimizing with respect to the overall number of additional gates in this section. In the following section, we show the flexibility of the A*-based approach by extending the cost function such that other objectives are supported. Recall that the cost function f of a node $f(x) = g(x) + h(x)$ is composed of the *path cost* as well as the *heuristic cost* that estimates the remaining cost for reaching a goal state.

The current cost of a node x is determined by its depth in the search tree since this describes the number of SWAP gates required to reach the mapping described by x. Since a SWAP gate is composed of 7 elementary operations (3 CNOTs and 4 Hadamard gates), the path cost could be defined by $g(x) = 7 \cdot depth(x)$. However, in order to make this value better comparable to the cost functions of other objectives, just the number of SWAPs is used as cost, i.e., $g(x) = depth(x)$.

Usually, it is harder to find a good heuristic to estimate the remaining path cost for reaching a goal state since the heuristic shall be as accurate as possible (to prune large parts of the search space) while being admissible (i.e., not overestimating the true remaining cost) if an optimal/minimal solution is desired. To get an admissible heuristic, one has to determine the distance (i.e., the number of edges) of the logical qubits[8] in the coupling map for each CNOT gate in the currently considered sub-circuit, and take the maximum of all these distances.[9] However, since we do not aim for a locally optimal solution anyway (since this often affects the overall solution negatively [22]), we drop the admissibility constraint and specify the heuristic cost by accumulating all these distances.

Having $g(x)$ and $h(x)$ allows to utilize the A^* search algorithm as introduced above. However, we can exploit the knowledge that it is called once for each sub-circuit G_i (except for the first one). Since we aim for a globally optimal solution rather than a local one, we additionally define lookahead cost $l(x, G_i)$ that estimates how the current mapping affects future sub-circuits. This term is added to the cost function, i.e., $f(x) = g(x) + h(x) + l(x, G_i)$. The lookahead cost contains an additive term for each subsequent sub-circuit G_j ($i < j < k$) that is computed as sum of the distances of the target and control qubits of the CNOTs (like the heuristic cost). However, these additive terms are weighted with factors that decrease exponentially with $j - i$.

Example 6 (continued). Figure 5 shows the search tree for finding the cheapest permutation circuit. The cost for the leftmost node (highlighted in gray) with depth 1 of the search tree has a path cost of $g(x) = 1$ since one SWAP operation (i.e., $Q_1 \leftrightarrow Q_2$) has been added to reach this mapping. The heuristic cost is determined as follows: After the SWAP, the distance between the logical qubits q_1 and q_4 is 2 (since they are mapped to the physical qubits Q_2 and Q_4, respectively). Similarly, the distance between the logical qubits q_2 and q_3 is also 2. Hence, $h(x) = (2 - 1) + (2 - 1) = 2$. Since the control and the target qubit of the CNOT in the next sub-circuit (i.e., $G_9 = \{CNOT(q_2, q_3)\}$) have also a distance of 2, the lookahead cost is $l(x, G_8) = (2 - 1) \cdot 0.75 = 0.75$) when using a weight of 0.75. Overall, this sums up to cost $f(x) = 1 + 2 + 0.75 = 3.75$. Similarly, the cost of the node highlighted in gray with depth 2 is $f(x') = 2$. Since this is a goal node, the new mapping is determined by inserting a permutation circuit composed of the SWAPS $Q_1 \leftrightarrow Q_2$ and $Q_2 \leftrightarrow Q_3$—eventually resulting in the mapped circuit shown in Fig. 6. This circuit has a gate count of $22 + 2 \cdot 7 = 36$, a depth of 25, as well as a workload distribution of 28.

3.3   Flexibility Regarding Different Objectives

Having the general scheme of A^*-based quantum-circuit mapping as discussed above, we eventually can discuss the flexibility of this solution with respect to different architectures and objectives. As already stated in Sect. 2.2, the A^* based approach is flexible regarding the architecture since coupling maps allow to specify not only IBM QX architectures, but also arbitrary ones like NN architectures

---

[8] More precisely, the distance of the physical qubits to which the logical ones are mapped is taken.

[9] Note that the distance might also include 4 Hadamard gates to indicate that the direction of the CNOT has to be switched.

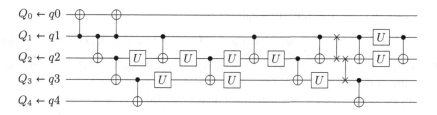

Fig. 6. Quantum circuit mapped to IBM QX5

(since the distance of two physical qubits in the coupling map can be easily determined in linear time using Dijkstra's algorithm). Besides that, the decision how to group gates also allows for a large flexibility when using A*-based mapping. In this section, we demonstrate that the algorithm is also flexible regarding certain cost metrics by providing a generic and parameterizable cost function that can be extended to take other cost metrics into account (e.g., qubit fidelity [28]) in the future.

The *path cost* $g(x)$ of a node x is generalized in such a way that it does not only include cost resulting from the gate count of the permutation circuit $cost_g$ (i.e., the depth of x in the search tree), but also cost resulting from the circuit depth $cost_d$ as well as cost resulting from the workload distribution $cost_w$ of part of the circuit that is already mapped (including the permutation circuits described by x), i.e.,

$$g(x) = cost_g/7 \cdot w_0 + cost_d/5 \cdot (1 - w_0) + cost_w \cdot w_1. \qquad (1)$$

Here, the additional weights w_0 and w_1 (with $0 \leq w_0, w_1 \leq 1$) allow to specify how much the algorithm shall focus on a certain cost metric.[10] For example, setting $w_0 = 1$ and $w_1 = 0$ results in the objective function described in the previous section—optimizing only the number of additional gates.

The heuristic cost (estimating the remaining cost based on the current mapping described by x) contains only the number of SWAPs to reach a goal node $cost_{hg}$ (this gives an estimate for gate count as well as for circuit depth):

$$h(x) = cost_{hg}/7 \qquad (2)$$

Like the path cost, also the lookahead cost for a subsequent sub-circuit G_j ($i < j < k$) is generalized to a sum of three terms:

- The sum of distances of the qubits occurring in the CNOTs of the sub-circuit G_j, i.e., $cost_{lg}$,
- the increase of circuit depth based on the distance of the qubits in the occurring CNOTs, i.e., $cost_{ld}$, and
- the change in the workload distribution based on the distance of the qubits in the occurring CNOTs, i.e., $cost_{lw}$.

---

[10] Note that we store the depth and the workload distribution for each physical qubit (considering the already mapped part of the circuit) to keep track of these values.

This leads to the generalized lookahead cost

$$l(x) = (cost_{lg}/7 \cdot w_0 + cost_{ld}/5 \cdot (1 - w_0) + cost_{lw} \cdot w_1) \cdot w_2^{j-i}. \qquad (3)$$

Here, the additional weight w_2 allows to exponentially decrease the contribution of future sub-circuits.

Overall, this leads to the generalized cost function

$$f(x) = g(x) + h(x) + \sum_{j=i+1}^{k} l(x, G_j) \qquad (4)$$

for a node x when currently considering a sub-circuit G_i.

Example 6 (continued). *Setting weights of the generalized cost and heuristic functions to $w_0 = 0.05$, $w_1 = 0$, $w_2 = 0.75$ allows to optimize for circuit depth at first hand and not for the gate count. Using this cost function in the mapping algorithm results in the circuit shown in Fig. 7. This circuit has now a depth of 22 (instead of 25) at the cost of increasing the gate count from 36 to $26 + 4 \cdot 7 = 54$.*

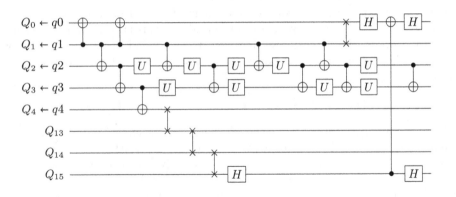

Fig. 7. Quantum circuit mapped to IBM QX5 using depth optimization

4   Experimental Evaluation

In this section, we experimentally evaluate the flexibility of A*-based mapping. To this end, we compare the generic solution proposed in this paper to dedicated solutions for 1D NN architectures developed over the past 10 years. Moreover, we evaluate how the parameters of the generalized objective function affect the cost of the mapped circuits. To this end, we have implemented the proposed general mapping approach in C++ and conducted several evaluations using benchmarks from RevLib [31] on a laptop with 2.6 GHz and 4 GB RAM.[11]

---

[11] Note that we grouped all gates that act on disjoint qubits into a sub-circuit as done in [21,22] (neglecting 1-qubit gates when forming the sub-circuits).

4.1   Flexibility Regarding the Considered Architecture

In a first series of evaluations, we compare the proposed generic mapping algorithm to dedicated solution for 1D NN architectures. As discussed in Sect. 2.2, these architectures can be modeled easily by using coupling maps, but are more restricted which makes it easier to develop dedicated optimizations. We compare the proposed approach to one of the first methods developed for these kind of architectures [17] as well as to one of the latest and most elaborated solutions [19] (this way, we showcase, how an adapted A*-based version compares to the initial NN-methods as well as today's state-of-the-art methods that emerged after several years of research on nearest neighbor optimization). Since both try to minimize the number of additional SWAP operations,[12] we also set our parameters $w_0 = 1$, $w_1 = 0$, and $w_2 = 0.75$ for $j - i = 1$ and to $w_2 = 0.5$ for $j > i + 1$.

Table 1 summarizes the obtained results when using the proposed approach for mapping all benchmark listed in the respective papers. The first three columns list the name of the benchmark, the number of qubits n, as well as the number of gates in the circuit to be mapped $|G|$. The next three columns list the obtained number of additional SWAP operations for the dedicated solutions presented in [17] and [19] as well as for the generic approach presented in this paper. The last two columns list the respectively achieved improvements. Runtimes are not provided since all mappings have been determined within a couple of seconds.

As can be seen in Table 1, the proposed generic approach significantly outperforms the dedicated approach presented in [17]. On average, 35.7% fewer SWAP operations are inserted. The generic approach even provides similarly good results compared to one of the most elaborated approaches for these specific architectures [19]. On average, the number of additionally required SWAP operations reduces even by 1.4%. These results are rather remarkable, since they indicate that dedicated solutions for, e.g., 1D NN architectures do not perform better than generic solutions applicable to any kind of envisioned architecture.

Overall, our evaluation shows that we reach significant and minor improvements compared to [17] and [19], respectively, even though the generality and flexibility of our approach does not allow to utilize dedicated optimization techniques when mapping to NN architectures. This is a clear testament of the power of A* as it shows that, using the proposed method allows to determine much better results as initial version and very competitive results compared to recent dedicated solutions.

4.2   Flexibility Regarding Different Cost Metrics

In a second round of experiments, we analyze the flexibility of the proposed method with respect to different objectives. In fact, changing a few parame-

---

[12] Note that no Hadamard operations have to be inserted since these architectures allow CNOTs in any direction between neighboring qubits.

Table 1. Comparison to dedicated solutions for 1D NN architectures

Benchmark			Required SWAP operations			Improvements	
Name	n	$|G|$	[17]	[19]	Proposed	w.r.t. [17]	w.r.t. [19]
3-17	3	13	5	6	4	−1	−2
4gt10-v1	5	36	29	24	22	−7	−2
aj-e11	5	59	43	33	29	−14	−4
hwb5	5	106	86	66	59	−27	−7
hwb6	6	146	140	111	104	−36	−7
mod5adder	6	81	79	46	54	−25	8
ham7	7	87	86	72	71	−15	−1
QFT7	7	21	29	18	21	−8	3
rd53	7	78	96	66	61	−35	−5
hwb7	8	2659	3480	2067	2015	−1465	−52
QFT8	8	28	41	31	34	−7	3
urf2	8	25150	23608	18428	16597	−7011	−1831
hwb8	9	16608	21767	13176	13546	−8221	370
QFT9	9	36	66	49	47	−19	−2
urf1	9	57770	62019	45730	42219	−19800	−3511
urf5	9	51380	54038	39852	37066	−16972	−2786
hwb9	10	20405	32979	18988	19495	−13484	507
QFT10	10	45	96	64	61	−35	−3
Shor3	10	2076	3353	2112	1982	−1371	−130
sym9	10	4452	5353	3103	4049	−1304	946
urf3	10	132340	140908	108321	100345	−40563	−7976
cycle10_2	12	1212	2193	966	1176	−1017	210
Shor4	12	10004	9510	5616	5410	−4100	−206
plus63mod4096	13	29019	54999	25617	29108	−25891	3491
plus127mod8192	14	65455	136820	63354	69470	−67350	6116
plus63mod8192	14	37101	77753	35472	38713	−39040	3241
Shor5	14	20530	22846	12221	11302	−11544	−919
ham15	15	458	803	531	537	−266	6
urf6	15	53700	91563	54815	51666	−39897	−3149
Shor6	16	37770	41551	22829	21159	−20392	−1670

ters allows to optimize for different cost metrics without changing any code or developing a new and dedicated solution.

Table 2 summarizes the obtained results. The first three columns list the name of the benchmark, the number of qubits n, the depth of the gate count of circuit to be mapped $|G|$. In the remaining columns, we list the gate count of the mapped circuit gc, its depth cd, as well as the workload distribution of the

Table 2. Evaluation of different parameter settings

Benchmark			Opt. gate count			Opt. depth			Opt. workload dist.		
Name	n	$|G|$	gc	cd	wd	gc	cd	wd	gc	cd	wd
3-17	3	36	105	63	14	112	64	9	138	74	10
rd32-v1	4	36	112	66	51	120	65	32	127	68	34
4_49	5	217	706	408	204	733	376	282	805	471	210
4gt10-v1	5	148	513	294	174	524	253	199	499	293	151
ex3	6	403	1345	762	447	1463	685	408	1338	768	333
hwb5	6	1336	4319	2512	1550	4689	2284	1666	4457	2547	1488
4mod5-bdd	7	70	270	151	116	285	130	87	274	145	98
ham7	7	320	1136	660	464	1287	609	392	1407	811	317
cm82a	8	650	2284	1242	531	2660	1131	697	2618	1454	630
urf5	9	164416	532100	294007	150186	612474	285427	163635	615963	332710	172780
sqn	10	10223	35572	19534	7354	41422	17673	10533	35860	19538	7144
urf3	10	125362	459017	250539	117506	560534	234612	144637	619623	324165	111370
9symml	11	34881	120708	67381	23653	149082	62038	33838	122708	68333	22098
dc1	11	1914	6841	3756	1264	7691	3337	1717	6369	3505	1466
life	11	22445	78395	44236	14841	95975	40431	21876	78548	44172	13975
rd84	12	13658	47471	25604	9203	58654	23878	12679	47833	25737	9101
sqrt8	12	3009	10910	5979	1906	12836	5352	2667	10923	6021	1917
sym10	12	64283	225510	126852	42949	278390	115416	60660	260146	146408	39162
adr4	13	3439	11569	6259	2616	14086	5990	3401	11878	6386	2360
dist	13	38046	133149	70751	22399	163240	64447	33983	133160	70283	22303
squar5	13	1993	6984	3630	1483	8282	3397	1940	7177	3678	1494
0410184	14	211	864	425	156	1147	347	184	891	452	107
pm1	14	1776	5971	3149	1454	6985	3046	1865	6451	3426	1110
sao2	14	38577	136483	71152	21215	169801	65420	35041	137215	71131	20456
co14	15	17936	64910	31600	6403	85351	29466	12829	70202	33803	5381
square_root	15	7630	26733	14022	4274	31663	12373	5895	27274	14244	3731
urf6	15	171840	617067	324396	88294	727960	307340	132278	628436	329294	74676
cnt3-5	16	175	555	204	44	674	224	79	579	220	49
inc	16	10619	36524	20579	6551	44182	18813	9890	37521	21126	4859
mlp4	16	18852	67821	37902	10773	83733	33734	15466	68415	37865	8728

qubits wd for the proposed circuit when optimizing for gate count (by setting $w_0 = 1$, $w_1 = 0$), for circuit depth (by setting $w_0 = 0.04$, $w_1 = 0$), and for the workload distribution (by setting $w_0 = 1$, $w_1 = 0.1$) when mapping the circuits to IBM QX5 (w_2 was the same for all three mappings and was 0.75 for $j - i = 1$ and 0.5 for $j > i + 1$).

Considering the optimization with respect to gate count as baseline, changing the parameters for optimizing with respect to circuit depth indeed results in a decrease of depth (on average by 7.7%) at the expense of inserting more SWAP and Hadamard operations (on average 17.1%). Similarly, the depth of the circuits optimized for depth is on average 12.3% smaller compared to those optimized for the workload distribution of the qubits. In contrast, their workload distribution is 39.3% worse compared to circuits optimized for that cost metric.

Overall, the experimental evaluation confirms the flexibility of the proposed approach with respect to different objectives. Moreover, this shows that optimizing for different objectives or architectures does not require to develop new algorithms, but only to adjust very few parameters in the objective functions. By this, we provide a mapping solution which is inherently applicable for future architectures just by employing suitable parameters or by slightly modifying the cost function.

5   Conclusions

In this work, we evaluated the flexibility of A* for mapping quantum circuit to physical quantum computers. By using coupling maps to model restrictions in the qubit interactions of these devices, one can specify arbitrary quantum architectures (e.g., NN architectures or IBM QX architectures). Since we additionally provide a generic and parameterizable cost function, our approach allows to optimize for different design objectives (like gate count, circuit depth, or workload distribution) just by changing parameters and without writing any code—inherently providing a customized mapping algorithm. Our experimental evaluation shows, that this generic approach is competitive with dedicated approaches for NN architectures and that changing the parameters indeed significantly influence the design objectives as desired.

Acknowledgements. This work has partially been supported by the LIT Secure and Correct System Lab funded by the State of Upper Austria and the European Union through the COST Action IC1405.

References

1. Nielsen, M., Chuang, I.: Quantum Computation and Quantum Information. Cambridge University Press, Cambridge (2000)
2. Shor, P.W.: Polynomial-time algorithms for prime factorization and discrete logarithms on a quantum computer. SIAM J. Comput. **26**(5), 1484–1509 (1997)
3. Grover, L.K.: A fast quantum mechanical algorithm for database search. In: Symposium on Theory of Computing, pp. 212–219 (1996)
4. Montanaro, A.: Quantum algorithms: an overview. NPJ Quantum Inf. **2**, 15023 (2016)
5. Debnath, S., Linke, N., Figgatt, C., Landsman, K., Wright, K., Monroe, C.: Demonstration of a small programmable quantum computer with atomic qubits. Nature **536**(7614), 63–66 (2016)
6. Linke, N.M., et al.: Experimental comparison of two quantum computing architectures. In: Proceedings of the National Academy of Sciences (2017). https://doi.org/10.1073/pnas.1618020114
7. IBM Q Team: IBM Q. https://www.research.ibm.com/ibm-q/. Accessed 02 May 2019
8. Nay, C.: IBM unveils world's first integrated quantum computing system for commercial use. https://newsroom.ibm.com/2019-01-08-IBM-Unveils-Worlds-First-Integrated-Quantum-Computing-System-for-Commercial-Use. Accessed 02 May 2019

9. Preskill, J.: Quantum computing in the NISQ era and beyond. arXiv preprint arXiv:1801.00862 (2018)
10. Sete, E.A., Zeng, W.J., Rigetti, C.T.: A functional architecture for scalable quantum computing. In: International Conference on Rebooting Computing, pp. 1–6 (2016)
11. Neill, C., et al.: A blueprint for demonstrating quantum supremacy with superconducting qubits. Science **360**(6385), 195–199 (2018)
12. Barenco, A., et al.: Elementary gates for quantum computation. Phys. Rev. A **52**(5), 3457 (1995)
13. Amy, M., Maslov, D., Mosca, M., Roetteler, M.: A meet-in-the-middle algorithm for fast synthesis of depth-optimal quantum circuits. Trans. Comput. Aided Des. Integr. Circ. Syst. **32**(6), 818–830 (2013)
14. Miller, D.M., Wille, R., Sasanian, Z.: Elementary quantum gate realizations for multiple-control Toffoli gates. In: International Symposium on Multi-valued Logic, pp. 288–293 (2011)
15. Siraichi, M., Dos Santos, V.F., Collange, S., Pereira, F.M.Q.: Qubit allocation. In: International Symposium on Code Generation and Optimization, pp. 1–12 (2018)
16. Botea, A., Kishimoto, A., Marinescu, R.: On the complexity of quantum circuit compilation. In: Symposium on Combinatorial Search (2018)
17. Saeedi, M., Wille, R., Drechsler, R.: Synthesis of quantum circuits for linear nearest neighbor architectures. Quantum Inf. Process. **10**(3), 355–377 (2011)
18. Wille, R., Lye, A., Drechsler, R.: Exact reordering of circuit lines for nearest neighbor quantum architectures. Trans. Comput. Aided Des. Integr. Circ. Syst. **33**(12), 1818–1831 (2014)
19. Wille, R., Keszocze, O., Walter, M., Rohrs, P., Chattopadhyay, A., Drechsler, R.: Look-ahead schemes for nearest neighbor optimization of 1D and 2D quantum circuits. In: Asia and South Pacific Design Automation Conference, pp. 292–297 (2016)
20. Hattori, W., Yamashita, S.: Quantum circuit optimization by changing the gate order for 2D nearest neighbor architectures. In: Kari, J., Ulidowski, I. (eds.) RC 2018. LNCS, vol. 11106, pp. 228–243. Springer, Cham (2018). https://doi.org/10.1007/978-3-319-99498-7_16
21. IBM Q Team: QISKit Python SDK Version 0.4.15. https://github.com/QISKit/qiskit-sdk-py. Accessed 02 May 2019
22. Zulehner, A., Paler, A., Wille, R.: An efficient methodology for mapping quantum circuits to the IBM QX architectures. Trans. Comput. Aided Des. Integr. Circ. Syst. (2018)
23. Zulehner, A., Wille, R.: Compiling SU(4) quantum circuits to IBM QX architectures. In: Asia and South Pacific Design Automation Conference, pp. 185–190 (2019)
24. Itoko, T., Raymond, R., Imamichi, T., Matsuo, A., Cross, A.W.: Quantum circuit compilers using gate commutation rules. In: Proceedings of the 24th Asia and South Pacific Design Automation Conference, pp. 191–196 (2019)
25. Dueck, G.W., Pathak, A., Rahman, M.M., Shukla, A., Banerjee, A.: Optimization of circuits for IBM's five-qubit quantum computers. In: Euromicro Conference on Digital System Design, pp. 680–684 (2018)
26. Wille, R., Burgholzer, L., Zulehner, A.: Mapping quantum circuits to IBM QX architectures using the minimal number of SWAP and H operations. In: Design Automation Conference (2019)
27. Zulehner, A., Wille, R.: Advanced simulation of quantum computations. Trans. Comput. Aided Des. Integr. Circ. Syst. (2018)

28. Tannu, S.S., Qureshi, M.K.: Not all qubits are created equal: a case for variability-aware policies for NISQ-era quantum computers. In: International Conference on Architectural Support for Programming Languages and Operating Systems, pp. 987–999 (2019)

29. Kelly, J.: A preview of Bristlecone, Google's new quantum processor (2018). https://ai.googleblog.com/2018/03/a-preview-of-bristlecone-googles-new.html

30. IBM Q Team: IBM Q 16 Rueschlikon backend specification v1.1.0. https://ibm.biz/qiskit-rueschlikon. Accessed 02 May 2019

31. Wille, R., Große, D., Teuber, L., Dueck, G.W., Drechsler, R.: RevLib: an online resource for reversible functions and reversible circuits. In: International Symposium on Multi-valued Logic, pp. 220–225 (2008). RevLib: http://www.revlib.org

Evaluating ESOP Optimization Methods in Quantum Compilation Flows

Giulia Meuli[1][✉], Bruno Schmitt[1], Rüdiger Ehlers[2], Heinz Riener[1], and Giovanni De Micheli[1]

[1] École Polytechnique Fédérale de Lausanne, Lausanne, Switzerland
giulia.meuli@epfl.ch
[2] University of Bremen, Bremen, Germany

Abstract. Exclusive-or sum-of-products (ESOP) expressions are used as intermediate representations in quantum circuit synthesis flows, and their complexity impacts the number of gates of the resulting circuits. Many state-of-the-art techniques focus on minimizing the number of product terms in a ESOP expression, either exactly or in a heuristic fashion.

In this paper, we investigate into ESOP optimization considering two recent quantum compilation flows with opposite requirements. The first flow generates Boolean functions with a small number of Boolean variables, which enables the usage of methods from exact synthesis; the second flow generates Boolean functions with many Boolean variables, such that heuristics are more effective. We focus on the reduction of the number of T gates, which are expensive in fault-tolerant quantum computing and integrate ESOP optimization methods into both flows. We show an average reductions of 36.32% in T-count for the first flow, while in the second flow an average reduction of 28.23% is achieved.

Keywords: Reversible Logic Synthesis · Logic optimization · ESOP · Quantum circuit

1 Introduction

Quantum compilation is the problem of translating a computational description of a quantum algorithm into basic quantum operations. Two main approaches are used in practice: (1) manual compilation, where a designer manually synthesizes (and optimizes) each component of the computational description and generates the final quantum circuit by hand, and (2) automatic compilation, which supports designers in the synthesis task by offering fast and scalable solutions to systematically explore the design space. On the one hand, automatic synthesis allows designers to deal with larger problems that are too complex to be tackled manually; on the other hand, systematic design space exploration enables designers to identify optimization capabilities otherwise overlooked.

© Springer Nature Switzerland AG 2019
M. K. Thomsen and M. Soeken (Eds.): RC 2019, LNCS 11497, pp. 191–206, 2019.
https://doi.org/10.1007/978-3-030-21500-2_12

Recent attempts in the field of automatic quantum compilation include *LUT-based Hierarchical Reversible Logic Synthesis* (*LHRS*) [25] and *Decomposition Based Synthesis* (*DBS*) [23]. The former framework, *LHRS*, uses a hierarchical method to synthesize quantum circuits from specifications provided in form of combinational logic designs. The designs are first decomposed into networks of look-up tables (LUTs). Then, a quantum circuit is assembled by translating each LUT into quantum gates. The latter framework, *DBS*, uses Young-subgroup based reversible synthesis [3] to compile quantum state permutations into quantum circuit. Both frameworks, *LHRS* and *DBS*, use *exclusive-or sum-of-products* (ESOPs) as representations of reversible logic gates generated during the translation process.

ESOPs are a classical two-level logic representation consisting of one level of AND-gates, followed by one level of XOR-gates. They provide a compact logic representation of Boolean functions, and are, for some classes of functions, exponentially more compact when compared to the sum-of-products (SOP) representation [21]. This compactness can be particularly recognized when XOR-intensive circuits, such as the parity function, need to be represented and makes ESOPs useful to describe arithmetic and cryptographic primitives [15].

Over the years, many advanced synthesis and optimization methods have been discovered for ESOPs. Exact methods [16,19,20] target the minimization of the number of product terms in an ESOP, such that the number becomes provably minimal. Their applicability, however, is limited to Boolean functions with at most 7 Boolean variables. Moreover, they often require large tables of pre-computed information and need a substantial amount of runtime to guarantee minimality.

Heuristic methods [13,20,27] are capable of reducing large-scale ESOPs with thousands of cubes by repeatedly applying simple cube transformation rules that first expand and then collapse cubes. Such transformation-based optimization strategies are fast, lead to significant reductions, and can be applied even if ESOPs with many Boolean variables are considered. Heuristic methods, however, cannot guarantee optimality and their progress often strongly degrades over time—the chances of finding a pair of cubes that can be collapsed decreases and the improvement saturates.

Overall, in this work, we target fault-tolerant quantum computation and analyze the impact of ESOP optimization methods on the number of T gates of the final quantum circuit. The T gates have been recognized as the most expensive gates in fault-tolerant quantum computing [1].

We integrate advanced ESOP optimization methods, both heuristic and exact, into recent quantum compilation flows. In particular, we consider *LHRS* and *DBS* as two possible application scenarios with opposite requirements: *DBS* uses simple specifications, such that only a few Boolean functions with a relatively small number of Boolean variables have to be synthesized. In this case, exact synthesis methods are useful and allow us to generate ESOPs of provably minimal size. In *LHRS*, however, ESOP optimization has to deal with many and larger Boolean functions. In this case, we advocate heuristic ESOP optimization methods to keep the approach scalable.

In our analysis, we consider two de-facto standard cost functions from logic synthesis—the number of product terms and the number of literals—and propose a novel exact synthesis procedure for ESOPs. Our procedure allows users to specify costs for each cube, considered during the synthesis process. We formulate the synthesis problem by introducing a weighted-version of the Helliwell equation [17], and solve the problem using partial weighted MAX-SAT.

2 Preliminaries

2.1 ESOP Representation of Boolean Functions

Definition 1. *An ESOP over n Boolean variables, $x_1, \ldots, x_n \in \mathbb{B}$, is an expression of form $t_1 \oplus \cdots \oplus t_k$, where each $t_i = l_{i,1} \cdots l_{i,l_i}$ is a product term (or cube) of literals $l_{i,j} \in \{x_1, \ldots, x_n, \bar{x}_1, \ldots, \bar{x}_n\}$ for $1 \leq i \leq k$ and $1 \leq j \leq l_i$. The symbol $\oplus$ denotes the modulo-2 addition (XOR-operation), and $\bar{x}_i$ denotes the negated Boolean variable x_i for $1 \leq i \leq n$.*

An ESOP expression can be interpreted as a two-level logic circuit, which realizes a possibly incompletely-specified Boolean function $f : \{0, 1, -\}^n \to \mathbb{B}$, i.e., $f(x_1, \ldots, x_n) = t_1 \oplus \cdots \oplus t_k$ for all possible valuations of the Boolean variables $x_1, \ldots, x_n$.

2.2 ESOP-Based Reversible Logic Synthesis

Reversible circuits are logic networks with the same number of inputs and outputs, composed of reversible gates. The most commonly used gates are the single-target gates and the multiple-controlled Toffoli gates.

Definition 2. *Let $c : \mathbb{B}^k \to \mathbb{B}$ be a Boolean function, called control function. Also, let $C = \{x_1, \ldots, x_k\}$ be the control lines and let $x_t \notin C$ be a target line. Then the single-target gate $T_c(C, t) : \mathbb{B}^n \to \mathbb{B}^n$ is a reversible Boolean function which maps:*

$$(x_1, \ldots, x_n) \to \begin{cases} x_i & \text{if } i \neq t \\ x_t \oplus c(x_1, \ldots, x_k) & \text{otherwise} \end{cases}$$

Definition 3. *If the control function c can be expressed as a single product term $c = \bigwedge_{i=1}^{k}(x_i \oplus p_i)$ using a single-target gate $T_c(C, t)$, where p_i, $1 \leq i \leq k$, are the polarities of the controls, then we call the gate a multiple-controlled Toffoli gate.*

A multiple-controlled Toffoli gate is a reversible gate acting on the bits in $x_1, \ldots, x_k, x_t$, such that the bits in C remain unchanged and the bit x_t flips if the control function $c(x_1, \ldots, x_k)$ evaluates to true.

ESOP-based reversible synthesis methods are based on the observation that an ESOP can be directly translated into a reversible circuit, as each term of the expression corresponds to a multiple-controlled Toffoli gate [5,6]. The method generates as many Toffoli gates as cubes in the expression, all cascaded and targeting the same bit.

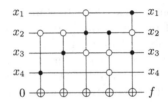

Fig. 1. Example of a reversible circuit of mixed-polarity multiple-controlled Toffoli gates

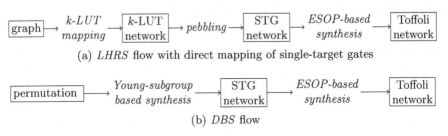

(a) *LHRS* flow with direct mapping of single-target gates

(b) *DBS* flow

Fig. 2. Two different state-of-the-art compilation flows for Boolean functions that use ESOP-based reversible synthesis

Example 1. The Toffoli network in Fig. 1 corresponds to the ESOP expression:

$$x_4\overline{x}_2 \oplus x_3\overline{x}_2 \oplus \overline{x}_3x_2\overline{x}_1 \oplus \overline{x}_4\overline{x}_3x_2 \oplus x_3\overline{x}_2x_1$$

Some optimization techniques aiming at reducing the cost of the generated reversible circuits have been proposed in literature [12,28]. The final circuit reflects the quality of the ESOP expression, so the synthesis process is crucial for this application.

3   Optimal ESOP for Quantum Compilation

The problem of automatically compiling a Boolean function into a universal quantum library is largely addressed in literature [7,9,22].

Among the available synthesis methods, hierarchical flows have the capability of being scalable, as they are based on a logic network representation [18], e.g., *LHRS* [26]. The input to *LHRS* is a classical logic network, e.g., provided in a hardware description language; the output is a quantum network realized in terms of Clifford+T gates. The framework is based on the usage of k-feasible Boolean logic networks (k-LUT networks), which consist of look-up tables (LUTs) with at most k inputs. Synthesis proceeds in two steps: (i) each k-LUT is mapped into a reversible single-target gate with k control lines, (ii) each reversible single-target gate is mapped into a Clifford+T network. *LHRS* provides different methods to perform the second step. One method, the so-called *direct mapping*, makes use of the ESOP representation of the control function of a reversible single-target gate, which can be *directly* translated into multiple-controlled Toffoli gates [6] (see Sect. 2.2) and further translated into quantum gates [11]. The flow of this method is shown in Fig. 2(a).

A second strategy (Fig. 2(b)) for quantum compilation is based on decomposing the initial function, given as a permutation, using the Young-subgroup method described in [3]. It only differs from the first one for the function's specification and the decomposition strategy employed. Differences that will result in a less scalable flow. The final steps are shared between the two flows: ESOP-based reversible synthesis is used to generate a Toffoli network and successively each Toffoli gate is compiled into quantum operations from the Clifford+T library using the method described in [11].

In this work, we address the Clifford+T universal quantum library, and try to optimize the number of T gates by applying ESOP optimization to the compilation flows. Nevertheless, our analysis and methods are applicable to the other quantum libraries, as far as the implementations of Toffoli gates are known.

4   Motivation

In the following, we introduce the problem of finding the right ESOP synthesis method to generate reversible circuits, which can be compiled into quantum circuits with optimal characteristics: minimal number of T gates and reduced number of Clifford gates.

Example 2. Given the Boolean function $f(x) = \overline{x}_1\overline{x}_3x_4 \vee \overline{x}_2\overline{x}_3x_4 \vee \overline{x}_1x_2x_3\overline{x}_4 \vee x_1\overline{x}_2x_3\overline{x}_4$ with $x = x_1, \ldots, x_4$, two possible ESOP expressions for f are:

$$A(x) = \quad x_3x_1 \oplus \overline{x}_4x_1 \oplus x_3x_2 \oplus x_1 \oplus \overline{x}_4x_2 \oplus x_2 \oplus x_4\overline{x}_3\overline{x}_2\overline{x}_1$$
$$B(x) = \quad \overline{x}_4x_3x_1 \oplus x_4\overline{x}_3x_2x_1 \oplus \overline{x}_4x_3x_2 \oplus x_4\overline{x}_3$$

The first expression $A(x)$ is composed of 7 product terms while the other expression, $B(x)$, is smaller and has size 4. We can use these ESOPs to synthesize a reversible network for f and successively we can compile them into quantum gates using the algorithm described in [11]. The resulting networks and the composition of the quantum circuits are reported in Fig. 3: H is the number of Hadamard gates, NOT and $CNOT$ are respectively the number of X and the number of controlled-X gates, T is the number of T gates. It is clearly shown how the second ESOP, independently from the smaller size, generates a quantum circuit with more gates. Differently, the first ESOP, that has larger size, shows characteristics allowing the compiler to create a circuit with reduced T gates, and fewer gates in general. We want to identify which are the characteristics that lead to a better quantum circuit. With this in mind, we can notice how the first ESOP has cubes with less literals, with respect to the second ESOP. Thus $A(x)$ generates a reversible circuit with multiple-controlled Toffoli gates with less controls and consequently a quantum circuit with less T gates.

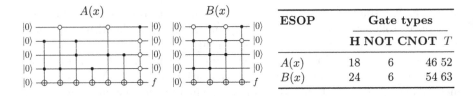

Fig. 3. Synthesis results of two different ESOPs for the same function f

It is evident how the quantum compilation problem can take advantage of optimal ESOP synthesis strategies. Consequently, in this work we apply state-of-the-art ESOP synthesis and optimization methods, e.g., the heuristic *EXOR-CISM* [14], into recent quantum compilation flows. In addition, we present a constraint-based ESOP synthesis method that accepts an arbitrary cost function, as Example 2 suggests that different cost metrics should be considered for ESOPs in quantum compilation.

5   Constraint-Based ESOP Synthesis

The problem of finding an ESOP expression that realizes a Boolean function is known as *ESOP synthesis*. The seminal work of Perkowski and Chrzanowska-Jeske [17] introduces the *Helliwell decision function* to characterize the solution space of ESOP synthesis for a given Boolean function.

5.1   Helliwell Decision Function

The Helliwell decision function $H_f(g_1, \ldots, g_K)$, $K \leq 3^n$, for a given Boolean function $f(x_1, \ldots, x_n)$ describes synthesis as an odd-even covering problem in terms of the minterms of f. For each possible product term in n Boolean variables, a decision variable g_i, $1 \leq i \leq K$, is introduced. The Helliwell decision function is then defined by the logic equation

$$\bigwedge_{m \in f} \left(\left(\bigoplus_{g \in I(m)} g \right) \oplus f(m) \oplus 1 \right), \tag{1}$$

where $m \in f$ denotes that m is a minterm of f and I maps each minterm to the decision variables $g_{i_1}, \ldots, g_{i_l}$ whose product terms are covered by m.

The logic equation (1) is constructed in such a way that every satisfying assignment $\hat{g}$ for $g = g_1, \ldots, g_K$ for $H(g)$ directly corresponds to an ESOP expression functionally equivalent to f.

Example 3. Given the Boolean function $f(x_1, x_2) = x_1 \vee x_2$ with Boolean variables x_1 and x_2, the Helliwell decision function using 9 Boolean variables $g_1, \ldots, g_9$, that are,

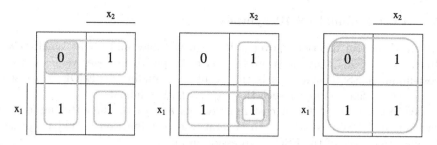

Fig. 4. Three possible ESOP covering for the function $f = x_1 \vee x_2$

$$g_1 = \overline{x}_1\overline{x}_2 \quad g_2 = \overline{x}_1 x_2 \quad g_3 = x_1\overline{x}_2 \quad g_4 = x_1 x_2$$
$$g_5 = x_1 \quad g_6 = \overline{x}_1 \quad g_7 = x_2 \quad g_8 = \overline{x}_2$$
$$g_9 = 1.$$

The SAT solver will find a selection of the cubes such that minterms for which f evaluates to one are covered an odd number of times, whether minterms for which f evaluates to false are covered an even number of times. Constraints must be added to the problem in order for the SAT solver to find a valid solution. The overall Helliwell decision function for f is:

$$H(g) = (g_1 \oplus g_6 \oplus g_8 \oplus g_9 \oplus 0 \oplus 1) \wedge (g_2 \oplus g_7 \oplus g_6 \oplus g_9 \oplus 1 \oplus 1) \wedge$$
$$(g_3 \oplus g_5 \oplus g_8 \oplus g_9 \oplus 1 \oplus 1) \wedge (g_4 \oplus g_5 \oplus g_7 \oplus g_9 \oplus 1 \oplus 1)$$

Figure 4 shows three possible ESOP covers on the Karnaugh map: g_4, g_6, g_8 and g_4, g_5, g_7 and g_6, g_9.

5.2   Size-Minimal ESOP Synthesis

Size-minimal ESOP synthesis is the problem of finding an ESOP expression for a given Boolean function f with a minimum number of product terms. Utilizing logic equation (1), the problem can be solved by computing minimum satisfying assignments for $H_f(g)$. An assignment $\hat{g}$ is minimum satisfying if the two conditions

$$\text{(a) } H_f(\hat{g}) \text{ and (b) } \forall g : (g \not\to \hat{g} \wedge H_f(g)) \implies g \not\to \hat{g}, \tag{2}$$

hold, i.e., if $\hat{g}$ satisfies H_f and no other assignment that satisfies H_f implies $\hat{g}$.

In the following, the idea of utilizing the Helliwell decision function for synthesizing size-minimum ESOP expression is generalized to synthesizing cost-minimal ESOP expressions, where the cost function is provided as a part of the input.

5.3   Cost-Minimal ESOP Synthesis

Given a Boolean function f over n Boolean variables and a cost function $\kappa :$ $\{0, 1, -\}^n \to \mathbb{N}_{>0}$, that maps product terms to positive integer values (costs), cost-minimal ESOP synthesis is the problem of finding an ESOP expression $t_1 \oplus \cdots \oplus t_k$ that realizes f such that $\bigwedge_{i=1}^{k} \kappa(t_i)$ is minimal.

We present two different cost function, κ_0 and κ_1 to illustrate the idea of cost-minimal ESOP synthesis. In general, the cost function should be picked keeping the usage of the ESOP expression in mind.

The constant function

$$\kappa_0(t) = 1 \tag{3}$$

defines unit costs for all product terms. If used, each ESOP expression obtained as solution of cost-minimal ESOP synthesis has a minimum number of product terms. The cost function

$$\kappa_1(t) = |t| + 1, \tag{4}$$

where $|t|$ counts the number of literals in t, weights each product term by the number of appearing literals. The additional 1 ensures that all costs—including the costs of the empty product term—are greater than 0.

Example 4. Consider the Boolean function $f_1(x) = \bar{x}_1\bar{x}_2 x_3 x_4 \vee \bar{x}_1 x_2 \bar{x}_3 x_4 \vee \bar{x}_1 x_2 x_3 \bar{x}_4 \vee x_1 \bar{x}_2 \bar{x}_3 x_4 \vee x_1 \bar{x}_2 x_3 \bar{x}_4 \vee x_1 x_2 \bar{x}_3 \bar{x}_4$ with $x = x_1, \ldots, x_4$. A cost-minimal ESOP expression that realizes f_1 with respect to cost function κ_0 is

$$\bar{x}_1 x_2 \bar{x}_4 \oplus x_2 \bar{x}_3 \oplus \bar{x}_2 x_3 \bar{x}_4 \oplus \bar{x}_1 \bar{x}_2 x_3 \oplus x_1 \bar{x}_3 x_4,$$

whereas a cost-minimal ESOP expression for the same Boolean function with respect to cost functions κ_1 is

$$x_1 \oplus x_2 \oplus \bar{x}_3 \oplus x_4 \oplus \bar{x}_1 \bar{x}_2 \bar{x}_3 \bar{x}_4 \oplus x_1 x_2 x_3 x_4.$$

5.4   Computing Cost-Minimal ESOPs

Next, we present the proposed SAT-based procedure for computing cost-minimal ESOP expressions using (weighted) maximum satisfiability (MAX-SAT) [10].

MAX-SAT deals with solving over-constrained constraint satisfaction problems modulo Boolean logic. The problems consist of hard and soft clauses, where each soft clause is associated with an integer weight greater than 0. The constraint satisfaction problem initially is unsatisfiable and the task of a MAX-SAT oracle is to find a minimal-cost relaxation of the soft clauses, i.e., the oracle has to remove a subset of the soft clauses, such that the problem becomes satisfiable while a given cost function is minimized.

Given a Boolean function f over n Boolean variables and a cost function $\kappa :$ $\{0, 1, -\}^n \to \mathbb{N}_{>0}$, cost-minimal ESOP synthesis is solved in three steps:

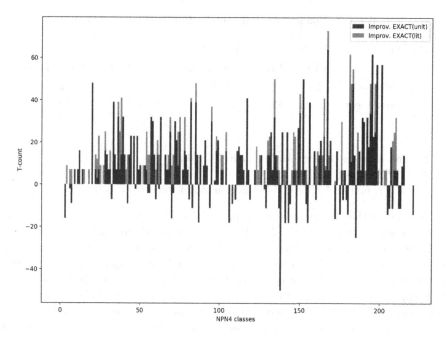

Fig. 5. Histogram showing the improvement over exact methods over *PKRM* with respect to two different cost functions: number of terms (*EXACT(unit)*) and number of literals (*EXACT(lit)*)

1. Formulate the Helliwell decision function $H(g)$ as described in (1).
2. Invoke a MAX-SAT oracle to find a satisfying assignment $\hat{g} = \hat{g}_1, \ldots, \hat{g}_K$ that minimizes $\sum_{i=1}^{K} \kappa(g_i)$ subject to $\text{CNF}[H(g)] \wedge (\bigwedge_{i=1}^{n} \bar{g}_i)$, where CNF translates the XOR-clauses to *conjunctive normal form* (CNF).
3. Construct the ESOP from the satisfying assignment $\hat{g}$.

The described approach is independent of the choice of the MAX-SAT oracle and the translation to CNF, but uses them as black-boxes.

6   Results

6.1   NPN4 Equivalence Classes

In this section, we evaluate the effect of different ESOP optimization methods on simple Boolean functions. As benchmarks, we use the 222 representatives of the NPN4 equivalence classes. We evaluate the number of product terms in the ESOP, as well as, the number of T gates in the generated quantum circuits considering different ESOP synthesis methods and the proposed constraint-based approach:

1. *Positive Polarity Reed Muller* (*PPRM*) [29],

Table 1. Comparison of different ESOP synthesis methods

Cost function	ESOP synthesis method				
	PPRM	PKRM	EXORCISM	EXACT(unit)	EXACT(lit)
avg. ESOP size	7.77	4.69	3.41	3.41	3.42
avg. num. T gates	87.35	82.32	59.05	67.50	58.19

2. *Pseudo-Kronecker Reed Muller* (*PKRM*) [4],
3. *EXORCISM* [14] and
4. *EXACT(unit)* and *EXACT(lit)* minimizing respectively κ_0 and κ_1.

We report the average number of product terms (size) and the average number of T gates for each of the ESOP synthesis methods in Table 1. *PPRM* and *PKRM* are special cases of general ESOP expressions, that can be easily derived from a given Boolean function but are sub-optimal when considering the number of product terms. They are often used as starting covers for ESOP optimization approaches. We report them to enable better comparability of the achieved reduction. *EXORCISM* is a fast cube transformation heuristic, capable of finding close to optimal ESOP expressions, starting from a PKRM cover of the Boolean function. Nevertheless, *EXORCISM* is an heuristic method and does not guarantee the minimality of the solution. In many cases, reducing the size of an ESOP also leads to a reduction of the number of T gates. Consequently, *EXORCISM*, *EXACT(unit)*, and *EXACT(lit)* improve over *PPRM* and *PRKM*. Reducing the number of literals also has a positive effect on the T gates, i.e., *EXACT(lit)* achieves a better reduction than *EXACT(unit)*. Moreover, *EXORCISM* also improves over the *EXACT(unit)* method because its heuristic prefers don't cares over concrete values and reduces the overall number of literals in an ESOP expression.

The histogram in Fig. 5 gives a more detailed overview of the improvement in T-count of *EXACT(lit)* and *EXACT(unit)* over *PKRM*, respectively, for all the 222 representatives in NPN4 equivalent classes.

Optimizing size and literals, however, does not minimize the number of T gates, which we illustrate by example: consider the two equivalent ESOPs

$$C(x_1, x_2, x_3) = 1 \oplus \bar{x}_1 x_2 \oplus x_1 x_2 x_3 \quad \text{and} \quad D(x_1, x_2, x_3) = x_1 x_2 \bar{x}_3 \oplus \bar{x}_2 \oplus \bar{x}_1. \tag{5}$$

Both ESOPs have the same number of product terms and the same number of literals. To realize $C(x_1, x_2, x_3)$ as quantum circuit, however, 23 T gates are required, whereas for realizing $D(x_1, x_2, x_3)$ 16 T gates are needed. This results suggest that in future work it would be valuable to identify more fitting cost functions than the number of literals. In addition, future technology developments could themselves require different cost functions. Our proposed constraint-based method could provide the flexibility to enable future research in this direction.

6.2   Integration into Quantum Compilation Flows

In this section, we show the result of integrating the advanced ESOP optimization methods into the quantum compilation flows *DBS* and *LHRS*.

To integrate optimized ESOP synthesis methods, we propose a pseudo-optimal portfolio approach as described in Algorithm 1. For each symmetric control function, the ESOP expression *esop* is computed using the *PKRM* method, that is optimum in this case. If the number of inputs is smaller or equal to 4, we use the exact methods to minimize the number of literals. For larger functions the heuristic *EXORCISM* is used (command & *exorcism -q* of abc [2]).

First we evaluate the improvement of the proposed method integrated into *DBS* (Fig. 2(b)). In Table 2 we show the synthesis results for reversible permutations from Maslov's reversible benchmark[1]. In addition we created reversible functions $MOD_{n/g} : \mathbb{B}^n \to \mathbb{B}^n$, where:

$$MOD_{n/g} = \begin{cases} 0 & \text{if } x = 0 \\ g^x mod(2^n - 1) & \text{if } 1 \leq x \leq 2^n - 2 \\ 2^n - 1 & \text{otherwise} \end{cases}$$

The data are showing a reduction in the number of T gates, with respect to the *PKRM* method, for both the *EXACT* approaches. Nevertheless, we can see how, if the synthesis is performed to minimize the number of literals in each cube, the T-count can be further improved. In fact, the *unit* approach gets to 22.66% improvement, while *lit* gives 28.23% improvement.

Algorithm 1. Pseudo-exact optimal ESOP

---

input   : control function $f : \mathbb{B}^n \to \mathbb{B}$
output: optimized ESOP expression of f
begin

    if $f \in cache$ **then**
        └ **return** $cache[f]$

    if f *is symmetric* **then**
        └ $esop \leftarrow PKRM(f)$

    else if $n \leq 4$ **then**
        └ $esop \leftarrow EXACT_{LIT}(f)$

    else
        └ $esop \leftarrow EXORCISM(f)$

    $cache.insert(f, esop)$
    └ **return** $esop$

In a second experiment, we evaluate the integration into the *LHRS* framework. In Table 3 we show results of synthesizing the arithmetic designs of

---

[1] http://webhome.cs.uvic.ca/~dmaslov.

Table 2. Comparison between exact method and heuristic for small reversible functions

Permutation	Q	PKRM		EXACT(lit)		EXACT(unit)	
		T	t[s]	T	t[s]	T	t[s]
hwb4	4	123	0.0	109	0.1	116	0.0
hwb5	5	514	0.0	337	59.9	447	0.3
hwb6	6	1361	0.0	993	0.9	993	0.9
hwb7	7	5331	0.0	3066	1.0	3066	1.1
hwb8	8	13562	0.0	7654	1.2	7654	1.2
mod5_11	5	453	0.0	350	36.5	368	0.2
mod5_12	5	453	0.0	361	59.1	400	0.2
mod5_13	5	428	0.0	329	38.2	343	0.1
mod5_17	5	478	0.0	382	64.3	414	0.3
mod5_21	5	433	0.0	352	34.9	482	0.1
mod5_22	5	469	0.0	354	25.0	391	0.1
mod5_24	5	503	0.0	405	61.4	448	0.3
mod5_3	5	494	0.0	386	34.8	411	0.2
mod7_14	7	5201	0.0	2936	1.0	2936	1.0
mod7_3	7	4945	0.0	2957	1.0	2957	1.0
mod7_7	7	4859	0.0	3039	1.0	3039	1.0
prime4	4	102	0.0	95	0.0	106	0.0
prime5	5	367	0.0	271	28.5	289	0.1
prime6	6	1054	0.0	786	0.8	786	0.7
prime7	7	3600	0.0	2283	1.0	2283	0.9
prime8	8	8302	0.0	4420	1.1	4420	1.0

avg. reduction $EXACT(lit) = 28.23\%$
avg. reduction $EXACT(unit) = 22.66\%$

the EPFL benchmark[2] into quantum circuits. As explained in the preliminary section, the first steps of the flow generate a reversible circuit made of single-target gates, each one with a control function of maximum k inputs, where k is the LUT size used to build the k-LUT network. An ESOP expression is synthesized for each control function and translated into quantum circuits as described in [6,11]. We compare a flow integrating our pseudo-exact approach against a flow using $PKRM$ for the mapping of single-target gates. We report synthesis results for LUT size (k) from 4 to 10. We obtain a maximum reduction of number of T gates in the case of $k = 10$ equal to 36.32% and a minimum reduction in the case of $k = 4$ equal to 17.86%.

---

[2] https://github.com/lsils/benchmarks.

Table 3. Synthesis of the EPFL arithmetic benchmark

k		Q	PKRM		Opt.			Q	PKRM		Opt.	
			T	t[s]	T	t[s]			T	t[s]	T	t[s]
4	adder	511	5398	0.0	5356	0.4	bar	1415	76816	0.2	56320	1.8
5		448	16061	0.1	15151	0.5		1031	95576	0.3	63694	2.9
6		448	16271	0.1	15279	0.6		647	52750	0.2	50944	1.8
7		427	37259	0.1	36110	0.7		647	52750	0.3	50944	1.9
8		427	37963	0.1	36654	0.7		647	52750	0.3	50944	1.9
9		416	84076	0.2	72338	0.8		647	52750	0.3	50944	1.9
10		416	85509	0.2	72985	0.9		647	52750	0.3	50944	1.9
4	div	26467	757193	5.8	635999	12.4	hyp	64630	2448872	25.3	2208000	37.5
5		24474	851035	6.8	690622	15.1		56568	2647894	26.1	2156087	40.5
6		24083	876636	8.0	709586	19.0		50118	2860466	28.2	2145634	46.6
7		23944	939887	9.6	742327	23.8		48399	3501767	31.0	2817812	51.8
8		23808	1034583	11.2	773058	26.6		47581	4540244	36.9	3546120	66.7
9		23711	1204407	13.0	831482	30.5		46992	5379295	43.0	4158260	79.1
10		23633	1710038	15.4	875766	34.3		46933	6238649	50.0	4596940	94.4
4	log	10420	458335	2.4	380787	12.8	max	1484	54422	0.2	42684	5.4
5		9661	623957	3.2	492501	24.1		1346	76507	0.2	60597	6.4
6		8156	1033225	4.3	768429	49.4		1256	104109	0.3	79853	6.4
7		8141	1507690	5.1	883462	103.7		1149	148355	0.4	102310	6.0
8		4658	2196359	6.2	1228593	48.1		1067	209851	0.6	140106	6.9
9		4456	3393095	8.4	1912337	65.8		977	323027	0.8	200270	5.9
10		3697	5786642	10.8	3268408	74.8		929	355341	1.1	230118	5.6
4	mult	8194	359422	1.8	270268	6.2	sin	1962	71409	0.4	64103	14.5
5		8100	479930	2.2	368062	8.8		1818	82386	0.5	71471	19.4
6		6706	1034190	2.8	579420	11.6		1608	115107	0.7	92659	25.7
7		7050	1448336	3.7	847558	15.2		1553	137989	0.9	104092	27.3
8		5101	1371054	3.7	818914	16.6		1449	249964	1.2	157332	32.5
9		5165	2115333	5.2	1410009	18.3		915	794521	1.5	362082	33.2
10		4006	3657831	8.0	2417393	23.9		878	1241237	2.2	542136	37.2
4	sqrt	8686	317522	1.7	255275	6.4	square	6909	354552	1.5	240636	11.5
5		8351	344049	2.3	265948	6.8		6092	553311	1.9	308262	18.0
6		8332	391900	2.9	285310	7.8		4195	299574	1.8	206683	16.1
7		8152	448518	3.4	301246	8.4		4213	368160	2.0	261272	22.8
8		7986	709282	4.4	358215	9.5		3764	477446	2.3	341092	24.3
9		7976	720144	5.3	359296	10.6		3724	658343	2.9	445505	32.5
10		7966	1413589	7.0	540586	12.4		3792	876884	3.7	532124	41.4

min avg. improvement k = 4 : 17.86%
max avg. improvement k = 10 : 36.32%
avg. improvement: 26.36%

7   Open Source Implementation

The proposed SAT-based exact synthesis method is implemented in the open source C++ library *easy*[3] [19,24] using our own C++ implementation of RC2 [8] as MAX-SAT oracle. The *easy* library provides implementations of various verification and synthesis algorithms for ESOP expressions.

For the quantum compilation results, we interfaced *easy* with *caterpillar*[4] and *tweedledum*[5]. The first library is dedicated to quantum compilation, hierarchical methods, and quantum memory management, whereas the second library implements state-of-the-art synthesis methods, e.g., Young subgroup decomposition based synthesis.

8   Conclusion

In this work, we integrate ESOP synthesis methods into quantum compilation flows in order to improve the quality of the produced quantum circuits. We target fault-tolerant quantum computing and aim at minimizing the number of expensive T gates. We consider two different compilation flows for Boolean functions that make use of ESOP-based reversible synthesis.

For both frameworks this integration leads to promising results, which show maximum T-count reductions of 28.23% in *DBS* and 36.32% in *LHRS* with respect to *PKRM*. In conclusion, advanced ESOP synthesis methods, both exact and heuristic, can be applied inside the quantum compilation flows that use ESOP-based reversible synthesis, to generate better circuits for fault-tolerant quantum computing.

Acknowledgments. This research was supported by the European COST Action IC 1405 'Reversible Computation', by the EPFL Open Science Fund and the Institutional Strategy of the University of Bremen, funded by the German Excellence Initiative.

References

1. Amy, M., Maslov, D., Mosca, M., Roetteler, M.: A meet-in-the-middle algorithm for fast synthesis of depth-optimal quantum circuits. IEEE Trans. Comput. Aided Des. Integr. Circ. Syst. **32**(6), 818–830 (2013)
2. Brayton, R., Mishchenko, A.: ABC: an academic industrial-strength verification tool. In: Touili, T., Cook, B., Jackson, P. (eds.) CAV 2010. LNCS, vol. 6174, pp. 24–40. Springer, Heidelberg (2010). https://doi.org/10.1007/978-3-642-14295-6_5
3. De Vos, A., Van Rentergem, Y.: Young subgroups for reversible computers. Adv. Math. Commun. **2**(2), 183–200 (2008)
4. Drechsler, R.: Pseudo-kronecker expressions for symmetric functions. IEEE Trans. Comput. **48**(9), 987–990 (1999)

---

[3] https://github.com/hriener/easy.
[4] https://github.com/gmeuli/caterpillar.
[5] https://github.com/boschmitt/tweedledum.

5. Drechsler, R., Finder, A., Wille, R.: Improving ESOP-based synthesis of reversible logic using evolutionary algorithms. In: Di Chio, C., et al. (eds.) EvoApplications 2011. LNCS, vol. 6625, pp. 151–161. Springer, Heidelberg (2011). https://doi.org/10.1007/978-3-642-20520-0_16

6. Fazel, K., Thornton, M., Rice, J.E.: ESOP-based Toffoli gate cascade generation. In: IEEE Pacific Rim Conference on Communications, Computers and Signal Processing, pp. 206–209 (2007)

7. Haener, T., Soeken, M., Roetteler, M., Svore, K.M.: Quantum circuits for floating-point arithmetic. In: Kari, J., Ulidowski, I. (eds.) RC 2018. LNCS, vol. 11106, pp. 162–174. Springer, Cham (2018). https://doi.org/10.1007/978-3-319-99498-7_11

8. Ignatiev, A., Morgado, A., Marques-Silva, J.: PySAT: a Python toolkit for prototyping with SAT oracles. In: Beyersdorff, O., Wintersteiger, C.M. (eds.) SAT 2018. LNCS, vol. 10929, pp. 428–437. Springer, Cham (2018). https://doi.org/10.1007/978-3-319-94144-8_26

9. JavadiAbhari, A., et al.: ScaffCC: a framework for compilation and analysis of quantum computing programs. In: Proceedings of the 11th ACM Conference on Computing Frontiers, p. 1. ACM (2014)

10. Li, C.M., Manyà, F.: MaxSAT, hard and soft constraints. In: Handbook of Satisfiability, pp. 613–631 (2009)

11. Maslov, D.: Advantages of using relative-phase Toffoli gates with an application to multiple control Toffoli optimization. Phys. Rev. A 93(2), 022311 (2016)

12. Miller, D.M., Wille, R., Drechsler, R.: Reducing reversible circuit cost by adding lines. In: 2010 40th IEEE International Symposium on Multiple-Valued Logic, pp. 217–222. IEEE (2010)

13. Mishchenko, A., Chatterjee, S., Brayton, R.K.: Improvements to technology mapping for LUT-based FPGAs. IEEE Trans. Comput. Aided Des. Integr. Circ. Syst. 26(2), 240–253 (2007)

14. Mishchenko, A., Perkowski, M.: Fast heuristic minimization of exclusive-sums-of-products. In: Proceedings of International Workshop on Applications of the Reed-Muller Expansion in Circuit Design, pp. 242–250 (2001)

15. Mizuki, T., Otagiri, T., Sone, H.: An application of ESOP expressions to secure computations. J. Circ. Syst. Comput. 16(02), 191–198 (2007)

16. Papakonstantinou, K., Papakonstantinou, G.: A nonlinear integer programming approach for the minimization of boolean expressions. J. Circ. Syst. Comput. 27(10), 1850163 (2018)

17. Perkowski, M., Chrzanowska-Jeske, M.: An exact algorithm to minimize mixed-radix exclusive sums of products for incompletely specified Boolean functions. In: ISCAS, pp. 1652–1655 (1990)

18. Rawski, M.: Application of functional decomposition in synthesis of reversible circuits. In: Krivine, J., Stefani, J.-B. (eds.) RC 2015. LNCS, vol. 9138, pp. 285–290. Springer, Cham (2015). https://doi.org/10.1007/978-3-319-20860-2_20

19. Riener, H., Ehlers, R., Schmitt, B., De Micheli, G.: Exact synthesis of ESOP forms. CoRR abs/1807.11103 (2018). http://arxiv.org/abs/1807.11103

20. Sasao, T.: EXMIN2: a simplification algorithm for exclusive-or-sum-of-products expressions for multiple-valued-input two-valued-output functions. IEEE Trans. Comput. Aided Des. Integr. Circ. Syst. 12(5), 621–632 (1993)

21. Sasao, T.: Representations of logic functions using EXOR operators. In: Sasao, T., Fujita, M. (eds.) Representations of Discrete Functions, pp. 29–54. Springer, Boston (1996). https://doi.org/10.1007/978-1-4613-1385-4_2

22. Soeken, M., Haener, T., Roetteler, M.: Programming quantum computers using design automation. In: Design, Automation & Test in Europe Conference & Exhibition (DATE), pp. 137–146. IEEE (2018)
23. Soeken, M., Mozafari, F., Schmitt, B., De Micheli, G.: Compiling permutations for superconducting QPUs. In: DATE (2019, to appear)
24. Soeken, M., Riener, H., Haaswijk, W., Micheli, G.D.: The EPFL logic synthesis libraries. CoRR abs/1805.05121 (2018). http://arxiv.org/abs/1805.05121
25. Soeken, M., Roetteler, M., Wiebe, N., De Micheli, G.: Logic synthesis for quantum computing. CoRR abs/1706.02721 (2017). http://arxiv.org/abs/1706.02721
26. Soeken, M., Roetteler, M., Wiebe, N., De Micheli, G.: LUT-based hierarchical reversible logic synthesis. IEEE Trans. Comput. Aided Des. Integr. Circ. Syst. (2018)
27. Stergiou, S., Daskalakis, K., Papakonstantinou, G.: A fast and efficient heuristic ESOP minimization algorithm. In: Proceedings of the 14th ACM Great Lakes symposium on VLSI, pp. 78–81. ACM (2004)
28. Wille, R., Soeken, M., Otterstedt, C., Drechsler, R.: Improving the mapping of reversible circuits to quantum circuits using multiple target lines. In: 2013 18th Asia and South Pacific Design Automation Conference (ASP-DAC), pp. 145–150. IEEE (2013)
29. Zhegalkin, I.: The technique of calculation of statementsin symbolic logic. Mathe. Sbornik. **34**, 9–28 (1927). (in Russian)

Applications and Implementations

Implementing NChooseK on IBM Q Quantum Computer Systems

Harsh Khetawat[1] , Ashlesha Atrey[1], George Li[1], Frank Mueller[1(✉)] ,
and Scott Pakin[2]

[1] North Carolina State University, Raleigh, NC, USA
{hkhetaw,amatrey,gpli,fmuelle}@ncsu.edu
[2] Los Alamos National Laboratory, Los Alamos, NM, USA
pakin@lanl.gov

Abstract. This work contributes a generalized model for quantum computation called NChooseK. NChooseK is based on a single parametrized primitive suitable to express a variety of problems that cannot be solved efficiently using classical computers but may admit an efficient quantum solution. We implement a code generator that, given arbitrary parameters for N and K, generates code suitable for execution on IBM Q quantum hardware. We assess the performance of the code generator, limitations in the size of circuit depth and number of gates, and propose optimizations. We identify future work to improve efficiency and applicability of the NChooseK model.

Keywords: IBM Q · Quantum computing · NChooseK

1 Introduction

Despite a number of quantum-computing hardware platforms that have recently become available and their theoretical potential to more efficiently solve problems that are of high computational complexity [12,23], few computational scientists have embraced these novel platforms other than to demonstrate how very small problems may be solved. A short-term challenge to adoption is hardware immaturity (low qubit counts, rapid decoherence, poor gate fidelities, etc. [21]). However, a longer-term impediment to using quantum computing as a practical resource for computational scientists is the difficulty of *programming* such systems. Several programming paradigms and languages have been proposed in prior work to address this issue but they are all variants of the same, low level of abstraction over the underlying hardware [13].

We address the quantum programmability issue by designing a new high-level quantum programming model that reduces the challenge for programmers to express their computational problems. We implement the software tools for generating programs expressed in our model to target contemporary quantum hardware. More specifically, we develop the NChooseK model that constrains "*N* bits such that *K* of those bits must be TRUE" (where *K* can be a set of

© Springer Nature Switzerland AG 2019
M. K. Thomsen and M. Soeken (Eds.): RC 2019, LNCS 11497, pp. 209–223, 2019.
https://doi.org/10.1007/978-3-030-21500-2_13

possibilities). This is of interest since one can express NP-complete problems as NChooseK. There are two unique aspects to our approach. First, the programming model we propose has a *classical* semantics, which makes it not only approachable by computational scientists who are not trained in quantum information theory but also easy to integrate into existing classical workflows. Second, the same program can be compiled *unmodified* on both gate-model quantum computers and quantum annealers. The model represents computational problems as satisfiability problems.

We first discuss our proposed programming model, NChooseK, and how it can be used to represent computational problems. We then provide an implementation via a code generator that generates code for IBM Q quantum computer systems [16] for any arbitrary parameters in the NChooseK programming model. We present results for the characteristics of the generated IBM Q circuit representation in terms of both circuit depth and gate count. Finally, we discuss the limitations of the code generator and explore future work to optimize and extend NChooseK to express more complex computation.

2 Background

A quantum Turing machine (or universal quantum computer) [11] is an abstract machine that models the behavior of a quantum computer. It can be used to formally express any quantum algorithm. A quantum circuit, which is computationally equivalent, is more widely used to model quantum algorithms rather than a quantum Turing machine. In the quantum circuit model, computation is described as a sequence of quantum gates on quantum registers. The model necessitates that any computation be reversible as quantum gates are unitary.

The code generator introduced in this work generates code for IBM Q quantum systems, which uses this model for computation. IBM Q systems use superconducting Josephson junctions [5] to implement the state of qubits. Other technologies, such as trapped ions [4] and optical lattices [2], have also been used to realize quantum computers in hardware. While these technologies realize quantum bits and gates through different substrates (materials) that exhibit quantum effects and operations, they follow a common quantum circuit model for operation.

Figure 1 depicts a 5 qubit IBM Q processor with the Josephson junctions for qubits, measuring circuits and interconnection between qubits. The image shows that there is no all-to-all connection between qubits as only certain qubits are connected to and may thus directly interact with one another.

3 The NChooseK Programming Model

We first describe the NChooseK programming model and then present our implementation on IBM Q systems. NChooseK is based on a single parameterized primitive, which can be used to express a wide variety of problems that quantum computer programmers might be interested in solving. The single NChooseK

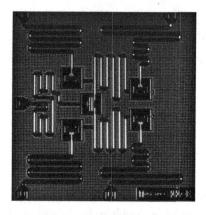

Fig. 1. IBM Q processor. Photo: IBM Research

primitive constrains k of n Boolean variables to TRUE. More precisely, given n Boolean variables and a set of K integers in the range $[0, n]$, executing the primitive sets exactly k of those Boolean values to TRUE for some $k \in K$.

Executing an entire NChooseK program results in the system assigning Boolean values that honor all of the program's constituent primitives. For example, using the notation "nck(V, K)" to indicate that of the n variables in the set $V, k \in K$ of them must be set to TRUE, Fig. 2 presents a trivial example of an NChooseK program. The program expresses the constrains that either 0 or 1 of the set of variables {a, b, c} must be TRUE, either 2 or 3 of the set of variables {b, c, d} must be TRUE, and exactly 1 of the set of variables {c, d, e} must be TRUE. Execution of this program amounts to computationally finding an assignment of variables that satisfies all three constrains. In this case, the sole solution is {b, d} = TRUE, {a, c, e} = FALSE.

$$\begin{array}{|l|}
\hline
nck(\{a, b, c\}, \{0, 1\}) \\
nck(\{b, c, d\}, \{2, 3\}) \\
nck(\{c, d, e\}, \{1\}) \\
\hline
\end{array}$$

Fig. 2. Trivial example of an NChooseK program

3.1   Implementing the NChooseK Model

The objective of this work is to convert the entire NChooseK program into a quantum black box (i.e., a unitary operator U_ω expressed as a quantum circuit) suitable for use in Grover's search algorithm [15]. Given a total of n Boolean variables in an NChooseK program, an exhaustive (classical) search for a satisfying assignment takes time $O(2^n)$. Grover's algorithm reduces the time to $O(\sqrt{2^n})$.

Consider the example in Fig. 3 depicting a quantum black box that corresponds to $nck(\{b, c, d\}, \{2, 3\})$. It maps a quantum state $|bcd\rangle|x\rangle$ to $|bcd\rangle|x \oplus 1\rangle$

when exactly 2 or 3 of $|b\rangle$, $|c\rangle$, and $|d\rangle$ are $|1\rangle$ and to $|bcd\rangle|x\rangle$ otherwise, as required by Grover's algorithm.

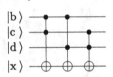

Fig. 3. A quantum black box for $nck(\{b,c,d\},\{2,3\})$

It is always possible to generate a circuit of the form used in Fig. 3 from an NChooseK expression of a problem by following the approach described by Younes [24]. Although the gates required by Younes's approach—CNOT, CCNOT, CCCNOT, etc.—are not provided natively by modern hardware (with the occasional exception of CNOT), standard transformations can be applied to map these gates onto the available gate set. Assuming a typical gate set of single-qubit gates plus CNOTs, these transformations would normally realize the circuit shown in Fig. 3 as a large (~40-qubit) circuit. To keep the depth more manageable for current hardware, which exhibits relatively short decoherence times, one could employ the techniques developed by Cincio et al. [3] to find shorter-depth equivalents. In the case of $nck(\{b,c,d\},\{2,3\})$, Cincio et al. find the 17-qubit circuit shown in Fig. 4.

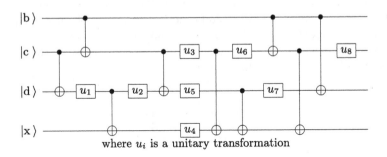

where u_i is a unitary transformation

Fig. 4. A short-depth implementation of $nck(\{b,c,d\},\{2,3\})$ using only single-qubit gates and CNOTs

3.2   Generality of the NChooseK Model

The NChooseK model is based on the single, easy-to-understand constraint of "K of N bits must be TRUE" (where K can be a set of possibilities). The key advantages of this model are that

1. it is sufficiently high-level as to abstract away the underlying hardware architecture so compilers and optimizers can target gate-model quantum computers, quantum annealers, and even classical computers and supercomputers;

2. it enables programs written to that model to be formally specified and exhibit a unique interpretation, even across disparate architectures; and
3. as a classical programming model, it can integrate easily into existing, classical, scientific workflows.

Let us next demonstrate that the NChooseK model is useful. Specifically, we show how one can express NP-complete problems [6]—loosely, problems that cannot efficiently be solved classically—using NChooseK.

Table 1. Adapting the truth table for OR for expression with NchooseK

A	B	A∨B	Valid?	#TRUE		A	B	A∨B	A∨B	Valid?	#TRUE
F	F	F	✓	0		F	F	F	F	✓	0
F	F	T		1		F	F	T	T		2
F	T	F		1		F	T	F	F		1
F	T	T	✓	2		F	T	T	T	✓	3
T	F	F		1		T	F	F	F		1
T	F	T	✓	2		T	F	T	T	✓	3
T	T	F		2		T	T	F	F		2
T	T	T	✓	3		T	T	T	T	✓	4

(a) Truth table for Boolean OR

(b) Truth table for Boolean OR with the third column repeated

Circuit Satisfiability. Given a Boolean expression, the goal of the circuit-satisfiability problem is to find a set of inputs for which the expression evaluates to TRUE or report that no such set exists. Figure 5 shows how one can construct the primitive operations needed to express circuit-satisfiability problems in terms of the NchooseK model.

The figure illustrates various NchooseK primitives as rectangles and the variables upon which they act as circles. The simplest primitives are shown in Figs. 5a and b. The former illustrates that variable A can be biased towards TRUE by expressing, "1 of out 1 input should be TRUE". Likewise, the latter illustrates that variable A can be biased towards FALSE by expressing, "0 of out 1 input should be TRUE". Figure 5c shows that an inverter can be expressed as "1 out of 2 inputs should be TRUE", which leads one of variables A and $\neg A$ to be TRUE and the other FALSE. Expressing OR and AND requires a modicum of creativity. For a 2-input OR, Table 1a indicates that $K = \{0, 2, 3\}$ corresponds to valid rows and $K = \{1, 2\}$ corresponds to invalid rows.

Because 2 appears in both the valid and invalid sets, one cannot use $nck(\{A, B, A\lor B\}, \{0, 2, 3\})$ to express OR. However, if one repeats the third column of the truth table as in Table 1b, then $K = \{0, 3, 4\}$ corresponds to valid rows and $K = \{1, 2\}$ corresponds to invalid rows. Because these are disjoint sets, OR can be expressed as in Fig. 5d. One can employ the same trick to find that AND can be expressed with $nck(\{A, B, A\lor B\}, \{0, 1, 4\})$ as in Fig. 5e.

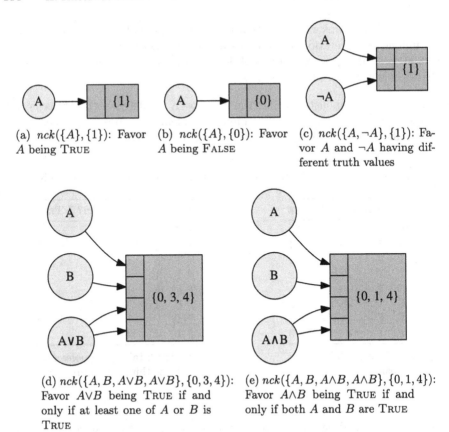

(a) $nck(\{A\}, \{1\})$: Favor A being TRUE

(b) $nck(\{A\}, \{0\})$: Favor A being FALSE

(c) $nck(\{A, \neg A\}, \{1\})$: Favor A and $\neg A$ having different truth values

(d) $nck(\{A, B, A \lor B, A \lor B\}, \{0, 3, 4\})$: Favor $A \lor B$ being TRUE if and only if at least one of A or B is TRUE

(e) $nck(\{A, B, A \land B, A \land B\}, \{0, 1, 4\})$: Favor $A \land B$ being TRUE if and only if both A and B are TRUE

Fig. 5. NchooseK building blocks for circuit satisfiability

A trivial circuit-satisfiability problem, corresponding to the function $x_6 = (x_1 \lor x_2) \land \neg x_3$, is illustrated in Fig. 6. Figure 6a depicts this function as a digital circuit, and Fig. 6b demonstrates how to find values of inputs x_1, x_2, and x_3 in the NChooseK model. x_4 is constrained to x_1 OR x_2 using the OR primitive defined in Fig. 5d; x_5 is constrained to the negation of x_3 using the inverter primitive defined in Fig. 5c; x_6 is constrained to x_4 AND x_5 using the AND primitive defined in Fig. 5e; and x_6 is further constrained to TRUE using the TRUE primitive defined in Fig. 5a.

Because AND, OR, and NOT constitute a universal (classical) gate set, the implication is that *any* Boolean function can be expressed in the NChooseK model, demonstrating its universality.

Map Coloring. Map coloring is another NP-complete problem. The goal is to color a map (a planar graph) using at most c colors, such that no two adjacent regions share a color, where is c is a constant, e.g., $c = 4$ to color a map of states

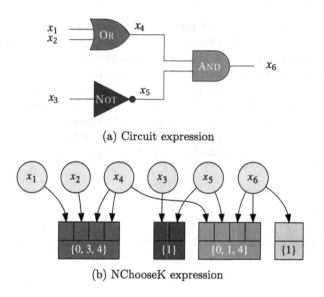

(a) Circuit expression

(b) NChooseK expression

Fig. 6. Example of expressing a circuit-satisfiability problem with NChooseK

or countries. Here, we show that the map-coloring problem, like the circuit-satisfiability problem, is easily expressed in the NChooseK model.

An NChooseK version of map coloring relies on only two primitives, which are illustrated in Fig. 7. Following the approach taken by Dahl [10] we use a unary encoding of each region of the map: one Boolean for each of red, orange, green, and blue. In NChooseK, this is expressed as "1 out of 4 inputs should be TRUE" and is illustrated in Fig. 7a. The other primitive ensures that for two

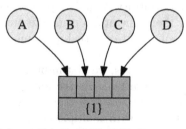

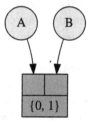

(a) $nck(\{A, B, C, D\}, \{1\})$: Favor coloring the current region with exactly one of colors A, B, C, or D

(b) $nck(\{A, B\}, \{0, 1\})$: Favor coloring at most one of regions A and B with the current color

Fig. 7. NChooseK building blocks for map coloring

adjacent regions, at most one of them is red—and likewise for each of orange, green, and blue. As Fig. 7b illustrates, an "either 0 or 1 of 2 inputs must be TRUE" NChooseK primitive expresses that constraint.

Figure 8 illustrates the construction of a two-region map-coloring problem using the building blocks from Fig. 7. The two regions are dubbed P and Q, and each is represented by four variables, one per color, yielding the eight variables P_r, P_o, P_g, P_b, Q_r, Q_o, Q_g, and Q_b. The four P variables connect to a block in Fig. 7a while the four Q variables connect to a block in Fig. 7a. The P and Q "red" variables connect to a block in Fig. 7b, and likewise for each of "orange", "green", and "blue".

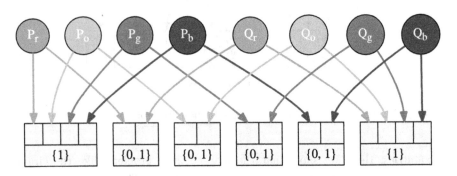

Fig. 8. Coloring two adjacent regions using NChooseK (Color figure online)

4   Implementation of the Code Generator

We implement a code generator for IBM Q Quantum Systems. It generates code for the IBM Qiskit API [17] given arbitrary N and K parameters for the NChooseK model. Our code generator then generates a complete program that can be executed on the IBM quantum simulator or actual quantum computing hardware.

To demonstrate how the code generator works, we first implement the basic logic gates, AND and OR, in Quirk [14]. Figure 9 depicts the implementation of the gates using Quirk for all $|0\rangle$ inputs (equivalent to FALSE in the following). Because Quirk allows the use of NOT gates with multiple controls and anti-controls, a circuit and its behavior can easily be visualized.

Figure 9a shows 6 conditions that would need to be addressed for the AND circuit. The first condition (all anti-controls) specifies that the output is TRUE if all inputs are FALSE. The next 4 conditions set the output to TRUE if one and only one of the inputs is TRUE (while the other 3 inputs are FALSE). The last condition sets the output to TRUE if all 4 inputs are TRUE. These 6 conditions correspond to the conditions required for the NChooseK primitive shown in Fig. 5e. So when the output is TRUE, this circuit represents an AND circuit of NChooseK combinations. Similarly, Fig. 9b uses 6 conditions to represent a

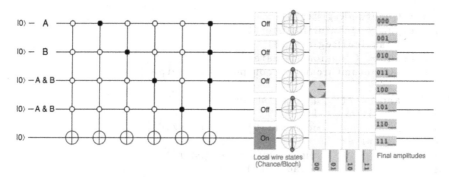

(a) AND of 6 NChooseK Combinations in Quirk

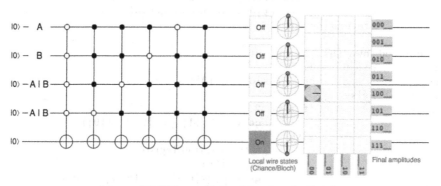

(b) OR of 6 NChooseK Combinations in Quirk

Fig. 9. Implementation of basic gates on quirk

multi-bit OR circuit of NChooseK combinations. In this case, the conditions represent those for the NChooseK primitive shown in Fig. 5d. For both Figs. 9a and b we need two qubits to represent A ∧ B and A ∨ B, respectively. The truth table and intuition for this is described in Table 1.

4.1   Code Generation Example

In this section we present an example code generated by our code generator. We choose the example of $nck(\{A, B, C\}\{0, 2\})$, which implements the XOR function $C = A \oplus B$ using the NChooseK primitive. The generated code is shown below. We exclude the initialization and measurement code for brevity.

```
1  q = QuantumRegister(3)
2  qoutput = QuantumRegister(1)
3  c = ClassicalRegister(3)
4  coutput = ClassicalRegister(1)
5  qc = QuantumCircuit(q, qoutput, c, coutput)
6
7  def andInner(t, qx, qz, m, qc):
8          if m == 1:
9                  qc.ccx(t[0], qx[0], qz[0])
10         else:
11                 tmp = QuantumRegister(1)
12                 qc.add(tmp)
13                 qc.ccx(t[0], qx[m-1], tmp[0])
14                 andInner(tmp, qx, qz, m-1, qc)
15                 qc.ccx(t[0], qx[m-1], tmp[0])
16         return qc
17
18 def and_nway(qx, qz, n, qc):
19         if n == 1:
20                 qc.cx(qx[0], qz[0])
21         else:
22                 if n == 2:
23                         qc.ccx(qx[1], qx[0], qz[0])
24                 else:
25                         t = QuantumRegister(1)
26                         qc.add(t)
27                         qc.ccx(qx[n-1], qx[n-2], t[0])
28                         andInner(t, qx, qz, n-2, qc)
29                         qc.ccx(qx[n-1], qx[n-2], t[0])
30         return qc
31
32 #Creating equal superposition.
33 qc.h(q)
34
35 qc.x(q)
36 and_nway(q, qoutput, 3, qc)
37 qc.x(q)
38
39 qc.x(q[0])
40 and_nway(q, qoutput, 3, qc)
41 qc.x(q[0])
42
43 qc.x(q[1])
44 and_nway(q, qoutput, 3, qc)
45 qc.x(q[1])
46
47 qc.x(q[2])
48 and_nway(q, qoutput, 3, qc)
49 qc.x(q[2])
50
51 qc.measure(q, c)
```

The Python code creates a 3-qubit register, q for the inputs, a single qubit register, $qoutput$ to represent the output. During measurement these registers map to their classical counterparts, c and $coutput$. The $andInner$ and and_nway functions create the necessary circuit required to implement an n-input AND gate using CCNOT gates. Finally, we add the gates for the necessary conditions of each k, where $k \in \{0, 2\}$, i.e., the first condition for $k = 0$ and the last three conditions for $k = 2$.

4.2   Evaluation

Because contemporary quantum hardware, including the IBM Q, does not support controlling a single gate by multiple controls, we use CCNOT and X gates (provided by IBM's Qiskit API) to create complex, multi-control gates. While complex logical circuits can be created using these previously described AND and OR circuits, our code generator supports more expressive NChooseK circuits by combining simpler ones. A programmer can thus more effectively describe their computational problem. The CCNOT operation is an expensive operation because it is composed of 9 single qubit and 6 two-qubit gates [22]. Because the cost of the circuit is dominated by CCNOT operations, we focus on the number of CCNOT gates required for a particular NChooseK computation. We also assess the depth of the circuit for different values of N and K.

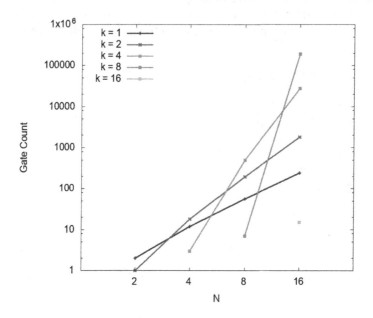

Fig. 10. Number of CCNOT gates required for arbitrary N and k

Figure 10 shows the number of CCNOT gates required for different combinations of N and k. We can see from the plot that the number of gates required is maximal when $k = \frac{N}{2}$, where $k \in K$. Also, the number of gates required increases exponentially with N. So while more complex computation can be expressed with larger values of N, programmers need to establish a trade-off between the using simpler circuits, such as AND and OR, and expressing more complex computation with larger values of N.

Figure 11 indicates the depth of CCNOT gates required for different combinations of N and k. Similar to the previous figure, the depth of the circuit is maximal when $k = \frac{N}{2}$, where $k \in K$. These results further confirm the need for programmers to establish a trade-off between expressing computation in high-level NChooseK primitives vs. using several small NChooseK primitives to express the same computation.

5   Related Work

It is projected that the number of qubits will approach 50 or more in the next few years, yet we are still addressing the quantum programmability issue to reduce the challenge for programmers to express quantum computational problems effectively and effortlessly.

Several attempts were made to address this issue. The first attempt was made by Deutsch [11] to define notations of quantum Turing machines (QTM). A formalized quantum programming language proposal given by Knill [18] defined pseudo code for implementation on a quantum random access machine (QRAM) but was not precise enough to be implementable as a quantum programming

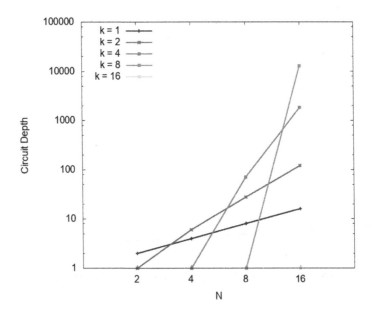

Fig. 11. Depth of circuit in CCNOT gates for arbitrary N and k

language. The first real quantum computing language, QCL [20], was developed by Omer with syntax similar to C and provides a range of high level quantum programming features such as memory management and automatic derivation of conditional versions of operators. Another high-level language based on C++ was developed by Bettelli [1]. A quantum programming language based on probabilistic predictive programming, guarded-command language, quantum lambda calculus with operational semantics and an equational theory were defined. A first-order functional programming language, QML in which control as well as data suitable for quantum was defined. Quantum programming with Haskell by defining basic elements of quantum mechanics as data types and functions was also implemented. These solutions still failed to reduce the challenges faced to solve quantum computational problems efficiently [13].

Recently, many open-source quantum software projects are being developed and many major companies are trying to develop their own solutions. An open source framework Qiskit [17] was developed by IBM Research in 2017 for creating and manipulating quantum programs [7]. Qiskit uses the Python programming language to eventually translate a quantum programs to the OpenQASM [8] representation of circuits of quantum gates. Microsoft has defined a new programming language, Q#, with simulators working either on local systems or a cloud platform [19]. D-Wave Systems's Qbsolv solves QUBO problems on quantum processors as well as classical hardware architecture [9]. Our solution is different from these solutions as we are providing a way to express a variety of problems in a generalized model of computation called NChooseK. It makes the process of describing a problem efficient by requiring users to define problems in terms of the model so that software can generate the code to execute the problem.

6 Conclusion and Future Work

In this work we present a novel model, NChooseK, for expressing quantum computation. We show how this model can be used to express computation for a circuit based universal quantum computer like the IBM Q. We demonstrate the generality of the programming model using 2 important applications, circuit satisfiability and map coloring. Finally, we describe the implementation of our code generator, which can generate Qiskit code for arbitrary inputs of N and K along with an example of the XOR gate. Our evaluation shows how the gate count and circuit depth is affected by different input parameters. In this context we discuss the trade-offs involved in using a single NChooseK primitive for more expressiveness vs. several smaller primitives to keep the gate count and circuit depth low.

We would like to further extend our code generator to combine multiple NChooseK primitives to express complex computational problems. The code generator/compiler can even explore the aforementioned trade-off space to automatically break down large NChooseK primitives into smaller more efficient subprimitives allowing the programmer to use larger, more expressive constructs.

We are also looking at code generation of NChooseK primitives for quantum annealing systems such as the D-Wave.

Acknowledgments. Research presented in this article was supported in part by NSF grants 1525609 and 1813004 and by the Laboratory Directed Research and Development program of Los Alamos National Laboratory under project numbers 20160069DR and 20190065DR. This work was also supported by the U.S. Department of Energy through Los Alamos National Laboratory. Los Alamos National Laboratory is operated by Triad National Security, LLC for the National Nuclear Security Administration of the U.S. Department of Energy (contract no. 89233218CNA000001).

References

1. Bettelli, S., Calarco, T., Serafini, L.: Toward an architecture for quantum programming. Eur. Phys. J. D At. Mol. Opt. Plasma Phys. **25**(2), 181–200 (2003)
2. Brennen, G.K., Caves, C.M., Jessen, P.S., Deutsch, I.H.: Quantum logic gates in optical lattices. Phys. Rev. Lett. **82**(5), 1060 (1999)
3. Cincio, L., Subaşı, Y., Sornborger, A.T., Coles, P.J.: Learning the quantum algorithm for state overlap. arXiv preprint arXiv:1803.04114 (2018)
4. Cirac, J.I., Zoller, P.: Quantum computations with cold trapped ions. Phys. Rev. Lett. **74**(20), 4091 (1995)
5. Clarke, J., Wilhelm, F.K.: Superconducting quantum bits. Nature **453**(7198), 1031 (2008)
6. Cook, S.A.: The complexity of theorem-proving procedures. In: Proceedings of the Third Annual ACM Symposium on Theory of Computing, pp. 151–158. ACM (1971)
7. Cross, A.: The IBM Q experience and QISKit open-source quantum computing software. Bull. Am. Phys. Soc. **63**(1) (2018). BAPS.2018.MAR.L58.3
8. Cross, A.W., Bishop, L.S., Smolin, J.A., Gambetta, J.M.: Open quantum assembly language. arXiv:1707.03429 (2017). http://arxiv.org/abs/1707.03429
9. D-Wave Systems Inc: Qbsolv. https://docs.ocean.dwavesys.com/projects/qbsolv/
10. Dahl, E.D.: Programming with D-Wave: Map coloring problem. D-Wave Official Whitepaper (2013)
11. Deutsch, D.: Quantum theory, the Church-Turing principle and the universal quantum computer. Proc. R. Soc. Lond. A Math. Phys. Sci. **400**(1818), 97–117 (1985)
12. Feynman, R.P.: Simulating physics with computers. Int. J. Theor. Phys. **21**(6–7), 467–488 (1982)
13. Gay, S.J.: Quantum programming languages: survey and bibliography. Math. Struct. Comput. Sci. **16**(4), 581–600 (2006)
14. Gidney, C.: Quirk: a drag-and-drop quantum circuit simulator. http://algassert.com/quirk
15. Grover, L.K.: A fast quantum mechanical algorithm for database search. In: Proceedings of the Twenty-Eighth Annual ACM Symposium on Theory of Computing, pp. 212–219. ACM (1996)
16. IBM: IBM Q Experience. https://quantumexperience.ng.bluemix.net/qx
17. IBM: IBM Qiskit (2019). https://qiskit.org/
18. Knill, E.: Conventions for quantum pseudocode. Technical report LA-UR-96-2724, Los Alamos National Laboratory, June 1996

19. Microsoft Research: Microsoft quantum development kit samples (2019). https://github.com/Microsoft/Quantum
20. Ömer, B.: A Procedural Formalism for Quantum Computing. Master's thesis, Department of Theoretical Physics, Technical University of Vienne, July 1998
21. Schneider, S., Milburn, G.J.: Decoherence and fidelity in ion traps with fluctuating trap parameters. Phys. Rev. A **59**(5), 3766 (1999)
22. Shende, V.V., Markov, I.L.: On the CNOT-cost of TOFFOLI gates. arXiv preprint arXiv:0803.2316 (2008)
23. Shor, P.W.: Algorithms for quantum computation: Discrete logarithms and factoring. In: 35th Annual Symposium on Foundations of Computer Science, Proceedings, pp. 124–134. IEEE (1994)
24. Younes, A.: Using Reed-Muller expansions in the synthesis and optimization of Boolean quantum circuits. In: Stepney, S., Adamatzky, A. (eds.) Inspired by Nature. ECC, vol. 28, pp. 113–141. Springer, Cham (2018). https://doi.org/10.1007/978-3-319-67997-6_5

Reversible In-Place Carry-Lookahead Addition with Few Ancillae

Torben Ægidius Mogensen[(✉)]

DIKU, University of Copenhagen,
Universitetsparken 5, 2100 Copenhagen O, Denmark
torbenm@di.ku.dk

Abstract. We present a reversible, in-place carry-lookahead adder that uses fewer ancillae than previous designs. Specifically, an N-bit adder uses only roughly N ancillae, where previous designs have used roughly $2N$ ancillae. The cost is 20% higher gate count and 50% higher gate delay.

1 Introduction

Reversible circuits often employ *ancilla* and *garbage* bits. An ancilla bit (or just ancilla) is an output bit that always has the same constant valure, regardless of which valid input is given, and a garbage bit is a non-constant output bit that does not contain useful information. Use of ancilla bits can often dramatically reduce circuit complexity (for example, from exponential to linear size), but they can be a problem, in particular in quantum circuits, where each ancilla bit uses a qubit, which is a sparse resource in quantum computers. Even in classical reversible circuitry, excessive use of ancilla bits should be avoided as they increase the width of the circuit.

Garbage bits limit the usability of a reversible circuit for calculating the inverse of the function computed by the applying the circuit in the forwards direction: You have to guess the value of the garbage bits to do so. Sometimes non-constant output bits that are not part of the function result are needed for reversibility: If the function computed by the circuit is not injective, extra information needs to be output to distinguish the cases where the function result is the same even though the inputs differ. We will not consider this garbage. But non-constant outputs are sometimes added even though they are not required for injectivity, because that may make circuits simpler or faster. This is what we call garbage. A common example is addition: Addition is not injective, for example both $3 + 5$ and $4 + 4$ yield 8 as result. If you, in addition to the sum, output one of the arguments, you will, however, get an injective function. So instead of mapping both $(3, 5)$ and $(4, 4)$ to 8, we can map $(3, 5)$ to $(3, 8)$ and $(4, 4)$ to $(4, 8)$, both of which can, by subtraction, be mapped back to unique inputs. We

This work was partially supported by the European COST Action IC 1405: Reversible Computation - Extending Horizons of Computing.

© Springer Nature Switzerland AG 2019
M. K. Thomsen and M. Soeken (Eds.): RC 2019, LNCS 11497, pp. 224–237, 2019.
https://doi.org/10.1007/978-3-030-21500-2_14

cann such adders *in-place* adders, as the outputs use at most one more bit (for the most significant bit of the sum) than the inputs. You often see *out-of-place* adders, where all the inputs are repeated in the output alongside the result, so (3, 5) and (4, 4) are, for example, mapped to (3, 5, 8) and (4, 4, 8), respectively. This makes the computed function trivially injective, but it means you can no longer use the circuit in reverse for subtraction – at least not without already knowing the answer. There is not a total agreement in literature about which of these outputs should be considered garbage – if you define the functionality of an adder to retain one or both inputs as outputs, you can argue that they are not garbage. Since we consider non-constant outputs garbage if they are not needed for injectivity, we, for adders, will not consider a copy of *one* of the outputs garbage, as that is the minimum extra information in addition to the sum that is needed to make the adder injective. But if copies of *both* inputs are output in addition to the sum, one of these must be considered garbage.

Out-of-place adders can be smaller and faster than in-place adders (that only output one of the arguments in addition to the result), so they do have some value. In this paper, we study in-place adders, as we want to retain the ability to use the adders in reverse for subtraction. This means that comparisons to out-of-place adder designs is largely meaningless, so we will limit comparison to in-place adders.

While we have identified ancilla bits and garbage bits as output bits, the number of input bits to a reversible circuit is the same as the number of output bits. This means that adding an ancilla bit requires addition of an input bit as well, which is typically a constant input. Similarly, adding garbage bits on top of the minimum required for reversibility also implies adding extra inputs, which will typically also be constant inputs.

Any irreversible circuit can be trivially implemented using reversible gates if there is no limit on ancilla and garbage bits, so a challenge in reversible circuit design is to limit the number of garbage bits to the minimal needed for inversion, and to reduce the number ancilla bits to the minimum required for achieving a given logic depth. There will, however, often be a trade-off between logic depth and the number of ancillae. If one circuit uses fewer ancillae but has a higher gate delay, and another uses more ancillae but has a lower gate delay, one is not obviously better than the other – this depends on the problem to which the circuit is applied and the technology used to implement the circuit. So it can be an advantage to have a number of different, logically equivalent, designs that trade off ancillae and logic depth in various ways, so you can choose the design that fits the given purpose and technology best.

Reversible ripple-carry adders, such as the Van Rentergem adder [5], typically reduces garbage bits to the minimum required, i.e., a copy of one of the inputs, unless there is a non-constant carry-in bit to the addition, in which case this is typically output as extra garbage. If the carry-in bit is known to be zero, the corresponding output is also constant, so it is an ancilla output instead of a garbage output. Additionally, since the result of the addition has one more bit than the largest input, there is a constant (zero) input which in the output is used to hold the most significant bit of the sum.

Ripple-carry adders have a gate delay proportional to the number of bits. Carry-lookahead adders can reduce the gate delay to $O(\log N)$, where N is the number of bits. In reversible logic, the cost is that $O(N)$ ancilla bits are needed, typically around $2N$ when N is a power of 2 [1,4].

The contribution in this paper is to show a way to roughly halve the number of ancillae compared to previous in-place carry-lookahead adder designs, so the number of ancilla bits is only around N when N is a power of 2. The cost is a higher gate delay (by roughly 50%), so there is a definite trade-off.

2 Carry-Lookahead Addition

Carry-Lookahead addition has been known since at least 1957, when Gerald Rosenberger of IBM filed a patent on the method [3]. The idea is that, even if you do not know the incoming carry, you can compute which of the following three cases hold:

0 The outgoing carry will be 0.
1 The outgoing carry will be 1.
P The outgoing carry will be the same as the incoming carry.

where P stands for "pass through".

If we have two bits a_i and b_i from the addends, it is easy to see that the outgoing carry will be 0 if $a_i = b_i = 0$, the outgoing carry will be 1 if $a_i = b_i = 1$, and it will be identical to the incoming carry if $a_i \neq b_i$. Usually, the three cases are represented by two bits p (pass) and g (generate), where $p = 1$ if the carry is passed through and $g = 1$ if the outgoing carry is 1. They can not both be 1, so only three of the four combinations are used. For two bits a_i and b_i, we have $p_i = a_i \oplus b_i$ and $g_i = a_i b_i$.

We want to compute p and g not just for individual bits, but for blocks of bits. If p_i^{j-1}, g_i^{j-1}, p_j^k, and g_j^k represent pass and generate for the blocks spanning from i to $j - 1$ and j to k, respectively, we can find pass and generate for the combined block spanning from i to k by

$$p_i^k = p_i^{j-1} p_j^k \tag{1}$$

$$g_i^k = g_i^{j-1} p_j^k \vee g_j^k \tag{2}$$

Since p_j^k and g_j^k can not both be 1, we can use exclusive-or ($\oplus$) instead of a normal logical or ($\vee$) in the formula for g_i^k.

So we can recursively combine blocks to find carry-propagation information for N bits in $O(\log N)$ logic depth.

The next step is to generate the actual carries. For this, we use that c_j, the carry-in to bit number j, can be found by

$$c_j = g_i^{j-1} \oplus p_i^{j-1} c_i \tag{3}$$

When we have computed g_0^{j-1} and p_0^{j-1} for all j that are powers of 2, we can from c_0 (the carry-in to the whole addition) immediately find c_j for these j. By using c_j, g_j^k and p_j^k, we can find $c_{(k+1)}$. By applying this recursively to blocks of decreasing size, we can find all the carry bits in $O(\log N)$ logic depth. A final step computes the bits of the sum as $s_i = a_i \oplus b_i \oplus c_i$.

3   A Reversible Carry-Lookahead Adder

Reversible in-place carry-lookahead adders were first presented by Draper, Kutin, Rains, and Svore [1]. First, an out-of-place carry-lookahead adder that takes A and B and produces $A + B$, A and B as outputs is presented, and then this is used to make an in-place adder that produces only $A + B$ and A as output. It is the latter in-place adder in which we are primarily interested. We will only look at adders for $N = 2^m$ bits, both for simplicity and because this is the common case. Both the adder by Draper et al. and the adder we present later can, however, be modified to work for other values of N.

The in-place adder consists of two parts:

1. An adder ADD that produces $S = A + B$, A and C, where C is the string of carry bits.
2. A slightly modified inverse of ADD that has the net effect of preserving $A + B$ and A while uncomputing C.

ADD consists of six steps:

1. Generating $g_i = a_i b_i$ and $p_i = a_i \oplus b_i$ for all bits i. g_i is generated on a new line, while p_i overwrites b_i.
2. Recursively generating p_i^k (on new lines) for larger and larger blocks.
3. Recursively generating g_i^k for larger and larger blocks. g_i^k overwrites g_j^k for the previous smaller block.
4. Recursively generating c_k first using the larger blocks and then smaller blocks. c_k overwrites g_j^k.
5. Uncomputing p_i^k by running step 2 backwards.
6. Adding (with $\oplus$) c_i to p_i (which is equal to $a_i \oplus b_i$) to get $s_i = a_i \oplus b_i \oplus c_i$, the i'th bit of the sum.

Figure 1 shows this for an 8-bit adder.

To uncompute the carry bits, Draper et al. make the observation that (in two's complement arithmetic modulo 2^N), if $S = A + B$, then the carry bits generated by the addition $\overline{B} = A + \overline{S}$ are the same as by the addition $S = A + B$, where $\overline{B}$ and $\overline{S}$ are the bitwise negations of B and S. So if we replace S by $\overline{S} \oplus A = S \oplus \overline{A}$, run steps 1 to 5 of ADD backwards, and negate the b-bits, we clear the c-bits, and the b bits now hold $A + B$. To preserve the carry-out bit that holds the most significant bit of the sum, the part of ADD that computed this bit should not be uncomputed.

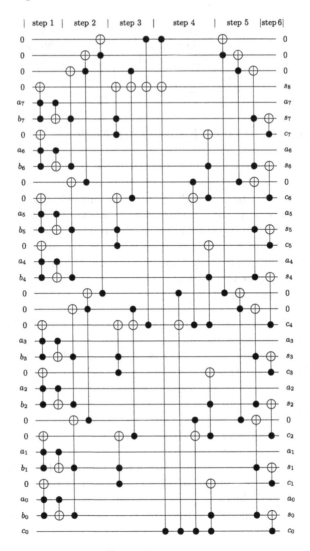

Fig. 1. The ADD part of Draper et al.'s in-place adder

This non-obvious observation is critical to making the in-place adder work, and it has been used in later carry-lookahead adder designs, such as [4], which uses the same number of ancilla bits as Draper et al.'s, but slightly fewer gates (mostly because it uses a wider selection of different gates).

The complete 8-bit in-place adder is shown in Fig. 2.

Simplifications can be made if we know c_0 to be 0: Carry generations of the form $c_{k+1} = g_{0k} \oplus p_{0k}c_0$ reduce to $c_{k+1} = g_{0k}$. This means that we don't need p_{0k} for $k > 0$, so we can omit the gates that compute and uncompute these and the ancilla lines that hold them. Figure 3 shows the 8-bit in-place adder optimised

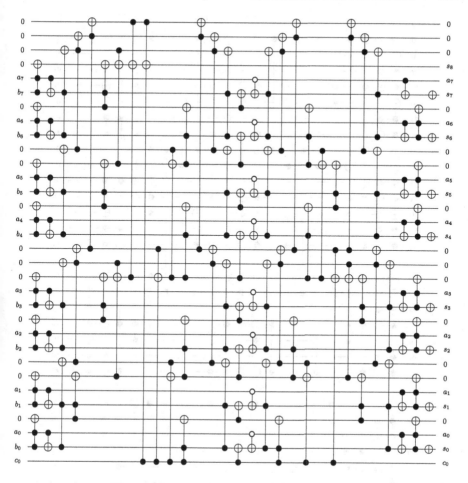

Fig. 2. Draper et al.'s complete in-place adder

this way. We have left gaps where lines are removed to make it clearer where this happens.

If N is a power of 2, Draper et al.'s in-place adder uses $2N - 2$ ancillae. If $c_0 = 0$, this is reduced by $\log_2 N$, as the lines for computing the $\log_2 N$ occurrences of p_{0k} are not needed. For eight bits, the non-optimised adder uses $2 \times 8 - 2 = 14$ ancillae and the optimised adder uses $2 \times 8 - 2 - \log_2 8 = 11$ ancillae.

4 Reducing the Number of Ancillae

We note that the adder presented above uses one ancilla for every bit to compute $g_i = a_i b_i$. We will try to avoid this by relaxing the requirement that p_i and g_i can not both be 1 (i.e., that $p_i g_i = 0$). We can do this by saying that we ignore the value of g_i when $p_i = 1$. If $p_i = 0$, $a_i = b_i$, so we can define $g_i = a_i$.

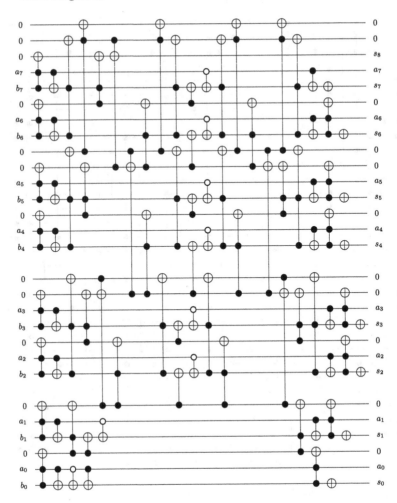

Fig. 3. Draper et al.'s in-place adder optimised for $c_0 = 0$

In general, we use all four combinations of p and g to mean

p	g	meaning
0	0	$c_{out} = 0$
0	1	$c_{out} = 1$
1	0	$c_{out} = c_{in}$
1	1	$c_{out} = c_{in}$

It is the last of these four combinations that we must now be able to handle.

In presenting Draper et al.'s adder, we used the property $p_j^k g_j^k = 0$ to rewrite $g_i^k = g_i^{j-1} p_j^k \vee g_j^k$ to $g_i^k = g_i^{j-1} p_j^k \oplus g_j^k$. But if $p_j^k g_j^k$ can be 1, this no longer holds. Instead we must use

$$g_i^k = g_i^{j-1} p_j^k \oplus g_j^k \overline{p_j^k} \tag{4}$$

Similarly, we must change the formula for the carry bits:

$$c_j = c_i p_i^{j-1} \oplus g_i^{j-1} \overline{p_i^{j-1}} \tag{5}$$

It looks like we now need an ancilla for each new g_i^k as well as two Toffoli gates to compute it. But we can avoid this by using a Fredkin gate: A Fredkin gate is a conditional swap gate that takes three inputs x, y, z and swaps the contents of y and z if and only if $x = 1$. There are two widely used notations for Fredkin gates:

While the notation on the right may be more intuitive, it breaks down when the lines that need to be swapped are not adjacent, so we will use the notation on the left in this paper.

The effect of applying a Fredkin gate can be written as

$$y' = y\overline{x} \oplus zx \tag{6}$$
$$z' = yx \oplus z\overline{x} \tag{7}$$

where overlines indicate negation.

We note that the formula for z' has the same "shape" as $g_i^k = g_i^{j-1} p_j^k \oplus g_j^k \overline{p_j^k}$, using p_j^k for x, g_i^{j-1} for y and g_j^k for z. So we can compute g_i^k onto the line that holds g_j^k using a single Fredkin gate. The cost is that the line that holds g_i^{j-1} is overwritten with nonsense, but we can uncompute this nonsense later.

We can from g_i^{j-1}, p_i^{j-1}, g_j^k, and p_j^k compute g_i^k and $_i^k$ using the following circuit

$$
\begin{array}{ll}
0 & \quad p_i^k \\
g_j^k & \quad g_i^k \\
p_j^k & \quad p_j^k \\
g_i^{j-1} & \quad \hat{g}_i^k \\
p_i^{j-1} & \quad p_i^{j-1}
\end{array}
$$

where $\hat{g}_i^k = g_i^{j-1} \overline{p_j^k} \oplus g_j^k p_j^k$ is garbage that later needs to be uncomputed to restore g_i^{j-1}.

The next step is to compute the carry bits. Draper et al.'s circuit computes $c_k = g_i^k \oplus c_i p_i^k$ on top of g_i^k, since this is not needed anymore. We need to uncompute g_i^k to restore g_i^{j-1} and g_j^k, which will eventually be needed as $a_i = g_i$, so we will instead compute c_k on top of p_i^k as $p_i^k \oplus c_i$ (note that this is the incoming carry bit and not the outgoing carry bit as in Draper et al.'s circuit) and from this compute $p_i^{j-1} \oplus c_i$ and $p_j^k \oplus c_j$. This has the benefit that we, at the end, get $p_i \oplus c_i = s_i$, so we do not need an extra step to compute the sums. On the downside, the circuit for propagating the carries becomes a bit more complex, partly because we need to restore g_i^{j-1} and g_j^k and partly because we no longer have $p_i^{j-1}g_i^{j-1} = 0$, which makes the formula for c_j somewhat more complex than previously $c_j = c_i p_i^{j-1} \oplus g_i^{j-1}\overline{p_i^{j-1}}$. The circuit for propagating carries is shown below.

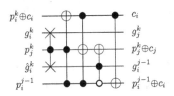

Note that c_i is not needed afterwards, so it is garbage that must be uncomputed later if we want an in-place adder.

To get an adder that has these carry bits as garbage (equivalent to the ADD part of Draper et al.'s adder), we use the following steps:

1. Compute $p_i = a_i \oplus b_i$ on the b_i lines.
2. Recursively apply the circuit that combines p and g until we have p_0^{n-1} and g_0^{n-1}.
3. Compute $s_n = c_n = c_0 p_0^{n-1} \oplus g_0^{n-1}\overline{p_0^{n-1}}$.
4. Overwrite the line p_0^{n-1} with $p_0^{n-1} \oplus c_0$.
5. Recursively apply the carry progagation circuit until we have $s_i = p_i \oplus c_i$ and $a_i = g_i$.

The combined circuit for 8 bits is shown in Fig. 4. Compared to Fig. 1, the new circuit uses a total of 25 lines compared to 32 for Draper et al.'s design, but it has a gate delay of 25 compared to 16 for Draper et al.'s design. Also note that only the even carries are output as garbage, but some of these multiple times. It is easy to eliminate the copies, so no carry bit occurs twice in the output, but since we plan to uncompute all carry bits anyway, we do not do this. To uncompute the carries, we use the same idea as Draper et al. – negating s_i if $a_i = 0$, apply the inverse of the ADD circuit except for the parts that add the carries to the sum and the part that computes the high sum bit. The new in-place adder for 8 bits is shown in Fig. 5, rotated to fit on a page. Again, this has 25 lines (8 of which are ancillae) compared to 32 lines (15 of which are ancillae) for Draper et al.'s design. And, again, the gate delay is about 50% higher.

As with Draper et al.'s adder, we can optimise for the case when $c_0 = 0$, removing the c_0 line and all gates and lines that become redundant as a consequence of $c_0 = 0$. Again, p_0^j are not needed, as we know that, if a carry is passed from input to bit j, this will be 0. As in the design of Draper et al., this removes $\log N$ ancillae from the circuit. The optimised circuit is shown in Fig. 6. It uses only four ancillae compared to 11 for the adder in Fig. 3, but the gate delay is 35 compared to 22, again an increase of roughly 50%.

5   A Detailed Comparison

For a more detailed comparison of the in-place adder design by Draper et al. and the one presented in this paper, we assume N is a power of 2.

5.1   Gate Count

For both designs, the gate count is dominated by the ADD part of the adder and its inverse. The optimisation for when $c_0 = 0$ and not uncomputing the carry-out both give an $O(\log N)$ reduction in gate count, so except for small N, they are relatively small. The total gate count is, hence, here simplified to twice that of the ADD part of the in-place adder. While this is a simplification, it affects both designs equally, so the comparison is still fair.

Draper et al.'s ADD design uses in step 1 N Toffoli gates and N C-not gates. Step 2 uses $N - 1$ Toffoli gates, as do step 4 and 5. Step 3 uses N toffoli gates,

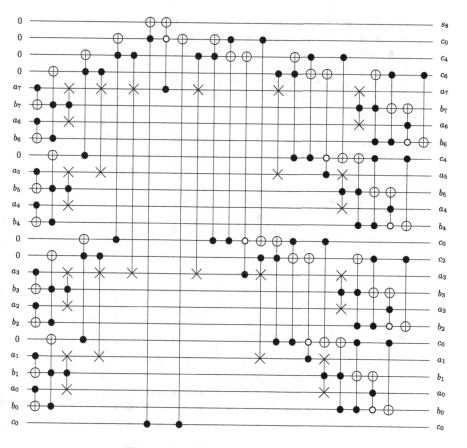

Fig. 4. The ADD part of the new adder

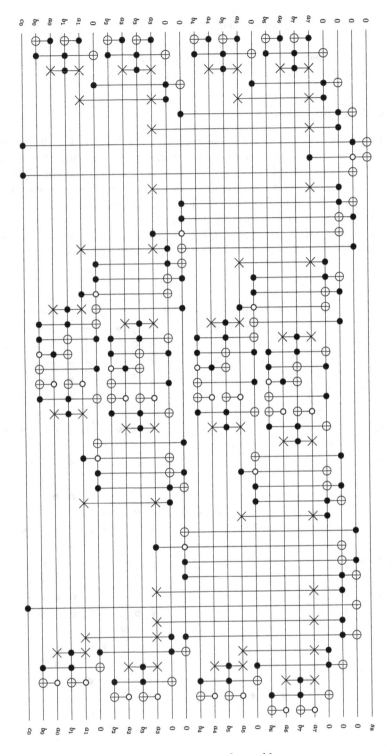

Fig. 5. The new in-place adder

and step 6 uses N C-not gates. The total is, hence $5N - 3$ Toffoli gates and $2N$ C-not gates.

Our design uses for the equivalent of step 1 N C-not gates. The equivalents of steps 2 and 3 combined use $N - 1$ Fredkin gates and $N + 1$ Toffoli gates. The equivalent of step 4, 5 and 6 combined use $N - 1$ Fredkin gates, $3N - 3$ Toffoli gates and $N - 1$ C-not gates. The total is, hence, $4N - 2$ Toffoli gates, $2N - 2$ Fredkin gates and $2N - 1$ C-not gates. If the cost of Toffoli and Fredkin gates are equal (as they are in both quantum cost and pass-gate cost), our design is roughly 20% more expensive in gates.

5.2   Gate Delay

Again, we use the ADD parts of the adder for our comparison. The total gate delay is very close to twice that of the ADD part – not uncomputing the carry out and the optimisation for $C_0 = 0$ reduce the gate delay by little, and the glue between the ADD part and its inverse is very small. Also, the simplification affects both designs roughly equally.

Step 1 of Draper et al.'s ADD design gives a gate delay of 1 Toffoli gate and one C-not gate. Step 2, 4, and 5 each give a delay of $\log N$ Toffoli gates, step 3 gives a delay of $\log N + 1$ Toffoli gates, and step6 gives a delay of 1 C-not gate. The total is $4 \log N$ Toffoli gates and 3 C-not gates.

The equivalent of step 1 in our design gives a delay of 1 C-not gate. The equivalent of step 2 and 3 combined give a delay of $\log N$ Fredkin gates and $\log N + 2$ Toffoli gates. The equivalents of step 4, 5 and 6 combined give a delay of $\log N$ Fredkin gates, $3 \log N$ Toffoli gates and $\log N$ C-not gates. The total is $2 \log N$ Fredkin gates, $4 \log N + 2$ Toffoli gates and $\log N$ C-not gates. If we, again, count Fredkin gates and Toffoli gates as equal, our design has slightly more than 50% higher gate delay.

5.3   Ancillae

Initially, we will look at the case that is not optimised for $c_0 = 0$.

Step 1 of Draper et al.'s ADD design uses N constant inputs. Step 2 uses $N-1$ constant inputs. The remaining steps do not introduce new constant inputs. The second part of the adder returns all except one of the constant inputs to 0, as one is used for the carryout bit, which becomes the most significant bit of the sum. So the in-place adder uses $2N - 2$ ancillae.

Our design uses no constant inputs for the equivalent of step 1 of Draper et al.'s design, and N constant inputs for the equivalent of steps 2 and 3. All but the one used for the carry-out bit are uncomputed in the in-place adder, so it uses $N - 1$ ancillae.

In both cases, optimising for $c_0 = 0$ removes $\log N$ ancillae, so Draper et al.'s design uses a total of $2N - \log N - 2$ ancillae while our design uses a total of $N - \log N - 1$ ancillae, so less than half.

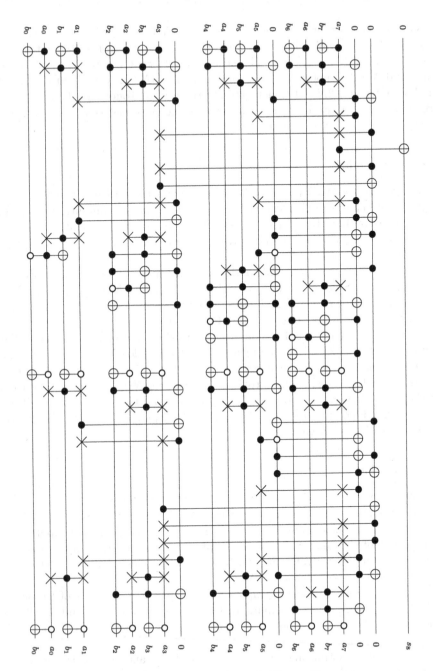

Fig. 6. The optimised new in-place adder

5.4   Thapliyal et al.'s Design

This design is very similar to that of Draper et al. The only difference is that the Toffoli gate and the C-not gate used in step 1 of the ADD part are replaced by a single gate of the author's design, called a TR gate. The authors argue that this is an improvement because the quantum cost of a TR gate is 4 compared to a total of 6 for a Toffoli gate and a C-not gate. No comparison of gate delay is made, and the number of ancillae is unchanged.

6   Conclusion

We have presented a design for a reversible carry-lookahead adder that uses less than half the ancillae of previous designs, at a cost of increasing the gate count by roughly 20% and the gate delay by roughly 50%. This makes the new design useful in contexts where low line count is more important than low gate delay and low gate count.

We have simulated at gate level the presented 8-bit adders on all 256×256 inputs and have found the results to be correct.

The observation that makes the reduction in ancillae possible is that if the "pass" bit is 1, the "generate" bit can be arbitrary, which allows us to use $g_i^i = a_i$, instead of $g_i^i = a_i b_i$, so we don't need an ancilla line on which to calculate g_i^i. This, however, complicates calculation of carry bits, which causes increased gate count and (in particular) gate delay.

Future work will look at reducing the gate delay and at using the adder in a previously proposed multiplier/divisor design [2], which in its current form uses a variant of Draper et al.'s in-place adder.

References

1. Draper, T.G., Kutin, S.A., Rains, E.M., Svore, K.M.: A logarithmic-depth quantum carry-lookahead adder. Quantum Info. Comput. **6**(4), 351–369 (2006)
2. Mogensen, T.Æ.: Garbage-free reversible multiplication and division. In: Kari, J., Ulidowski, I. (eds.) RC 2018. LNCS, vol. 11106, pp. 253–268. Springer, Cham (2018). https://doi.org/10.1007/978-3-319-99498-7_18
3. Rosenberger, G.B.: Simultaneous carry adder. US Patent 2,966,305A (1957)
4. Thapliyal, H., Jayashree, H.V., Nagamani, A.N., Arabnia, H.R.: Progress in reversible processor design: a novel methodology for reversible carry look-ahead adder. Trans. Comput. Sci. **17**, 73–97 (2013)
5. Van Rentergem, Y., De Vos, A.: Optimal design of a reversible full adder. Int. J. Unconventional Comput. **1**, 339–355 (2005)

Controlling Reversibility in Reversing Petri Nets with Application to Wireless Communications
Work-in-Progress Paper

Anna Philippou[1], Kyriaki Psara[1(✉)], and Harun Siljak[2]

[1] Department of Computer Science, University of Cyprus, Nicosia, Cyprus
{annap,kpsara01}@cs.ucy.ac.cy
[2] CONNECT Centre, Trinity College Dublin, Dublin, Ireland
harun.siljak@tcd.ie

Abstract. Petri nets are a formalism for modelling and reasoning about the behaviour of distributed systems. Recently, a reversible approach to Petri nets, Reversing Petri Nets (RPN), has been proposed, allowing transitions to be reversed spontaneously in or out of causal order. In this work we propose an approach for controlling the reversal of actions of an RPN, by associating transitions with conditions whose satisfaction/violation allows the execution of transitions in the forward/reversed direction, respectively. We illustrate the framework with a model of a novel, distributed algorithm for antenna selection in distributed antenna arrays.

1 Introduction

Reversibility is a phenomenon that occurs in a variety of systems, e.g., biochemical systems and quantum computations. At the same time, it is often a desirable system property. To begin with, technologies based on reversible computation are considered to be the only way to potentially improve the energy efficiency of computers beyond the fundamental Landauer limit. Further applications are encountered in programming languages, concurrent transactions, and fault-tolerant systems, where in case of an error a system should reverse back to a safe state.

As such, reversible computation has been an active topic of research in recent years and its interplay with concurrency is being investigated within a variety of theoretical models of computation. The notion of causally-consistent reversibility was first introduced in the process calculus RCCS [1], advocating that a transition can be undone only if all its effects, if any, have been undone beforehand. Since then the study of reversibility continued in the context of process calculi [2–6], event structures [7], and Petri nets [8–10].

A distinguishing feature between the cited approaches is that of controlling reversibility: while various frameworks make no restriction as to when a transition can be reversed (uncontrolled reversibility), it can be argued that some

© Springer Nature Switzerland AG 2019
M. K. Thomsen and M. Soeken (Eds.): RC 2019, LNCS 11497, pp. 238–245, 2019.
https://doi.org/10.1007/978-3-030-21500-2_15

means of controlling the conditions of transition reversal is often useful in practice. For instance, when dealing with fault recovery, reversal should only be triggered when a fault is encountered. Based on this observation, a number of strategies for controlling reversibility have been proposed: [2] introduces the concept of irreversible actions, and [11] introduces compensations to deal with irreversible actions in the context of programming abstractions for distributed systems. Another approach for controlling reversibility is proposed in [12] where an external entity is employed for capturing the order in which transitions can be executed in the forward or the backward direction. In another line of work, [13] defines a roll-back primitive for reversing computation, and in [4] roll-back is extended with the possibility of specifying the alternatives to be taken on resuming the forward execution. Finally, in [14] the authors associate the direction of action reversal with energy parameters capturing environmental conditions of the modelled systems.

In this work we focus on the framework of reversing Petri nets (RPNs) [9], which we extend with a mechanism for controlling reversibility. This control is enforced with the aid of conditions associated with transitions, whose satisfaction/violation acts as a guard for executing the transition in the forward/backward direction, respectively. The conditions are enunciated within a simple logical language expressing properties relating to available tokens. The mechanism may capture environmental conditions, e.g., changes in temperature, or the presence of faults. We present a causal-consistent semantics of the framework. Note that conditional transitions can also be found in existing Petri net models, e.g., in [15], a Petri-net model that associates transitions and arcs with expressions.

We conclude with the model of a novel antenna selection (AS) algorithm which inspired our framework. Centralized AS in DM MIMO (distributed, massive, multiple input, multiple output) systems [16] is computationally complex, demands a large information exchange, and the communication channel between antennas and users changes rapidly. We introduce an RPN-based, distributed, time-evolving solution with reversibility, asynchronous execution and local condition tracking for reliable performance and fault tolerance.

2   Reversing Petri Nets

In this section we extend the reversing Petri nets of [9] by associating transitions with conditions that control their execution and reversal, and allow tokens to carry data values of specific types (clauses (2), (6) and (7) in the following definition). We introduce a causal-consistent semantics for the framework.

Definition 1. A *reversing Petri net* (RPN) is a tuple $(P, T, \Sigma, A, B, F, C, I)$ where:

1. P is a finite set of *places* and T is a finite set of *transitions*.
2. Σ forms a finite set of data types with V the associated set of data values.

3. A is a finite set of *bases* or *tokens* ranged over by $a, b, \ldots$. $\overline{A} = \{\overline{a} \mid a \in A\}$ contains a "negative" instance for each token and we write $\mathcal{A} = A \cup \overline{A}$.

4. $B \subseteq A \times A$ is a set of undirected *bonds* ranged over by $\beta, \gamma, \ldots$. We use the notation $a-b$ for a bond $(a, b) \in B$. $\overline{B} = \{\overline{\beta} \mid \beta \in B\}$ contains a "negative" instance for each bond and we write $\mathcal{B} = B \cup \overline{B}$.

5. $F : (P \times T \cup T \times P) \to 2^{\mathcal{A} \cup \mathcal{B}}$ is a set of directed labelled *arcs*.

6. $C : T \to \text{COND}$ is a function that assigns a condition to each transition t such that $type(C(t)) = Bool$.

7. $I : A \to V$ is a function that associates a data value from V to each token a such that $type(I(a)) = type(a)$.

RPNs are built on the basis of a set of *tokens* or *bases* which correspond to the basic entities that occur in a system. Tokens have a type from the set Σ, and we write $type(e)$ to denote the type of a token or expression in the language. Values of these types are associated to tokens of an RPN via function I. Tokens may occur as stand-alone elements but as computation proceeds they may also merge together to form *bonds*. Transitions represent events and are associated with conditions COND defined over the data values associated with the tokens of the model and functions/predicates over the associated data types. *Places* have the standard meaning. Directed arcs connect places to transitions and vice versa and are labelled by a subset of $\mathcal{A} \cup \mathcal{B}$. Intuitively, these labels express the requirements for a transition to fire when placed on arcs incoming the transition, and the effects of the transition when placed on the outgoing arcs. Graphically, a Petri net is a directed bipartite graph where tokens are indicated by •, places by circles, transitions by boxes, and bonds by lines between tokens.

The association of tokens to places is called a *marking* such that $M : P \to 2^{\mathcal{A} \cup \mathcal{B}}$ where $a-b \in M(x)$, for some $x \in P$, implies $a, b \in M(x)$. In addition, we employ the notion of a *history*, which assigns a memory to each transition $H : T \to 2^{\mathbb{N}}$. Intuitively, a history of $H(t) = \emptyset$ for some $t \in T$ captures that the transition has not taken place, and a history of $k \in H(t)$, captures that the transition was executed as the kth transition occurrence and it has not been reversed. Note that $|H(t)| > 1$ may arise due to cycles in a model. A pair of a marking and a history, $\langle M, H \rangle$, describes a *state* of a RPN with $\langle M_0, H_0 \rangle$ the initial state, where $H_0(t) = \emptyset$ for all $t \in T$.

We introduce the following notations. We write $\circ t = \{x \in P \mid F(x, t) \neq \emptyset\}$ and $t\circ = \{x \in P \mid F(t, x) \neq \emptyset\}$ for the incoming and outgoing places of transition t, respectively. Furthermore, we write $\text{pre}(t) = \bigcup_{x \in P} F(x, t)$ and $\text{post}(t) = \bigcup_{x \in P} F(t, x)$. Finally, we define $\text{con}(a, C)$, where a is a token and $C \subseteq A \cup B$ a set of connections, to be the tokens connected to a via a sequence of bonds in B, together with the bonds creating these connections.

In what follows we assume that: (1) transitions do not erase tokens ($A \cap \text{pre}(t) = A \cap \text{post}(t)$), and (2) tokens/bonds cannot be cloned into more than one outgoing places of a transition ($F(t, x) \cap F(t, y) = \emptyset$ for all $x, y \in P, x \neq y$). Furthermore, we assume for all $a \in A, |\{x \mid a \in M_0(x)\}| = 1$, i.e., there exists exactly one base of each type in M_0. Note that we extend the exposition of [9] by allowing transitions to break bonds and by permitting cyclic structures.

2.1   Forward Execution

For a transition to be forward-enabled in an RPN the following must hold:

Definition 2. Consider a RPN $(P, T, \Sigma, A, B, F, C, I)$, a transition t, and a state $\langle M, H \rangle$. We say that t is *forward-enabled* in $\langle M, H \rangle$ if:

1. If $a \in F(x, t)$ (resp. $\beta \in F(x, t)$) for some $x \in \circ t$, then $a \in M(x)$ (resp. $\beta \in M(x)$), and if $\overline{a} \in F(x, t)$ (resp. $\overline{\beta} \in F(x, t)$) for some $x \in \circ t$, then $a \notin M(x)$ (resp. $\beta \notin M(x)$),
2. If $\beta \in F(t, x)$ for some $x \in t \circ$ and $\beta \in M(y)$ for some $y \in \circ t$ then $\beta \in F(y, t)$,
3. $E(C(t)) = \text{True}$.

Thus, t is enabled in state $\langle M, H \rangle$ if (1) all tokens and bonds required for the transition are available in t's incoming places and none of the tokens/bonds whose absence is required exists in t's incoming place, (2) if a pre-existing bond appears in an outgoing arc of a transition, then it is also a precondition of the transition to fire, and (3) the transition's condition $C(t)$ evaluates to true. We write $E(c)$ for the value of the condition based on the assignment function I.

When a transition t is executed in the forward direction, all tokens and bonds occurring in its outgoing arcs are relocated from the input to the output places along with their connected components. The history of t is extended accordingly:

Definition 3. Given a RPN $(P, T, \Sigma, A, B, F, C, I)$, a state $\langle M, H \rangle$, and a transition t enabled in $\langle M, H \rangle$, we write $\langle M, H \rangle \xrightarrow{t} \langle M', H' \rangle$ where:

$$M'(x) = M(x) - \bigcup_{a \in F(x,t)} \mathsf{con}(a, M(x))$$
$$\cup \bigcup_{a \in F(t,x), y \in \circ t} \mathsf{con}(a, M(y) - \mathsf{pre}(t) \cup F(t, x))$$

and $H'(t') = H(t') \cup \{\max(\{0\} \cup \bigcup_{t'' \in T} H(t'')) + 1\}$, if $t' = t$, and $H(t')$, otherwise.

2.2   Causal Order Reversing

We now move on to *causal-order reversibility*. The following definition enunciates that a transition t is *co-enabled* ('*co*' standing for causal-order reversing) if it has been previously executed and all the tokens on the outgoing arcs of the transition are available in its outplaces. Furthermore, to handle causality in the presence of cycles, clause (1) additionally requires that all bonds involved in the connected components of such tokens have been constructed by transitions t' that have preceded t. Furthermore, clause (2) of the definition requires that the condition of the transition is not satisfied.

Definition 4. Consider a RPN $(P, T, \Sigma, A, B, F, C, I)$, a state $\langle M, H \rangle$, and a transition $t \in T$ with $k = \max(H(t))$. Then t is *co-enabled* in $\langle M, H \rangle$ if: (1) for all $a \in F(t, y)$ then $a \in M(y)$, and if $\mathsf{con}(a, M(y)) \cap \mathsf{post}(t') \neq \emptyset$ for some $t' \in T$ with $k' \in H(t')$, then $k' \leq k$, and, (2) $E(C(t)) = \text{False}$.

When a transition t is reversed all tokens and bonds in the pre-conditions of t, as well as their connected components, are transferred to t's incoming places.

Definition 5. Given a RPN a state $\langle M, H \rangle$, and a transition t co-enabled in $\langle M, H \rangle$ with history $k \in H(t)$, we write $\langle M, H \rangle \overset{t}{\rightsquigarrow} \langle M', H' \rangle$ where:

$$M'(x) = M(x) - \bigcup_{a \in F(t,x)} \text{con}(a, M(x))$$
$$\cup \bigcup_{y \in to, a \in F(x,t)} \text{con}(a, M(y) - \text{post}(t) \cup F(x,t))$$

and $H'(t') = H(t') - \{k\}$ if $t' = t$, and $H(t')$, otherwise.

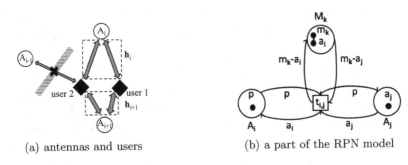

(a) antennas and users   (b) a part of the RPN model

Fig. 1. RPN for antenna selection in DM MIMO (large antenna array).

3   Case Study: Antenna Selection in DM MIMO

The search for a suitable set of antennas is a sum capacity maximization problem:

$$\mathcal{C} = \max_{\mathbf{P}, \mathbf{H_c}} \log_2 \det \left(\mathbf{I} + \rho \frac{N_R}{N_{TS}} \mathbf{H_c} \mathbf{P} \mathbf{H_c}^H \right) \tag{1}$$

where ρ is the signal to noise ratio, N_{TS} the number of antennas selected from a total of N_T antennas, N_R the number of users, $\mathbf{I}$ the $N_{TS} \times N_{TS}$ identity matrix, $\mathbf{P}$ a diagonal $N_R \times N_R$ power matrix. $\mathbf{H_c}$ is the $N_{TS} \times N_R$ submatrix of $N_T \times N_R$ channel matrix $\mathbf{H}$ [16]. Instead of centralized AS, in our approach (1) is calculated locally for small sets of antennas (neighborhoods), switching on only antennas which improve the capacity: in Fig. 1(a), antenna A_{i-1} will not be selected. In the RPN interpretation, we present the antennas by places $A_1, \ldots, A_n$, where $n = N_T$, and the overlapping neighbourhoods by places $M_1, \ldots, M_h$. These places are connected together via transitions $t_{i,j}$, connecting A_i, A_j and M_k, whenever there is a connection link between antennas A_i and A_j. The transition captures that, based on the neighbourhood knowledge in place M_k, antenna A_i may be preferred over A_j or vice versa (the transition may be reversed).

To implement the intended mechanism, we employ three types of tokens. First, we have the power tokens $p_1, \ldots, p_l$, where l is the number of enabled antennas. If token p is located on place A_i, antenna A_i is considered to be on. Transfer of these tokens results into new antenna selections, ideally converging to a locally optimal solution. Second, tokens $m_1, \ldots, m_h$, each represent one neighbourhood. Finally, $a_1, \ldots, a_n$, represent the antennas. The tokens are used as follows: Given transition $t_{i,j}$ between antenna places A_i and A_j in neighbourhood M_k, transition $t_{i,j}$ is enabled if token p is available on A_i, token a_j on A_j, and bond (a_i, m_k) on M_k, i.e., $F(A_i, t_{i,j}) = \{p\}$, $F(A_j, t_{i,j}) = \{a_j\}$, and $F(M_k, t_{i,j}) = \{(a_i, m_k)\}$. This configuration captures that antennas A_i and A_j are on and off, respectively. (Note that the bonds between token m_k and tokens of type a in M_k capture the active antennas in the neighbourhood.) Then, the effect of the transition is to break the bond (a_i, m_k), and release token a_i to place A_i, transferring the power token to A_j, and creating the bond (a_j, m_k) on M_k, i.e., $F(t_{i,j}, A_i) = \{a_i\}$, $F(t_{i,j}, A_j) = \{p\}$, and $F(t_{i,j}, M_k) = \{(a_j, m_k)\}$. The mechanism achieving this for two antennas can be seen in Fig. 1(b).

Finally, to capture the transition's condition, an antenna token a_i is associated with data vector $I(a_i) = \mathbf{h}_i$, $type(\mathbf{h}_i) = \mathbb{R}^2 (= \mathbb{C})$, i.e., the corresponding row of $\mathbf{H}$. The condition constructs the matrix $\mathbf{H}_c$ of (1) by collecting the data vectors $\mathbf{h}_i$ associated with the antenna tokens a_i in place M_k: $\mathbf{H}_c = (\mathbf{h}_1, ..., \mathbf{h}_n)^T$ where $\mathbf{h}_i = I(a_i)$ if $a_i \in M_k$, otherwise $\mathbf{h}_i = (0 \ldots 0)$. The transition $t_{i,j}$ will occur if the sum capacity calculated for all currently active antennas (including a_i), $\mathcal{C}_{a_i}$, is less than the sum capacity calculated for the same neighbourhood with the antenna A_i replaced by A_j, $\mathcal{C}_{a_j}$, i.e., $\mathcal{C}_{a_i} < \mathcal{C}_{a_j}$. Note that if the condition is violated, the transition may be executed in the reverse direction.

Results of the RPN-based approach on an array consisting of 64 antennas serving 16 users, varying the number of selected antennas from 16 to 64 are shown in Fig. 2 [17]. If we run five RPN models in parallel and select the one with the best performance for the final selection, the results are consistently superior to those of a centralised (greedy) algorithm, and if we run just one (equivalent to the average of the performance of these five models) the results are on par with those of the centralised algorithm.

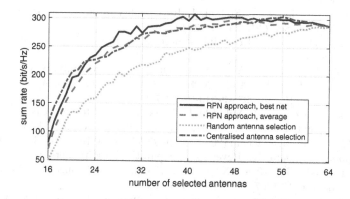

Fig. 2. Results of antenna selection on a distributed 64 antenna array.

4   Conclusions

We have extended RPNs with conditions that control reversibility by determining the direction of transition execution, and we have applied our framework to model an AS algorithm. Preliminary results show superior performance to centralised approaches. Our experience strongly suggests that resource management can be studied and understood in terms of RPNs as, along with their visual nature, they offer a number of relevant features. In subsequent work, we plan to extend RPNs for allowing multiple tokens of the same base/type to occur in a model and for developing out-of-causal-order reversibility semantics in the presence of conditional transitions as well as the destruction of bonds.

Acknowledgments. This work was partially supported by the European COST Action IC 1405: Reversible Computation - Extending Horizons of Computing, Science Foundation Ireland (SFI) and European Regional Development Fund under Grant Number 13/RC/2077, and the EU Horizon 2020 research & innovation programme under the Marie Sklodowska-Curie grant agreement No 713567.

References

1. Danos, V., Krivine, J.: Reversible communicating systems. In: Gardner, P., Yoshida, N. (eds.) CONCUR 2004. LNCS, vol. 3170, pp. 292–307. Springer, Heidelberg (2004). https://doi.org/10.1007/978-3-540-28644-8_19
2. Danos, V., Krivine, J.: Transactions in RCCS. In: Abadi, M., de Alfaro, L. (eds.) CONCUR 2005. LNCS, vol. 3653, pp. 398–412. Springer, Heidelberg (2005). https://doi.org/10.1007/11539452_31
3. Phillips, I., Ulidowski, I.: Reversing algebraic process calculi. In: Aceto, L., Ingólfsdóttir, A. (eds.) FoSSaCS 2006. LNCS, vol. 3921, pp. 246–260. Springer, Heidelberg (2006). https://doi.org/10.1007/11690634_17
4. Lanese, I., Lienhardt, M., Mezzina, C.A., Schmitt, A., Stefani, J.-B.: Concurrent flexible reversibility. In: Felleisen, M., Gardner, P. (eds.) ESOP 2013. LNCS, vol. 7792, pp. 370–390. Springer, Heidelberg (2013). https://doi.org/10.1007/978-3-642-37036-6_21
5. Lanese, I., Mezzina, C.A., Stefani, J.: Reversibility in the higher-order π-calculus. Theor. Comput. Sci. **625**, 25–84 (2016)
6. Cardelli, L., Laneve, C.: Reversible structures. In: Proceedings of CMSB 2011, pp. 131–140. ACM (2011)
7. Ulidowski, I., Phillips, I., Yuen, S.: Concurrency and reversibility. In: Yamashita, S., Minato, S. (eds.) RC 2014. LNCS, vol. 8507, pp. 1–14. Springer, Cham (2014). https://doi.org/10.1007/978-3-319-08494-7_1
8. Barylska, K., Koutny, M., Mikulski, Ł., Piątkowski, M.: Reversible computation vs. reversibility in Petri nets. In: Devitt, S., Lanese, I. (eds.) RC 2016. LNCS, vol. 9720, pp. 105–118. Springer, Cham (2016). https://doi.org/10.1007/978-3-319-40578-0_7
9. Philippou, A., Psara, K.: Reversible computation in Petri nets. In: Kari, J., Ulidowski, I. (eds.) RC 2018. LNCS, vol. 11106, pp. 84–101. Springer, Cham (2018). https://doi.org/10.1007/978-3-319-99498-7_6
10. Barylska, K., Gogolinska, A., Mikulski, Ł., Philippou, A., Piatkowski, M., Psara, K.: Reversing computations modelled by coloured Petri nets. In: Proceedings of ATAED 2018, vol. 2115, pp. 91–111. CEUR Workshop Proceedings (2018)

11. Lanese, I., Mezzina, C.A., Stefani, J.-B.: Controlled reversibility and compensations. In: Glück, R., Yokoyama, T. (eds.) RC 2012. LNCS, vol. 7581, pp. 233–240. Springer, Heidelberg (2013). https://doi.org/10.1007/978-3-642-36315-3_19

12. Phillips, I., Ulidowski, I., Yuen, S.: A reversible process calculus and the modelling of the ERK signalling pathway. In: Glück, R., Yokoyama, T. (eds.) RC 2012. LNCS, vol. 7581, pp. 218–232. Springer, Heidelberg (2013). https://doi.org/10.1007/978-3-642-36315-3_18

13. Lanese, I., Mezzina, C.A., Schmitt, A., Stefani, J.-B.: Controlling reversibility in higher-order Pi. In: Katoen, J.-P., König, B. (eds.) CONCUR 2011. LNCS, vol. 6901, pp. 297–311. Springer, Heidelberg (2011). https://doi.org/10.1007/978-3-642-23217-6_20

14. Bacci, G., Danos, V., Kammar, O.: On the statistical thermodynamics of reversible communicating processes. In: Corradini, A., Klin, B., Cîrstea, C. (eds.) CALCO 2011. LNCS, vol. 6859, pp. 1–18. Springer, Heidelberg (2011). https://doi.org/10.1007/978-3-642-22944-2_1

15. Jensen, K., Kristensen, L.M.: Coloured Petri Nets - Modelling and Validation of Concurrent Systems. Springer, Heidelberg (2009). https://doi.org/10.1007/b95112

16. Gao, X., Edfors, O., Tufvesson, F., Larsson, E.G.: Massive mimo in real propagation environments: do all antennas contribute equally? IEEE Trans. Commun. 63(11), 3917–3928 (2015)

17. Siljak, H., Psara, K., Philippou, A.: Distributed antenna selection for massive MIMO using reversing Petri nets. IEEE Wirel. Commun. Lett. (2019, under review)

Author Index

Printed in the United States
By Bookmasters